W9-CCF-197

WASHINGTON STANDARD

BY

Steve Robinson

THREE-TIME WORLD CHAMPION

EIGHTEEN-TIME NORTH AMERICAN CHAMPION

A complete system using a convention card as an outline of:

1. Strong notrumps.
2. Five-card majors.
3. Two-over-one game-forcing.
4. Defenses against opponents's methods based on the Law of
        Total Tricks.
5. Carding methods.

WASHINGTON STANDARD

BY

STEVE ROBINSON

EDITED BY MARVIN ELSTER

WITH HELP FROM FRED STEINBERG

Copyright 1996 © by Steve Robinson

All rights reserved. No part of this
book may be reproduced in any form
without the permission of Steve Robinson
and Devyn Press.

Printed in the United States of America.

Devyn Press, Inc.
3600 Chamberlain Lane, Suite 230
Louisville, KY 40241
1-800-274-2221

ISBN 0-939460-59-9

WASHINGTON STANDARD

TABLE OF CONTENTS

INTRODUCTION

I asked several players three questions. After responder bids two notrump as a forcing four-card major-suit raise (Jacoby), what is opener's double of a three-club overcall? I got two diverse answers, penalties and club shortness. After responder bids two spades transferring to three clubs following a one-notrump opener, what does responder's three-of-a-major follow-up show? Again I got two diverse answers, length and shortness. What does a six-club response to the Grand Slam Force show? Again I got two diverse answers, extra values and weakness. Read on. These and a myriad of other bids are explained in a clear, logical fashion in this book.

What I have done is to create a complete five-card major, two-over-one game-forcing system with defenses and carding agreements. This book defines the meanings of all of the basic conventions which make up the system, such as Jacoby Two Notrump, four-suit transfers and the Grand Slam Force; as well as follow-ups, such as the meanings of the double of the three-club overcall, responder's three-of-a-major follow-up, and a six-club response to the Grand Slam Force so that newly formed partnerships have a complete system and old partnerships can fine tune their system. If two players who have never played with each other read this book and sit down to play, they will have a much better system with fewer misunderstandings than the same two players taking two hours filling out a convention card. They will both know that the double of three clubs is for penalties, three-of-a-major shows shortness, and six clubs is answerer's weakest response.

Washington Standard, derived from Eastern Scientific, contains many conventions and understandings that define suit lengths which will help you follow the Law of Total Tricks. All of the conventions used in Washington Standard are played in some form by top-flight players throughout the country. If you want to become a top-flight player, learning what's in this book is a must. If you're not familiar with the basics of this system, start slowly. Start with conventions you already know, for instance Jacoby Transfers or Negative Doubles. Use this book as a reference manual and refine your understandings of these conventions. Slowly incorporate one or two new conventions every month, and when you have mastered them, try others. Don't bite off more than you can chew.

I have used the 1988 version of the ACBL convention card as an outline in writing this book. Because of this, some sections should be read out of order. You should start this book with sections 25.1 through 25.3 - Roman Keycard Blackwood, and section 12.11 - Last Train. RKC and the Last Train are used throughout the book. You should also read section 26.4 - Smith Echoes, and section 13.6 - Support Doubles and Redoubles. If you learn only two conventions, Smith Echoes and Support Doubles, the book will be worth what you paid for it.

Washington Standard has four main characters. The character who appears in every auction is Opener, and he/she starts the bidding; Responder, who's Opener's partner; Responder has good days when he/she jumps around causing havoc to the opponents and bad days when he/she doesn't have enough strength to do anything. This book has two villains. Overcaller, who most of the time doesn't have the values that Opener has, is first of the villains to speak. Overcaller is always trying to steal the contract from Opener and Responder. Last, but not least, there's Advancer, Overcaller's partner in crime, who only gets to speak after both Opener and Overcaller have had their say. This book is about the constant struggles between Opener and his/her sidekick Responder against Overcaller and his/her sidekick Advancer. In the movie version of this book, and I've already gotten offers from Hollywood, I expect Opener to be played by Beth Palmer, who has been studying for this part for about 20 years. Her partner, Responder, will be played by Lynn Deas. Overcaller will be played by Peter Boyd, and I will take time off from my writings to play the part of Advancer.

To make this book easier to read, I shortened 'he/she' down to 'he' and 'he' can just as easily be a woman or a man. To help keep straight who is bidding what, I try to keep the number of he's to a minimum. I have tried to use the lowest possible spot cards to fill out hands. I understand that a hand with 8's and 9's is more valuable than the same hand with 2's and 3's, and I assume that at the table you will take that into account.

CHAPTER 1 - ONE NOTRUMP OPENER

1.1 -- OPENING NOTRUMP 15-17. BAD 18 CAN BE OPENED. IF 18 THEN 4-3-3-3, NO TENS, FEWER THAN EIGHT HONOR CARDS.

One notrump shows 15 to a bad 4-3-3-3 18 HCPs. The only way to show 4-3-3-3 hands, 4-4-3-2 hands, and 5-3-3-2 hands with a five-card minor, which have 15 to 17 HCPs, is to open one notrump. Some 18 point hands should be opened one notrump. If you do not open one notrump with 4-3-3-3 bad 18's, you have to open one-of-a-minor and jump to two notrump. I like a two-notrump jump rebid to show a hand that has play for three notrump opposite an average six-point hand. ♠A43♥A32♦A543♣AQ2 is a horrible 18-point hand if partner wants to play notrump. Notice that there are only five honor cards. Give partner ♠K76♥K876♦Q65♣765 and you have 26 HCPs between you; yet three notrump needs a club finesse, the diamond king onside and a 3-3 break in a red suit. However, ♠AJT♥QT9♦JT9♣AJT9, a 13-point hand with ten honor cards, will make three notrump opposite ♠K76♥K876♦Q65♣765, if you are a good guesser, more often than not. Honor cards are important. A432 opposite 1098 will never produce three tricks, and will produce two tricks only 36% of the time, while KJ32 opposite 1098 will produce three tricks 50% of the time. All other things being equal, the more honor cards you and your partner have, the more tricks you will take.

To decide whether to open a hand one notrump with two doubletons, you must think about your second and third bid. Any hand with four spades and five clubs can be opened one club, since you can rebid one spade. Holding ♠KJ32♥A2♦K2♣A5432, you can open one club and can rebid one spade over partner's red-suit response. It's your third bid which is a problem. What are you going to do when partner rebids one notrump? You can raise to two notrump and find partner with a six-count or you can pass one notrump and find partner with a ten-count. If you open one notrump with all 2-2-4-5, 2-2-5-4, 2-4-5-2, 4-2-2-5 and 4-2-5-2 hands containing 15 or 16 HCPs with honors in your short suits, you will avoid all rebid problems. Open one notrump with ♠KJ♥KJ32♦A5432♣KJ, ♠K2♥AQ32♦K2♣QJ432, ♠K2♥K2♦AQ432♣K432 and ♠Q2♥K2♦AQ32♣KQ432. With pure hands containing 15 or 16 HCPs, open your five-card suit and rebid your four-card suit. Open one diamond with ♠32♥AQ32♦AKQ32♣32 and rebid two hearts. Open one diamond with ♠32♥32♦AKQ32♣AQ32 and rebid two clubs. Open one club with ♠32♥AKQ2♦32♣AQ432 and rebid hearts. Open one club with ♠32♥32♦AKQ2♣AQ432 and rebid diamonds. With 17 HCPs, you will always have enough strength to reverse. You might even find some hands with singleton honors that are better described by opening one notrump. ♠Q32♥AK32♦KJ432♣K and ♠Q♥KQ32♦KQ432♣A32 look like notrump openers.

Hands with six-card minors should not be opened one notrump. An exception would be if opening one-of-a-minor and then jumping to three-of-a-minor does not describe your hand. ♠AQ♥AQ2♦Q2♣Q65432 contains enough strength to open one club and jump to three clubs. However, responder expects a better club suit, and would think that his club king solidifies your club suit. ♠AQ♥Q32♦32♣AKJ432, a hand with rebiddable clubs, should be opened one club.

A two-small suit should not deter you from opening one notrump. The only way you can describe ♠32♥AK43♦AQ32♣K32 is to open one notrump.

1.2 -- CAN HAVE A FIVE-CARD MAJOR.

If opener opens one notrump with a five-card major, opener should get to the correct level. However, opener might miss a 5-3 or 5-4 major-suit fit. If opener holds ♠AQ543♥K2♦QJ2♣KJ2 and opens one spade, opener bids two clubs over responder's forcing notrump and corrects responder's two-spade preference to two notrump. If responder has six HCPs, two notrump will be played from responder's side rather then one notrump from opener's side. On the other hand, if opener opens one notrump with a five-card spade suit, responder with six HCPs and four-card support passes and opener will miss his 5-4 fit. If opener opens one heart with ♠K2♥AQ543♦QJ2♣KJ2, what is opener going to bid if responder responds one spade? With an extra jack, however, opener jumps to two notrump.

The answer is to open one notrump with a five-card major only if you might have a rebid problem. If you are 5-3-3-2 with a five-card heart suit, open one notrump with 15 or 16 HCPs. If you open one heart and partner responds one spade, you don't have a good rebid with 15 or 16 HCPs. Open one heart with 17 HCPs, and jump to two notrump over a one-spade response, or raise a one-notrump response to two notrump.

If you are 5-3-3-2 with a five-card spade suit, open one spade with 15 HCPs and treat it like a minimum opener. Over a one-notrump response, rebid two-of-a-minor and pass a two-spade preference. Open one notrump with 16 HCPs. Open one spade with 17 HCPs, and raise a one-notrump response to two notrump.

1.3 -- NON-FORCING STAYMAN. WITH BOTH FOUR-CARD MAJORS OPENER RESPONDS HEARTS FIRST. WITH A FIVE-CARD MAJOR OPENER JUMPS.

Opener (1)	Responder	Opener (2)	Responder
♠32 ♦AQJ2	♠J654 ♦543	♠32 ♦AQJ2	♠JT54 ♦T3
♥K32 ♣AQ32	♥A54 ♣K54	♥K32 ♣AQ32	♥A54 ♣KT54
1NT	Pass	1NT	2clubs
		2diamonds	2NT
		3NT	Pass

Responder shows a balanced invitational hand with a good eight or any nine HCPs by bidding two clubs and following with two notrump over opener's response. Bidding two clubs and then bidding two notrump does not promise a four-card major nor does it deny a four-card major. Responder does promise a four-card major if he bids two clubs and then bids three notrump. Responder should pass one notrump with 4-3-3-3 eight-count unless the hand contains three ten's. Responder should also pass one notrump with 4-4-3-2 eight-count containing honors in his short suits.

With 4-4 in the majors, opener responds two hearts. Bidding hearts first allows responder to bid two spades showing an invitational hand with four spades (see section 1.8). If opener always responds hearts first, responder will know that if opener responds two spades, opener can not have four hearts.

In example (1), responder with a 4-3-3-3 eight-count passes one notrump. In example (2), responder is 4-3-2-4 with three ten's and has honors in his long suits. Responder invites and opener accepts, reaching a good three-notrump contract. Even if the ten of diamonds is a small diamond, three notrump will usually make if the king of diamonds is onside.

Opener jumps to three spades to show a five-card spade suit with exactly 16 HCPs or jumps to three hearts to show a five-card heart suit with 15 or 16 HCPs.

1.4 -- TRANSFERS.

Two diamonds, Jacoby, transfers to two hearts, the anchor suit and shows at least five hearts, any strength. Responder can have anywhere from ♠32♥65432♦432♣432 or ♠32♥8765432♦32♣32 to ♠AKQ♥AK432♦A32♣32 or ♠-♥AK5432♦2♣AK5432. Two hearts, Jacoby, transfers to two spades, the anchor suit and shows at least five spades, any strength. Be consistent. Anytime responder has a five-card major, responder transfers.

Two spades transfers to three clubs and shows at least five clubs. Responder can have anywhere from ♠543♥432♦2♣765432 to ♠AKQ♥32♦AQ2♣AJ432, enough to try for a grand. Two notrump transfers to three diamonds and shows at least five diamonds. Responder can have anywhere from ♠543♥432♦765432♣2 to ♠AKQ♥32♦AQ432♣AJ2, enough to try for a grand. If responder has a sign-off or an invitational hand, responder will always have at least six clubs to transfer to clubs and at least six diamonds to transfer to diamonds. Only in game-forcing situations might responder have only five clubs or only five diamonds.

1.5 -- TEXAS.

Opener	(1)	Responder		Opener	(2)	Responder	
♠J54	♦A54	♠32	♦K32	♠J54	♦A54	♠32	♦32
♥J87	♣AKQ4	♥KQ5432	♣32	♥J87	♣AKQ4	♥QT965432	♣2
1NT		4diamonds		1NT		4diamonds	
4hearts		Pass		4hearts		Pass	

Opener	(3)	Responder		Opener	(4)	Responder	
♠J876	♦A5	♠AK5432	♦K432	♠J876	♦A5	♠AK5432	♦KQJ2
♥AKQ3	♣J54	♥2	♣32	♥AKQ3	♣J54	♥2	♣KQ
1NT		4hearts		1NT		4hearts	
4spades		Pass		4spades		4NT	
				5spades		6NT	

Four diamonds transfers to four hearts and shows at least six hearts. Four hearts transfers to four spades and shows at least six spades. Use Texas to set the trump suit in order to use Roman Keycard Blackwood. If an opponent doubles a Texas four-diamond bid, opener shows whether or not he has a diamond control just in case responder is planning on bidding RKC. If opener does not have a diamond control, opener passes four-diamonds doubled. If opener has a diamond control, opener bids four hearts if it doesn't make a difference who plays the hand or redoubles to let responder play the hand. Holding ♦A3, opener redoubles four-diamonds doubled just in case responder holds ♦Q2. If a Texas four-heart bid gets doubled, the logic is the same.

Examples (1) and (2) are examples of minimum four-diamond calls. In example (2), responder holding eight hearts wants to be in four hearts because either four hearts makes or it will be a good sacrifice. In example (3), responder with ten HCPs and a six-card spade suit wants to play four spades. Responder bids four hearts and although opener has a super hand for spades, opener respects responder's judgment and simply completes the transfer. In example (4), responder wants to be in slam unless two keys are missing. Responder bids four hearts, requiring opener to bid four spades. Responder then bids four notrump RKC. Since responder promises at least six spades for his Texas bid, opener responds five spades showing two keycards with the spade queen or a ten-card fit. Responder, missing one ace, counts 12 tricks and bids six notrump.

10

1.6 -- ONE NOTRUMP - TWO CLUBS - TWO DIAMONDS - TWO HEARTS IS WEAK WITH BOTH MAJORS (4-4), (4-5) or (5-5).

With 5-4 or 5-5 in the majors and a weak hand, responder bids Stayman in order to play in a major at the two-level. With 4-4 in the majors and fewer than eight HCPs, responder can take a position to try to find a 4-4 fit by bidding Stayman. I would be more likely to try Stayman with 4-4-4-1 or 4-4-5-0 then with 4-4-3-2 distribution. If opener responds a major, responder happily passes. If opener responds two diamonds, responder passes holding four or more diamonds, or bids two hearts showing a weak hand with both majors with an emphasis on hearts. Sometimes responder ends up playing a 4-3 fit when opener does not have a four-card major, or possibly a 4-2 fit on the rare occasion when opener opens one notrump with 2-2 in the majors.

With four spades and five hearts, responder has a better chance of getting to a reasonable fit, since he will play a 4-3 fit only if opener has exactly three spades and two hearts. If opener has three spades and two hearts, opener corrects two hearts to two spades, since responder might have only four hearts. ♠J432♥5432♦2♣J432, ♠J5432♥Q5432♦32♣2, ♠J432♥K5432♦32♣32 are examples of two clubs followed by two hearts after a two-diamond response.

1.7 -- ONE NOTRUMP - TWO CLUBS - TWO DIAMONDS - TWO SPADES IS WEAK WITH EXACTLY FOUR HEARTS AND AT LEAST FIVE SPADES.

Opener (1)	Responder	Opener (2)	Responder
♠K76 ♦A54	♠J5432 ♦32	♠K76 ♦A654	♠J5432 ♦32
♥AK65 ♣J54	♥J432 ♣32	♥AK5 ♣J54	♥J432 ♣32
1NT	2clubs	1NT	2clubs
2hearts	Pass	2diamonds	2spades
		Pass	

One notrump -- two clubs -- two diamonds -- two spades is a sign-off showing a weak hand with at least five spades and four hearts. If opener responds two hearts to two clubs, responder passes. If opener responds two diamonds, responder signs-off in two spades.

In examples (1) and (2), responder has a weak hand with five spades and four hearts. In example (1), responder bids two clubs and passes two hearts. In example (2), responder bids two clubs and corrects two diamonds to two spades.

1.8 -- AFTER ONE NOTRUMP - TWO CLUBS - TWO HEARTS; TWO SPADES SHOWS FOUR SPADES AND IS INVITATIONAL; TWO NOTRUMP DENIES FOUR SPADES.

Opener	(1)	Responder		Opener	(2)	Responder	
♠K765	♦A5	♠A432	♦K32	♠K765	♦A5	♠A32	♦K432
♥AK54	♣J65	♥Q32	♣432	♥AK54	♣J65	♥Q32	♣432

Opener (1)	Responder	Opener (2)	Responder
1NT	2clubs	1NT	2clubs
2hearts	2spades	2hearts	2NT
Pass		Pass	

One notrump -- two clubs -- two hearts -- two spades shows an invitational hand with four spades and fewer than four hearts. Over responder's two-spade bid, opener with four-card spade support passes two spades with a 15-count or a 4-3-3-3 16-count, raises to three spades with a 4-4-3-2 16-count and raises to four spades with more. Without four spades, opener bids two notrump with a minimum notrump and three notrump with a maximum notrump.

In example (1), responder shows exactly four spades and an invitational hand by bidding two spades. Opener, who also has four spades, knows that he can play in spades, and since opener has a minimum notrump, opener passes two spades.

Responder can't use one notrump -- two notrump as an invitational raise without a major since that sequence is a transfer to diamonds (see section 1.11). Therefore, one notrump -- two clubs -- two hearts -- two notrump shows an invitational hand without a four-card major. Two notrump must be alerted, since in a Standard system, two clubs followed by two notrump promises a four-card major. Over responder's two-notrump bid, opener passes with a minimum and raises to three notrump with a maximum. In example (2), responder shows an invitational hand without four hearts or four spades by bidding two clubs followed by two notrump. Opener with a minimum notrump passes. With a maximum, opener bids three notrump. Spades are never in the picture.

Opener	(3)		Responder		Opener	(4)		Responder	
♠K32	◆A32		♠QJ65	◆K54	♠K432	◆A32		♠QJ65	◆K54
♥AK32	♣K32		♥QJ4	♣654	♥AK32	♣K2		♥QJ4	♣654
1NT			2clubs		1NT			2clubs	
2hearts			2spades		2hearts			2spades	
3NT			Pass		4spades			Pass	

Opener	(5)		Responder		Opener	(6)		Responder	
♠K432	◆A2		♠QJ5	◆K654	♠K32	◆A32		♠QJ65	◆K654
♥AK32	♣K32		♥QJ4	♣654	♥AK32	♣J32		♥QJ4	♣54
1NT			2clubs		1NT			2clubs	
2hearts			2NT		2hearts			2spades	
3NT			Pass		2NT			Pass	

In examples (3) through (6), responder bids two clubs and opener responds two hearts. In examples (3) and (4), responder shows an invitational hand with four spades by bidding two spades. In example (3), opener has a maximum notrump without four spades and jumps to three notrump. In example (4), opener has a maximum notrump with four spades. Since responder promises four spades and invitational values, opener jumps to four spades. In example (5), responder shows an invitational hand without four hearts or four spades by bidding two notrump. Responder raises hearts with four hearts and bids two spades with four spades. Opener with a maximum notrump bids three notrump rather than four spades, since responder's two-notrump bid denies holding four spades. In example (6), responder shows an invitational hand with four spades by bidding two spades. Opener has a minimum notrump without four spades and corrects two spades to two notrump.

1.9 -- ONE NOTRUMP - TWO CLUBS - TWO ANY - THREE-OF-A-MINOR IS FORCING TO GAME.

Two clubs followed by three-of-a-minor shows a four-card major and a longer minor and is forcing to game. If responder has a minimum game-force, responder should have an outside singleton or void. Responder uses this sequence to avoid playing three notrump when a suit is unstopped, as well as to try to get to slam. With a one-suited minor hand without a four-card major, responder starts out by bidding two spades, transferring to clubs, or two notrump, transferring to diamonds (see section 1.11).

If opener responds two-of-a-major in response to two clubs, responder's three-of-a-minor shows the other major. If opener denies a four-card major by responding two diamonds, opener doesn't know which major responder has when responder bids three-of-a-minor. Opener's first duty is to evaluate whether the hand belongs in three notrump. If opener has wasted values in responder's short suit, the hand probably belongs in three notrump and is unlikely to belong in slam. Only with a super fit will opener try for slam. Responder can bid above three notrump if he's interested in slam.

Opener	(1)	Responder		Opener	(2)	Responder	
♠KQJ	♦K32	♠A432	♦AQ654	♠KQJ	♦K32	♠A432	♦AQJ54
♥432	♣AK32	♥5	♣654	♥432	♣AK32	♥5	♣QJ4

Opener (1)	Responder	Opener (2)	Responder
1NT	2clubs	1NT	2clubs
2diamonds	3diamonds	2diamonds	3diamonds
3spades	4diamonds	3spades	4spades
5diamonds	Pass	5clubs	6diamonds

In examples (1) and (2), responder shows five or more diamonds and a four-card major. Opener does not know which major responder has. Opener bids three spades showing spade values and denying heart values. Responder, with a singleton heart, knows by opener's failure to bid three hearts or three notrump that three notrump is not the right contract. If opener bids three hearts showing heart values, instead of three spades showing spade values, responder holding four spades bids three notrump. In example (1), responder has a minimum game force and slows the auction with a four-diamond call. Some partnerships, with prior agreement, can play four diamonds as non-forcing. In example (2), responder has a game force and cuebids four spades leading to a good six-diamond contract.

Opener (3)		Responder		Opener (4)		Responder	
♠KQJ	♦K32	♠2	♦AQ654	♠KQJ	♦K32	♠2	♦AQ654
♥432	♣AK32	♥A765	♣765	♥KJ2	♣K432	♥A765	♣765

Opener (3)	Responder	Opener (4)	Responder
1NT	2clubs	1NT	2clubs
2diamonds	3diamonds	2diamonds	3diamonds
3spades	3NT	3NT	Pass
Pass			

Opener (5)		Responder		Opener (6)		Responder	
♠AQJ2	♦K32	♠43	♦AQ7654	♠AQJ2	♦K32	♠3	♦AQ654
♥KQJ	♣432	♥AT32	♣5	♥KQJ	♣432	♥T432	♣KQJ

Opener (5)	Responder	Opener (6)	Responder
1NT	2clubs	1NT	2clubs
2spades	3diamonds	2spades	3diamonds
3hearts	4diamonds	3hearts	3NT
4hearts	Pass	Pass	

In examples (3) and (4), responder's three-diamond bid shows five or more diamonds and a four-card major. In example (3), opener bids three spades showing spade values and denying heart values. Opener knows that responder has a four-card major but he doesn't know which one. Responder, with a singleton opposite opener's strength, bids three notrump. In example (4), opener has both majors, as well as clubs, well stopped and, therefore, bids three notrump. One of opener's kings will be opposite shortness and therefore wasted for slam purposes.

In examples (5) and (6), responder's three-diamond bid shows five or more diamonds and four hearts. Responder must have four hearts since responder has a four-card major and doesn't have four spades. RESPONDER DENIES FOUR-CARD SUPPORT FOR OPENER'S MAJOR WHEN HE BIDS THREE-OF-A-MINOR. In example (5), opener shows a heart fragment since he's worried about clubs. Opener denied holding four hearts when he bid two spades, since with two four-card majors opener always bids hearts first. Responder, holding a singleton club, bypasses three notrump. Over four diamonds, opener suggests playing a 4-3 heart fit and responder accepts. In example (6), opener shows four spades and a heart fragment. Responder holds good clubs and knows that three notrump will be a reasonable contract.

15

Opener	(7)		Responder		Opener	(8)		Responder	
♠AQJ2	♦K32		♠K543	♦AQ7654	♠AQJ	♦K32		♠K543	♦AQ7654
♥KQJ2	♣32		♥43	♣5	♥KQJ2	♣432		♥43	♣5

Opener (7)	Responder	Opener (8)	Responder
1NT	2clubs	1NT	2clubs
2hearts	3diamonds	2hearts	3diamonds
3spades	4diamonds	3hearts	4diamonds
4spades	Pass	5diamonds	Pass

If opener bids two hearts and responder bids three-of-a-minor, a 4-4 spade fit can still exist. Over three-of-a-minor, opener bids three spades with four spades. With fewer than four spades, opener bids three notrump with the other minor well stopped, bids three hearts with a tenuous stopper in the other minor, or bids at the four-level with great support for responder's minor. Since opener holds four hearts and responder holds four spades, major-suit stoppers should not be a problem.

In examples (7) and (8), responder bids three diamonds showing five or more diamonds and exactly four spades. Opener knows that responder has four spades since three diamonds promises a four-card major and responder did not raise hearts. In example (7), opener bids three spades showing four spades and setting spades as trumps. Responder bids four diamonds trying for slam. If opener's hearts are Axxx instead of KQJx, six spades is odds on. Opener with no outside aces and KQJx of hearts opposite a singleton or doubleton signs-off in four spades. In example (8), opener does not have four spades and does not have a club stopper. Opener bids three hearts denying four spades and denying a club stopper. If opener has five hearts, he jumps to three hearts over two clubs, so rebidding hearts does not show five hearts. Responder doesn't have a club stopper and bids four diamonds. An excellent five diamond contract is reached.

1.10 -- ONE NOTRUMP - TWO CLUBS - TWO DIAMONDS - THREE MAJOR IS SMOLEN (JUMP IN FOUR-CARD MAJOR SHOWS FIVE OR MORE IN OTHER MAJOR).

After opener responds two diamonds denying a four-card major, responder, holding four spades and five hearts, knows there can't be a 4-4 spade fit, but there can be a 5-3 heart fit.[1] If responder jumps in his four-card major instead of his five-card major, responder gains the advantage of opener being the declarer. Responder's jump to three spades, his four-card major, shows exactly four spades and five or more hearts. Over three spades, opener bids three notrump holding only two hearts. HOLDING THREE HEARTS, OPENER BIDS FOUR HEARTS WITH BAD VALUES FOR SLAM, FOUR CLUBS, ARTIFICIAL, WITH GOOD VALUES FOR SLAM. Four clubs allows responder to bid four diamonds, transfer, so opener can play four hearts. If opener always bids four clubs with a slam try, opener always gets to play four hearts and, more important, opener doesn't give the opening leader any information to help him make a better opening lead. With six hearts and four spades and game-forcing values (♠AK32♥QJ5432♦Q2♣2) responder starts out the same, one notrump -- two clubs -- two diamonds -- three spades. When opener bids three notrump showing only two hearts, responder bids four hearts showing a six-card suit.

With five or more spades and exactly four hearts, responder jumps to three hearts, responder's four-card major, over opener's two-diamond denial. Over three hearts, opener bids three notrump holding only two spades. Holding three spades, opener bids three spades with bad values for slam, four clubs, artificial, with good values for slam. Four clubs allows responder to bid four hearts, transfer, so opener can play four spades. If responder has six spades and four hearts, responder starts out the same, one notrump -- two clubs -- two diamonds -- three hearts. When opener bids three notrump showing exactly two spades, responder bids four hearts showing a six-card spade suit and forcing opener to bid four spades.

If responder wants to bid RKC after using Smolen, responder does so only after a response which shows a fit. If responder bids four notrump over three notrump, responder shows a 4-5-2-2 or 4-5-3-1 quantitative raise.

---

[1] In Standard Bridge, responder jumps to three hearts over opener's two-diamond denial to show five or more hearts and four spades with game-forcing values. Three hearts gives opener a choice between three notrump and four hearts. This has the disadvantage of making responder the declarer in four hearts.

Opener	(1)	Responder		Opener	(2)	Responder	
♠QJ4 ♦A43		♠AK32 ♦Q2		♠QJ4 ♦A543		♠AK32 ♦Q2	
♥AK6 ♣K654		♥QJ432 ♣32		♥AK ♣K654		♥QJ5432 ♣2	

Opener (1)	Responder	Opener (2)	Responder
1NT	2clubs	1NT	2clubs
2diamonds	3spades(4-5)	2diamonds	3spades (4-5)
4clubs	4diamonds	3NT	4hearts (4-6)
4hearts	Pass	Pass	

Opener	(3)	Responder		Opener	(4)	Responder	
♠Q6 ♦A543		♠AK432 ♦Q2		♠Q6 ♦A543		♠AK5432 ♦2	
♥AK4 ♣K654		♥QJ32 ♣32		♥AK4 ♣K654		♥QJ32 ♣32	

Opener (3)	Responder	Opener (4)	Responder
1NT	2clubs	1NT	2clubs
2diamonds	3hearts (5-4)	2diamonds	3hearts(5-4)
3NT	Pass	3NT	4hearts(6-4)
		4spades	Pass

In examples (1) and (2), responder's jump to three spades shows exactly four spades and five or more hearts. In example (1), opener bids four clubs, showing three hearts and good values for slam. Responder bids four diamonds, transferring to four hearts. Opener bids four hearts, which ends the auction. In example (2), opener shows two hearts by bidding three notrump. Responder holds six hearts and signs-off in four hearts.[2]

In examples (3) and (4), responder's jump to three hearts shows exactly four hearts and five or more spades. In example (3), opener shows two spades by bidding three notrump and responder holding five spades passes. In example (4), opener shows two spades by bidding three notrump. Responder holds six spades and bids four hearts, transfer, forcing opener to bid four spades. Four hearts can't be to play, since responder's jump to three hearts shows exactly four hearts.

---

[2]   Responder can only transfer to four hearts with four diamonds when opener has shown a fit. If no fit has been found, four diamonds is needed to show a 4-5-4-0 hand trying to find a diamond fit.

Opener (5)	Responder	Opener (6)	Responder
♠J54 ♦AQ3	♠KQ32 ♦K2	♠J4 ♦A543	♠KQ32 ♦K2
♥765 ♣AKQJ	♥AQ432 ♣32	♥K65 ♣AK54	♥AQ432 ♣32
1NT	2clubs	1NT	2clubs
2diamonds	3spades (4-5)	2diamonds	3spades(4-5)
4hearts	Pass	4clubs	4NT
		5clubs	6hearts

Opener (7)	Responder	Opener (8)	Responder
♠AK4 ♦Q543	♠QJ32 ♦A2	♠AK4 ♦K543	♠QJ32 ♦A2
♥Q4 ♣A543	♥AKT32 ♣Q2	♥QJ ♣A543	♥AKT32 ♣Q2
1NT	2clubs	1NT	2clubs
2diamonds	3spades (4-5)	2diamonds	3spades(4-5)
3NT	4NT	3NT	4NT
Pass		6NT	Pass

In examples (5) and (6), responder's jump to three spades shows exactly four spades and five or more hearts. Holding three hearts, opener has two choices; four hearts to show a bad hand for slam, or four clubs, artificial, to show a good hand for slam. Whether a hand is good or bad is based on aces and honors in the majors, not the number of HCPs. ♠J32♥J32♦KQJ♣AKQJ, an 18-count, is a minimum while ♠A2♥AQ2♦A32♣5432, a 14-count, is a maximum.

In example (5), opener bids four hearts showing three hearts and a bad hand for slam. Opener does have 17 HCPs, but has only one HCP in the majors. Responder passes four hearts. In example (6), opener bids four clubs showing three hearts and a good hand for slam. Opener has only 15 HCPs, but has three keycards and a ruffing value. Responder bids four notrump, RKC for hearts, and finds opener with three keycards. Responder bids six hearts.

In examples (7) and (8), responder with 16 HCPs bids four notrump quantitative, asking opener to bid six notrump with a maximum. Four notrump can't be keycard since there isn't a trump suit.

Interference: If overcaller doubles two clubs or bids two diamonds, opener bids a four-card major if he has one. IF OPENER PASSES TWO-CLUBS DOUBLED OR PASSES TWO DIAMONDS, DENYING A FOUR-CARD MAJOR, RESPONDER USES SMOLEN TO DESCRIBE HIS MAJOR-SUIT HOLDING. RESPONDER JUMPS IN FOUR-CARD SUIT TO SHOW LENGTH IN THE OTHER MAJOR.

1.11 -- ONE NOTRUMP - TWO SPADES TRANSFERS TO CLUBS, CAN BE WEAK, INVITATIONAL (KQ5432 AND OUT), OR STRONG DEPENDING UPON FOLLOW-UP, (TWO NOTRUMP ACCEPTS CLUB INVITATION). ONE NOTRUMP - TWO NOTRUMP TRANSFERS TO DIAMONDS, CAN BE WEAK, INVITATIONAL (KQ5432 AND OUT), OR STRONG DEPENDING UPON FOLLOW-UP, (THREE CLUBS ACCEPTS DIAMOND INVITATION).

Two spades by responder shows at least five clubs and denies a four-card major and may be to get out in three clubs, invite three notrump, give choice of games (three notrump or five clubs) or make a slam try. Two notrump by responder shows at least five diamonds and denies a four-card major and may be to get out in three diamonds, invite three notrump, give choice of games (three notrump or five diamonds) or make a slam try. If responder has a weak or invitational hand, he will always have at least a six-card minor. Only in game-forcing situations will responder with only a five-card minor initiate a minor-suit transfer.

Over two spades transfer to clubs, opener's choices are to sign-off in three clubs or bid two notrump (pre-accept). Over two notrump transfer to diamonds opener's choices are to sign-off in three diamonds or bid three clubs (pre-accept). Opener pre-accepts if opener accepts an invitation to three notrump. To accept the invitation, opener must have a fit as well as stoppers. The perfect acceptance is ♠A32♥A32♦A432♣A32. Opener counts six tricks in responder's minor and three aces. Qxx in responder's minor is enough of a fit to accept. Responder does not invite three notrump with a suit that does not need a fit to run, such as AKQ432 or AQJ432. Responder just bids three notrump. Most likely three-notrump invitational holdings are KQ5432, KJ5432, QJ5432, AJ5432. Besides a fit, opener needs to take nine tricks before the opponents take five. Stoppers and quick tricks are important. Holding ♠432♥KQJ♦KQJ♣KQ32, opener declines the invitation because even if responder has one spade stopper, the opponents will take at least three spades and two aces before opener takes nine tricks. Holding ♠JT32♥A32♦AQ2♣A32, opener accepts the invitation because the opponents will not be able to take five spade tricks.

Opener doesn't deny a fit by signing off. Opener simply doesn't think he can make three notrump opposite KQ5432 and out. Opener can have a great fit and a great hand for slam but still decline the invitation to three notrump because opener has a worthless doubleton or tripleton.

With a weak club hand, responder passes opener's three-club rejection or bids three clubs over opener's two-notrump pre-acceptance. With an invitational club hand, responder bids three notrump over opener's two-notrump pre-acceptance and passes opener's three-club rejection. With a club slam try, responder bids higher than three clubs over opener's three-club rejection and makes any bid other than three clubs or three notrump over opener's two-notrump pre-acceptance. With a balanced slam try in clubs, responder jumps to four notrump, quantitative, over opener's two-notrump pre-acceptance. Three notrump is a sign-off over opener's two-notrump pre-acceptance. Over opener's three-club rejection, three notrump is a slam try and shows a balanced 15-count while four notrump shows a 16 or 17-count.

With a weak diamond hand, responder passes opener's three-diamond rejection or bids three diamonds over opener's three-club pre-acceptance. With an invitational diamond hand, responder bids three notrump over opener's three-club pre-acceptance and passes opener's three-diamond rejection. With a diamond slam try, responder bids higher than three diamonds over opener's three-diamond rejection, and makes any bid other than three diamonds or three notrump over opener's three-club pre-acceptance. With a balanced diamond slam try, responder jumps to four notrump, quantitative, over opener's three-club pre-acceptance. Three notrump is a sign-off over opener's three-club pre-acceptance. Over opener's three-diamond rejection, three notrump is a slam try and shows a 15-count while four notrump shows a 16 or 17-count.

Opener	(1)		Responder		Opener	(2)		Responder	
♠QJ4	♦QJ54		♠32	♦32	♠654	♦KQJ4		♠32	♦32
♥AK5	♣A65		♥432	♣KQJ432	♥KQJ	♣A65		♥432	♣KQJ432

Opener (1)	Responder	Opener (2)	Responder
1NT	2spades	1NT	2spades
2NT	3NT	3clubs	Pass

In examples (1) and (2), responder bids two spades transferring to clubs. In example (1), opener counts nine tricks and bids two notrump accepting responder's possible invitation. If opener thinks he can take nine tricks opposite KQ5432, responder is willing to put opener to the test and bids three notrump. I know a heart lead beats three notrump, but opener is very likely to get a diamond or a spade lead. In example (2), opener has a great club fit and can count nine tricks; however, opener knows the opponents can take at least five tricks first, so opener bids three clubs, rejecting the invitation.

Opener	(3)	Responder		Opener	(4)	Responder	
♠QJ4	♦QJ54	♠32	♦32	♠A54	♦A654	♠32	♦32
♥AK4	♣A87	♥J32	♣J65432	♥AKQ4	♣87	♥J32	♣J65432
1NT		2spades		1NT		2spades	
2NT		3clubs		3clubs		Pass	

Opener	(5)	Responder		Opener	(6)	Responder	
♠7654	♦AJ6	♠32	♦KQ5432	♠54	♦AJ6	♠32	♦KQ5432
♥AKJ	♣A43	♥432	♣J2	♥KQJ	♣AQ43	♥432	♣J2
1NT		2NT		1NT		2NT	
3clubs		3NT		3diamonds		Pass	

In examples (3) and (4), responder bids two spades, transferring to clubs. In example (3), opener bids two notrump, pre-acceptance, accepting a possible club invitation. However, responder is so weak that responder bids three clubs, declining the acceptance. In example (4), opener has a maximum with aces, but bids three clubs rejecting a possible club invitation because his clubs are so bad. In examples (5) and (6), responder bids two notrump, transferring to diamonds. In example (5), opener counts nine tricks and bids three clubs, accepting responder's possible invitation, since with opener holding four spades, the opponents are unlikely to be able to take five spade tricks. Responder with an invitational hand bids three notrump. In example (6), opener has a great diamond fit and can count nine tricks; however, opener knows the opponents can take at least five tricks first, so opener bids three diamonds, rejecting the invitation.

Examples (2), and (6) are good examples where opener rejects an invitation to three notrump, but if the small cards happen to be opposite shortness, opener will accept a slam invitation. Examples (1), and (3) are just the opposite. Opener accepts a three-notrump invitation, but because one of the QJx's will be opposite shortness, rejects most slam invitations. Example (4) is a good example where opener rejects an invitation to three notrump because his clubs are so bad but accepts a slam invitation because he has a maximum with aces. Opener does not necessarily need good support to accept a slam try. Example (5) is a good example where opener accepts all invitations because he has a maximum, he has aces and he has great support.

1.12 -- TRANSFER TO THREE CLUBS OR THREE DIAMONDS FOLLOWED BY A NEW SUIT SHOWS SHORTNESS AND SHOWS SLAM INTEREST.

Opener	(1)	Responder		Opener	(2)	Responder

♠QJ3 ♦QJ43   ♠2 ♦AK2   ♠543 ♦QJ43   ♠2 ♦AK2
   ♥KQ4 ♣A65   ♥J32 ♣KQJ432   ♥AKQ ♣A65   ♥J32 ♣KQJ432

1NT	2spades	1NT	2spades
3clubs	3spades	3clubs	3spades
3NT	Pass	4hearts	4NT
		5hearts	6clubs
		Pass	

Once responder transfers to a long minor, the next step is for responder to show shortness[3] and where it is. Responder wants to avoid getting to three notrump with an unstopped suit, and get to slam if opener has fitting cards. Three-of-a-major, after transferring to diamonds, or any three-level bid after transferring to clubs, is forcing to game and shows shortness in that suit. Opener bids three notrump if opener has responder's short suit well stopped and has no interest in getting to slam.

In examples (1) and (2), responder transfers to clubs and then bids three spades, showing game-forcing values with spade shortness. In example (1), opener, with a spade stopper and a bad hand for slam, signs-off in three notrump. In example (2), opener with three little spades knows that his hand is golden. However, opener can't bid RKC because if responder holds one keycard and answers five diamonds, opener would get to slam with two keycards missing. Opener has to be satisfied cuebidding four hearts. Responder is able to bid RKC. With responder's club and diamond holdings, it's impossible for opener to cuebid four hearts without at least two keycards. Responder signs-off in six clubs with one keycard missing.

Since transferring to a minor followed directly by four notrump is quantitative, in order to ask for keycards after transferring, responder has to show an unbalanced hand first. Therefore, responder has to show a singleton before bidding four notrump. If responder wants to bid RKC but has a balanced hand, responder bids three-of-either-major first, a white lie, and then bids four notrump. Once responder shows an unbalanced hand, four notrump is always RKC.

---

[3] Shortness denotes singleton or void

1.13 -- AFTER ONE NOTRUMP - TWO CLUBS - TWO SPADES. THREE HEARTS SHOWS FOUR SPADES WITH SOME SHORTNESS. FOUR CLUBS IS ROMAN KEYCARD GERBER FOR SPADES. FOUR DIAMONDS IS A BALANCED SLAM TRY WITH FOUR SPADES.

Opener	(1)	Responder		Opener	(2)	Responder	
♠AJ54	♦7654	♠KQ32	♦32	♠AJ54	♦7654	♠KQ32	♦2
♥AKQ	♣K6	♥2	♣AQ5432	♥AKQ	♣K6	♥32	♣AQ5432

Opener (1)	Responder	Opener (2)	Responder
1NT	2clubs	1NT	2clubs
2spades	3hearts	2spades	3hearts
3spades	3NT	3spades	4diamonds
4clubs	4hearts	4NT	5spades
4spades	Pass	6spades	Pass

After one notrump -- two clubs -- two spades, responder bids three hearts, artificial, to show four-card spade support, shortness somewhere and a slam try. Shortness means singleton or void. Responder needs to have a slam try to bid three hearts. With ♠AJ32♥AJ32♦2♣5432, responder is not strong enough to bid three hearts over two spades. Responder signs-off in four spades over two spades. If opener is interested in knowing where responder's shortness is, opener bids three spades asking. With ♠KQJ2♥QJ2♦QJ2♣QJ2, opener does not bother asking where responder's shortness is, he just signs-off in four spades. Over opener's three-spade ask, responder answers three notrump showing heart shortness, four clubs showing club shortness and four diamonds showing diamond shortness.

In examples (1) and (2), responder bids three hearts, artificial, showing a slam try with four spades and shortness somewhere. Opener bids three spades asking. In example (1), responder answers three notrump showing heart shortness. Opener has a super maximum in support of spades but holding AKQ opposite heart shortness, can only invite slam. Opener invites slam by bidding four clubs, his cheapest control. Since responder has implied length in clubs by showing shortness elsewhere, kings as well as aces can be shown. Responder, with his club suit filled in, is able to cuebid four hearts. A cuebid below game is not a slam commitment, just a slam try. Opener, knowing that a diamond control is missing, signs-off in four spades. In example (2), responder answers four diamonds, showing diamond shortness. Opener with a maximum notrump, good controls, and diamond length with no wasted diamond honors, takes control with RKC and signs-off in six spades when one keycard is missing. If opener's diamond holding is KJxx or KQxx, opener signs-off in four spades.

Opener (3)		Responder		Opener (4)		Responder	
♠J543	♦AQ43	♠AKQ2	♦2	♠J543	♦KQJ3	♠AKQ2	♦2
♥AQ3	♣K6	♥2	♣AQJ5432	♥KQ3	♣K6	♥2	♣AQJ5432

Opener (3)	Responder	Opener (4)	Responder
1NT	2clubs	1NT	2clubs
2spades	4clubs	2spades	4clubs
4spades	5clubs	4diamonds	4spades
5NT	7NT	Pass	

Opener (5)		Responder		Opener (6)		Responder	
♠KQ54	♦AJ43	♠AJ32	♦2	♠Q654	♦KQJ3	♠AJ32	♦2
♥A43	♣J6	♥2	♣AKQ5432	♥KQJ	♣J6	♥2	♣AKQ5432

Opener (5)	Responder	Opener (6)	Responder
1NT	2clubs	1NT	2clubs
2spades	4clubs	2spades	4clubs
4diamonds	4spades	4diamonds	4spades
5spades	7NT	Pass	

After one notrump -- two clubs -- two spades, responder bids four clubs, Roman Keycard Gerber, asking for keycards with spades as the trump suit. Opener answers four diamonds showing zero or three keycards, four hearts showing one or four keycards, four spades showing two keycards without the spade queen and four notrump showing two keycards with the spade queen. Responder can ask for keycards, find out that he is missing two keycards, or one keycard and the trump queen, and still sign-off in four spades.

In examples (3) through (6), responder bids four clubs asking for keycards with spades as the trump suit. In example (3), responder finds out that opener has two keycards. Responder continues with five clubs promising all the keycards and asking for specific kings up the line. Opener answers five notrump showing the king of clubs and denying the diamond king and the heart king. Five notrump shows the king of the king-asking suit. Responder counts 13 tricks and bids seven notrump. In example (4), responder finds out that opener doesn't have any keycards. Responder, missing two keycards signs-off in four spades. In examples (5) and (6), responder, not knowing whether opener has zero or three keycards, signs-off in four spades. In example (5), opener bids five spades showing three keycards, and the spade queen, but denying any outside kings (see section 25.2). Over five spades, responder bids seven notrump. In example (6), opener holding zero keycards passes four spades and a disaster is averted.

25

Opener	(7)	Responder		Opener	(8)	Responder	
♠KJ54	♦AQJ5	♠AQ32	♦432	♠KJ54	♦AQJ5	♠AQT9	♦432
♥543	♣A4	♥A2	♣KQ32	♥543	♣A4	♥A2	♣KQJ2
1NT		2clubs		1NT		2clubs	
2spades		4diamonds		2spades		4diamonds	
4hearts		4spades		4hearts		4NT	
Pass				5clubs		6spades	

Opener	(9)	Responder		Opener	(10)	Responder	
♠A654	♦KQJ	♠KQ32	♦32	♠AJ54	♦KQJ	♠KQ32	♦32
♥K5	♣A432	♥A432	♣KQJ	♥KJ	♣5432	♥A432	♣KQJ
1NT		2clubs		1NT		2clubs	
2spades		4diamonds		2spades		4diamonds	
4NT		5spades		4spades		Pass	
6spades		Pass					

After one notrump -- two clubs -- two spades, responder bids four diamonds to show a balanced slam try, 15-17 HCPs, with four spades. Responder bids four diamonds instead of jumping to five spades as a quantitative invitation. Over four diamonds, opener signs-off in four spades with a minimum. With a maximum, opener commits to slam unless two keys are found to be missing. With an in-between hand, a minimum hand in high cards but with good controls or a hand with 16 HCPs, opener bids four hearts, the Last Train (see section 12.11).

In examples (7) through (10), responder jumps to four diamonds, showing four-card spade support and a slam try. In examples (7) and (8), opener has enough to cooperate but not enough to insist on slam, so he compromises and bids four hearts, the Last Train. Opener does not promise a heart control by bidding four hearts. In example (7), responder, with a minimum slam try, signs-off in four spades. In example (8), responder with a maximum invitation, bids RKC and bids slam. In this case, responder does not have to bid five notrump showing all the keycards, since opener's hand is limited. In example (9), opener with prime values has enough to commit the hand to slam unless two keys are missing. Opener bids four notrump, RKC, and then bids six spades when responder shows two keycards and the spade queen. In example (10), opener with a minimum notrump and jacks which can be wasted values, signs-off in four spades.

1.14 -- AFTER ONE NOTRUMP - TWO CLUBS - TWO HEARTS. THREE SPADES SHOWS FOUR HEARTS WITH SOME SHORTNESS. FOUR CLUBS IS ROMAN KEYCARD GERBER FOR HEARTS. FOUR DIAMONDS IS A BALANCED SLAM TRY WITH FOUR HEARTS.

Opener	(1)	Responder		Opener	(2)	Responder
♠KQJ3 ♦KQJ		♠2 ♦32		♠A543 ♦KQ4		♠2 ♦32
♥QJ54 ♣76		♥AK32 ♣KQ5432		♥QJ54 ♣A6		♥AK32 ♣KQ5432

Opener (1)	Responder	Opener (2)	Responder
1NT	2clubs	1NT	2clubs
2hearts	3spades	2hearts	3spades
4hearts	Pass	3NT	4hearts
		4NT	5hearts
		6hearts	Pass

After one notrump -- two clubs -- two hearts, responder bids three spades, artificial, to show four-card heart support, shortness somewhere and a slam try. Singleton is assumed, but responder can show the void through void responses to RKC (see section 25.6). If opener is interested in knowing where responder's shortness is, opener bids three notrump asking. Responder answers four clubs showing club shortness, and four diamonds showing diamond shortness. With spade shortness, responder answers four hearts if responder's willing to be passed in four hearts, or four spades if responder is too strong to be passed out in four hearts.

In examples (1) and (2), responder bids three spades, artificial, showing a slam try with four hearts and shortness somewhere. In example (1), opener has wasted values in all suits, a minimum with poor controls. Since opener is not required to ask where responder's shortness is, opener just signs-off in four hearts. In example (2), opener bids three notrump, asking. Responder answers four hearts, showing a minimum slam try with a singleton or void in spades. Opener, with Axxx of spades opposite shortness, has an easy RKC bid and signs-off in six hearts when one keycard is missing. With wasted spade values such as KQ2 or KJ2, opener passes four hearts. If responder's hand is ♠2♥AK32♦K2♣KQ5432, a king more than the example hand, responder answers four spades to opener's three-notrump ask instead of four hearts. Holding only two keycards, responder can't bid RKC over two hearts, since opener can have ♠KQJ♥J654♦QJ2♣AJ6. However, once opener shows more than a minimum by his three-notrump ask, responder can bid above game.

Opener	(3)	Responder		Opener	(4)	Responder	
♠AQJ3 ♦AK3		♠2 ♦2		♠AQJ3 ♦AK3		♠K2 ♦2	
♥J654 ♣76		♥AKQ2 ♣AQJ5432		♥J654 ♣76		♥AQ32 ♣KQJ432	

Opener	Responder	Opener	Responder
1NT	2clubs	1NT	2clubs
2hearts	4clubs	2hearts	4clubs???
4spades	5clubs	4spades	5hearts
5diamonds	6clubs	Pass	
6hearts	Pass		

After one notrump -- two clubs -- two hearts, responder bids four clubs, Roman Keycard Gerber, asking for keycards with hearts as trumps. SINCE A FOUR-SPADE RESPONSE SHOWS TWO KEYCARDS AND IS FORCING TO THE FIVE-LEVEL, ASKER, IN ORDER TO BID FOUR CLUBS, MUST HAVE AT LEAST THREE OF THE SIX KEYS (FOUR ACES AND KQ OF TRUMPS) OR MUST HAVE AT LEAST 17 HCPS. The key here is that responder doesn't want to play at the five-level and possibly go minus. If there is any chance that two keys can be missing, responder shows shortness by bidding three spades over two hearts, or makes a balanced slam try by bidding four diamonds.

In example (3), responder needs opener to have two aces and the club king to make seven hearts, and just needs opener to have one ace to have a play for six hearts. Responder bids four clubs, RKC for hearts. Opener answers four spades showing two keycards and denying the heart queen. If opener doesn't have any keycards and answers four diamonds, zero or three keycards, responder signs-off in four hearts. If opener has one keycard and answers four hearts, responder jumps to six hearts. Over four spades, responder bids five clubs showing all the keycards and asking for specific kings up the line. Opener answers five diamonds showing the king of diamonds, his cheapest king. Bidding five diamonds does not deny holding the club or spade king. A five-spade answer shows the king of spades and denies the king of diamonds. Bidding five spades does not deny holding the club king. A five-notrump answer shows the king in the king-ask suit, clubs, and denies any other kings. A five-heart answer denies any outside kings. Over five diamonds, responder is interested in the club king and bids six clubs asking opener to bid seven if opener has the club king. Opener does not have the club king and signs-off in six hearts. If opener has the club king, he bids anything other than six hearts. In example (4), responder makes a big mistake bidding four clubs, keycard for hearts. Over four clubs, opener answers four spades showing two keycards. Responder, missing two keycards, has to play in five hearts which can go down if suits split badly.

Opener (5)		Responder		Opener (6)		Responder	
♠KQJ	♦KQJ5	♠32	♦432	♠A54	♦AKQ	♠32	♦432
♥KJ54	♣32	♥AQ32	♣AKQJ	♥KJ54	♣432	♥AQ32	♣AKQJ

Opener	Responder	Opener	Responder
1NT	2clubs	1NT	2clubs
2hearts	4diamonds	2hearts	4diamonds
4hearts	Pass	4spades	4NT
		5clubs	6hearts

Opener (7)		Responder		Opener (8)		Responder	
♠AQ3	♦KQJ	♠K2	♦32	♠A43	♦KQJ	♠K2	♦32
♥K543	♣654	♥AQJ2	♣KQJ32	♥K543	♣A54	♥AQJ2	♣KQJ32

Opener	Responder	Opener	Responder
1NT	2clubs	1NT	2clubs
2hearts	4diamonds	2hearts	4diamonds
4hearts	Pass	4spades	4NT
		5clubs	6NT

After one notrump -- two clubs -- two hearts, responder bids four diamonds to show a balanced slam try, 15-17 HCPs, with four hearts. Over four diamonds, opener signs-off in four hearts with 15 HCPs and bids above four hearts with 17 HCPs. With 16 HCPs, opener accepts with keycards and rejects with queens and jacks.

In examples (5) and (6), responder needs opener to have a maximum to have any play for slam. In example (5), opener has 16 HCPs but has no aces, and signs-off in four hearts. In example (6), opener has enough to try for slam. Opener notices, however, that if he bids RKC, responder might have only one keycard and respond five diamonds. Opener will not be able to ask for the heart queen and might get to slam missing one keycard and the queen of hearts. Opener solves the problem by bidding four spades. Responder asks for keycards and bids six hearts. Responder can't be embarrassed by any of opener's answers. In examples (7) and (8), responder needs opener to have at least three keycards to have any play for slam. Responder can't bid four clubs, Roman Keycard Gerber, since opener might have only two keycards and five hearts might go down if suits split badly. In example (7), opener has a minimum and signs-off in four hearts. In example (8), opener has a maximum with good controls. Opener bids four spades to force responder to bid keycard. Responder bids keycard and finds one keycard missing. Since one keycard is missing and opener has a maximum, six notrump should be a better contract than six hearts, avoiding possible bad splits and ruffs.

29

1.15 -- ONE NOTRUMP - THREE CLUBS SHOWS BOTH MINORS, AT LEAST 5-5, AND IS WEAK.

Opener	(1)	Responder		Opener	(2)	Responder

♠AQJ3   ♦K65   ♠2   ♦QJ432   ♠KQ43   ♦AK65   ♠2   ♦QJ432
   ♥AQJ4 ♣65   ♥32   ♣QJ432   ♥KQ   ♣765   ♥32   ♣QJ432

Opener (1)	Responder	Opener (2)	Responder
1NT	3clubs	1NT	3clubs
3diamonds	Pass	Pass	

If responder is 5-5 or longer in the minors (♠32♥2♦Q5432♣Q5432) with a weak hand, responder wants to play in three-of-a-minor rather than one notrump. With three or more clubs, opener passes three clubs, otherwise opener bids three diamonds.

In example (1), opener has only two clubs, so opener corrects three clubs to three diamonds. In example (2), opener has four diamonds and only three clubs. However, opener passes three clubs, hoping to buy the contract. Opener knows that the opponent's have a nine-card major-suit fit, and by passing three clubs, opener gives only LHO a chance to balance. The extra outstanding club makes it is less likely that LHO will be short enough to balance. Also, there is a likely club ruff in a diamond contract.

1.16 -- ONE NOTRUMP - THREE DIAMONDS SHOWS BOTH MINORS AT LEAST 5-5, AND IS GAME FORCING.

Opener	(1)	Responder	Opener	(2)	Responder
♠AQJ3 ♦Q76		♠2 ♦A5432	♠AK43 ♦KQJ6		♠2 ♦A5432
♥AQJ4 ♣43		♥32 ♣AKQJ2	♥A54 ♣43		♥32 ♣AKQJ2

Opener (1)	Responder	Opener (2)	Responder
1NT	3diamonds	1NT	3diamonds
3NT	Pass	3spades	4clubs
		4hearts	4NT
		5clubs	5hearts
		5spades	7NT

Responder bids three diamonds to show at least 5-5 in the minors with game-forcing values. Opener is in a good position to decide whether this hand belongs in three notrump, five-of-a-minor or slam. THE MOST IMPORTANT STEP IN HAVING A GOOD SLAM SEQUENCE IS SETTING TRUMPS AS SOON AS POSSIBLE. I recommend using three hearts to set clubs as trumps and three spades to set diamonds as trumps. This way, both partners know what the trump suit is, and four notrump can then be RKC for that minor. If opener has a choice, opener sets clubs as trumps to get the benefit of the opening lead. Follow-ups can vary from simple cuebids to complicated asking bids, depending upon partnerships. If opener has a super maximum without a fit, ♠AKQJ♥AQJT♦876♣43 for instance, opener jumps to four notrump (natural).

In example (1), opener has only two points in the minors and signs-off in three notrump. In example (2), opener has four-card diamond support and sets diamonds as trumps by bidding three spades. Over three spades, responder can show a minimum hand by bidding either three notrump or four diamonds. Responder shows a sound slam try by cuebidding four clubs. Opener who can show all of his honors through keycard, cuebids four hearts encouraging responder to bid keycard. Responder bids four notrump, RKC for diamonds. When opener shows three keycards, responder bids five hearts asking for the diamond queen. Since five hearts is higher than five diamonds, five hearts promises all the keycards and is a grand slam try. Over five hearts, opener bids five spades showing the queen of diamonds and the king of spades. Six diamonds denies the queen of diamonds. Responder counts 13 tricks and bids seven notrump. Opener showed 16 of his 17 HCPs.

1.17 -- ONE NOTRUMP - THREE HEARTS SHOWS BOTH MAJORS AT LEAST 5-5 AND IS INVITATIONAL TO GAME.

Opener	(1)	Responder		Opener	(2)	Responder	
♠KQ6 ♦A54		♠A5432	♦32	♠876 ♦KQJ4		♠A5432	♦32
♥AQ5 ♣6543		♥KJ432	♣2	♥Q65 ♣AKJ		♥KJ432	♣2

1NT		3hearts		1NT		3hearts	
4spades		Pass		3spades		Pass	

Responder bids three hearts showing at least 5-5 in the majors with invitational values. Over three hearts, opener is in a good position to decide whether this hand belongs in game or in a partscore. If opener is 2-2 in majors, good luck. Aces and honors in the majors are valuable, kings and queens in the minors are not. If possible, opener plays the hand in spades to get benefit of the opening lead.

In example (1), even though opener has only 15 HCPs, all of his cards are working, so opener jumps to four spades. In example (2), opener has 16 HCPs, but only one honor in the majors, so opener rejects responder's invitation. Even though opener's hearts are better than his spades, opener bids three spades. If opener gets a club lead into his AKJ, opener can take one more trick.

1.18 -- ONE NOTRUMP - THREE SPADES SHOWS BOTH MAJORS AT LEAST 5-5 AND IS JUST CHOICE OF GAMES.

One notrump -- three spades is 5-5 or better in the majors and is limited to choice of games. Responder just wants to play in game and doesn't want to get to the five-level. ♠AQ432♥QJ432♦32♣2 is a typical hand where responder wants to be in just game opposite a notrump opener. Opener, if equal in the majors, plays in hearts to get benefit of the opening lead. Opener can have a super maximum in support of hearts, such as ♠K2♥K432♦AK32♣A32, and can make a slam try by bidding four clubs, setting hearts as trumps. Over four clubs, responder bids four diamonds as a transfer, since opener has not yet bid hearts. Opener can also have a super maximum in support of spades, such as ♠K432♥K2♦AK32♣A32, and can make a slam try by bidding four diamonds, setting spades as trumps. Over four diamonds, responder bids four spades as a sign-off and four hearts as an artificial forward-going bid. Responder has already bid spades, so there is no need to transfer.

1.19 -- ONE NOTRUMP - TWO HEARTS - TWO SPADES - THREE HEARTS SHOWS BOTH MAJORS AT LEAST 5-5 AND IS A SLAM TRY.

Opener (1)	Responder	Opener (2)	Responder
♠A432 ♦A32	♠KQJ65 ♦54	♠A2 ♦AQ32	♠KQJ65 ♦54
♥QJ ♣A432	♥AK654 ♣5	♥QJ32 ♣K32	♥AK654 ♣5

1NT	2hearts	1NT	2hearts
2spades	3hearts	2spades	3hearts
3spades	4clubs	4clubs	4diamonds
4NT	5spades	4NT	5hearts
5NT	6hearts	6hearts	Pass
7spades	Pass		

Responder transfers to spades and then bids three hearts to show a slam try with at least 5-5 in the majors. This auction allows the trump suit to be set at a low level, and the sooner both partners know which major is the trump suit, the better the constructive auction will be. After one notrump -- two hearts -- two spades -- three hearts, opener with wasted minor-suit honors signs-off in four-of-a-major. Opener signs-off in three notrump with either 2-2 in the majors or a hand without any major-suit honors (♠J32♥J2♦KQJ9♣AKQ2). With a maximum, opener bids three spades, setting spades as trumps, or cuebids four-of-either-minor, setting hearts as trumps. A direct four notrump by opener is RKC for hearts. If opener wants to keycard for spades, opener bids three spades first and then bids four notrump.

WHENEVER RESPONDER SHOWS A TWO-SUITER, OPENER'S FIRST DUTY IS TO SET TRUMPS AS SOON AS POSSIBLE. With equal majors, opener sets spades as trumps to get the benefit of the opening lead and to keep the auction lower.

In examples (1) and (2), responder shows a slam try with at least 5-5 in the majors. In example (1), opener bids three spades, setting spades as trumps. Responder bids four clubs, showing a club control. Opener bids keycard for spades and finds responder with two keycards and the queen of spades. Opener bids five notrump asking for specific kings. When responder shows the king of hearts, opener bids seven spades, knowing that he can use responder's heart suit for discards. In example (2), opener bids four clubs, a cuebid setting hearts as trumps. If possible, opener tries to bid four clubs, which leaves room for responder to bid four diamonds. Responder, with extras, bids four diamonds, the Last Train. Opener bids keycard for hearts and then bids six hearts.

Opener (3)		Responder		Opener (4)		Responder	
♠A32	♦KQJ	♠KQJ54	♦43	♠A2	♦KQJ2	♠KQJ54	♦43
♥Q32	♣QJ32	♥AK654	♣4	♥Q32	♣QJ32	♥AK654	♣4

Opener (3)	Responder	Opener (4)	Responder
1NT	2hearts	1NT	2hearts
2spades	3hearts	2spades	3hearts
4spades	Pass	4hearts	Pass

Opener (5)		Responder		Opener (6)		Responder	
♠A432	♦KQJ	♠KQJ65	♦43	♠A2	♦KQJ2	♠KQJ65	♦43
♥Q32	♣QJ2	♥AK876	♣3	♥5432	♣KQ2	♥AK876	♣3

Opener (5)	Responder	Opener (6)	Responder
1NT	2hearts	1NT	2hearts
2spades	3hearts	2spades	3hearts
3spades	4clubs	4clubs	4diamonds
4spades	Pass	4hearts	Pass

In examples (3) through (6), responder describes a slam-going hand with at least 5-5 in the majors. In example (3), opener, holding no outside aces and only two major-suit honors, jumps to four spades, his most discouraging action in support of spades. Responder with a minimum slam try, passes. In example (4), opener bids four hearts, his most discouraging action in support of hearts. Responder passes. In example (5), opener, holding four spades, bids three spades, setting spades as trumps. If opener has four spades and has any reason to think his hand might be of any value, he should bid only three spades. Holding four cards in a major is enough to make a forward-going bid. Responder bids four clubs showing extras. Opener, who couldn't have a worse notrump opener, signs-off in four spades and responder passes. In example (6), opener, holding four hearts, bids four clubs, setting hearts as trumps. If opener has four hearts and has any reason to think his hand might be of any slam value, he cuebids. Responder bids four diamonds showing extras, and opener signs-off in four hearts ending the auction.

1.20 -- AFTER JACOBY, OPENER CAN SHOW FOUR TRUMPS (SUPER ACCEPT) BY BIDDING A DOUBLETON (RESPONDER SHOULD RETRANSFER) OR BY JUMPING TO THREE-OF-A-MAJOR.

Opener (1)		Responder		Opener (2)		Responder	
♠54	♦J54	♠32	♦32	♠AK54	♦J54	♠32	♦AK
♥AQJ6	♣AQJ6	♥K5432	♣5432	♥AQJ6	♣76	♥K5432	♣A432

Opener (1)	Responder	Opener (2)	Responder
1NT	2diamonds	1NT	2diamonds
2spades	3diamonds	3clubs	3diamonds
3hearts	Pass	3hearts	4clubs
		4diamonds	4NT
		5spades	6hearts

Over responder's Jacoby transfer, opener is expected to complete the transfer by bidding two-of-the-anchor-suit. If responder bids two diamonds, opener is expected to bid two hearts, the anchor suit. If responder bids two hearts, opener is expected to bid two spades, the anchor suit. However, if opener has four or five-card support, opener is allowed to show it, to super accept, by bidding above two-of-the-anchor suit. Any bid higher than the anchor suit is a super accept and shows a doubleton in the bid suit with four or more of the anchor suit. Even with a minimum notrump it's very important to show where the doubleton is. Opener bids two notrump to show a 4-3-3-3 maximum with at least three-card support. Opener jumps in the anchor suit with a doubleton in the transfer suit or to conceal his distribution. Opener can't show a doubleton in the transfer suit because responder needs to be able to bid that suit to retransfer. Having opener play the hand is sometimes worth a trick. Responder's first duty after the super accept is to retransfer. After retransferring, responder passes, bids game or makes a slam try depending on his strength. Responder's best possible holding is four small opposite opener's doubleton. Responder's worst holding is two small.

In examples (1) and (2), responder transfers to hearts. In example (1), opener bids two spades, showing four or more hearts and exactly two spades. Responder bids three diamonds, retransfer, and then passes three hearts. If three hearts goes down, the opponents should be able to make at least two spades. In example (2), opener bids three clubs showing four or more hearts and exactly two clubs. Responder bids three diamonds, retransfer, and then, knowing this is a good fitting hand, cuebids four clubs. With good trumps and the AK of spades, opener has just enough to bid four diamonds, the Last Train. Responder bids keycard and bids six hearts.

Opener	(3)	Responder		Opener	(4)	Responder	
♠AJ76	♦KQJ4	♠Q5432	♦A2	♠K76	♦AKQ	♠Q5432	♦32
♥A54	♣76	♥32	♣5432	♥K54	♣K876	♥32	♣AJ32

Opener	Responder	Opener	Responder
1NT	2hearts	1NT	2hearts
3clubs	3hearts	2NT	3hearts
3spades	4spades	3spades	4spades

Opener	(5)	Responder		Opener	(6)	Responder	
♠QJ65	♦A4	♠432	♦32	♠QJ65	♦KJ	♠432	♦32
♥AQJ6	♣QJ4	♥K5432	♣K32	♥AQJ6	♣QJ4	♥K5432	♣K32

Opener	Responder	Opener	Responder
1NT	2diamonds	1NT	2diamonds
3hearts	Pass	2hearts	Pass

In examples (3) and (4), responder bids two hearts planning on passing two spades. In example (3), opener's three-club bid, showing four spades and only two clubs, makes responder's hand worth bidding game. Responder bids three hearts, retransferring to spades, and raises to game. In example (4), two notrump shows a 4-3-3-3 maximum or super maximum. Responder retransfers and then raises three spades to game. This is the rare exception when opener can super accept with only three-card support. At IMPs, I would always super accept, since I expect my opponent at the other table to open my hand one club and jump to two notrump. At matchpoints, however, I would bid only two spades. In example (5), opener jumps to three hearts showing four or more hearts and possibly a doubleton diamond. NOTICE THAT OPENER CAN'T BID THREE DIAMONDS BECAUSE THAT IS RESERVED FOR RETRANSFERRING. Responder also has a doubleton diamond and passes three hearts.

Just because opener has four-card support doesn't mean opener has to super accept. Opener might not super accept with Qx, QJ, KQ or AJ in the doubleton suit. Opener might not super accept vulnerable with a minimum. Opener might not super accept holding four cards in the other major. Opener might not super accept holding cards which will be useful on defense but not on offense. Opener might not super accept if he's 4-3-3-3.

Example (6) is a type of hand when opener might not super accept holding four-card support. Holding four cards in the other major, honors in the doubleton suit, jacks which can be more valuable on defense than on offense, all point to trying to buy this hand as cheaply as possible.

1.21 -- JACOBY FOLLOWED BY A THREE-LEVEL MINOR BID IS GAME FORCING, SHOWS A SECOND SUIT AND IS A MILD SLAM TRY.

Opener	(1)	Responder		Opener	(2)	Responder	
♠AQJ3 ♦AQJ4		♠2 ♦32		♠AQJ3 ♦AQJ4		♠2 ♦32	
♥K6 ♣765		♥A5432 ♣AQ432		♥K76 ♣65		♥A5432 ♣AQ432	

Opener (1)	Responder	Opener (2)	Responder
1NT	2diamonds	1NT	2diamonds
2hearts	3clubs	2hearts	3clubs
3NT	Pass	3hearts	4hearts

Responder transfers to his major and bids three-of-his-minor to show a five-card major, a four or five-card minor, and enough strength to force to game. With a five-card major, a four-card minor, and a singleton, responder needs at least 12 HCPs to transfer to his major and bid three-of-a-minor. ♠KJ432♥Q32♦3♣AQ32 is the minimum needed to transfer to two spades and bid three clubs with five spades and four clubs and a singleton. With 5-4-2-2, responder with nine to thirteen HCPs should transfer to his major and rebid three notrump. With a five-card major, a four-card minor and eight or nine HCPs, responder transfers to his major and rebids two notrump. With a five-card major and a five-card minor, eight HCPs is enough for responder to transfer to his major and bid three-of-his-minor. ♠Q5432♥32♦2♣AQ432 is a minimum needed to transfer to two spades and bid three clubs with five spades and five clubs.

IF OPENER HAS AT LEAST THREE-CARD SUPPORT OF RESPONDER'S MAJOR, OPENER MUST SET RESPONDER'S MAJOR AS TRUMPS BY BIDDING THREE-OF-RESPONDER'S-MAJOR. Unless responder is a passed hand, opener should not jump to four-of-responder's-major, just in case responder wants to make a slam try. IF OPENER BIDS ANYTHING OTHER THAN THREE-OF-RESPONDER'S-MAJOR, OPENER DENIES THREE-CARD SUPPORT. If opener has two cards in responder's major, opener bids three notrump with both unbid suits well stopped.

In examples (1) and (2), responder shows five hearts and at least four clubs with game-forcing values. In example (1), opener has only two hearts and bids three notrump. Opener has diamonds and spades well stopped and will have wasted values opposite responder's shortness. In example (2), opener has three-card heart support and sets hearts as trumps by bidding three hearts. Responder, with a minimum hand, raises to four hearts. While opener will usually pass four hearts, opener, with ♠A32♥K32♦A2♣KQ432, for instance, can check for keycards and bid at least six clubs.

Opener (3)	Responder			Opener (4)	Responder		
♠J43 ♦AKQ4	♠2	♦32		♠A43 ♦AK54	♠2	♦32	
♥KQ ♣7654	♥AJ432	♣AQJ32		♥K5 ♣K654	♥AJ432	♣AQJ32	

Opener (3)	Responder	Opener (4)	Responder
1NT	2diamonds	1NT	2diamonds
2hearts	3clubs	2hearts	3clubs
3diamonds	4clubs	4NT	5spades
4hearts	Pass	7clubs	Pass

Opener (5)	Responder			Opener (6)	Responder		
♠Q43 ♦AKQ4	♠J2	♦32		♠Q43 ♦AKQ4	♠J2	♦32	
♥KQ ♣J654	♥A5432	♣AQ32		♥KQ6 ♣J54	♥A5432	♣AQ32	

Opener (5)	Responder	Opener (6)	Responder
1NT	2diamonds	1NT	2diamonds
2hearts	3NT	2hearts	3NT
Pass		4hearts	Pass

In example (3), responder shows at least five hearts and at least four clubs with game-forcing values. Opener has only two hearts and can't support hearts. Since opener's spade holding is suspect, opener bids three diamonds, which shows diamond values and denies spade values. Responder doesn't have spade values, so responder can't bid three notrump. Responder rebids his club suit. With a minimum and wasted values in diamonds, opener shows his good two-card heart support. Responder passes four hearts, ending the auction. The key is to avoid three notrump without a spade stopper. In example (4), responder shows hearts and clubs with game-forcing values. Opener with four-card club support and all aces and kings, bids keycard for clubs. When responder shows two keycards and the club queen, opener bids seven clubs. If responder doesn't have five clubs, he has extra values, such as ♠32♥AQJ32♦32♣AQJ2, and all seven clubs needs is a 3-2 club break. Four notrump is keycard for clubs, since opener did not bid three hearts setting hearts as trumps. In examples (5) and (6), responder with 2-5-2-4 distribution does not have enough strength to transfer and bid a new suit. Responder transfers to hearts and jumps to three notrump. Responder wants to play in four hearts if opener has at least three hearts, and wants to play in three notrump if opener has only two hearts. In example (5), opener has only two hearts and passes three notrump. In example (6), opener with three hearts corrects three notrump to four hearts. Every once in a while, opening leader will have K109xx of clubs, and you will be thankful that clubs were never bid.

1.22 -- ONE NOTRUMP - TWO DIAMONDS - TWO HEARTS - TWO SPADES IS INVITATIONAL WITH FIVE HEARTS AND FOUR SPADES.

Opener (1)	Responder	Opener (2)	Responder
♠7654 ♦AQ4	♠AJ32 ♦32	♠KQ54 ♦AQ4	♠AJ32 ♦32
♥QJ6 ♣KQJ	♥K5432 ♣32	♥AQ6 ♣654	♥K5432 ♣32
1NT	2diamonds	1NT	2diamonds
2hearts	2spades	2hearts	2spades
Pass		4spades	Pass

Opener (3)	Responder	Opener (4)	Responder
♠K54 ♦AQ54	♠AJ32 ♦32	♠K54 ♦AQ54	♠AJ32 ♦32
♥Q6 ♣KQJ4	♥K5432 ♣32	♥J6 ♣KQJ4	♥K5432 ♣32
1NT	2diamonds	1NT	2diamonds
2hearts	2spades	2hearts	2spades
3NT	Pass	2NT	Pass

Responder shows five hearts and four spades with around eight HCPs by transferring to two hearts and then bidding two spades. With game-forcing values, responder uses Smolen. If opener holds four spades, opener passes two spades with a minimum and jumps to four spades with a maximum. If opener is in the middle, opener invites with three spades. With heart support, opener bids three hearts with a minimum or bids four hearts with a maximum. If opener does not have three hearts or four spades, opener bids two notrump with a 15-16 HCPs and three notrump with 17 HCPs. Opener bids conservatively, since responder is usually counting distribution as part of his invite.

In examples (1) through (4), responder transfers to two hearts and then bids two spades, showing five hearts, four spades and around eight HCPs. In example (1), opener with four spades and a bare minimum passes two spades. In example (2), opener with a maximum notrump and fits in both majors wants to be in game. Opener bids four spades rather than four hearts, since the 4-4 spade fit sometimes takes more tricks than the 5-3 heart fit. If opener holds three hearts and four spades, opener has to weigh the advantages of playing in a 4-4 spade fit with the disadvantages of having the lead come through him. In examples (3) and (4), opener has only three spades and two hearts and, therefore, cannot play in a major. In example (3), opener, with 17 HCPs, jumps to three notrump. In example (4), opener, with 16 HCPs, stops in two notrump.

1.23 -- ONE NOTRUMP - TWO DIAMONDS - TWO HEARTS - FOUR HEARTS OR ONE NOTRUMP - TWO HEARTS - TWO SPADES - FOUR SPADES ARE MILD BALANCED SLAM TRIES.

Opener (1)	Responder	Opener (2)	Responder
♠QJ3 ♦QJ43	♠AK2 ♦K2	♠43 ♦AQ43	♠AK2 ♦K2
♥76 ♣AKQ4	♥KJ5432 ♣32	♥AQ6 ♣K654	♥KJ5432 ♣32
1NT	2diamonds	1NT	2diamonds
2hearts	4hearts	2hearts	4hearts
Pass		4NT	5hearts
		6hearts	Pass

Opener (3)	Responder	Opener (4)	Responder
♠765 ♦QJ4	♠AQJ432 ♦K32	♠765 ♦QJ4	♠AQJ432 ♦K32
♥AQJ4 ♣KQ4	♥K2 ♣32	♥AQJ4 ♣KQ4	♥32 ♣32
1NT	2hearts	1NT	4hearts
2spades	4spades	4spades	Pass

Playing Texas and Jacoby, responder has a choice of how to get to game holding a six-card or longer major. Responder can transfer at the four-level, Texas, or responder can transfer at the two-level, Jacoby, and jump to game. Jacoby followed by a jump to game is a non-forcing mild slam try denying an outside singleton or void, while Texas is either a sign-off or is used to set trumps in order to bid RKC. Texas is preemptive and makes it more difficult for the opponents to compete. Responder uses Jacoby when responder needs opener to have a fit along with aces and kings to make a slam.

In examples (1) and (2), responder transfers to two hearts and then bids four hearts, a mild balanced slam try. In example (1), opener passes four hearts because he has only one ace, one king and no fit. In example (2), opener bids RKC because his hand contains a fit, two aces, one king and a possible ruffing value. In example (3), responder transfers to two spades and then jumps to four spades showing a mild balanced slam try. Opener with a minimum passes four spades. In example (4), responder wants to play in four spades. Responder transfers at the four-level and passes four spades.

Jumps to game after Jacoby in competition are not slam tries (see section 1.26).

1.24 -- AFTER JACOBY TRANSFERS, JUMPS SET TRUMPS AND ARE SPLINTERS.

Opener (1)		Responder	
♠QJ4	♦QJ54	♠A32	♦K32
♥65	♣AKQ3	♥KQJ432	♣2

Opener	Responder
1NT	2diamonds
2hearts	4clubs
4hearts	Pass

Opener (2)		Responder	
♠KQJ	♦AQ54	♠A32	♦K32
♥65	♣A543	♥KQJ432	♣2

Opener	Responder
1NT	2diamonds
2hearts	4clubs
4NT	5spades
6hearts	Pass

Opener (3)		Responder	
♠KJ3	♦AQ54	♠2	♦K32
♥65	♣KQJ4	♥KQJ432	♣A32

Opener	Responder
1NT	2diamonds
2hearts	3spades
4hearts	Pass

Opener (4)		Responder	
♠543	♦AQ4	♠2	♦K32
♥A65	♣KQJ4	♥KQJ432	♣A32

Opener	Responder
1NT	2diamonds
2hearts	3spades
4NT	5spades
6hearts	Pass

After responder transfers to two-of-a-major and opener completes the transfer, a jump by responder in a new suit shows a good six-card or longer major with shortness in the bid suit. After one notrump -- two diamonds -- two hearts, jumps to three spades, four clubs and four diamonds by responder show at least six good hearts, a slam try, and shortness in the bid suit. Similarly, after one notrump -- two hearts -- two spades, a jump to four clubs, four diamonds and four hearts by responder shows at least six good spades, a slam try and shortness in the bid suit. Opener needs aces and kings with very little wastage in the splinter suit to bid above game.

In examples (1) and (2), responder transfers to hearts and then jumps to four clubs, showing a heart slam try with club shortness. In example (1), opener, with values in clubs, signs-off in four hearts. In example (2), opener with no wasted club values bids keycard and bids a slam. In examples (3) and (4), responder shows a heart slam try with spade shortness. In example (3), opener with KJ of spades signs-off. In example (4), opener with three little spades has enough to take charge by bidding RKC. After responder shows two keycards and the heart queen, opener bids six hearts.

1.25 -- AFTER JACOBY TRANSFER A JUMP TO FOUR NOTRUMP IS NATURAL.

Opener	(1)	Responder		Opener	(2)	Responder	
♠QJ3	♦QJ54	♠AK2	♦K32	♠Q43	♦AQ54	♠AK2	♦K32
♥54	♣AKQ4	♥KQJ32	♣32	♥54	♣AKQ4	♥KQJ32	♣32

Opener	Responder	Opener	Responder
1NT	2diamonds	1NT	2diamonds
2hearts	4NT	2hearts	4NT
Pass		6NT	Pass

Opener	(3)	Responder		Opener	(4)	Responder	
♠Q3	♦A654	♠AK2	♦K32	♠Q3	♦AQ54	♠AK2	♦K32
♥A54	♣KQ54	♥KQJ32	♣32	♥A54	♣KQ54	♥KQJ32	♣32

Opener	Responder	Opener	Responder
1NT	2diamonds	1NT	2diamonds
2hearts	4NT	2hearts	4NT
5hearts	Pass	6hearts	Pass

Jacoby followed by a jump to four notrump is similar to a one notrump -- four notrump bid but with a five-card major. A typical hand has 15 or 16 HCPs. Responder is always 5-3-3-2. If responder is 5-4, he transfers and then bids his four-card minor or bids Smolen if he's 5-4 in the majors. If opener has only two-card support for responder's major, opener passes four notrump with 15 or a bad 16 and bids six notrump with 17 or a good 16. With heart support, opener bids five hearts with a minimum, six hearts with a maximum.

In examples (1) through (4), responder has a balanced hand with five hearts and 16 HCPs. Responder transfers to hearts and then bids four notrump quantitative. In examples (1) and (2), opener has only two hearts so he can't support hearts. In example (1), opener has only 15 HCPs, so opener passes four notrump. In example (2), opener has 17 HCPs so opener jumps to six notrump. In examples (3) and (4), opener has heart support. In example (3), opener has a minimum notrump and signs-off in five hearts. In example (4), opener has a maximum notrump and jumps to six hearts.

1.26 -- IF JACOBY GETS DOUBLED.

Opener	(1)	Responder		Opener	(2)	Responder	
♠32 ♦AQJ2		♠QJT65 ♦543		♠432 ♦AQJ2		♠QJT65 ♦543	
♥K32 ♣AQ32		♥Q4 ♣654		♥K32 ♣AQ2		♥Q4 ♣654	

Open	Advnc	Resp	Over	Open	Advnc	Resp	Over
1NT	Pass	2♥	Dbl	1NT	Pass	2♥	Dbl
Pass	Pass	2♠	Pass	2♠	Pass	Pass	

If an opponent doubles two diamonds, opener passes the double with two-card heart support. Over opener's two-card-heart-support pass, responder with a weak hand bids two hearts, completing the transfer. If responder has an invitational hand and only a five-card heart suit, responder bids two notrump. If responder has an invitational hand and a six-card heart suit, responder jumps to three hearts. If responder was planning on bidding Jacoby and jumping to game showing a mild slam try, responder uses four diamonds, Texas, instead. After the double, any bid by responder other than two hearts, three hearts, four diamonds or two notrump is forcing to game and carries the same meaning as if the transfer has not been doubled. If responder has a game-forcing hand and is worried about stoppers in the doubled suit, responder can cuebid or bid a new suit.

With three-card heart support, opener accepts the transfer. With four-card heart support, opener bids either two hearts or three hearts depending upon his hand (see section 1.20). In competition, if opener has four-card support, it's more important to preempt the auction then to show a doubleton. Redouble shows at least four diamonds and only two hearts, and suggests the ability to play two-diamonds redoubled.

The same logic applies if two-hearts is doubled. Opener passes two-hearts doubled to show exactly two spades. Opener bids two spades with three-card support. With four-card support opener bids either two spades or three spades depending upon his hand.

In examples (1) and (2), overcaller doubles responder's two-heart transfer. In example (1), opener, holding two spades, passes the double. Responder with a weak hand bids two spades completing the transfer, and opener passes. This is a situation where two spades gets played from the wrong side. In example (2), opener holds three spades and completes the transfer. Responder with a weak hand passes two spades.

Opener	(3)	Responder		Opener	(4)	Responder	
♠K2 ♦AQJ2		♠QJT43 ♦K43		♠K2 ♦AQJ2		♠QJT43 ♦K43	
♥432 ♣AQJ2		♥A5 ♣543		♥432 ♣AQJ2		♥65 ♣K43	

Open	Advnc	Resp	Over	Open	Advnc	Resp	Over
1NT	Pass	2♥	Dbl	1NT	Pass	2♥	Dbl
Pass	Pass	3♥	Pass	Pass	Pass	2NT	Pass
3♠	Pass	4♠	Pass	3♠	Pass	4♠	Pass

Opener	(5)	Responder		Opener	(6)	Responder	
♠432 ♦AQJ2		♠QJT65 ♦K43		♠432 ♦AQJ2		♠QJT65 ♦543	
♥K32 ♣AQ2		♥Q4 ♣KJ3		♥K32 ♣AQ2		♥Q4 ♣KJ3	

Open	Advnc	Resp	Over	Open	Advnc	Resp	Over
1NT	Pass	2♥	Dbl	1NT	Pass	2♥	Dbl
2♠	Pass	4♠	Pass	2♠	Pass	3♠	Pass
Pass	Pass			4♠	Pass		

In examples (3) and (4), opener, holding two spades, passes the double. In example (3), responder, with a game-forcing hand, cuebids. He knows opener has only two spades, but if opener doesn't have help in hearts, four spades can be a better contract than three notrump. Opener bids three spades and responder raises to game. If opener has the heart king instead of the spade king he bids three notrump. In example (4), responder, holding nine HCPs, bids two notrump invitational, the same bid he would have made had two hearts not been doubled. Opener with a maximum without a heart stopper bids three spades showing two-card support. Responder raises to four spades.

In examples (5) and (6), opener holds three spades and completes the transfer. In example (5), with 12 HCPs and an eight-card fit, responder jumps to four spades. This is not a mild slam try. Responder's original intention was to transfer and then bid three notrump, giving opener a choice between three notrump and four spades. Since opener promises at least three spades when he accepts the transfer after the double, responder can jump straight to four spades. If responder's original intention was to transfer and jump to four spades as a mild slam try, responder cuebids instead. In example (6), responder with nine HCPs invites. Since opener promises three spades, opener invites with three spades rather than two notrump. Opener with 16 good points and the working king of hearts accepts.

CHAPTER 2 - IF THE OPPONENTS COMPETE AGAINST OUR NOTRUMP

2.1 -- PENALTY DOUBLE -- REDOUBLE FORCES TWO CLUBS TO SIGN-OFF IN A MINOR, AND REST OF SYSTEM IS ON.

Opener	(1)	Responder		Opener	(2)	Responder	
♠A5	♦A765	♠432	♦32	♠A5	♦A765	♠432	♦KJ432
♥AK65	♣Q65	♥432	♣KJ432	♥AK65	♣Q65	♥432	♣32

Open	Over	Resp	Advnc	Open	Over	Resp	Advnc
1NT	Dbl	Rdbl	Pass	1NT	Dbl	Rdbl	Pass
2♣	Pass	Pass	Pass	2♣	Pass	2♦	Pass

When overcaller doubles one notrump for penalties, a direct two clubs by responder is Stayman. Pass by responder says that he wants to play one-notrump doubled. Sometimes responder is 4-3-3-3 and a 4-3-3-3 hand opposite a 4-3-3-3 hand usually does better playing in notrump. Redouble by responder forces opener to bid two clubs. Responder, holding clubs, passes opener's forced two-club bid or, holding diamonds, bids two diamonds to play. Holding a five-card or longer minor, the odds are that two-of-your-minor will play as well if not better than one-notrump doubled.

In examples (1) and (2), overcaller doubles one notrump for penalties. Responder wants to play this hand in two-of-a-minor. Responder redoubles overcaller's penalty double, forcing opener to bid two clubs. In example (1), responder with a weak club hand passes two clubs. In example (2), responder wants to play this hand in two diamonds. Over opener's forced two-club bid, responder corrects to two diamonds.

Any call by responder after a penalty double other than redouble carries the same meaning as if overcaller had passed. Two clubs is Stayman, two diamonds and two hearts are Jacoby, etc. Since there are two ways for responder to show a one-suited club hand, redouble forcing two clubs and two spades transferring to three clubs, two spades shows a hand with at least six clubs. Since there are two ways for responder to show a one-suited diamond hand, redouble forcing two clubs followed by two diamonds and two notrump transferring to three diamonds, two notrump shows a hand with at least six diamonds. If responder holds 5432♥5432♦5432♣2, responder bids two clubs and passes any response by opener.

Opener	(3)	Responder		Opener	(4)	Responder	
♠65 ♦AQJ8		♠432 ♦32		♠65 ♦AQJ8		♠32 ♦K765432	
♥AK65 ♣Q65		♥QJ432 ♣432		♥AK65 ♣Q65		♥2 ♣432	

Open	Over	Resp	Advnc	Open	Over	Resp	Advnc
1NT	Dbl	2♦	Pass	1NT	Dbl	2NT	Pass
3♥	Pass	Pass	Pass	4♦	Pass	Pass	Pass

Opener	(5)	Responder		Opener	(6)	Responder	
♠87 ♦AQJ4		♠5432 ♦32		♠87 ♦AQJ4		♠65432 ♦32	
♥AK5 ♣Q654		♥QJ432 ♣32		♥AK5 ♣Q654		♥QJ32 ♣32	

Open	Over	Resp	Advnc	Open	Over	Resp	Advnc
1NT	Dbl	2♣	Pass	1NT	Dbl	2♣	Pass
2♦	Pass	2♥	Pass	2♦	Pass	2♠	Pass

In example (3), responder wants to play the hand in two hearts. Over overcaller's penalty double, responder bids two diamonds, Jacoby. Opener with four hearts super-accepts by jumping to three hearts. Showing a doubleton spade doesn't figure to help responder but can help the opponents. In example (4), responder has seven diamonds and wants to play this hand in at least three diamonds. Responder bids two notrump which is a transfer to three diamonds. Opener has great diamond support but does not pre-accept with three clubs because of his two little spades. Since opener knows that responder has at least six diamonds, he follows the Law and bids to the ten-trick level.

In examples (5) and (6), responder bids two clubs, Stayman, and opener responds two diamonds, denying a four-card major. In example (5), responder bids two hearts showing a weak hand with at least 4-4 in the majors. Opener passes two hearts. With three spades and only two hearts, opener must correct two hearts to two spades since responder might have only four hearts. In example (6), responder bids two spades showing a weak hand with five spades and four hearts and opener passes two spades.

2.2 -- DOUBLE OTHER THAN PENALTIES -- REDOUBLE IS STRONG AND SYSTEM IS ON.

Opener	(1)	Responder		Opener	(2)	Responder	

♠54   ♦AQJ5   ♠AQ32 ♦432   ♠54   ♦AQJ5   ♠32   ♦K432
  ♥AK54 ♣Q54   ♥32   ♣KJ32   ♥AK54 ♣Q54   ♥QJ32 ♣AJ2

Open	Over	Resp	Advnc	Open	Over	Resp	Advnc
1NT	Dbl*	Rdbl	2♦	1NT	Dbl**	Rdbl	Pass
Dbl	2♥	Pass	Pass	Pass	2♠	Pass	Pass
Dbl	Pass	Pass	Pass	3♥	Pass	4♥	Pass

Opener	(3)	Responder		Opener	(4)	Responder	

♠65   ♦AQJ5   ♠AQ432 ♦432   ♠65   ♦AQJ5   ♠32   ♦432
  ♥AK65 ♣Q65   ♥32   ♣432   ♥AK65 ♣Q65   ♥QJ432 ♣432

Open	Over	Resp	Advnc	Open	Over	Resp	Advnc
1NT	Dbl*	2♥	Dbl	1NT	Dbl**	2♦	Pass
Pass	Pass	2♠	Pass	3♥	Pass	Pass	Pass

*four card major & longer minor   **unspecified one-suiter

If overcaller's double is some form of takeout double, redouble shows a penalty oriented hand. In example (1), responder redoubles to let opener know that the opponents could be in trouble. Responder is happy to double the black suits, and maybe opener can double the red suits. Advancer bids two diamonds, choice of majors, which opener doubles. Overcaller bids two hearts. Responder passes two hearts around to opener, who doubles. Happy ending! In example (2), responder redoubles to tell opener that they have the balance of power. Overcaller bids two spades which responder passes around to opener. Opener, with two small spades, can't double two spades. Since opener can't pass two spades, opener bids three hearts and responder raises to four hearts. If opener does not have four hearts, he bids two notrump with a spade stopper or bids three-of-a-minor.

If responder doesn't have a penalty oriented hand, responder ignores the double. Responder bids two-clubs Stayman, two-diamonds and two-hearts Jacoby, etc. In examples (3) and (4), responder has a weak hand with a five-card major. In example (3), responder bids two hearts, Jacoby. Advancer doubles. Since opener has only two spades, opener passes the double. Responder signs-off in two spades. In example (4), responder transfers to hearts, and opener, following total-trick concepts, jumps to three hearts.

2.3 -- TWO CLUBS NATURAL, TRANSFER OR CAPPELLETTI, DOUBLE IS STAYMAN AND REST OF SYSTEM IS ON.

Opener	(1)	Responder		Opener	(2)	Responder	
♠65 ♦A65		♠K432 ♦K432		♠Q65 ♦AQJ5		♠32 ♦K432	
♥AQJ5 ♣KQJ4		♥32 ♣A32		♥AQJ5 ♣54		♥K432 ♣A32	

Open	Over	Resp	Advnc	Open	Over	Resp	Advnc
1NT	2♣*	Dbl	Pass	1NT	2♣*	Dbl	Pass
Pass	2♥	Pass	Pass	2♥	Pass	4♥	Pass
Dbl	Pass	Pass	Pass	Pass	Pass		

Opener	(3)	Responder		Opener	(4)	Responder	
♠65 ♦AQJ5		♠AQ432 ♦432		♠65 ♦AQJ5		♠32 ♦432	
♥AK65 ♣Q65		♥32 ♣432		♥AK65 ♣Q65		♥QJ432 ♣432	

Open	Over	Resp	Advnc	Open	Over	Resp	Advnc
1NT	2♣*	2♥	Pass	1NT	2♣*	2♦	Pass
2♠	Pass	Pass	Pass	3♥	Pass	Pass	Pass

Over overcaller's two clubs, which is either natural, a transfer to diamonds, an unspecified one-suiter or an unspecified two-suiter, responder's double is Stayman. Opener with at least three clubs and defensive prospects passes the double of two clubs for penalties. If opener has only two clubs, opener bids a four-card major or bids two diamonds without one. Responder doesn't promise a four-card major since doubling two clubs and then bidding two notrump is the way responder invites three notrump. All other bids carry the same meaning as if overcaller had passed. Two diamonds and two hearts are Jacoby, two notrump is a transfer to diamonds, etc. Responder can double two clubs with fewer than eight points if responder can pass any response opener makes or responder can bid two-of-a-major showing a weak hand with both majors.

In examples (1) through (4), overcaller bids two clubs showing an unspecified one-suiter. Responder doubles two clubs, which is Stayman. In example (1), opener, with clubs, passes responder's double. Opener can double clubs or hearts and hopes that responder can double diamonds or spades. Overcaller bids two hearts showing a heart one-suiter. Responder passes two hearts, allowing opener to double. In example (2), opener, with only two clubs, bids two hearts and responder raises to four. In examples (3) and (4), responder transfers to two-of-his-major.

2.4 -- TWO CLUBS OR TWO DIAMONDS SHOWING BOTH MAJORS -- DOUBLE IS A PENALTY DOUBLE OF ONE OR BOTH MAJORS OR A STRONG HAND WITH BOTH MINORS. PASS THEN DOUBLE IS COOPERATIVE. TWO HEARTS SHOWS CLUBS AND TWO SPADES SHOWS DIAMONDS (UNUSUAL OVER UNUSUAL) WITH INVITATIONAL STRENGTH OR BETTER.

Opener	(1)	Responder		Opener	(2)	Responder	
♠54 ♦Q65		♠AQ32 ♦KJ32		♠AQ4 ♦AQJ5		♠32 ♦K432	
♥AK54 ♣AQJ5		♥32 ♣432		♥54 ♣Q765		♥QJ32 ♣AJ2	

Open	Over	Resp	Advnc	Open	Over	Resp	Advnc
1NT	2♣*	Dbl	Pass	1NT	2♣*	Dbl	2♠
Pass	2♥	Pass	Pass	Pass	Pass	3♠	Pass
Dbl	Pass	Pass	Pass	3NT	Pass	Pass	Pass

* majors

If two clubs or two diamonds shows both majors, it becomes unnecessary to try to get to a major-suit fit. You are very unlikely to need Stayman or Jacoby transfers. What is necessary is to be able to double the opponents if they are out of line or to be able to have a constructive minor-suit auction. It is more efficient to play UNUSUAL OVER UNUSUAL rather than Systems On.

Responder's double of overcaller's major-showing two clubs or major-showing two diamonds shows a semi-balanced defensive oriented hand. Responder is prepared to double the opponents if they bid one of his four-card suits, pass opener's four-card penalty double, or strongly invite game. Responder with a singleton in one of the majors should try to find another call since the opponents will very likely have at least an eight-card fit. After responder's double, opener or responder needs a very good reason to double with only three cards in the opponent's suit. A maximum with good defensive cards, vulnerable opponents, playing matchpoints and state of the match are reasons for making a three-card speculative double.

In examples (1) and (2), overcaller bids two clubs showing both majors. Responder, who can make a penalty double of one of the majors, doubles two clubs. In example (1), opener holds four hearts and doubles two hearts for penalties. Responder is very happy to defend. In example (2), opener has three spades, so opener can either make a speculative double and lead trumps or opener can pass to see if responder can double two spades. Responder can't double two spades, so responder cuebids looking for the best game.

Opener	(3)	Responder	
♠543 ♦Q54		♠AQ2 ♦KJ32	
♥AK5 ♣AQJ5		♥432 ♣432	

Open	Over	Resp	Advnc
1NT	2♣*	Pass	2♥
Pass	Pass	Dbl	Pass
Pass	Pass		

Opener	(4)	Responder	
♠43 ♦Q54		♠AQ2 ♦KJ32	
♥AK65 ♣AQJ5		♥432 ♣432	

Open	Over	Resp	Advnc
1NT	2♣*	Pass	2♠
Pass	Pass	Dbl	Pass
3♣	Pass	3NT	Pass
Pass	Pass		

Opener	(5)	Responder	
♠654 ♦QJ3		♠Q32 ♦AK2	
♥K54 ♣AKQJ		♥Q32 ♣5432	

Open	Over	Resp	Advnc
1NT	2♣*	Pass	2♠
Pass	Pass	Double	Pass
2NT	Pass	3NT	Pass
* majors			

Opener	(6)	Responder	
♠54 ♦QJ3		♠Q32 ♦AK2	
♥K54 ♣AKQJ6		♥Q32 ♣5432	

Open	Over	Resp	Advnc
1NT	2♣*	Pass	2♥
Pass	Pass	Dbl	Pass
2NT	Pass	3NT	Pass
Pass	Pass		

If responder wants to make a cooperative three-card double, responder passes overcaller's major-showing two clubs or major-showing two diamonds and then doubles at his next opportunity. Responder has enough strength to bid game. Opener pulls the double with two cards in the opponent's suit and passes with three or more cards in the opponent's suit. Opener pulls responder's double if opener has a five-card or longer minor or strength concentrated in a minor. The opponents won't be doubled if they are in an eight or nine-card fit and will likely be doubled if they are in a seven-card or worse fit.

In examples (3) through (6), overcaller bids two clubs showing both majors. Responder has a cooperative three-card double rather than a penalty double type hand. Responder passes two clubs and then doubles when advancer bids his better major. In example (3), opener has three hearts and happily passes responder's cooperative three-card double. In example (4), opener has only two spades and pulls responder's cooperative three-card double to his four-card club suit. Responder with a spade stopper bids three notrump. In examples (5) and (6), opener with a good club suit does not sit for responder's three-card cooperative double. Defending at the two-level, you don't want your AKQJ of clubs taking at most one trick on defense. Opener removes the double to two notrump and responder bids three notrump.

```
Opener    (7)      Responder           Opener    (8)      Responder

♠54    ♦654      ♠32  ♦AKJ32        ♠54    ♦654      ♠32  ♦AKQJ2
   ♥AK54  ♣AKJ5     ♥J32    ♣432       ♥AK54  ♣AKJ5     ♥QJ2    ♣432
```

Open	Over	Resp	Advnc	Open	Over	Resp	Advnc
1NT	2♣*	2♠	Pass	1NT	2♣*	2♠	Pass
3♦	Pass	Pass	Pass	3♦	Pass	3♥	Pass
* majors				4♣	Pass	5♦	Pass

If responder has a hand with a five-card or longer minor, responder bids UNUSUAL OVER UNUSUAL (see section 12.3) over the major-showing two clubs or major-showing two diamonds. Responder bids two hearts to show a club suit with at least invitational values, and bids two spades to show a diamond suit with at least invitational values. After bidding UNUSUAL OVER UNUSUAL, responder can pass any minimum response by opener.

Over two clubs showing both majors, two diamonds and three clubs by responder are natural and to play, showing less than invitational values. Over two diamonds, showing both majors, three clubs and three diamonds by responder are natural and to play, showing less than invitational values. Since two notrump is not needed as Lebensohl, it can be natural and invitational. A jump to three notrump is to play and says nothing about major-suit stoppers.

In examples (7) and (8), overcaller overcalls two clubs showing both majors. Responder bids two spades, UNUSUAL OVER UNUSUAL, showing a diamond suit and at least invitational values. Opener, with a minimum notrump, signs-off in three diamonds. In example (7), responder with an invitational diamond hand passes three diamonds. In example (8), responder with a game-forcing hand bids three hearts showing values in hearts and denying a spade stopper. WHEN THERE ARE TWO OPPONENT'S SUITS TO CUEBID, AND YOU'RE TRYING FOR THREE NOTRUMP, CUEBID THE SUIT YOU HAVE STRENGTH IN. Opener doesn't have spades stopped, so opener bids four clubs showing club values. Responder jumps to five diamonds. With only 11 HCPs, responder can bid a non-forcing four diamonds.

Even though the two-club or two-diamond bidder shows both majors, every once in a while opener and responder can have an eight or even a nine-card major-suit fit. Therefore, responder's jumps to three-of-a-major are natural and forcing, and Texas transfers apply.

2.5 -- IF OVERCALLER BIDS A NATURAL TWO HEARTS OR TWO SPADES OVER ONE NOTRUMP, TWO NOTRUMP IS LEBENSOHL, DOUBLE IS NEGATIVE.

Opener (1)		Responder		Opener (2)		Responder	
♠65 ♦AQJ4		♠432 ♦32		♠65 ♦AQJ4		♠32 ♦32	
♥AK6 ♣Q765		♥432 ♣KQJ32		♥AK6 ♣Q765		♥QJ5432 ♣432	

Open	Over	Resp	Advnc	Open	Over	Resp	Advnc
1NT	2♠	2NT	Pass	1NT	2♠	2NT	Pass
3♣	Pass	Pass	Pass	3♣	Pass	3♥	Pass

Opener (3)		Responder		Opener (4)		Responder	
♠54 ♦AQJ4		♠32 ♦K32		♠54 ♦AQJ4		♠32 ♦K32	
♥AK5 ♣Q654		♥QJ2 ♣AKJ32		♥AK5 ♣Q654		♥QJ432 ♣AK2	

Open	Over	Resp	Advnc	Open	Over	Resp	Advnc
1NT	2♠	3♣	Pass	1NT	2♠	3♥	Pass
3♥	Pass	3♠	Pass	4♥	Pass	Pass	Pass
4♣	Pass	5♣	Pass				

If overcaller bids a natural two hearts or a natural two spades, responder's two notrump is Lebensohl and forces opener to bid three clubs. IF OPENER HAS OPENED ONE NOTRUMP WITH A FIVE-CARD MAJOR, OPENER BIDS THE FIVE-CARD MAJOR INSTEAD OF AUTOMATICALLY BIDDING THREE CLUBS. Responder, with a sign-off in clubs, passes three clubs. With a sign-off in diamonds or hearts, responder corrects three clubs to three diamonds or three hearts. New suits by responder at the three-level are forcing to game.

In examples (1) through (4), overcaller bids two spades. In example (1), responder wants to play in three clubs. Responder bids two notrump forcing opener to bid three clubs, which responder passes. In example (2), responder wants to play in three hearts. Responder bids two notrump, forcing opener to bid three clubs. Responder then bids three hearts, which is to play. In example (3), responder bids three clubs, which is natural and game forcing. Opener bids three hearts, showing heart values. Responder, not sure where he is headed, bids three spades, the Last Train for three notrump, denying a spade stopper. Opener shows his club support, and responder raises to game. In example (4), responder, with a game-forcing heart hand, bids three hearts forcing. Opener with three-card support raises to four hearts.

Opener	(5)	Responder	
♠54 ♦AQJ4		♠K32 ♦32	
♥AK65 ♣Q65		♥Q32 ♣AK432	

Open	Over	Resp	Advnc
1NT	2♠	2NT	Pass
3♣	Pass	3NT	Pass
Pass	Pass		

Opener	(6)	Responder	
♠54 ♦AQJ4		♠K32 ♦32	
♥AK65 ♣Q65		♥Q432 ♣AJ32	

Open	Over	Resp	Advnc
1NT	2♠	2NT	Pass
3♣	Pass	3♠	Pass
4♥	Pass	Pass	Pass

Opener	(7)	Responder	
♠54 ♦AQJ4		♠K32 ♦32	
♥AK5 ♣Q765		♥Q432 ♣AJ32	

Open	Over	Resp	Advnc
1NT	2♠	2NT	Pass
3♣	Pass	3♠	Pass
3NT	Pass		

Opener	(8)	Responder	
♠54 ♦AQJ		♠K32 ♦32	
♥AK765 ♣Q65		♥Q32 ♣AK432	

Open	Over	Resp	Advnc
1NT	2♠	2NT	Pass
3♥	Pass	4♥	Pass
Pass	Pass		

Using Lebensohl (slow), game-forcing auctions that go through two notrump show a stopper in the opponent's suit. If responder goes through two notrump and cuebids, responder shows four of the other major plus a stopper in the opponent's suit. If responder goes through two notrump and then bids three notrump, responder shows enough strength to play in three notrump and a stopper in the opponent's suit. Playing Lebensohl you can't play two notrump.

In example (5), responder holds 12 HCPs and a spade stopper. Responder bids two notrump, forcing opener to bid three clubs. Responder then bids three notrump. Opener passes three notrump even though he has two little spades, since responder promises a spade stopper. In examples (6) and (7), responder has ten HCPs and four hearts. Responder bids two notrump, forcing opener to bid three clubs. Responder then cuebids three spades, showing four hearts and a spade stopper, and enough strength to bid game. In example (6), opener, with four-card support, bids four hearts. In example (7), opener does not have four hearts so he can't bid four hearts. Even though opener does not have a spade stopper, opener bids three notrump, knowing that responder has a spade stopper. In example (8), responder is expecting the auction to be the same as example (5). However, when opener shows a five-card heart suit, responder raises to four hearts.

Opener	(9)		Responder		Opener	(10)		Responder	
♠65	♦AQJ3		♠432	♦K2	♠K5	♦A543		♠432	♦K2
♥AK54	♣Q65		♥Q32	♣AK432	♥AK54	♣Q65		♥Q32	♣AK432

Open	Over	Resp	Advnc	Open	Over	Resp	Advnc
1NT	2♠	3NT	Pass	1NT	2♠	3NT	Pass
4♦	Pass	5♣	Pass	Pass	Pass		

Opener	(11)		Responder		Opener	(12)		Responder	
♠54	♦AQJ4		♠32	♦K32	♠54	♦AQJ4		♠32	♦K32
♥AK76	♣Q54		♥5432	♣AK32	♥AK6	♣Q654		♥5432	♣AK32

Open	Over	Resp	Advnc	Open	Over	Resp	Advnc
1NT	2♠	3♠	Pass	1NT	2♠	3♠	Pass
4♥	Pass	Pass	Pass	4♣	Pass	Pass	Pass

Using Lebensohl (slow), game-forcing auctions that bypass two notrump deny a stopper in the opponent's suit. A direct three notrump by responder denies four of the other major and denies a stopper in overcaller's suit. A direct cuebid by responder shows four of the other major and denies a stopper in overcaller's suit. With a partial stopper, or even no stopper, responder shows a stopper if three notrump figures to be as good a contract as four-of-a-minor. RESPONDER MAKES A BID DENYING A STOPPER ONLY IF HE CAN SUPPORT OPENER BIDDING FOUR-OF-A-MINOR. Even if you don't have a stopper the suit may block or they may lead some other suit.

In examples (9) and (10), responder bids a direct three notrump which denies a spade stopper and denies four hearts. If opener does not have a spade stopper, responder, with a five-card club suit, has a good alternative strain. In example (9), opener does not have a spade stopper so he bids four diamonds. Responder corrects to five clubs, ending the auction. In example (10), opener has a spade stopper and passes three notrump. In examples (11) and (12), responder cuebids three spades directly, which shows four hearts but denies a spade stopper. With a doubleton spade, responder has a good chance of finding an alternative strain if opener does not have four hearts and does not have a spade stopper. In example (11), opener has four hearts and bids four hearts. In example (12), opener doesn't have four hearts so he can't bid four hearts. Since opener doesn't have a spade stopper, opener can't bid three notrump either. Opener bids four clubs and responder with a minimum passes.

Opener	(13)	Responder		Opener	(14)	Responder	
♠654	♦AQ7	♠J32	♦5432	♠654	♦AQ7	♠A2	♦J65432
♥QJ54	♣AK4	♥AK2	♣Q32	♥QJ54	♣AK4	♥K32	♣Q2

Open	Over	Resp	Advnc	Open	Over	Resp	Advnc
1NT	2♠	2NT	Pass	1NT	2♠	3NT	Pass
3♣	Pass	3NT	Pass	4♣	Pass	4♦	Pass
Pass	Pass			5♦	Pass		

Example (13) is a good example of a hand where the only contract responder wants to play is three notrump. You might not make three notrump, but any other contract can be a disaster. Does responder really want to play a 4-3 or a 4-2 fit at the four-level if opener does not have a spade stopper? Since responder has no safety at the four-level, responder shows a spade stopper and hopes for the best. Example (14) is just the opposite. Responder has a hand where one spade stopper might not be enough to make three notrump. If opener does not have help in spades, five diamonds might be a better contract than three notrump. Responder bids a direct three notrump, denying a spade stopper. Opener does not have a stopper and runs to four clubs. Responder bids four diamonds, and opener, with nothing wasted in spades, raises, and a good five diamond contract is reached.

If overcaller shows a six-card or longer major, responder is very unlikely to have a penalty double. How often is responder going to have four cards in overcaller's suit? More likely responder is going to be short in overcaller's suit. Therefore double of a one-suited natural two-of-a-major overcall is negative and promises four cards in the other major with at least six HCPs. Responder doesn't promise a rebid and can pass any bid opener makes.

Over responder's negative double, opener bids a four-card or longer major. Otherwise opener bids a four-card minor, or bids two notrump with stoppers in overcaller's suit. If opener has a choice, opener bids a four-card minor rather then bid notrump. Since responder doubled to show the other major rather than going through Lebensohl, opener should be conservative.

If overcaller's two-of-a-major is conventional and can be a five-card or shorter suit, then responder's double is penalties.

2.6 -- IF OVERCALLER BIDS A NATURAL TWO DIAMONDS OVER ONE NOTRUMP, TWO NOTRUMP IS LEBENSOHL, DOUBLE IS NEGATIVE.

Opener (1)   Responder   Opener (2)   Responder

♠QJ5   ♦543   ♠432   ♦2   ♠QJ5   ♦543   ♠AK2   ♦2
  ♥AKQJ ♣QJ7   ♥432   ♣A65432   ♥AKQJ ♣QJ7   ♥432   ♣AK5432

Open	Over	Resp	Advnc
1NT	2♦	2NT	Pass
3♣	Pass	Pass	Pass

Open	Over	Resp	Advnc
1NT	2♦	3♣	Pass
3♥	Pass	3♠	Pass
4♥	Pass	6♣	Pass

Opener (3)   Responder   Opener (4)   Responder

♠QJ4   ♦654   ♠K32   ♦32   ♠654   ♦K54   ♠K32   ♦32
  ♥AKQJ ♣QJ5   ♥432   ♣AK432   ♥AKQJ ♣QJ5   ♥432   ♣AK432

Open	Over	Resp	Advnc
1NT	2♦	3NT	Pass
4♣	Pass	Pass	Pass

Open	Over	Resp	Advnc
1NT	2♦	3NT	Pass
Pass	Pass		

Over a natural two diamonds, two notrump is slow Lebensohl and is similar to bidding over a two-of-a-major overcall. If responder has a game-forcing hand without a four-card major, responder jumps directly to three notrump without a stopper, and bids two notrump followed by three notrump with a stopper. To check for majors with game-forcing values, responder can go through Slow Lebensohl with a stopper or Fast Lebensohl without a stopper.

In example (1), responder wants to play in three clubs. Responder bids two notrump, slow Lebensohl, forcing opener to bid three clubs. In example (2), responder wants to investigate a club slam. Responder bids three clubs forcing. Opener bids three hearts, denying a diamond stopper. Responder bids three spades showing spade values. Opener rebids his hearts, showing a five-card or strong four-card suit. Responder, facing a hand with nothing wasted in diamonds, takes a chance with six clubs. In examples (3) and (4), responder doesn't have a diamond stopper and doesn't have a four-card major, so responder jumps directly to three notrump. In example (3), opener doesn't have a diamond stopper and runs to four clubs. Since responder didn't make a negative double or bid Stayman, responder must have a club suit for his three-notrump jump. Responder has a minimum three-notrump bid and passes four clubs. In example (4), opener has a diamond stopper, so he passes three notrump.

Opener	(5)	Responder		Opener	(6)	Responder	
♠Q654	♦A4	♠KJ32	♦K32	♠Q54	♦A54	♠KJ32	♦K32
♥AK54	♣QJ5	♥32	♣K432	♥AK54	♣QJ5	♥32	♣K432

Open	Over	Resp	Advnc	Open	Over	Resp	Advnc
1NT	2♦	Dbl	Pass	1NT	2♦	Dbl	Pass
2♥	Pass	3NT	Pass	2♥	Pass	3NT	Pass
4♠	Pass	Pass	Pass	Pass	Pass		

Opener	(7)	Responder		Opener	(8)	Responder	
♠Q654	♦A4	♠KJ32	♦32	♠Q654	♦A4	♠KJ32	♦32
♥AK65	♣QJ5	♥Q432	♣432	♥AK65	♣QJ5	♥Q432	♣A32

Open	Over	Resp	Advnc	Open	Over	Resp	Advnc
1NT	2♦	Dbl	Pass	1NT	2♦	Dbl	Pass
2♥	Pass	Pass	Pass	2♥	Pass	4♥	Pass

Responder's double of a natural two-diamond overcall or two-diamond balance is negative and promises at least one four-card major and at least five HCPs. If opener responds two notrump or three clubs to responder's negative double denying a four-card major, responder uses Smolen to show various major-suit lengths.

In examples (5) and (6), responder's negative double followed by three notrump shows a four-card major with a diamond stopper. If responder doesn't have a diamond stopper, responder cuebids after opener bids two-of-the-other-major. In example (5), opener knows responder has at least one major and corrects three notrump to four spades. In example (6), opener passes three notrump. In example (7), responder has a six-point hand with both majors. Responder doubles and passes any bid opener makes. If responder bids two spades over opener's two hearts, responder has fewer than eight HCPs with four spades and four or more clubs. If opener responds two spades to the negative double and responder corrects to three clubs, responder has fewer than eight HCPs with four hearts and four or more clubs. In example (8), responder has a game-forcing hand with both majors. Responder doubles and then bids game.

Two-level bids by responder are natural and non-forcing. Jumps to the three-level by responder are game forcing and show at least a five-card major. If responder has an invitational hand with a five-card or longer major, responder bids two notrump forcing opener to bid three clubs. Responder then bids three-of-a-major invitational.

57

2.7 -- DEFENSE AGAINST TWO DIAMONDS SHOWING ONE MAJOR.

Opener	(1)	Responder			Opener	(2)	Responder	
♠65 ♦AQJ4		♠432 ♦32			♠65 ♦AQJ4		♠32 ♦32	
♥AK6 ♣Q765		♥432 ♣KQJ32			♥AK6 ♣Q765		♥QJ5432 ♣432	

Open	Over	Resp	Advnc		Open	Over	Resp	Advnc
1NT	2♦	2NT	Pass		1NT	2♦	2♥	Pass
3♣	Pass	Pass	Pass		Pass	2♠	Pass	Pass
					3♥	Pass	Pass	Pass

If two diamonds shows an unspecified major, responder can describe his hand directly or can force overcaller to revel his major and then describe his hand. If responder has a hand which is easily described, and responder does not want to try to penalize overcaller, responder bids directly. Two-of-either-major is natural and non-forcing. All direct three-level bids are natural and game forcing, showing at least a five-card suit. Three notrump says responder wants to play three notrump. Texas transfers apply. A direct two notrump by responder is Lebensohl, forcing opener to bid three clubs. Over opener's forced three-club bid, responder passes three clubs with weak clubs, bid three diamonds with weak diamonds, or bids three-of-a-major with invitational values and at least a five-card suit.

In example (1), responder bids two notrump, forcing opener to bid three clubs, Responder with a weak club hand passes three clubs. In example (2), responder bids two hearts non-forcing. After overcaller balances with two spades, opener with two little spades competes with three hearts.

If responder wants to penalize overcaller or bid Stayman for the other major, responder starts by doubling two diamonds. Responder's double of two diamonds is forcing to three notrump or four-of-a-minor. Doubling two diamonds followed by doubling overcaller's major is a penalty double. Doubling two diamonds followed by passing overcaller's major is forcing, shows at least two cards in overcaller's suit and allows opener to make a four-card penalty double. All subsequent bids by responder after doubling two diamonds carry the same meaning as if the major was directly overcalled. Lebensohl and Stayman with or without stoppers apply.

Opener	(3)		Responder
♠54	♦AQJ5	♠32	♦K32
♥AK54	♣Q54	♥QJ32	♣AJ32

Open	Over	Resp	Advnc
1NT	2♦	Dbl	2♥*
Dbl	2♠	3♠	Pass
4♥	Pass	Pass	Pass
* Pass or correct			

Opener	(4)		Responder
♠54	♦AQJ5	♠K2	♦432
♥AK54	♣Q54	♥QJ32	♣AJ32

Open	Over	Resp	Advnc
1NT	2♦	Dbl	2♥*
Dbl	2♠	2NT	Pass
3♣	Pass	3♠	Pass
4♥	Pass	Pass	Pass

Opener	(5)		Responder
♠A54	♦AQJ5	♠KJ32	♦432
♥54	♣A654	♥AJ32	♣Q2

Open	Over	Resp	Advnc
1NT	2♦	Dbl	2♥*
Pass	Pass	Dbl	Pass
*pass or correct			

Opener	(6)		Responder
♠A54	♦AQJ5	♠Q2	♦432
♥54	♣A654	♥AJ32	♣KJ32

Open	Over	Resp	Advnc
1NT	2♦	Dbl	2♥*
Pass	2♠	Pass	Pass
2NT	Pass	3NT	Pass

In examples (3) through (6), responder doubles two diamonds, planning on doubling at least one major and hoping opener can double the other major. Advancer bids two hearts pass or correct. Overcaller will pass if hearts is his major or bid two spades if spades is his major. In examples (3) and (4), opener with four hearts doubles two hearts and overcaller corrects to two spades. In example (3), responder bids a direct three spades showing four hearts and denying a spade stopper. This allows opener to play four hearts. In example (4), responder goes through two notrump to show four hearts and a spade stopper. This gives opener a chance to play three notrump instead of the 4-4 heart fit. In example (5), overcaller's suit is hearts. Responder with four hearts doubles, so two-hearts doubled becomes the final contract. In example (6), opener passes two hearts denying four hearts. Overcaller corrects to two spades. Responder passes two spades showing two or three spades, hoping opener can double. Opener doesn't have four spades, so he can't double. Since opener is forced to bid, opener bids two notrump and responder raises to three notrump. Any bid by opener or responder over two spades is natural and forcing.

If responder passes two diamonds, responder can later double to show a three-card cooperative double, bid a new suit, which is non-forcing, or bid two notrump, choice of minors.

2.8 -- TABLE OF COUNTER DEFENSES TO NOTRUMP DEFENSES.

	2♣	2♦	2♥	2♠	2NT	3♣	3♦	3♥	3♠	3NT
Double	Stay 6+	Tr ♥ 4+	Tr ♠ 4+	Tr ♣ 4+	Tr ♦ 4+	♣ ♦ 4-7	♣ ♦ 8+	♥ ♠ 7-8	♥ ♠ 9+	Bal 9+

	Dbl	2♦	2♥	2♠	2NT	3♣	3♦	3♥	3♠	3NT
2♣ Natural Don't, Capp	Stay 4+	Tr ♥ 4+	Tr ♠ 4+	Tr ♣ 4+	Tr ♦ 4+	♣ ♦ 4-7	♣ ♦ 8+	♥ ♠ 7-8	♥ ♠ 9+	Bal 9+
2♣ Landy	Bal 8+	♦ 4-7	♣ 8+	♦ 8+	Nat 7-8	♣ 4-7	♦ 4-7	♥ 8+	♠ 8+	Bal 9+
2♣ Astro ♥ and lower	Bal 8+	♦ 4-7	Stay 8+	♠ 4-7	Leb♥ 4+	♣ 8+	♦ 8+	♥ 8+	♠ 8+	No ♥ Stop
2♣ Brozel ♥ and ♣	Bal 8+	♦ 4-7	Stay 8+	♠ 4-7	Leb♥ 4+	♣ 8+	♦ 8+	♥ 8+	♠ 8+	No ♥ Stop

The above chart shows various double and two-club defenses to one notrump and what responder's bids mean. (4-7) bids are non-forcing. (8+) bids are game forcing. (7-8) bids are invitational. (4+) bids are either weak or strong depending upon follow-up. (Leb) is Lebensohl forcing three clubs and uses the Lebensohl section logic. Since the opponents can have only a four-card suit, responder has to be able to play in the opponent's suit, therefore most three-level bids are natural and Texas Transfers apply. Since your meaning is dependant upon the meaning of two clubs, it's important that you always inquire.

	Dbl	2♥	2♠	2NT	3♣	3♦	3♥	3♠	3NT	Comment
2♦ Natural Don't	Neg 4+	♥ 4-7	♠ 4-7	Leb 4+	♣ 8+	Stay 8+	♥ 9+	♠ 9+	No ♦ Stop	
2♦ one major	Bal 8+	♥ 4-7	♠ 4-7	Leb 4+	♣ 8+	♦ 8+	♥ 9+	♠ 9+	Bal	Pos Dbl
2♦ Transfer ♥	Bal 8+	Stay 8+	♠ 4-7	Leb 4+	♣ 8+	♦ 8+	♥ 9+	♠ 9+	No ♥ Stop	2♥ Stayman
2♦ Both majors	Bal 8+	♣ 8+	♦ 8+	Nat 7-8	♣ 4-7	♦ 4-7	♥ 8+	♠ 8+	Bal 9+	Unusual Unusual
2♦ Brozel ♦ & ♥	Bal 8+	Stay 8+	♠ 4-7	Leb♥ 4+	♣ 8+	♦ 8+	♥ 8+	♠ 8+	No ♥ Stop	2♥ Stayman
2♥ Both majors	Pen 8+		♦ 8+	Nat 7-8	♣ 4-7	♦ 4-7	♣ 8+	♠ 8+	Bal 8+	Unusual Unusual
2♥ Transfer ♠	Bal 8+		Stay 8+	Leb♠ 4+	♣ 8+	♦ 8+	♥ 9+	♠ 9+	No ♠ Stop	2♠ Stayman
2♥ Natural	Neg 4+		Nat 4-7	Leb♥ 4+	♣ 8+	♦ 8+	Stay 9+	♠ 9+	No ♥ Stop	Leb
2♥ ♥ & Min	Pen 8+		Nat 4-7	Leb♥ 4+	♣ 8+	♦ 8+	Stay 9+	♠ 9+	No ♥ Stop	
2♠ Natural	Neg 4+			Leb♠ 4+	♣ 8+	♦ 8+	♥ 9+	Stay 9+	No ♠ Stop	Leb
2♠ ♠ & Min	Pen 8+			Leb♠ 4+	♣ 8+	♦ 8+	♥ 9+	Stay 9+	No ♠ Stop	
2♠ Transfer ♣	Bal 8+			Leb♣ 4+	Stay 9+	♦ 8+	♥ 9+	♠ 9+	No ♣ Stop	

The above chart shows various two-diamond, two-heart and two-spade defenses to one notrump and what responder's bids mean. (4-7) bids are non-forcing. (8+) bids are game forcing. (7-8) bids are invitational. (4+) bids are either weak or strong depending upon follow-up. (Leb) is Lebensohl.

61

2.9 -- TEXAS IF YOU CAN JUMP.

Opener	(1)	Responder		Opener	(2)	Responder	
♠KQJ	♦43	♠AT5432	♦KQJ	♠KQJ	♦43	♠432	♦2
♥QJ76	♣KQJ4	♥432	♣2	♥QJ76	♣KQJ4	♥AK5432	♣A32

Open	Over	Resp	Advnc	Open	Over	Resp	Advnc
1NT	3♣	4♥	Pass	1NT	3♦	4♥	Pass
4♠	Pass	Pass	Pass	Pass	Pass		

After an overcall, if responder has a game-forcing hand with a six-card or longer major and responder can jump to four diamonds, then responder's jump to four diamonds is Texas, a transfer to four hearts, and responder's jump to four hearts is a transfer to four spades. If responder can't jump to four diamonds, responder has to declare four-of-a-major. If the overcall is three clubs or lower, then Texas applies. If the overcall is three diamonds or higher, then responder's four-level bids are natural. In example (1), over overcaller's three-club bid, responder jumps to four hearts, Texas, transferring to four spades. In example (2), over overcaller's three-diamond bid, responder bids four hearts, natural.

2.10 -- NEGATIVE DOUBLES AT THREE-LEVEL OR HIGHER.

If overcaller bids at the three-level or higher against one notrump or two notrump, responder's double is negative, not penalties. Responder needs at least six HCPs to make a negative double if the opening bid is one notrump, only three HCPs if the opening bid is two notrump. After a one-notrump opener, if responder has only six HCPs, responder has to be able to pass any bid by opener. Opener with length and strength in overcaller's suit can convert the negative double to penalties. If responder passes, opener is not required and is very unlikely to reopen with a takeout double. Therefore, responder with a penalty-double type hand has no way to penalize overcaller and has to be satisfied bidding three notrump. If the overcall is three-of-a-major, responder's negative double promises the unbid major. If the overcall is three-of-a-minor, responder's negative double promises only one major. If responder doubles three clubs and opener bids three diamonds, responder uses Smolen. All three-level bids by responder are forcing. Only if responder is willing to pass any bid by opener, can responder not have a game-forcing hand.

Opener	(1)		Responder
♠KQ54	♦765	♠AJ32	♦J432
♥AK54	♣A3	♥QJ32	♣2

Open	Over	Resp	Advnc
1NT	3♣	Dbl	Pass
3♥	Pass	4♥	Pass

Opener	(2)		Responder
♠KQ54	♦765	♠AJ32	♦QJ432
♥AK54	♣A3	♥QJ2	♣2

Open	Over	Resp	Advnc
1NT	3♣	Dbl	Pass
3♥	Pass	3NT	Pass
4♠	Pass	Pass	Pass

Opener	(3)		Responder
♠KQ54	♦543	♠AJ2	♦KJ32
♥AK54	♣A5	♥Q32	♣432

Open	Over	Resp	Advnc
1NT	3♦	3NT	Pass
Pass	Pass		

Opener	(4)		Responder
♠KQ4	♦QJT3	♠AJ32	♦2
♥AK4	♣Q65	♥QJ32	♣J432

Open	Over	Resp	Advnc
1NT	3♦	Dbl	Pass
Pass	Pass		

In example (1), responder has a perfect negative double, nine HCPs and support for all the unbid suits. Opener bids three hearts and responder raises to game. In example (2), responder has enough to bid game but wants to try to find a spade fit. Responder makes a negative double and bids three notrump when opener bids three hearts. Since responder promises a four-card major with his negative double, opener corrects three notrump to four spades. Responder does not need a stopper to bid three notrump. Responder assumes that opener has a stopper, the suit will block, or overcaller won't lead the suit. If responder bids a new suit over three hearts, it is natural and forcing and denies four-card heart support.

In example (3), responder wants to double three diamonds for penalties but his double would be negative. Responder can't afford to pass, since opener doesn't have to reopen and in this case, opener wouldn't. Responder has to be satisfied bidding three notrump. In example (4), responder with both majors makes a negative double. Opener, with a strong four-card diamond holding, converts the double to penalties. Example (4), where opener has a penalty pass, is much more likely to occur then example (3), where responder has a penalty double.

2.11 -- DOUBLES OF NATURAL BIDS BY THE NOTRUMP OPENER ARE FOR TAKEOUT IN ALL SEATS UNLESS PARTNER HAS BID. OPENER SHOULD DOUBLE WITH TWO LITTLE IN OPPONENT'S SUIT.

Opener	(1)	Responder		Opener	(2)	Responder	
♠AK65 ♦AQJ5		♠432 ♦K432		♠65 ♦AQJ5		♠432 ♦32	
♥Q65 ♣65		♥432 ♣K32		♥AK65 ♣Q65		♥Q432 ♣K432	

Open	Advnc	Resp	Over	Open	Over	Resp	Advnc
1NT	Pass	Pass	2♣	1NT	2♠	Pass	Pass
Dbl	Pass	2♦	Pass	Dbl	Pass	2NT	Pass
Pass	Pass			3♦	Pass	3♥	Pass

If opener has a doubleton in overcaller's natural-bid suit, even sitting behind overcaller, opener makes a takeout double for all three suits, or, holding both minors, bids two notrump. A GOOD RULE ON COMPETITIVE BIDDING IS THAT WHEN YOU ARE SHORT IN THE OPPONENT'S SUIT, YOU COMPETE. Holding Qx in the opponent's suit, opener might not double. Over opener's takeout double, responder bids any five-card suit, or a four-card suit at the two-level. If responder must bid at the three-level and has two four-card suits, responder bids two notrump for takeout, asking opener to bid his lowest four-card suit. If responder is 3-3-3-4, responder bids his four-card club suit or bids two notrump, giving opener a choice. Opener then bids four-card suits up the line. If responder has four cards in the opponent's suit, responder passes the double for penalties, knowing that the opponents are in a seven-card fit.

In example (1), overcaller bids two clubs, natural. Opener with a doubleton club and support for all suits, doubles for takeout. [4] Responder bids his four-card diamond suit. If opener passes, responder holding three clubs and knowing opener has at least three clubs, sells out. In example (2), opener has a doubleton spade. Knowing that the opponents can be in an eight-card fit, opener doubles for takeout. Responder, holding four clubs and four hearts, bids two notrump, choice of suits. If opener bids three clubs, responder passes, since any 4-4 fit is good. Since opener bids three diamonds, responder bids three hearts and the 4-4 heart fit is found.

---

[4] If two clubs is conventional, opener's double shows clubs.

Opener	(3)		Responder			Opener	(4)		Responder	

♠AK76 ◆AQJ6   ♠5432 ◆K432   ♠AK76 ◆AQJ6   ♠432 ◆5432
   ♥65   ♣Q43   ♥432   ♣K2   ♥65   ♣Q43   ♥QJ32 ♣K2

Open	Over	Resp	Advnc	Open	Over	Resp	Advnc
1NT	2♥*	Pass	Pass	1NT	2♥*	Pass	Pass
Dbl	Pass	2♠	Pass	Dbl	Pass	Pass	Pass
Pass	Pass		* hearts & minor				

Opener	(5)		Responder			Opener	(6)		Responder	

♠A6 ◆AQJ5   ♠5432 ◆K432   ♠A6 ◆AQJ5   ♠5432 ◆432
   ♥65 ♣KQ543   ♥432   ♣J2   ♥65 ♣KQ543   ♥QJ32 ♣J2

Open	Over	Resp	Advnc	Open	Over	Resp	Advnc
1NT	2♥*	Pass	Pass	1NT	2♥*	Pass	Pass
2NT	Pass	3◆	Pass	2NT	Pass	Pass	Pass
Pass	Pass		* both majors				

In examples (3) and (4), overcaller bids two hearts, showing hearts and a minor. With a doubleton heart and support for all of the unbid suits, opener doubles for takeout. His double is for takeout even if it is RHO who bids two hearts. In example (3), responder bids his four-card spade suit. In example (4), responder holding four hearts knows the opponents are in a seven-card fit and passes opener's takeout double.

In examples (5) and (6), overcaller bids two hearts, showing hearts and spades. Opener with a doubleton heart and support for both minors bids two notrump. In example (5), responder bids three diamonds and the 4-4 diamond fit is found. In example (6), responder with two heart stoppers passes opener's two-notrump takeout bid. Two notrump figures to be as good as if not better than the likely 4-3 diamond fit.

CHAPTER 3 - TWO NOTRUMP OPENER

3.1 -- OPENING TWO NOTRUMP SHOWS 20-21.

An opening two notrump shows 20-21 HCPs. Opener can have a five-card major. A two-little suit should not deter you from opening two notrump. I've even seen players open two notrump with a singleton honor.

3.2 -- TWO NOTRUMP - THREE CLUBS - THREE DIAMONDS - THREE-OF-A-MAJOR IS SMOLEN FORCING TO GAME.

Opener	(1)	Responder		Opener	(2)	Responder	
♠KQJ ♦KQJ		♠A5432 ♦32		♠KQJ ♦KQJ		♠A432 ♦32	
♥AQ6 ♣K654		♥K432 ♣32		♥AQ6 ♣K654		♥K5432 ♣A2	

Opener (1)	Responder	Opener (2)	Responder
2NT	3clubs	2NT	3clubs
3diamonds	3hearts	3diamonds	3spades
4clubs	4hearts	4clubs	4diamonds
4spades	Pass	4hearts	4spades
		4NT	5clubs
		6NT	Pass

Responder with 4-5, 4-6, 5-4 or 6-4 in the majors, starts off with Stayman. Over three diamonds, responder uses Smolen (see section 1.10). Since there are no weak sign-offs over two notrump, Smolen over two notrump doesn't have to be a jump. The follow-ups are similar to those after one notrump.

In examples (1) and (2), responder bids Stayman and opener denies a four-card major. In example (1), responder bids three hearts, showing exactly four hearts and five or more spades. Opener bids four clubs, artificial, showing a maximum in support of spades. Responder bids four hearts, transfer, and opener is obligated to bid four spades, ending the auction. In example (2), responder bids three spades, showing exactly four spades and five or more hearts. Opener, with a maximum and three-card heart support, bids four clubs, artificial. Responder bids four diamonds, forcing opener to bid four hearts. Responder is unable to bid keycard since if opener responds five diamonds, responder can't ask for the heart queen. Responder bids four spades and opener bids keycard. When responder answers five clubs, opener, counting 12 tricks in notrump, bids six notrump.

3.3 -- TWO NOTRUMP - THREE CLUBS - THREE HEARTS - THREE SPADES SHOWS FOUR HEARTS AND A SLAM TRY.

Opener	(1)	Responder		Opener	(2)	Responder	
♠AQ43	♦AKQ	♠2	♦432	♠KQJ	♦KQJ	♠2	♦432
♥AQ65	♣54	♥K432	♣AQJ32	♥AQ65	♣K54	♥K432	♣AQJ32

Opener (1)	Responder	Opener (2)	Responder
2NT	3clubs	2NT	3clubs
3hearts	3spades	3hearts	3spades
4NT	5hearts	4hearts	Pass
5NT	6hearts		

After two notrump -- three clubs -- three hearts, responder holding four hearts has to be able to set hearts as trumps and investigate slam. THREE SPADES, THE OTHER MAJOR, IS AN ARTIFICIAL SLAM TRY SETTING HEARTS AS TRUMPS, AND REPLACES A JUMP TO FIVE HEARTS AS A HEART SLAM TRY. IF RESPONDER BIDS ANYTHING OTHER THAN THREE SPADES, EXCEPT A NON-SLAM-TRY RAISE TO FOUR HEARTS, RESPONDER DENIES FOUR-CARD HEART SUPPORT.

In examples (1) and (2), responder bids Stayman and finds opener with four hearts. Responder bids three spades, showing four hearts and a slam try. In example (1), opener, with a maximum, bids RKC. Responder shows his two keycards. Opener bids five notrump, promising all the keycards, asking for specific kings. Responder bids six hearts denying a king. Since responder's hand is unlimited, with all six keys present, opener has to bid five notrump. If responder holds a solid suit, for instance ♠2♥AJ32♦43♣AKQ432, responder can bid seven hearts only if opener bids four notrump followed by five notrump. In example (2), opener has nothing to cuebid over three spades and signs-off in four hearts. If opener can't cuebid anything then there probably isn't a slam, so responder passes four hearts. If hearts are 4-1, ten tricks can be the limit.

After two notrump -- three clubs -- three hearts, four notrump by responder is quantitative, asking opener to bid slam with a maximum, and denies four-card heart support. Since three clubs promises a four-card major, there can still be a 4-4 spade fit. With a minimum, opener passes four notrump or signs-off in five spades. With a maximum, opener jumps to six spades or six notrump. If opener bids five-of-a-minor, it shows a five-card suit. If responder wants to bid keycard for hearts, responder first has to bid three spades, artificial, setting hearts as trumps. After three spades, four notrump is keycard for hearts by both opener and responder.

3.4 -- TWO NOTRUMP - THREE CLUBS - THREE SPADES - FOUR HEARTS SHOWS FOUR SPADES AND A SLAM TRY.

Opener	(1)	Responder		Opener	(2)	Responder	
♠KQJ5	♦KQJ	♠A432	♦432	♠KQJ5	♦KJ5	♠A432	♦432
♥AQ3	♣K65	♥2	♣AQ432	♥KQJ	♣KJ5	♥2	♣AQ432

Opener (1)	Responder	Opener (2)	Responder
2NT	3clubs	2NT	3clubs
3spades	4hearts	3spades	4hearts
4NT	5hearts	4spades	Pass
6spades	Pass		

After two notrump -- three clubs -- three spades, responder holding four spades has to be able to set spades as trumps and investigate slam. Four hearts, the other major, which is not needed as a natural bid, is an artificial slam try setting spades as trumps and replaces a jump to five spades as a spade slam try. If responder bids anything other than four hearts, except a non-slam-try raise to four spades, responder denies spade support. Over four hearts, opener looks at his aces and kings, his extra values, his 4-4-3-2 distribution or lack thereof, and decides whether to sign-off in four spades or make a further slam try.

In examples (1) and (2), responder bids Stayman and finds opener with four spades. Responder bids four hearts, showing four spades and a slam try. In example (1), opener, with a maximum, bids RKC. Responder shows two keycards. Opener bids six spades, ending the auction. In example (2), opener has a minimum with no aces, and signs-off in four spades. Responder, with only a mild slam try, passes four spades. With a heart lead and a diamond return, ten tricks can be the limit.

After two notrump -- three clubs -- three spades, four notrump by responder is quantitative, asking opener to bid six notrump with a maximum and denies four-card spade support. With a minimum, opener passes four notrump. If opener bids five-of-a-minor, it shows a five-card suit. If responder wants to bid keycard for spades, responder has to first bid four hearts, artificial, setting spades as trumps. After four hearts, four notrump is keycard for spades by both opener and responder.

3.5 -- TWO NOTRUMP - THREE CLUBS - THREE ANY - FOUR-OF-A-MINOR IS A ONE-SUITED SLAM TRY AND RESPONDER MAY HAVE A FOUR-CARD MAJOR.

1.	2.	3.	4.	5.	6.	7.
2NT 3♣	2NT 3♣	2NT 3♣	2NT 3♣	2NT 3♣	2NT 3♣	2NT 3♣
3♥ 4♣	3♥ 4♣	3♥ 4♣	3♥ 4♣	3♥ 4♣	3♥ 4♣	3♥ 4♣
4♦	4NT	5NT	4♠ 4NT	4♠ 5♣	4♠ 5♦	4♠ 5NT

8.	9.	10.	11.	12.	13.	14.
2NT 3♣	2NT 3♣	2NT 3♣	2NT 3♣	2NT 3♣	2NT 3♣	2NT 3♣
3♥ 4♦	3♥ 4♦	3♥ 4♦	3♥ 4♦	3♥ 4♦	3♥ 4♦	3♥ 4♦
4♥	4NT	5NT	4♠ 4NT	4♠ 5♦	4♠ 5♣	4♠ 5NT

Responder shows a slammish hand with a four-card major and a longer minor or with a one-suited minor by bidding three clubs Stayman, and then bidding his minor at the four-level, unless opener bids responder's four-card major. IF OPENER BIDS RESPONDER'S FOUR-CARD MAJOR, RESPONDER MUST SET THAT MAJOR AS TRUMPS BY BIDDING THE OTHER MAJOR (SEE SECTIONS 3.3 AND 3.4).

Since there are not many natural calls between responder's four-of-a-minor call and four notrump, opener bids four diamonds over four clubs as keycard for clubs, auction (1), or four hearts over four diamonds as keycard for diamonds, auction (8). After opener finds out how many keycards responder has, opener is in a very good position to determine the level. Without a fit, opener signs-off in four notrump with a minimum, auctions (2) and (9) and jumps to five notrump with a maximum, auctions (3) and (10). Responder with a combined minimum of 34 HCPs never plays below six notrump. At IMPs, responder plays in six-of-a-minor with a combined 34 HCPs only if he knows that there isn't a slow trump loser.

If opener is 4-4 in the majors, opener bids three hearts first and then bids four spades over any bid responder makes. If responder does not have four spades, responder signs-off in four notrump with a minimum slam try, auctions (4) and (11). If responder wants to force, he rebids his minor showing a six-card suit and asking for keycards, auctions (5) and (12), or he bids five notrump, showing enough for slam with only a five-card minor, auctions (7) and (14). If responder also has four spades, responder bids the other minor setting spades as trumps and asking for keycards, auctions (6) and (13).

Opener	(1)	Responder		Opener	(2)	Responder	
♠KQ2	♦AQ	♠A543	♦432	♠KQ2	♦AQ	♠A543	♦K5432
♥AQ32	♣K432	♥4	♣AQ765	♥AQ32	♣K432	♥4	♣A65

Opener (1)	Responder	Opener (2)	Responder
2NT	3clubs	2NT	3clubs
3hearts	4clubs	3hearts	4diamonds
4diamonds	5clubs	4NT	Pass
5diamonds	6clubs		

Opener	(3)	Responder		Opener	(4)	Responder	
♠KQ32	♦AQ	♠A654	♦K5432	♠KQ32	♦AQ	♠A54	♦K5432
♥AQ32	♣K32	♥4	♣A54	♥AQ32	♣K32	♥54	♣A54

Opener (3)	Responder	Opener (4)	Responder
2NT	3clubs	2NT	3clubs
3hearts	4diamonds	3hearts	4diamonds
4spades	5clubs	4spades	4NT
5diamonds	6spades	Pass	

In example (1), responder bids three clubs and then four clubs, showing a club slam try. Opener, with good club support, bids four diamonds keycard for clubs. Responder answers five clubs, showing two keycards and the club queen. Since responder's hand is unlimited, opener bids five diamonds, the next higher forcing bid, promising all the keycards and asking for specific kings. Responder answers six clubs denying any outside kings. If responder has 13 or more HCPs, responder signs-off in six notrump. After opener asks for keycards, opener continues asking for the queen or outside kings using the next higher forcing bid. If clubs is the trump suit, then four notrump over a four-spade keycard response continues asking, and five clubs is a sign-off. All other four-notrump calls by opener are sign-offs.

In example (2), responder shows a diamond slam try by bidding four diamonds. Opener with only two diamonds and a minimum, signs-off in four notrump. Over four diamonds, four hearts by opener is keycard for diamonds, four spades is natural showing 4-4 in the majors. In examples (3) and (4), responder shows a diamond slam try, possibly with four spades, and opener bids four spades showing 4-4 in the majors. Four spades neither promises nor denies extra values. In example (3), responder bids five clubs, the other minor, setting spades as trumps and asking for keycards. Opener shows three keycards, and responder bids six spades. In example (4), responder signs-off in four notrump, denying four spades and showing a minimum. Opener, with a minimum without a diamond fit, passes four notrump.

3.6 -- JACOBY TRANSFERS.

Opener	(1)	Responder		Opener	(2)	Responder	
♠KQJ	♦KQJ2	♠54	♦43	♠AK32	♦A2	♠54	♦43
♥KQ2	♣KJ2	♥AJ543	♣AQ54	♥KQ2	♣KJ32	♥AJ543	♣AQ54

Opener (1)	Responder	Opener (2)	Responder
2NT	3diamonds	2NT	3diamonds
3hearts	4clubs	3hearts	4clubs
4hearts	Pass	4diamonds	5clubs
		7clubs	Pass

Three diamonds shows at least five hearts any strength. Three hearts shows at least five spades any strength. Two-level rules apply if the three-level transfer gets doubled (see section 1.26). If responder transfers and then bids three notrump, opener, holding three of responder's major, must remember that responder is weak and might have an unbalanced hand. Holding ♠2♥QJ432♦2♣Q65432, responder transfers to three hearts and then bids three notrump.

JACOBY TRANSFER FOLLOWED BY FOUR-OF-A-MINOR SHOWS FIVE OF A MAJOR AND AT LEAST FOUR OF THE MINOR, AND IS A SLAM TRY. Over four-of-a-minor, opener needs to be able to sign-off, support responder's major, bid keycard for responder's major and bid keycard for responder's minor. There's only one method to accomplish all of the above. After responder's four-of-a-minor, opener, with a minimum, bids four-of-responder's-major to show three or four-card support or bids five-of-responder's-minor with support for the minor. Opener bids four notrump to deny a fit for either suit. Opener bids the lower off-suit as keycard for both of responder's suits. Since there are two trump suits, there are six keycards, four aces and two kings. There are also two queens. The first and second steps show zero or three and one or four. The third step shows two keycards and either zero or two queens. The fourth step shows two keycards and one queen.

In examples (1) and (2), responder shows a slam try with hearts and clubs. In example (1), opener, with no aces, signs-off with four hearts. Responder with a minimum slam try passes four hearts. In example (2), opener has a great hand in support of a heart-club slam try. Opener bids four diamonds, keycard for both clubs and hearts. Responder answers five clubs, the fourth step, showing two of the six possible keycards and one queen. Opener can count five hearts, five clubs, assuming a ruff, two spades and one diamond with decent splits, so opener bids seven clubs.

71

Opener	(3)	Responder		Opener	(4)	Responder	
♠KQJ2	♦KQ2	♠54	♦AJ54	♠AK32	♦KQ32	♠54	♦AJ54
♥A2	♣KQ32	♥KQ543	♣54	♥A2	♣AJ2	♥KQ543	♣54

Opener (3)	Responder	Opener (4)	Responder
2NT	3diamonds	2NT	3diamonds
3hearts	4diamonds	3hearts	4diamonds
4NT	Pass	4spades	5hearts
		5spades	6diamonds
		Pass	

Opener	(5)	Responder		Opener	(6)	Responder	
♠KQJ2	♦KQ2	♠43	♦AJ54	♠AQJ2	♦KQ32	♠43	♦AJ54
♥A2	♣KQ32	♥KQ543	♣A4	♥A2	♣KQ2	♥KQ543	♣A4

Opener (5)	Responder	Opener (6)	Responder
2NT	3diamonds	2NT	3diamonds
3hearts	4diamonds	3hearts	4diamonds
4NT	6NT	4spades	4NT
		5clubs	5hearts
		7diamonds	Pass

In examples (3) through (6), responder transfers to three hearts and bids four diamonds, showing at least five hearts, at least four diamonds and at least a mild slam try. In example (3), opener with only two hearts, only three diamonds and only one ace, signs-off in four notrump. In example (4), opener has a diamond fit and four of the six keycards. Opener bids the lower off-suit, four spades, keycard for diamonds and hearts. Opener bids four hearts to show three or four-card heart support and a minimum, four notrump to deny a fit for either suit and five diamonds to show a minimum with a diamond fit but without a heart fit. Over four spades, responder answers five hearts, showing two keycards and one queen. Opener bids five spades showing that all six keycards and the two queens are present. Responder with a minimum slam try signs-off in six diamonds. Opener converts to six hearts with heart support. In example (5), opener with a minimum and no fit signs-off in four notrump. Responder with 14 HCPs bids six notrump. In example (6), opener with a diamond fit bids four spades keycard for diamonds and hearts. Responder answers four notrump, showing zero or three keycards. Opener bids five clubs, the cheapest forcing call, asking for queens. Responder answers five hearts showing one queen. Five diamonds, the cheapest step, would deny any queens. Opener bids seven diamonds. Since there are two queens, the responses are different from normal RKC. If opener wants to ask for kings, opener bids five spades.

Opener	(7)	Responder		Opener	(8)	Responder	
♠KQJ ♦AK32		♠A5432 ♦4		♠KQJ ♦AK32		♠65432 ♦4	
♥K32 ♣A32		♥AQ654 ♣54		♥K32 ♣A32		♥AJ654 ♣54	

Opener (7)	Responder	Opener (8)	Responder
2NT	3diamonds	2NT	3hearts
3hearts	3spades	3spades	4hearts
4clubs	4diamonds	4spades	Pass
4NT	5spades		
7NT	Pass		

Responder with 5-5 or better in the majors has two choices. With a weak hand and at least 5-5 in the majors, responder bids three hearts, transfer to spades, and then bids four hearts non-forcing. This sequence is strictly choice of major-suit games. Opener either passes four hearts or bids four spades. WITH 5-4 OR 6-4 IN THE MAJORS, RESPONDER USES SMOLEN.

With a slam try and at least 5-5 or better in the majors, responder bids three diamonds, transfer to hearts, and then bids three spades. Over the slam try 5-5, opener bids three notrump with 2-2 in the majors or a hand with concentrated strength in the minors. With a slam oriented hand, opener bids four clubs, which sets hearts as trumps, or bids four diamonds, which sets spades as trumps. If possible, opener sets hearts as trumps to get the benefit of the opening lead. IT'S VERY IMPORTANT THAT THE TRUMP SUIT BE SET AS SOON AS POSSIBLE SO EACH PARTNER MAY BETTER EVALUATE HIS HAND AND RKC CAN BE USED EFFECTIVELY. Opener signs-off in four-of-a-major with a non-slam oriented hand.

In example (7), responder shows a slam try with both majors, 5-5 or better. Opener bids four clubs setting hearts as trumps so opener can later bid keycard and ask for the heart queen. Responder, with a sound slam try, bids four diamonds, the Last Train. Opener bids four notrump, keycard for hearts. When responder answers two keycards and the heart queen, opener can count 13 tricks, so opener bids seven notrump. If opener bids four diamonds, setting spades as trumps, responder can bid four hearts as a Last-Train bid. In example (8), responder shows 5-5 in the majors, choice of games. Responder wants to play in four hearts or four spades, and has no interest in getting to slam. Opener chooses four spades to get the benefit of the opening lead.

3.7 -- JACOBY FOLLOWED BY A RAISE TO GAME IS A MILD SLAM TRY. TEXAS IS A SIGN-OFF.

Opener	(1)	Responder		Opener	(2)	Responder	
♠KQ4	♦KQJ5	♠32	♦432	♠AK54	♦A5	♠32	♦432
♥K76	♣KQJ	♥AJ5432	♣A2	♥KQ6	♣KJ43	♥AJ5432	♣A2

Opener	Responder	Opener	Responder
2NT	3diamonds	2NT	3diamonds
3hearts	4hearts	3hearts	4hearts
Pass		4NT	5hearts
		6hearts	

Opener	(3)	Responder		Opener	(4)	Responder	
♠A87	♦KQJ4	♠KJ65432	♦32	♠A87	♦KQJ4	♠KJ65432	♦32
♥A54	♣KQJ	♥32	♣32	♥A54	♣KQJ	♥32	♣A2

Opener	Responder	Opener	Responder
2NT	4hearts	2NT	3hearts
4spades	Pass	3spades	4spades
		4NT	5spades
		6spades	Pass

Similar to over a one-notrump opener, holding a six-card or longer major and playing both Jacoby and Texas transfers, responder can get to game by transferring at the three-level and raising to game, or by transferring at the four-level. If responder wants to set trumps and then bid keycard, responder uses Texas. Transferring at the three-level (Jacoby) and raising to game is a non-forcing mild slam try. Opener needs aces and mild trump support to accept.

In examples (1) and (2), responder transfers to three hearts and bids four hearts showing a mild slam try with at least six hearts. In example (1), opener, missing all four aces, knows that responder can't hold three aces and make a non-forcing bid. Opener therefore passes four hearts. In example (2), opener has three keycards, the queen of trumps and two kings. Opener bids four notrump, RKC, and over responder's five-heart response, signs-off in six hearts. Responder's hand is limited, so opener doesn't bid five notrump showing all the keys. In example (3), responder uses Texas to sign-off in four spades. In example (4), responder uses Jacoby to make a mild spade slam try. Opener, needing only a good spade suit and one outside ace for slam, bids RKC. Responder with a seventh spade shows two keycards and the queen or extra length, and opener bids slam.

74

Opener	(5)	Responder	
♠AK32	♦AQ	♠54	♦432
♥K32	♣KJ32	♥AQ7654	♣54

Opener	Responder
2NT	4diamonds
4hearts	Pass

Opener	(6)	Responder	
♠AK32	♦AQ	♠54	♦432
♥K32	♣KJ32	♥AQJ654	♣A4

Opener	Responder
2NT	4diamonds
4hearts	4NT
5clubs	5NT
6clubs	6hearts
Pass	

Opener	(7)	Responder	
♠AJ2	♦AJ2	♠43	♦543
♥KJ	♣KQJ32	♥AQ5432	♣A4

Opener	Responder
2NT	3diamonds
3hearts	4hearts
4NT	5spades
7NT	Pass

Opener	(8)	Responder	
♠AJ2	♦AJ2	♠Q3	♦543
♥KJ	♣KQJ32	♥AQ5432	♣A4

Opener	Responder
2NT	4diamonds
4hearts	4NT
5clubs	5NT
7NT	

In example (5), responder wants to play in four hearts, so he transfers at the four-level and passes opener's forced response. In example (6), responder wants to play in six hearts unless two keycards are missing. Responder transfers to four hearts and over opener's forced response, bids four notrump RKC. After finding that all keycards are present, responder bids five notrump just in case opener can count 13 tricks. Sometimes opener has KQJxx of a side suit. In example (7), responder transfers to three hearts and raises to four showing a mild slam try. Opener with three keys bids RKC. Responder answers five spades showing two keycards and the heart queen. Opener counts 13 tricks -- six hearts, five clubs, and two aces -- and bids seven notrump. In example (8), responder has enough to bid slam if enough keycards are present. Responder bids four diamonds forcing opener to bid four hearts. Responder then bids four notrump RKC. Opener answers five clubs showing three keycards. With all six keys present, responder bids five notrump. Opener counts 13 tricks and bids seven notrump. WHEN PARTNER BIDS FOUR NOTRUMP AND THEN BIDS FIVE NOTRUMP, YOU SHOULD ALWAYS TRY TO SEE IF THERE ARE 13 TRICKS FIRST, BEFORE ANSWERING SPECIFIC KINGS.

3.8 -- THREE SPADES IS MINOR-SUIT STAYMAN.

Opener	(1)	Responder		Opener	(2)	Responder	
♠AQ3	♦KQJ5	♠2	♦A432	♠AQ3	♦KQJ	♠2	♦A432
♥AK5	♣J65	♥432	♣AQ432	♥AK5	♣J765	♥432	♣AQ432

Opener (1)	Responder	Opener (2)	Responder
2NT	3spades	2NT	3spades
4diamonds	4spades	4clubs	4diamonds
4NT	5hearts	4hearts	4spades
5NT	6diamonds	4NT	5spades
Pass		6clubs	Pass

Responder bids three spades showing at least 4-4 in the minors and slam-invitational values, asking opener to bid a four-card minor. If opener has a four-card minor, he bids it. If opener has a five-card minor, he bids four hearts holding five clubs or bids four spades holding five diamonds. Opener bids three notrump to deny a four-card minor. Opener should deny a four-card minor if he is 4-3-3-3 with very strong major-suit holdings. Over three notrump, if responder then bids a minor, responder is showing exactly four of that minor and at least five of the other minor, similar to Smolen. If responder bids four-of-a-major over three notrump, responder is showing at least 5-5 in the minors with shortness in that major. If responder bids three spades and follows with four notrump over three notrump or over four-of-a-minor, he is making a non-forcing mild slam try.

If opener bids three notrump and then four notrump, it's a sign-off. If opener wants to make a positive response to responder's four-of-a-minor slam try, he cuebids. If opener wants to make a positive response to responder's four-of-a-major slam try, he bids five-of-a-minor setting that minor as trumps and asking for keycards. If opener wants to make a negative response, he bids four notrump.

In example (1), responder asks for four-card minors, and opener shows his four-card diamond suit. Responder cuebids four spades and opener bids keycard. Responder shows two keycards. Opener bids five notrump in case responder has solid clubs. Responder bids six diamonds denying the club king. If responder has 14 or more HCPs, he denies any kings by bidding six notrump instead. With at least 34 HCPs between you, you don't want to play in six-of-a-minor. In example (2), opener shows his four-card club suit. After three cuebids, opener bids keycard. Responder shows two keycards and the club queen. Opener signs-off in six clubs. If responder has 14 or more HCPs, he corrects six clubs to six notrump.

Opener	(3)		Responder		Opener	(4)		Responder	
♠KQJ5	♦KJ5		♠432	♦AQ432	♠KQJ5	♦KJ		♠432	♦AQ432
♥AQJ3	♣K5		♥2	♣A432	♥AQJ3	♣K65		♥2	♣A432

Opener	Responder	Opener	Responder
2NT	3spades	2NT	3spades
3NT	4clubs	3NT	4clubs
4hearts	4spades	4NT	Pass
4NT	5spades		
6diamonds	Pass		

Opener	(5)		Responder		Opener	(6)		Responder	
♠AKQ3	♦QJ6		♠2	♦A5432	♠AQ3	♦KQJ		♠2	♦A5432
♥AK5	♣J65		♥32	♣AQ432	♥AK54	♣J65		♥32	♣AQ432

Opener	Responder	Opener	Responder
2NT	3spades	2NT	3spades
3NT	4spades	3NT	4spades
4NT	Pass	5clubs	5NT
		6NT	Pass

In examples (3) and (4), responder asks for four-card minors and opener bids three notrump denying. Responder bids four clubs showing exactly four clubs and five or more diamonds. In example (3), opener cuebids showing diamond support and slam-going values. Since opener denies holding four clubs and responder shows exactly four clubs, clubs cannot be the trump suit. Responder bids four spades, allowing opener to bid RKC for diamonds. Responder shows two keycards and the diamond queen. Opener signs-off in six diamonds. In example (4), opener holding only two diamonds and a minimum, signs-off in four notrump. In examples (5) and (6), responder bids four spades showing 5-5 in the minors with a singleton or void in spades. In example (5), opener signs-off in four notrump. In example (6), opener bids five clubs, setting clubs as trumps and asking for keycards. Opener sets clubs as trumps so he can find out about the club king and queen as well as the diamond ace. Responder bids five notrump showing two keycards and the club queen. Knowing a keycard is missing and able to count 12 tricks, opener signs-off in six notrump.

Four notrump is only RKC after a positive response. In examples (4) and (5), there weren't any positive responses, so four notrump is a sign-off.

CHAPTER 4 - THREE NOTRUMP OPENER

4.1 -- GAMBLING THREE NOTRUMP. SOLID SEVEN-CARD OR LONGER MINOR WITH NO OUTSIDE ACE OR KING IN FIRST OR SECOND POSITION. IN THIRD OR FOURTH POSITION YOU CAN HAVE ANYTHING AND YOU ARE RESPONSIBLE FOR RUNNING IF DOUBLED.

1.	2.	3.
♠432♥2♦AKQ5432♣32	♠5432♥2♦AKQ5432♣2	♠K32♥2♦AKQ5432♣32
♠Q2♥2♦Q32♣AKQ5432	♠2♥J432♦2♣AKQ5432	♠2♥2♦QJ32♣AKQ5432
♠2♥32♦32♣AKQ65432	♠-♥432♦32♣AKQ65432	♠2♥2♦32♣AKQ765432
		♠K2♥K3♦AKJ5432♣K2
		♠Q2♥AQ♦432♣AKQJ32

An opening three notrump in first or second position shows a seven or eight-card minor headed by the AKQ without any outside aces or kings. Opener may have outside queens or jacks. Opener should not have a void or an outside four-card suit. In third or fourth position, opener can have anywhere from a solid minor without any outside aces or kings to a twenty-point hand with a semi-solid minor suit. A third or fourth seat strong three-notrump opener should not have three of either major. Opener doesn't want to miss a major-suit fit. Opposite a first or second seat opener, responder is the Captain. Opposite a third or fourth seat opener, opener is the Captain. The Captain is the one who decides whether three notrump or three notrump doubled will be the final contract.

Hands from column (1) can be opened three notrump in any seat. Opener is responsible for running from three notrump if his third or fourth seat three notrump opener from column (1) gets doubled. Hands from column (2) are too distributional to be opened three notrump in any seat. Hands from column (3) are too strong to be opened three notrump in first or second seat, but can be opened three notrump in third or fourth seat.

4.2 -- THREE NOTRUMP - FOUR CLUBS OR THREE NOTRUMP - FIVE CLUBS ASKS OPENER TO PASS IF SUIT IS CLUBS AND BID DIAMONDS IF SUIT IS DIAMONDS.

Opener	(1)	Responder		Opener	(2)	Responder
♠432 ♦AKQ5432		♠QJ65 ♦76		♠432 ♦AKQ5432		♠98765 ♦76
♥2 ♣32		♥43 ♣AQJ54		♥2 ♣32		♥A3 ♣AQJ4

Opener	Responder		Opener	Responder
3NT	4clubs		3NT	Pass
4diamonds	Pass			

Opener	(3)	Responder		Opener	(4)	Responder
♠2 ♦432		♠A543 ♦AK765		♠2 ♦432		♠AQ43 ♦AQ765
♥32 ♣AKQ5432		♥4 ♣876		♥32 ♣AKQ5432		♥AQ54 ♣-

Opener	Responder		Opener	Responder
3NT	5clubs		3NT	5clubs

If responder is void in a minor, responder can't pass three notrump. To pass a first or second seat three-notrump opener, responder needs at least one card in opener's presumed minor and stoppers or length in all of the other suits. To pass a third or fourth seat three-notrump opener, responder needs at least one card in opener's presumed minor. If responder decides to bid over three notrump and wants to play in four-of-opener's-minor, responder bids four clubs. Over four clubs, opener passes with clubs and corrects to four diamonds with diamonds. Since four diamonds is conventional asking for shortness, responder can never sign-off in four diamonds. With stronger or preemptive hands, responder can sign-off at the five or six-level. All of responder's minor-suit bids other than four diamonds are pass or correct. Opener passes if responder bids his minor. Opener corrects to his minor if responder bids the other minor. All major-suit bids by responder are to play.

In examples (1) and (3), responder doesn't have a heart stopper. In example (1), responder bids four clubs, pass or correct, and opener corrects to four diamonds, which is better than three notrump. In example (3), responder can count 11 tricks if opener can ruff a heart in the short hand, so responder bids five clubs. In examples (2) and (4), responder has all of the side suits stopped or has extra length, and can count nine tricks. In example (2), responder passes three notrump. In example (4), however, responder is void in clubs, and cannot pass three notrump. Five clubs should have some play, especially with the lead coming into the Ace-Queens.

4.3 -- THREE NOTRUMP - FOUR DIAMONDS ASKS FOR SHORTNESS. FOUR NOTRUMP SHOWS 7-2-2-2. FIVE CLUBS SHOWS CLUB SUIT WITH DIAMONDS SHORTNESS. FIVE DIAMONDS SHOWS DIAMOND SUIT WITH CLUB SHORTNESS.

Opener (1)	Responder	Opener (2)	Responder
♠432 ♦AKQ5432	♠AKQ5 ♦876	♠32 ♦AKQ5432	♠AKQ5 ♦876
♥2 ♣32	♥54 ♣AK54	♥32 ♣32	♥54 ♣AK54
3NT	4diamonds	3NT	4diamonds
4hearts	6diamonds	4NT	5diamonds
Pass		Pass	

Opener (3)	Responder	Opener (4)	Responder
♠432 ♦AKQ5432	♠AKQ5 ♦876	♠432 ♦2	♠AKQ5 ♦AK76
♥32 ♣2	♥54 ♣AK76	♥32 ♣AKQ5432	♥54 ♣876
3NT	4diamonds	3NT	4diamonds
5diamonds	Pass	5clubs	Pass
Pass			

If responder wants to know if opener has shortness, responder asks with four diamonds. With a singleton or void in a major, opener bids the major. Opener bids four notrump if opener is 7-2-2-2. With a singleton in a minor, opener bids his solid minor, not his short minor. If opener happens to have diamond shortness, opener bids five clubs, which is passable, not five diamonds, which forces responder to bid six clubs.

In examples (1) through (4), responder is interested in slam but is worried about losing two heart tricks. Responder bids four diamonds, asking opener if he has shortness. In example (1), opener bids four hearts, showing a singleton heart. Responder, no longer worried about losing two heart tricks, jumps to six diamonds. In example (2), opener bids four notrump denying any shortness and responder signs-off in five diamonds. Since five and six diamonds are not conventional, responder, holding club honors, can sign-off in five or six diamonds. However, all club bids are pass or correct. In example (3), opener bids five diamonds, showing a diamond suit with club shortness. Responder knows that he has two heart losers and passes five diamonds. In example (4), opener bids five clubs showing a club suit with diamond shortness. Responder knows that he has two heart losers and passes five clubs.

4.4 -- THREE NOTRUMP - FOUR NOTRUMP ASKS HOW MANY CARDS (FIVE CLUBS = SEVEN, FIVE DIAMONDS = EIGHT).

If responder has three first-round controls and needs an eight-card suit to make seven, responder can place the contract at the correct level by bidding four notrump, asking opener how many cards he has in his long suit. Opener answers five clubs showing a seven-card suit. Five diamonds shows an eight-card suit. Four notrump is not needed for keycard since opener promises exactly two keycards and the queen of trumps. If responder is void in opener's suit and is interested in seven, responder bids five notrump asking opener if the suit is completely solid. REGARDLESS OF PREVIOUS CALLS, ALL FIVE NOTRUMP CALLS BY RESPONDER, ASK OPENER TO BID SEVEN-OF-HIS-SUIT IF OPENER CAN PLAY OPPOSITE A VOID. AKQJ432 or AKQ65432 are the minimum seven and eight-card suits needed for opener to bid seven.

4.5 -- OVER OPPONENTS GAMBLING THREE NOTRUMP, FOUR CLUBS IS TAKEOUT.

Overcaller (1)	Advancer		Overcaller (2)	Advancer	
♠AK432 ♦AQ2	♠QJ65 ♦K543		♠KQJ32 ♦KQ2	♠A765 ♦J543	
♥A432 ♣2	♥K65 ♣43		♥KQJ2 ♣2	♥765 ♣43	

Open	Over	Resp	Advnc	Open	Over	Resp	Advnc
3NT	Dbl	4♣	4♠	3NT	4♣	Pass	4♠
Pass	Pass	Pass		Pass	Pass	Pass	

If an opponent opens three notrump, double shows a good hand. However, there are some hands where overcaller would rather insist on declaring rather then defending. ♠KQJ32♥KQJ32♦KQ♣2 is great on offense, but the opponents could take seven clubs and three aces in three-notrump doubled. Four clubs is for takeout and ensures that overcaller won't have to defend against three notrump. Advancer bids his longer major, but can pass four clubs if he has a weak hand with a long club suit headed by an honor.

In example (1), overcaller, holding a good hand including three aces, doubles three notrump. Advancer bids his four-card spade suit, ending the auction. In example (2), overcaller cannot double three notrump since he has no guarantee that three notrump can be defeated. Overcaller therefore bids four clubs for takeout, and advancer bids four spades, ending the auction.

Chapter 5 - MAJOR OPENERS

5.1 -- FIVE-CARD MAJORS IN FIRST OR SECOND SEAT.

Opener	(1)	Responder		Opener	(2)	Responder	
♠KJ432	♦Q2	♠65	♦AKJ43	♠KJ432	♦Q2	♠Q65	♦AKJ43
♥2	♣AKQ32	♥KQJ3	♣J4	♥2	♣AKQ32	♥Q43	♣J4

1spade	2diamonds	1club	1diamond
3clubs	3NT	1spade	3NT

Opening a major in first or second seat promises at least five. Five-card majors helps in competitive situations where responder can raise to the two-level with three-card support, raise to the three-level with four-card support, and raise to the four-level with five-card support, all normally safe levels under the Law. Five-card majors also helps in constructive auctions where responder can always support opener with three-card support even if opener doesn't rebid his suit. I believe opener should open one-of-a-major whenever opener holds a five-card major, even if opener has a longer minor. It's important for responder to know when opener, who opens a minor, might also have a five-card major. If responder holds a major-suit singleton, he knows that the opponents have at least an eight-card fit if opener's minor-suit opening denies an outside five-card or longer major. I never have a five-card major if I open one-of-a-minor. Opening one-of-a-minor, denying a five-card major, takes the guess work out of some auctions. It allows opener to open a minor and later bid and rebid a four-card major if that's the best description of opener's hand. If I open one-of-a-minor and LHO jumps to four hearts and I reopen with four spades, my partner knows I have exactly four spades. If I open one club and LHO overcalls one spade and I reopen with two hearts, my partner knows I have exactly four hearts. I believe so strongly in this concept that I would open one spade with ♠65432♥-♦-♣AKQJ5432.

Examples (1) and (2) show why I always open one spade with five spades and five or more clubs. In example (1), opener knows that responder does not have three-card spade support and therefore he belongs in three notrump. In example (2), opener has to guess. If responder has the example hand, one with three-card spade support and maybe one heart stopper, the hand belongs in four spades. However, if responder has the hand from example (1), only two spades and KQJx of hearts, the hand belongs in three notrump. Wouldn't responder bid the same with either hand?

82

5.2 -- ONE NOTRUMP IS FORCING BY UNPASSED HAND.

Opener	(1)	Responder		Opener	(2)	Responder

```
Opener    (1)      Responder        Opener    (2)      Responder

♠432   ♦32      ♠QJ5   ♦KQ54       ♠32   ♦AJ2      ♠QJ5   ♦KQ54
  ♥AK432  ♣AJ2     ♥65     ♣8765      ♥AK432  ♣432     ♥65     ♣8765

1heart           1NT               1heart           1NT
2clubs           2hearts           2clubs           2hearts
Pass                               Pass
```

Opposite a first or second seat major-suit opener, one notrump is forcing for one round and shows five to twelve HCPs. Some rebids are easy: opener rebids a six-card or longer major, bids a lower ranking four-card or longer suit, raises to two notrump with 17 or 18 balanced, jumps to three notrump with 19 balanced, and jump shifts with game-forcing hands. Since opener can't pass one notrump, opener must sometimes respond in his cheaper three-card minor instead. Since opener's minor-suit rebid can be a three-card suit, responder with less than five-card support for the minor has to take a preference to opener's major any time responder has two-card support. Playing forcing notrump, one frequently plays 5-2 major-suit fits.

Opener doesn't have to rebid a six-card major. Knowing that responder is going to prefer his major any time responder has at least two, allows opener to bid two-of-a-minor on hands that are hard to describe. If opener doesn't want to jump to three-of-his-major because his major is weak and wouldn't play very well opposite a singleton or void, opener can bid two-of-a-minor instead, and then raise responder's preference. If responder passes two-of-a-minor, it can work out for the best. With six spades and four hearts, opener rebids two hearts unless the hearts are very weak.

In examples (1) and (2), opener passes a non-forcing notrump response, but has to bid his three-card minor over a forcing notrump response. In example (1), if responder's notrump is non-forcing, two clubs shows a four-card suit so responder passes two clubs and plays the 4-4 club fit. However, playing forcing notrump, opener might have only three clubs, so responder has to prefer hearts. If responder has only one heart, responder passes two clubs and hopes for the best. In example (2), opener bids his three-card club suit. With 3-3 in the minors, opener bids two clubs even though his diamonds are stronger than his clubs. Responder with four clubs and two hearts has to prefer hearts, since opener might have only three clubs.

Opener	(3)	Responder		Opener	(4)	Responder	
♠KQJ32	♦2	♠76	♦543	♠J5432	♦2	♠76	♦543
♥5432	♣KQ2	♥Q76	♣A6543	♥AKJ2	♣KQ2	♥Q76	♣A6543

Opener	Responder		Opener	Responder
1spade	1NT		1spade	1NT
2hearts	Pass		2hearts	Pass

Opener	(5)	Responder		Opener	(6)	Responder	
♠AQJ432	♦2	♠65	♦543	♠AKJ32	♦2	♠65	♦543
♥AJ32	♣K2	♥KQ4	♣A7654	♥AJ32	♣K32	♥KQ4	♣A7654

Opener	Responder		Opener	Responder
1spade	1NT		1spade	1NT
2hearts	2spades		2hearts	2spades
3spades	4spades		3clubs	5clubs
Pass			Pass	

In examples (3) through (6), responder with two spades and three hearts has to decide whether to pass two hearts or bid two spades. In example (3), two spades plays much better than two hearts. Playing two hearts, it's possible for the opponents to draw trumps and run diamonds. In example (4), two hearts plays much better than two spades. So how does responder know if opener's spades are better than his hearts, as in example (3), or opener's hearts are better than his spades, as in example (4)? Responder can't tell. What responder can do is prepare for examples (5) and (6). With sound values, values where responder is happy if opener makes a game try, responder takes a preference just in case opener makes a game try. With weak values, values where responder would not be happy if opener makes a game try, responder passes, in effect barring opener from making a game try. In examples (3) and (4), responder's hand is so weak that he will not be happy if opener makes a game try, so responder passes two hearts ending the auction. Responder hopes opener has the hand from example (4). In examples (5) and (6), responder with a sound response keeps the auction alive by bidding two spades. In example (5), opener bids three spades showing a good hand with six spades and four hearts and responder raises to four spades. In example (6), opener bids three clubs, showing a good hand with at least three clubs. Responder jumps to five clubs. If responder holds ♠76♥Q76♦543♣A6543, responder passes two hearts, keeping the auction low.

84

Opener	(7)	Responder		Opener	(8)	Responder	
♠AK432	♦KQ2	♠765	♦A543	♠AKQ32	♦KQ2	♠765	♦A543
♥432	♣32	♥QJ5	♣KJ4	♥432	♣32	♥QJ5	♣KJ4

Opener	Responder	Opener	Responder
1spade	1NT	1spade	1NT
2diamonds	3spades	2diamonds	3spades
Pass		4spades	

Opener	(9)	Responder		Opener	(10)	Responder	
♠KQJ32	♦KQ2	♠A54	♦6543	♠KQJ32	♦AKJ	♠A54	♦6543
♥432	♣32	♥5	♣KJ654	♥432	♣32	♥5	♣KJ654

Opener	Responder	Opener	Responder
1spade	3spades	1spade	3spades
Pass		4spades	Pass

If responder bids one notrump and then jumps to three-of-opener's-major, responder shows a balanced three-card limit raise with 11 HCPs. Sometimes responder has a bad 12, sometimes responder has a good ten, but opener should play responder for 11. Responder, with a balanced three-card limit raise, jumps to four-of-opener's-major if opener rebids his major showing a six-card suit. Responder also jumps to four-of-opener's-major if opener jumps shifts or if opener raises one notrump to two notrump. If responder has an unbalanced three-card limit raise, responder jumps directly to three-of-opener's-major. Responder usually has three trumps to an honor with an outside singleton to make a three-card limit raise. Since there is no way to show opener where his shortness is, responder wants opener to bid game with any excuse. A direct three-of-a-major is stronger then bidding one notrump first and then bidding three-of-a-major, therefore, opener will accept more often. Jumping directly to three-of-a-major gives the opponents less information to defend with. The opponents, thinking that you have a nine-card fit, might make a mistake and enter the auction.

In examples (7) and (8), responder has a balanced 11-point three-card spade raise. Responder bids one notrump and over opener's two-club rebid, jumps to three spades. In example (7), opener with only 12 HCPs passes three spades. In example (8), opener has 14 HCPs and accepts. In examples (9) and (10), responder has a three-card limit raise with an outside singleton. In example (9), opener with only 12 HCPs passes three spades. In example (10), opener has 14 HCPs and accepts. Give responder a singleton diamond instead of a singleton heart and a blind diamond lead still gives four spades a play.

Opener	(11)	Responder		Opener	(12)	Responder	
♠AKQ32	♦KQ2	♠65	♦A543	♠AK432	♦KQ2	♠65	♦A543
♥432	♣32	♥QJ5	♣KJ54	♥432	♣32	♥QJ5	♣KJ54

Opener	Responder	Opener	Responder
1spade	1NT	1spade	1NT
2diamonds	2NT	2diamonds	2NT
3NT	Pass	Pass	

Opener	(13)	Responder		Opener	(14)	Responder	
♠AJ5432	♦AK2	♠K6	♦Q765	♠AJ432	♦KJ432	♠K6	♦Q765
♥K32	♣2	♥QJ4	♣QJ43	♥K2	♣2	♥QJ4	♣QJ43

Opener	Responder	Opener	Responder
1spade	1NT	1spade	1NT
2diamonds	2NT	2diamonds	2NT
3spades	4spades	3diamonds	Pass

If responder bids one notrump and then bids two notrump, responder is showing 11 HCPs. Sometimes responder has 12, sometimes responder has only ten, but opener plays responder for 11. Opener, with 14, accepts all invitations. Since responder's hand is so well defined, only those bids by opener which force responder to prefer opener's lowest suit at the four-level are forcing.

In examples (11) through (14), responder has 11 HCPs and fewer than three spades. Responder bids one notrump and over opener's two-diamond bid, follows with two notrump. In example (11), opener with 14 HCPs bids three notrump. In example (12), opener with only 12 HCPs passes two notrump. In example (13), opener has a hand that is in-between a rebid of two and three spades. Since opener does not want to play in spades opposite a singleton, opener bids two diamonds, planning on bidding spades later, showing six spades and diamond values with enough strength to want to be in game opposite a sound two-card preference. If responder has a singleton spade and passes two diamonds, playing in two diamonds can work better than playing in three spades. Responder with 11 HCPs bids two notrump. Over two notrump, opener bids three spades, forcing, showing six spades, and responder raises to four spades. Three spades is forcing, since responder has to bid four diamonds to prefer diamonds. In example (14), opener bids three diamonds, non-forcing, and responder passes. If opener bids three clubs over two notrump, that is also non-forcing. Three hearts, however, is forcing, since responder has to bid four diamonds to prefer diamonds.

5.3 -- ONE-OF-A-MAJOR - TWO-OF-A-MAJOR IS MILDLY CONSTRUCTIVE. WILL ACCEPT AT LEAST ONE GAME TRY.

Opener	(1)	Responder	Opener	(2)	Responder
♠AK432 ♦K432		♠765 ♦Q65	♠AK432 ♦K432		♠765 ♦Q65
♥KQ2 ♣2		♥J43 ♣K543	♥KQ2 ♣2		♥J43 ♣K543

Opener (1)	Responder	Opener (2)	Responder
1spade	2spades	1spade	1NT
3diamonds	3spades	2diamonds	2spades
Pass		Pass	

A simple major-suit raise from one-of-a-major to two-of-a-major by an unpassed hand shows three or four-card support with seven to ten points. There is another route to get to two-of-opener's-major. Responder bids a forcing notrump and over opener's forced rebid, takes a preference to two-of-opener's-major. Going through the forcing-notrump sequence has the effect of slowing the auction down, since responder frequently has only two-card support for opener's major. If responder has three-card support for opener's major but wouldn't accept any game tries, responder doesn't want to end up at the three-level when the limit of the hand might be only eight tricks. If responder bids a forcing notrump and then takes a preference to two-of-opener's-major, opener will be conservative, since opener hasn't necessarily found an eight-card fit. After one spade -- two spades, opener has found an eight-card fit and might make an aggressive game try.

With four-card support, responder usually raises directly. Raising directly stops the opponents from making a cheap overcall. Only if responder has to choose between passing one-of-a-major or raising does responder go through the forcing notrump sequence. With three or four HCPs and four-card support, go through the forcing notrump sequence rather than pass. With a nine-card fit, you want to make it difficult for the opponents to enter the auction.

In example (1), see what happens when responder raises to two spades. Opener, with a known eight-card fit, needing to find responder with only QJx of spades and QJx of diamonds to have a play for four spades, makes a help-suit game try which responder rejects. Even two spades might go down. In example (2), responder bids a forcing notrump, and then over opener's two-diamond bid, takes a preference to two spades. Since responder is very likely to have only two spades, this becomes a point-count auction, with opener's 15 HCPs, opposite responder's maximum of ten HCPs, unlikely to produce a game.

5.4 -- ONE-OF-A-MAJOR - TWO-OF-A-MAJOR - FOUR-ANY IS 5-5 SLAM TRY.

Opener (1)	Responder	Opener (2)	Responder
♠AK432 ♦AQT32	♠Q65 ♦K54	♠AK432 ♦AQT32	♠765 ♦J54
♥AK ♣2	♥432 ♣Q543	♥AK ♣2	♥QJ2 ♣KQJ3

1spade	2spades	1spade	2spades
4diamonds	4hearts	4diamonds	4spades
4NT	5clubs	Pass	
5diamonds	5NT		
6spades	Pass		

Once responder has raised opener's major, a fit has been found. After a fit is found, opener's only problem is the level. If opener has a hand with two long and strong suits and responder has fitting cards, slam is a definite possibility. Opener is half-way there since responder already has shown a fit in opener's major and a hand that accepts at least one game try. Opener jumps in a second suit if two cover cards in responder's hand will produce a good play for slam. Cover cards are the AKQ of trumps or a fourth trump, AKQ of the side-suit, shortness in the side-suit with four-card trump support, and any of the missing two aces. Opener has to weigh getting to slam against the probability that the defenders will get vital information which will make it easier for them to defend.

If opener jumps in a new suit, responder has three choices. Responder signs-off in four-of-opener's-major with zero or one cover card, bids above four-of-opener's-major with three or more cover cards, and bids the in-between suit if possible with one or two cover cards. With one cover card, responder has to choose whether to be aggressive or conservative.

In example (1), opener is missing three cover cards (♠Q, ♦K, ♣A). If responder has two of them, opener wants to be in slam. Opener jumps to four diamonds showing a 5-5 hand which has grown to a three-loser hand by responder's raise. Responder with two cover cards bids four hearts, the Last Train, the only bid responder has to encourage without bidding above game. If responder can encourage, opener accepts. Opener bids keycard and then asks for the spade queen to make sure responder hasn't encouraged with just very good diamond values. Over five diamonds, responder bids five notrump showing the spade queen and diamond king. In example (2), responder has ten HCPs but zero cover cards, so responder signs-off in four spades.

5.5 -- ONE SPADE - TWO SPADES - THREE HEARTS - THREE SPADES - FOUR HEARTS CHOICE OF GAMES.

Jumping to four hearts after one spade -- two spades, is a two-suited slam try, therefore bidding three hearts followed by four hearts is choice of games. Opener wants to play in four hearts if responder has four or more hearts.

5.6 -- HELP SUIT GAME TRIES.

After one-of-a-major -- two-of-a-major, opener has available three types of game tries; two notrump, bidding three-of-opener's-major or bidding a new suit - a help suit game try. Remember from section 5.3 that responder will accept at least one game try. Opener bids two notrump to show a 5-3-3-2 17 or 18-count with at least one honor in every suit. Opener bids three-of-his-major to show a six-card suit, needing nine or ten HCPs.

Bidding a new suit is a help-suit game try. Using help-suit game tries, opener bids a xxx, xxxx, Axx, Axxx, Kxx, Kxxx, Qxx or a Qxxx suit. If responder holds xxx, Jxx, xxxx or Qxxx, responder usually rejects. Holding Ax, Kx, or KQx, responder accepts. With a choice of suits, opener bids the lowest in order to give responder a chance to bid an in-between suit. After one heart -- two hearts, bidding two spades allows responder to bid two notrump with scattered values, bid three clubs with values in clubs, or bid three diamonds with values in diamonds. Responder bids an in-between suit holding kings and queens in the suit, not aces. Aces are always good, but kings and queens can be worthless opposite shortness. Holding four trumps is always good. 4-4-3-2 is better than 4-3-3-3. Holding three trumps to an honor is better than holding three small trumps.

Since opener might be thinking about slam, if responder's hand is worth accepting a slam try as well as accepting a game try, responder bids four-of-his-better-minor instead of bidding game. Over one spade -- two spades -- three clubs, four clubs or four diamonds are natural bids. They accept opener's game try, and if opener is thinking about slam, responder has slam-going values, something like ♠Kxx♥xx♦xxx♣KQxxx. Over one spade -- two spades -- three clubs, four spades accepts opener's game try and denies slam-going values, something like ♠xxxx♥KQx♦KJxx♣xx.

Opener (1)	Responder	Opener (2)	Responder
♠K432 ♦A	♠A5 ♦8765	♠Q32 ♦K432	♠A5 ♦8765
♥AQ432 ♣Q32	♥765 ♣KJ54	♥AQ432 ♣A	♥765 ♣KJ54
1heart	2hearts	1heart	2hearts
2spades	3clubs	2spades	3clubs
4hearts	Pass	3hearts	Pass

Opener (3)	Responder	Opener (4)	Responder
♠KJ65432 ♦A	♠10987 ♦KQ32	♠KJ65432 ♦A	♠Q987 ♦32
♥A ♣AJ32	♥K32 ♣54	♥A ♣AJ32	♥432 ♣KQ54
1spade	2spades	1spade	2spades
3clubs	4spades	3clubs	4clubs
Pass		4NT	5clubs
		5diamonds	6clubs
		6spades	Pass

In example (1), opener makes a game try by bidding two spades. Responder, who happily would have accepted a club-game try, makes a counter try with three clubs, and opener accepts. A counter try of two notrump shows honors in both minors, which opener rejects. In example (2), opener makes his game try with two spades, not three diamonds. Two spades allows responder to make a counter try of three clubs, which slows opener down. If responder has honors in diamonds and spades instead of clubs and spades, four hearts has good play.

In examples (3) and (4), opener bids three clubs, trying for slam. In example (3), responder has a super maximum in HCPs along with four-card support and accepts opener's game try by bidding four spades. If opener is making a club slam try, responder with no honors in the black suits has a bad hand for slam. In example (4), responder has the best possible club holding and four-card trump support. Responder bids four clubs, accepting opener's game try and cooperating with a possible club slam try. Opener bids keycard, finds responder with the queen of trumps and bids a slam.

5.7 -- ONE-OF-A-MAJOR - THREE-OF-A-MAJOR IS FOUR-CARD OR UNBALANCED THREE-CARD LIMIT RAISE (11 SUPPORT POINTS).

Opener	(1)		Responder		Opener	(2)		Responder	
♠KQJ32	♦32	♠A654	♦654		♠KQJ32	♦32	♠A654	♦654	
♥A32	♣A32	♥KJT	♣K54		♥A32	♣A32	♥QJ4	♣QJ4	

1spade	3spades	1spade	2spades
4spades	Pass	Pass	

Opener	(3)		Responder		Opener	(4)		Responder	
♠KQJ32	♦2	♠A54	♦76543		♠KQJ32	♦2	♠A54	♦76543	
♥A432	♣A32	♥5	♣KQ54		♥A432	♣A32	♥KQ65	♣4	

1spade	3spades	1spade	1NT
4spades	Pass	2hearts	4hearts

A jump raise by responder shows 11 support points with four-card support. Since opener has to decide whether to bid game, responder wants to keep the range as small as possible. If responder has 11, maybe a good ten, maybe a bad 12, opener has a better chance of going right. Some partnerships allow limit raises with unbalanced three-card support, and I agree. To make a direct three-card limit raise in spades, responder should have good trumps, a ruffing value and fewer than four hearts. Responder doesn't want to miss a 4-4 heart fit.

In example (1), responder bids three spades showing 11 support points and usually four spades. Opener raises to game. Four spades is cold on a heart lead, cold if you can strip the hand and play a club, or on a heart guess otherwise. In example (2), responder has ten support points, is 4-3-3-3, and raises to two spades. In examples (3) and (4), responder has an unbalanced three-card limit raise in spades. Example (3) is a good example where responder bids three spades with only three-card support. A trump lead is a killer, and the less information you give opening leader, the better the chance opening leader will help you. Don't you lead the king of hearts holding ♠765♥KQJT♦98♣JT87 on the above auction, and don't you lead a trump if the auction goes one spade -- one notrump -- two hearts, etc. Example (4) is the exception. Holding four hearts, responder doesn't want to miss his 4-4 heart fit so responder bids one notrump planning on jumping to three spades. When opener bids two hearts, responder jumps to four hearts.

5.8 -- ONE HEART - ONE NOTRUMP - TWO-OF-A-MINOR - TWO SPADES SHOWS A GOOD MINOR-SUIT RAISE.

Opener (1)		Responder		Opener (2)		Responder	
♠432	♦K32	♠AQ5	♦AJ654	♠32	♦KQ32	♠AQ5	♦AJ654
♥KQJ32	♣A2	♥65	♣543	♥AQ432	♣A2	♥65	♣543

Opener (1)	Responder	Opener (2)	Responder
1heart	1NT	1heart	1NT
2diamonds	2spades	2diamonds	2spades
3diamonds	Pass	3NT	Pass

Opener (3)		Responder		Opener (4)		Responder	
♠2	♦A32	♠543	♦KQ4	♠2	♦A32	♠543	♦654
♥KQJ32	♣A432	♥54	♣KQ765	♥KQJ32	♣A432	♥54	♣KQ765

Opener (3)	Responder	Opener (4)	Responder
1heart	1NT	1heart	1NT
2clubs	2spades	2clubs	3clubs
3diamonds	5clubs	Pass	

After one heart -- one notrump -- two-of-either-minor, responder bids two spades, artificial, to show at least a nine-point raise of opener's minor. Two spades has to be artificial, since responder's one notrump denies holding more than four spades. A direct minor raise is therefore weaker then bidding two spades. Opener should not be afraid to play in three-of-a-minor with only a three-card suit, since responder usually has five-card support for his artificial two-spade bid.

In examples (1) and (2), responder bids a forcing notrump. Over opener's two-diamond bid, responder raises diamonds as strongly as responder can without getting overboard by bidding two spades. In example (1), opener, with a minimum, signs-off in three diamonds. Responder, having described his hand, passes. In example (2), opener has 15 HCPs and a semi-balanced hand. Opener jumps to three notrump over responder's diamond-support-showing two-spade bid. In example (3), responder bids two spades showing a good club raise. Opener with extras bids his diamond fragment, and responder with a good fit jumps to five clubs. In example (4), responder raises to three clubs, showing the weaker raise. Three clubs preempts the opponents out of their spade fit and keeps the auction alive just in case opener has a hand which will make game opposite just club support. Opener passes three clubs.

5.9 -- BY UNPASSED HAND, JUMP SHIFTS TO THREE-LEVEL ARE INVITATIONAL (ONE SPADE - THREE CLUBS SHOWS 10-12 POINTS WITH AT LEAST SIX CLUBS).

Opener (1)	Responder	Opener (2)	Responder
♠AQ432 ♦A32	♠5 ♦654	♠AQ432 ♦AJ32	♠65 ♦654
♥32 ♣QJ2	♥AQJ654 ♣K65	♥2 ♣432	♥AQJ654 ♣K5

Opener (1)	Responder	Opener (2)	Responder
1spade	3hearts	1spade	1NT
4hearts	Pass	2diamonds	3hearts
		Pass	

A jump shift to the three-level by responder after a major-suit opening is natural and invitational, and replaces Standard American's two-over-one followed by a rebid of the same suit. Responder shows a six-card or longer suit with somewhere around 11 points and at most two cards in opener's major. One-of-either-major -- three clubs, one-of-either-major -- three diamonds, and one spade -- three hearts, are all natural and invitational jump shifts. A jump to three hearts over one spade shows fewer than two spades or a hand with a heart suit that always wants to play in hearts, such as KQJT32. With six hearts, two spades and invitational values, responder bids a forcing notrump and over opener's two-of-a-minor bid, responder jumps to three hearts. If opener rebids two spades, responder jumps to four hearts, showing an invitational hand with six hearts and two spades. This maximizes the chances of getting to the better major-suit fit. Over responder's jump to four hearts, opener bids four spades with fewer than two hearts, thereby playing a 6-2 spade fit and avoiding a 6-1 heart fit. If opener has three hearts, opener passes four hearts playing the 6-3 heart fit instead of the 6-2 spade fit. With two hearts, opener has a choice between 6-2 major-suit fits. Over invitational jump shifts, all of opener's non-game bids are forcing. Since the jump shift is invitational opposite a minimum opener, any extras tips the scale and makes game playable.

In example (1), responder has a good six-card heart suit with ten HCPs and a singleton spade, and jumps to three hearts. Opener with a fit and a sound minimum raises to game. In example (2), responder has a similar hand except responder has a doubleton spade. Responder bids a forcing notrump and over opener's two-diamond bid, jumps to three hearts. Opener with a minimum without a fit passes three hearts.

5.10 -- TWO NOTRUMP RESPONSE IS A FOUR-CARD FORCING RAISE (JACOBY).

Opener	(1)	Responder		Opener	(2)	Responder	
♠AQ432	♦A32	♠K765	♦QJ65	♠QJ432	♦A432	♠K765	♦QJ65
♥32	♣QJ2	♥KQJ	♣43	♥2	♣KJ2	♥KQJ	♣43
1spade		2NT		1spade		2NT	
4spades		Pass		3hearts		4spades	

Opener	(3)	Responder		Opener	(4)	Responder	
♠AQJ32	♦A32	♠K654	♦QJ65	♠AQJ32	♦AK432	♠K654	♦QJ65
♥32	♣AQJ	♥KQJ	♣54	♥2	♣32	♥KQJ	♣54
1spade		2NT		1spade		2NT	
3spades		4spades		4diamonds		4spades	
Pass				Pass			

Responder's jump to two notrump shows a four-card game-forcing raise. Opener's first rebid describes his distribution and his strength. With a singleton or void, opener shows his shortness, regardless of his strength, by bidding his short suit at the three-level. If opener has a good second five-card or longer suit, he jumps to the four-level in his second suit. If opener has a minimum balanced hand, 11-13 HCPs 5-3-3-2 or 11-12 HCPs 6-3-2-2, opener jumps to four-of-his-major. If opener has more than a minimum, opener rebids three-of-his-major with 16 or more points and bids three notrump with fewer than 16 points.

In examples (1) through (4), responder has a minimum Jacoby raise, four trumps and 12 HCPs. The hand is a little too good for a limit raise. In example (1), opener jumps to four spades showing a balanced minimum opening bid. In example (2), opener bids three hearts showing a singleton or void in hearts, saying nothing about strength. Responder with a minimum hand jumps to four spades. In example (3), opener shows a balanced hand with at least 16 HCPs. When responder can't cuebid opposite a hand with at least 16 HCPs, opener realizes that there is a lack of values and conservatively passes. Eighteen HCPs opposite a balanced 12 does not always produce a slam. In example (4), opener jumps to four diamonds showing at least five diamonds with values in diamonds and spades. Responder signs-off in four spades.

Opener	(5)	Responder		Opener	(6)	Responder	
♠AQ432	♦AQ32	♠K765	♦54	♠AQ432	♦AQ32	♠K765	♦654
♥2	♣KJ2	♥KQJ3	♣A43	♥2	♣KJ2	♥AQJ	♣A43

Opener (5)	Responder	Opener (6)	Responder
1spade	2NT	1spade	2NT
3hearts	3spades	3hearts	3spades
4clubs	4spades	4clubs	4hearts
Pass		4spades	Pass

Opener	(7)	Responder		Opener	(8)	Responder	
♠AQJ32	♦KQ32	♠K654	♦A4	♠AQJ32	♦KQ32	♠K7654	♦AJ
♥2	♣KJ2	♥6543	♣AQ3	♥2	♣KJ2	♥6543	♣AQ

Opener (7)	Responder	Opener (8)	Responder
1spade	2NT	1spade	2NT
3hearts	4clubs	3hearts	4NT
4NT	5clubs	5diamonds	6spades
6spades	Pass	Pass	

After opener shows shortness, responder has five choices. In reverse order of strength, responder can sign-off in four-of-opener's-major, mark time with three-of-opener's-major or three notrump, which ever is lower and then sign-off, mark time with three-of-opener's-major or three notrump, whichever is lower and then cuebid, cuebid directly, or bid RKC.

In examples (5) through (8), opener bids three hearts showing a singleton or void in hearts. In example (5), responder has two keycards, a source of tricks and a possible ruffing value, so responder marks time with three spades and then signs-off. This shows a sound minimum hand, one with aces and kings but with some wasted values. Responder shows a minimum hand, one with queens and jacks and wasted values by jumping to four spades over three hearts. In example (6), responder has 11 working HCPs, which is strong enough to make a delayed cuebid, so responder bids three spades, the mark-time bid, followed by a cuebid. Cuebidding four hearts directly is a whole cuebid and shows at least 13 working HCPs. In example (7), responder with 13 working HCPs has a hand which is good enough for a direct cuebid. Opener doesn't need to hear any more. Opener keycards and signs-off in six spades when opener finds he's missing one keycard. In example (8), responder needs very little opposite heart shortness to have a play for slam, so responder bids keycard. Responder doesn't have to ask for the queen since responder knows that there is at least a ten-card fit.

Opener	(9)		Responder	

♠AK654 ♦AQJ5 ♠QJ32 ♦K432
  ♥43 ♣Q4 ♥AK2 ♣32

Open	Advnc	Resp	Over
1♠	Pass	2NT	3♣
Pass	Pass	4♠	Pass

Opener	(10)		Responder	

♠AK654 ♦AQJ5 ♠QJ32 ♦K432
  ♥43 ♣K4 ♥AK2 ♣32

Open	Advnc	Resp	Over
1♠	Pass	2NT	3♣
3♦	Pass	3♥	Pass
4NT	Pass	5♦	Pass
5♥	Pass	5NT	Pass
6♠	Pass	Pass	Pass

What does opener bid if overcaller enters his Jacoby auction? Bidding game directly has the same meaning as if overcaller had passed, a weak balanced hand. Since overcaller knows that you have at least a nine-card fit, and sometimes makes frivolous lead-directing overcalls, opener's double should be for penalties, promising at least four cards and two honors in overcaller's suit. If responder has two cards and opener has four-cards in overcaller's suit, overcaller will be in at best a seven-card fit. Doubling overcaller will always be right when opener can't make game, and will usually be satisfactory compensation at equal vulnerability, especially playing IMPs. Responder is allowed to pull the penalty double. If opener has extra values, opener shows whether or not he has first or second-round control in overcaller's suit. Opener can't have a slam if he has two or more losers in the opponent's suit. Opener passes to deny first or second-round control. With a control, opener bids a second suit, bids notrump with a balanced hand, cuebids with shortness in overcaller's suit, or rebids his own suit at the three-level with extra length. If overcaller bids Michaels, opener keys on the other major. If overcaller bids the Unusual Notrump, opener's minor-suit bids are natural cuebids.

In examples (9) and (10), overcaller bids three clubs. In example (9), opener passes three clubs, showing extra values but denying a club control. Responder, also lacking a club control, signs-off in four spades. In example (10), opener bids three diamonds showing extra values, diamond values and a club control. Responder, who doesn't have to worry about a club control, cuebids three hearts. Opener bids keycard and responder shows one keycard. Opener asks for the spade queen. Responder shows the queen and the king of hearts, by bidding five notrump which is the cheapest king he can show. Five spades denies the queen, and six spades shows the queen and denies any kings. With the queen, responder shows any outside kings up the line as naturally as possible. Opener signs-off in six spades.

5.11 -- TWO-TIER SPLINTERS.

1.

1spade	3NT
4clubs	4diamonds

♠AJ76♥543♦6♣A5432

2.

1spade	3NT
4clubs	4hearts

♠AJ76♥3♦KJ32♣QJ43

3.

1spade	3NT
4clubs	4spades

♠AJ76♥QJ32♦QJ32♣3

4.

1heart	3spades
3NT	4diamonds

♠KJ76♥K432♦6♣K543

5.

1heart	3spades
3NT	4hearts

♠3♥AJ32♦QJ32♣K543

6.

1heart	3spades
3NT	4clubs

♠KQJ6♥AJ32♦5432♣3

7.

1spade	4diamonds

♠AJ76♥KQJ3♦6♣A543

8.

1spade	4hearts

♠AJ76♥3♦KJ32♣A543

9.

1spade	4clubs

♠AJ76♥KJ32♦KQ32♣3

10.

1heart	4diamonds

♠KJ76♥KQJ3♦6♣A543

11.

1heart	3NT

♠3♥AJ32♦KJ32♣A543

12.

1heart	4clubs

♠KQ76♥AJ32♦KQ32♣3

In auctions (1), (2) and (3), responder bids three notrump over one spade, artificial, and in auctions (4), (5) and (6), responder bids three spades over one heart, artificial, showing four-card support for opener's major, 9-12 HCPs, and unspecified shortness. In auctions (1), (2) and (3), opener asks for shortness by bidding four clubs. In auctions (4), (5) and (6), opener asks for shortness by bidding three notrump. OPENER ASKS FOR SHORTNESS ONLY IF OPENER IS INTERESTED IN SLAM. Otherwise, opener signs-off in four-of-his-major. Auctions (1) through (6) are examples of how responder can force to game without getting overboard. In auctions (7) through (12), responder shows four-card support for opener's major, 13-15 HCPs, and except for auction (11), shortness in the bid suit. In column (1), responder shows diamond shortness. In column (2), responder shows shortness in the other major. In column (3), responder shows shortness in clubs. If responder has a void, he still splinters and then shows the void by cuebidding or during RKC (see section 25.6).

Opener	(1)		Responder		Opener	(2)		Responder	
♠AQ432	♦AQ32		♠K765	♦4	♠AQ432	♦AQ32		♠K765	♦7654
♥2	♣KJ2		♥AJ43	♣Q543	♥2	♣KJ2		♥AQ43	♣3

Opener	Responder		Opener	Responder
1spade	3NT		1spade	3NT
4clubs	4diamonds		4clubs	4spades
4hearts	4NT		Pass	
5spades	6spades			

Opener	(3)		Responder		Opener	(4)		Responder	
♠AK432	♦A432		♠Q765	♦5	♠AK432	♦A432		♠QJ65	♦KQ65
♥2	♣KJ2		♥AJ43	♣AQ43	♥2	♣KJ2		♥AJ43	♣3

Opener	Responder		Opener	Responder
1spade	4diamonds		1spade	4clubs
4NT	5spades		4diamonds	4hearts
6clubs	7clubs		4NT	5diamonds
7spades	Pass		5hearts	6diamonds
			6spades	Pass

In example (1), responder bids three notrump showing a four-card spade raise with unspecified shortness and 9-12 HCPs. Opener bids four clubs, asking, and responder shows his diamond shortness by bidding four diamonds. Opener needs responder to have two keycards so he bids four hearts the Last Train. Responder has two keycards, and bids RKC. Bidding four hearts is designed to stop opener from getting to the five-level opposite ♠KJ76♥KQJ3♦6♣6543 where a heart lead and a club return might beat five spades. In example (2), responder again bids three notrump showing a 9-12 unspecified splinter. Opener bids four clubs, asking, hoping for diamond shortness. When responder bids four spades, showing club shortness, opener passes, settling for game. In example (3), responder bids a direct four diamonds showing diamond shortness with at least 13 HCPs. Opener bids keycard, finds all keycards present, and then bids six clubs, asking responder to bid seven with third-round club control. Responder bids seven clubs showing the club queen. Opener converts to seven spades. If opener is interested in kings, he bids five notrump instead of six clubs. In example (4), opener with KJx opposite a 13+ club splinter makes a slam try with four diamonds. Responder bids four hearts, the Last Train, showing a minimum with prime values. With a maximum and prime values, responder forces to slam. With queens and jacks, responder signs-off in four spades. Opener has enough to be in slam opposite a hand with prime values, so opener bids keycard and bids six spades.

Opener (5)		Responder		Opener (6)		Responder	
♠432	♦AQ32	♠5	♦KJ54	♠432	♦AQ32	♠J765	♦4
♥AQ432	♣A	♥K765	♣K432	♥AQ432	♣A	♥K765	♣KQJ2

Opener (5)	Responder	Opener (6)	Responder
1heart	3spades	1heart	3spades
3NT	4hearts	3NT	4diamonds
4NT	5diamonds	4hearts	Pass
6hearts	Pass		

Opener (7)		Responder		Opener (8)		Responder	
♠Q32	♦2	♠4	♦AJ43	♠Q32	♦2	♠KJ54	♦KQJ3
♥AQ432	♣KQJ2	♥KJ65	♣A543	♥AQ432	♣KQJ2	♥KJ65	♣3

Opener (7)	Responder	Opener (8)	Responder
1heart	3NT	1heart	4clubs
4clubs	4diamonds	4hearts	Pass
4NT	5clubs		
6hearts	Pass		

In example (5), responder bids three spades showing, a four-card heart raise with unspecified shortness and 9-12 HCPs. Opener bids three notrump asking, and responder shows his spade shortness by bidding four hearts. Opener bids RKC and bids six hearts. In example (6), responder again bids three spades, showing four-card heart support, 9-12 HCPs and unspecified shortness. Opener bids three notrump, asking, hoping for spade shortness. When responder bids four diamonds showing diamond shortness, opener settles for game. Bidding higher than four hearts is too dangerous. While responder's black suits could be reversed, opener can't play responder for specific cards. Responder very rarely has them. In example (7), responder bids three notrump showing spade shortness with at least 13 HCPs. Opener bids keycard and then bids six hearts. In example (8), opener with KQJx opposite a 13+ club splinter signs-off in four hearts. Opener needs responder to have ♠AK,♥K,♦A, a specific holding, which is very unlikely.

5.12 -- TWO-OVER-ONE IS 100% GAME FORCING, EVEN BIDDING AND REBIDDING A SUIT.

After a major-suit opening, two-over-one sequences are game forcing. This doesn't include passed hand two-over-one sequences or if responder's right-hand-opponent has overcalled. Responder forces with at least 13 points. With 12 points, responder treats the hand as either limit or forcing depending upon texture, distribution and partner's opening bid style. Two-over-one gives up accuracy in game-invitational sequences, but gains in choice-of-game sequences and slam sequences. Two-over-one allows responder to set trumps at a lower level. Two-over-one allows responder to rebid two notrump, forcing, allowing opener to finish describing his hand. If responder has a one-suiter, responder can rebid his suit rather then inventing a bid in order to create a forcing auction, thus making all bids natural. Remember, responder shows a six-card suit and 10-12 HCPs with a direct jump (see section 5.9). Partnerships can make an exception if opener or responder bids his suit at the minimum level three times, but to keep it simple, two-over-one sequences are 100% forcing to game.

When responder has a choice of suits with which to bid two-over-one, responder's two-heart response shows a five-card or longer suit. Responder's two-diamond response shows a five-card or longer suit or at least a very strong four-card suit, and responder's two-club response shows all other game-forcing hands. With 3-4-4-2 after a spade opener or 4-3-4-2 after a heart opener, responder has to decide whether to respond two diamonds or two clubs. Since responder is going to support opener's major at his next call, it's better to respond two clubs on a doubleton than two diamonds on only a four-card suit. In other words, opener treats a two-club response as a suspect suit similar to a one-club opener, but treats two diamonds or two hearts as a real suit.

It's often better to respond two clubs rather than one spade in order to avoid having to go through a fourth-suit game-forcing sequence. With a ten or eleven point two-suiter, with which you wish to force to game, it's often better to start with a two-over-one and get both suits in. At least if opener has three-card support for either one of your suits, you'll find it.

100

Opener	(1)	Responder		Opener	(2)	Responder

Opener (1)		Responder		Opener (2)		Responder
♠AQ432 ♦AQ2		♠K5 ♦K43		♠AQ432 ♦AQ2		♠K5 ♦K43
♥32 ♣J32		♥AJ54 ♣K654		♥32 ♣J32		♥AQ654 ♣Q54

Opener (1)	Responder		Opener (2)	Responder
1spade	2clubs		1spade	2hearts
2spades	2NT		2NT	3NT
3NT	Pass		Pass	

After opening one-of-a-major, opener has to find a rebid after responder bids two-over-one. Since responder needs five hearts to respond two hearts, opener can raise hearts anytime he has at least three. Opener raises two hearts to four hearts with a minimum opener, 5-4-2-2 distribution and no aces or kings in either minor. If responder needs five diamonds to respond two diamonds, opener needs three-card support and a sound opening bid to raise. If responder can respond two diamonds with only four, opener needs four-card support and a sound opening bid to raise. Opener raises two clubs to three clubs with four-card support and a sound opening bid, one with at least 14 HCPs. Raising responder's minor shows either extra strength or extra distribution. Opener can always raise with five-card support. Opener raises two diamonds to four diamonds or two clubs to four clubs with a sound opener, at least 5-5 distribution with at least second-round control in both unbid suits.

If opener can't bid a new suit at the two-level, opener with 11-13 HCPs must either rebid his major or bid two notrump, depending upon the honors opener has in the unbid suits and the strength opener has in his major. Rebidding two-of-a-major does not promise a six-card suit. With 5-3-3-2 hands where opener has two or three little in an unbid suit, or 5-1-3-4 hands where opener does not have enough strength to bid three clubs, opener rebids his five-card major. Opener also rebids his five-card major if the major is strong enough to play opposite two small. Rebidding two-of-his-major allows responder to bid two notrump. If opener bids two notrump, he is usually 5-3-3-2. If responder bids two notrump, he can have any balanced or semi-balanced distribution. Therefore, opponents have a more difficult time defending the hand when responder plays three notrump.

In example (1), opener has to find a bid over responder's game-forcing two clubs. Since opener has two little hearts, opener rebids two spades rather than two notrump. In example (2), opener has at least one honor in the two unbid suits, so opener bids two notrump.

101

5.13 -- ONE SPADE - TWO DIAMONDS - THREE CLUBS AND ONE SPADE - TWO HEARTS - THREE-OF-A-MINOR SHOWS EXTRA VALUES.

Opener	(1)	Responder		Opener	(2)	Responder	
♠AQ432	♦A2	♠K5	♦KJ543	♠AQ432	♦A2	♠K5	♦KJ543
♥32	♣AJ32	♥AQ4	♣654	♥32	♣QJ32	♥AQ4	♣654

Opener (1)	Responder	Opener (2)	Responder
1spade	2diamonds	1spade	2diamonds
3clubs	3NT	2spades	2NT
Pass		3clubs	3NT

Opener	(3)	Responder		Opener	(4)	Responder	
♠AQ432	♦K2	♠K5	♦AJ3	♠AQ432	♦K2	♠K5	♦AJ3
♥K2	♣AK32	♥AQJ43	♣765	♥2	♣AJ432	♥AQJ43	♣765

Opener (3)	Responder	Opener (4)	Responder
1spade	2hearts	1spade	2hearts
3clubs	3NT	3clubs	3NT
4NT	6NT	Pass	

If opener bids a new suit at the three-level over responder's two-over-one, it shows extra values. One spade -- two hearts -- three-of-either-minor, one spade -- two diamonds -- three clubs, one heart -- two diamonds -- three clubs all show extra values. With a four-card suit, opener needs at least 15 HCPs. To bid a new suit at the three-level, opener doesn't need as much extra strength with a five-card or longer second suit.

In example (1), opener with a 5-2-2-4 15-count has a minimum three-club bid. Responder bids three notrump and opener with a minimum three-club bid passes three notrump. In example (2), opener does not have enough strength to bid three clubs, and does not want to bid two notrump with two little hearts. Therefore, opener must rebid two spades. Opener gets a chance to bid his clubs when responder bids two notrump. In example (3), opener has more than enough to bid three clubs. Over responder's three-notrump sign-off, opener raises to four notrump, natural, and with more than a minimum, responder bids six notrump. In example (4), with 5-5 in the black suits, opener has the minimum values for a three-club bid. Responder with only one black honor signs-off in three notrump, and opener with a minimum three-club bid passes.

5.14 -- OPENER'S JUMP REBID AFTER A TWO-OVER-ONE SHOWS A SOLID SUIT (USUALLY SEVEN OR MORE) AND MIGHT NOT HAVE EXTRA VALUES.

Opener	(1)		Responder		Opener	(2)		Responder	
♠AKQ5432	♦K2	♠6	♦AQ543		♠AKQ5432	♦K2	♠6	♦QJT543	
♥K32	♣2	♥AQ54	♣K43		♥K32	♣2	♥QJT	♣KQJ	

Opener (1)	Responder	Opener (2)	Responder
1spade	2diamonds	1spade	2diamonds
3spades	4clubs	3spades	4spades
4NT	5hearts	Pass	
6spades	Pass		

Opener	(3)		Responder		Opener	(4)		Responder	
♠AKQ5432	♦A2	♠6	♦KQJ43		♠AKQ5432	♦A2	♠6	♦KQJ43	
♥32	♣32	♥AK65	♣QJ4		♥432	♣2	♥AK65	♣QJ4	

Opener (3)	Responder	Opener (4)	Responder
1spade	2diamonds	1spade	2diamonds
3spades	4diamonds	3spades	4diamonds
4spades	Pass	4hearts	4NT
		5clubs	6spades

SINCE TWO-OVER-ONE IS 100% GAME FORCING, OPENER DOES NOT HAVE TO JUMP TO FORCE. A jump rebid shows a solid suit, one that will play opposite a void, and sets that suit as trumps. AKQxxxx or KQJTxxx are minimum suit holdings. Responder with slam interest shows controls or concentration of values. Four notrump is RKC for opener's major.

In examples (1) through (4), opener jumps to three spades, setting spades as trumps. In example (1), responder bids four clubs, showing club values and slam interest, which is all the incentive opener needs to bid RKC. In example (2), responder raises to four spades, in effect, denying any aces. If responder can't cuebid, even four spades can go down with foul splits. In examples (3) and (4), responder has a great hand but is worried about clubs. Responder bids four diamonds, showing a diamond control and denying a club control. Opener knows from responder's failure to bid four clubs that responder has at least two club losers. In example (3), opener, holding two little clubs and knowing that responder does not have first or second-round club control, signs-off in four spades. In example (4), opener has second-round club control and bids four hearts, the Last Train, to show further interest. Responder, knowing that opener has a club control, bids keycard. Notice that there were two cuebids and neither cuebid promised first-round control.

5.15 -- AFTER TWO-OVER-ONES, ALL JUMP SHIFTS ARE SPLINTERS.

1.	2.	3.	4.	5.	6.	7.
1♠ 2♣ 3♦	1♠ 2♣ 3♥	1♠ 2♦ 3♥	1♠ 2♦ 4♣	1♠ 2♥ 4♣	1♠ 2♥ 4♦	1♥ 2♣ 3♦

8.	9.	10.
1♥ 2♣ 3♠	1♥ 2♦ 3♠	1♥ 2♦ 4♣

11.	12.	13.	14.	15.	16.	17.
1♠ 2♣ 2♠ 4♦	1♠ 2♣ 2♠ 4♥	1♠ 2♦ 2♠ 4♣	1♠ 2♦ 2♠ 4♥	1♠ 2♥ 2♠ 4♣	1♠ 2♥ 2♠ 4♦	1♥ 2♣ 2♥ 3♠

18.	19.	20.	21.	22.	23.	24.
1♥ 2♣ 2♥ 4♦	1♥ 2♦ 2♥ 3♠	1♥ 2♦ 2♥ 4♣	1♠ 2♣ 2♦ 3♥	1♠ 2♣ 2♥ 4♦	1♠ 2♦ 2♥ 4♣	1♠ 2♦ 3♣ 4♥

25.	26.	27.	28.	29.
1♠ 2♥ 3♣ 4♦	1♥ 2♣ 2♦ 3♠	1♥ 2♣ 2♠ 4♦	1♥ 2♦ 2♠ 4♣	1♥ 2♦ 3♣ 4♠

Since two-over-one by responder is game forcing, opener doesn't need to jump shift to create a force. Therefore, jump shifts by opener are splinter bids. They show at least four-card support and a singleton or void in the splinter suit, and they promise sound opening values with some slam interest. You can splinter with a singleton ace or a void. You should try not to splinter without an honor in the unbid suit. Splinters above three notrump in support of a minor need significant extra values. It's very important for slam investigation to be able to show support and shortness at the same time. Auctions (1) through (10) are splinter auctions by opener.

Responder can splinter also. Auctions (11) through (29) are splinter auctions by responder for opener's last bid suit. They show sound values with a singleton or a void in the splinter suit, and promise three-card support in auctions (11) through (20), and four-card support, in opener's second suit, in auctions (21) through (29).

Opener	(1)	Responder		Opener	(2)	Responder	
♠AK432	♦KJ32	♠Q65	♦AQ654	♠AK432	♦KJ32	♠5	♦AQ654
♥KJ2	♣2	♥43	♣KQJ	♥KJ2	♣2	♥AQ43	♣543

Opener	Responder	Opener	Responder
1spade	2diamonds	1spade	2diamonds
4clubs	4spades	4clubs	4NT
Pass		5hearts	6diamonds

Opener	(3)	Responder		Opener	(4)	Responder	
♠AKQ32	♦2	♠65	♦A6543	♠AK432	♦2	♠5	♦KQJ3
♥Q432	♣AQ2	♥AK765	♣3	♥Q432	♣AQ2	♥KJ765	♣K43

Opener	Responder	Opener	Responder
1spade	2hearts	1spade	2hearts
4diamonds	4NT	4diamonds	4hearts
5spades	5NT	Pass	
7hearts	Pass		

Opener	(5)	Responder		Opener	(6)	Responder	
♠AK432	♦KJ32	♠65	♦AQ654	♠AK432	♦KJ32	♠65	♦AQ654
♥2	♣A32	♥KQJ	♣JT4	♥2	♣A32	♥JT3	♣KQJ

Opener	Responder	Opener	Responder
1spade	2diamonds	1spade	2diamonds
3hearts	3NT	3hearts	4clubs
Pass		4NT	5diamonds
		6diamonds	Pass

In examples (1) and (2), opener jumps to four clubs showing club shortness, four-card or longer diamond support and significant extra values. In example (1), responder with wasted club values signs-off in four spades. In example (2), responder, no longer worried about his three little clubs, bids RKC and signs-off in six diamonds. In examples (3) and (4), opener bids four diamonds showing four-card heart support with diamond shortness. In example (3), responder keycards and opener bids five spades showing two keycards and the heart queen. Responder bids five notrump promising all the keys, and opener bids seven hearts. In example (4), responder with the wasted KQJ of diamonds signs-off in four hearts. In examples (5) and (6), opener jumps to three hearts, showing four-card diamond support with heart shortness. In example (5), responder bids three notrump assuming opener has help in clubs. In example (6), with nothing wasted in hearts, responder bids four clubs. Opener bids RKC and bids six diamonds.

Opener	(7)		Responder		Opener	(8)		Responder	
♠AK5432	♦432	♠Q76	♦5		♠AK5432	♦432	♠Q76	♦AJ65	
♥KQ2	♣2	♥AJ43	♣AQ543		♥KQ2	♣2	♥3	♣AQ543	

Opener	Responder	Opener	Responder
1spade	2clubs	1spade	2clubs
2spades	4diamonds	2spades	4hearts
4NT	5spades	4spades	Pass
6spades	Pass		

Opener	(9)		Responder		Opener	(10)		Responder	
♠AK432	♦2	♠Q65	♦AK543		♠AK432	♦2	♠Q65	♦3	
♥AQ32	♣432	♥KJ54	♣5		♥AQ32	♣432	♥KJ54	♣AK765	

Opener	Responder	Opener	Responder
1spade	2diamonds	1spade	2clubs
2hearts	4clubs	2hearts	4diamonds
4NT	5hearts	4hearts	Pass
6hearts	Pass		

Opener	(11)		Responder		Opener	(12)		Responder	
♠A32	♦KJ32	♠4	♦AQ65		♠KQJ	♦J432	♠4	♦AQ65	
♥AQ432	♣2	♥K5	♣KQJT43		♥AQ432	♣2	♥K5	♣KQJT43	

Opener	Responder	Opener	Responder
1heart	2clubs	1heart	2clubs
2diamonds	3spades	2diamonds	3spades
4spades	4NT	3NT	Pass
5clubs	6diamonds		

In examples (7) and (8), over opener's two-spade rebid, responder's jump shows shortness and three-card spade support. In example (7), opener, with no wasted diamond honors, bids keycard and bids a slam. In example (8), opener with wasted heart honors signs-off in four spades. In examples (9) and (10), over opener's two-heart bid, responder's jump shows shortness and four-card heart support. SPLINTERS SHOW SUPPORT FOR THE LAST BID SUIT. If responder's spade holding is xxx, his worst possible holding, he should be content to just raise hearts. In example (9), opener, with no wasted club honors, bids keycard and bids a slam. In example (10), opener, with shortness in diamonds also, signs-off in four hearts. In examples (11) and (12), over opener's two-diamond bid, responder's jump shows shortness and four-card diamond support. In example (11), opener, with no wasted spade honors, invites slam. In example (12), opener, with wasted spade honors, bids three notrump.

106

5.16 -- ONE SPADE - TWO CLUBS - TWO HEARTS; TWO SPADES AND FOUR SPADES SHOW THREE SPADES. THREE SPADES SHOWS FOUR SPADES.

Opener	(1)	Responder		Opener	(2)	Responder
♠AK432 ♦Q2		♠Q65 ♦K43		♠AK432 ♦Q2		♠QJ65 ♦AKJ43
♥AKJ2 ♣32		♥Q43 ♣KQJ4		♥AKJ2 ♣32		♥43 ♣A4

Opener (1)	Responder		Opener (2)	Responder
1spade	2clubs		1spade	2diamonds
2hearts	4spades		2hearts	3spades
Pass			4diamonds	4NT
			5clubs	5NT
			6hearts	7spades/7NT

After one spade -- two clubs -- two-of-a-red-suit, one spade -- two diamonds -- two hearts or one heart -- two clubs -- two diamonds, responder has three ways to support opener's major. Responder can bid two, three or four-of-opener's-major. Jumps take up a lot of bidding room, so they show specific types of hands. Responder's jump to four-of-opener's-major shows exactly three of opener's major to one honor, no aces and no more than two kings. Opener's hand is unlimited, so responder's jump to four-of-opener's-major has to be weak and well defined. Responder's jump to three-of-opener's-major shows five or more of his first bid suit and four-card support for opener's major, with strength concentrated in the two suits. If responder has four-card support, but doesn't have a five-card suit with concentrated values, responder starts with Jacoby Two Notrump. Supporting opener at the two-level shows all other hands with three-card support. Over two-of-opener's-major, opener with a minimum hand rebids three-of-his-major since responder's hand is unlimited. Opener has to give responder a chance to make a slam try below game.

In example (1), responder bids two clubs and then jumps to four spades, showing a minimum two-over-one with three trumps to one honor and no aces. Opener, missing two aces, passes four spades. In example (2), responder bids two diamonds and then jumps to three spades, showing four spades and at least five diamonds. Opener bids four diamonds, showing diamond values or diamond length and denying club values. Responder, with a club control, bids RKC. Opener shows three keycards. Responder asks for specific kings and opener shows the king of hearts. At IMPs responder bids seven spades. At matchpoints responder can try seven notrump.

Opener	(3)		Responder		Opener	(4)		Responder	
♠KQ432	♦32		♠AJ5	♦654	♠KQ432	♦32		♠AJ5	♦KQ
	♥AKQ2	♣K2	♥43	♣AQJ43		♥AKQ2	♣K2	♥543	♣AQJ43

Opener (3)	Responder	Opener (4)	Responder
1spade	2clubs	1spade	2clubs
2hearts	2spades	2hearts	2spades
3clubs	3spades	3clubs	3diamonds
4hearts	4spades	4NT	5hearts
Pass		6spades	Pass

Opener	(5)		Responder		Opener	(6)		Responder	
♠KQ432	♦32		♠AJ5	♦654	♠KQ432	♦32		♠AJ5	♦KQ
	♥A432	♣K2	♥65	♣AQJ43		♥A432	♣K2	♥765	♣AQJ43

Opener (5)	Responder	Opener (6)	Responder
1spade	2clubs	1spade	2clubs
2hearts	2spades	2hearts	2spades
3spades	4spades	3spades	4clubs
		4hearts	4spades
		5clubs	6spades

In examples (3) through (6), responder shows game-forcing values with three-card spade support by bidding two-over-one followed by two spades. In example (3), opener cuebids twice. Kings as well as aces can be cuebid. With two little diamonds, opener passes four spades when responder fails to make a diamond cuebid. In example (4), opener shows club values and responder shows diamond values. Opener, no longer worried about his two little diamonds, bids RKC. When responder shows two keycards, opener bids six spades. At matchpoints, responder might bid six notrump. In examples (5) and (6), opener bids three spades showing a minimum opener. In example (5), responder has a minimum two-over-one and raises to four spades. In example (6), responder has extras and bids four clubs, showing club values and a slam try opposite a minimum opener. Opener has the best hand he can possibly have and not make a slam try over two spades. Opener cuebids the heart ace and then the club king. Responder bids a slam, counting ten tricks in the black suits and two tricks in the red suits.

Opener	(7)		Responder		Opener	(8)		Responder	
♠KQ432	♦432		♠J65	♦AK5	♠KQ432	♦432		♠AJ5	♦765
♥AKQ	♣K2		♥32	♣AQJ43		♥AKQ	♣K2	♥32	♣AQJ43

Opener	Responder	Opener	Responder
1spade	2clubs	1spade	2clubs
2spades	3spades	2spades	3spades
4clubs	4diamonds	4clubs	4spades
4NT	5hearts	Pass	
6spades			

Opener	(9)		Responder		Opener	(10)		Responder	
♠AKJ432	♦QJ2		♠Q98	♦K43	♠765432	♦AQJ		♠Q98	♦K43
	♥AKJ	♣2	♥Q32	♣KQJ3		♥AKQ	♣A	♥QJ2	♣KQJ3

Opener	Responder	Opener	Responder
1spade	2clubs	1spade	2clubs
2spades	4spades	2spades	4spades
Pass		Pass	

If opener rebids two spades, responder shows three or four-card support by raising to three spades or by splintering (see section 5.16, auctions (11) through (20), and examples (7) and (8)).

In examples (7) and (8), opener, with three little diamonds, decides to rebid two spades rather then jump to three notrump. Responder with three-card spade support raises to three spades. Opener with extra values cuebids four clubs. In example (7), responder cuebids four diamonds, showing diamond values. Opener, no longer worried about his three little diamonds, bids RKC, finds responder with two keycards and bids six spades. In example (8), when responder signs-off in four spades, denying control of either red suit, opener passes, knowing that he has at least two diamond losers.

As noted earlier, responder's jump to four-of-opener's-major over opener's two-of-a-major rebid shows exactly three of opener's major to one honor, no aces and no more than two kings. In examples (9) and (10), responder jumps to four spades showing an aceless hand with three spades to one honor. In example (9), opener knows that two aces are missing and passes four spades. In example (10), opener knows that the best trumps responder can have is KT9, which makes slam much lower than 50%.

5.17 -- JUMP SHIFT BY OPENER AFTER A FORCING NOTRUMP IS GAME FORCING.

One spade -- one notrump -- three-of-any-suit is 100% game forcing. Opener's jump shift is a commitment that opener will not pass a non-game bid. After the auction one spade -- one notrump -- three hearts, responder has six options. Option one is to raise three hearts to four hearts holding four or more hearts. Responder raises with three hearts only if responder wants to play a 4-3 heart fit. Option two is to jump to four spades holding three-card spade support with limit-raise values. With a bad hand with three spades, responder bids three spades and then bids four spades. Option three is to bid a natural four-of-minor with a seven-card or longer suit with shortness in spades.

Option four is to bid three notrump. When responder bids three notrump over opener's three-heart jump shift, responder denies three spades and usually does not have three hearts. Responder bids three notrump with three-card heart support only if he knows that three notrump will play better than a possible 5-3 heart fit. Over three notrump, if opener with 5-5 in the majors bids again, opener expects to be playing in at best a 5-2 fit. If opener is 6-5 or 6-6 and insists on playing in four-of-a-major, opener chooses the major. Option five is to bid four notrump keycard for hearts. If responder wants to keycard for spades, responder bids three spades and then bids four notrump.

Option six is to bid three spades. BIDDING THREE SPADES, EVEN WITH A SINGLETON SPADE, ALLOWS OPENER TO FINISH DESCRIBING HIS HAND. Option six is the default when responder doesn't have a clear bid. If responder has three hearts and wants to play in four hearts only if opener has five of them, responder bids three spades. Over three spades, opener with five hearts bids four hearts, opener with six spades bids four spades, opener with 5-4-4-0 shows his other four-card suit and opener with 5-4-2-2 or 5-4-3-1 bids three notrump.

Over one-of-a-major -- one notrump -- three-of-a-minor, responder has similar options. Unless responder has something clear to say, responder prefers opener's major, allowing opener to finish describing his hand. SINCE OPENER IS ALLOWED TO JUMP SHIFT INTO A THREE-CARD MINOR HOLDING A SOLID MAJOR, RESPONDER IS BARRED FROM JUMPING TO FIVE-OF-OPENER'S-MINOR. The jump shift is 100% game forcing, so four-of-opener's-minor is forcing and unlimited. If opener jump shifts to three-of-a-minor and then bids four-of-his-major, opener shows a self-sufficient major.

Opener	(1)		Responder		Opener	(2)		Responder
♠AKQ32	♦2	♠5	♦6543		♠AKQ432	♦2	♠5	♦6543
♥AKJ32	♣J2	♥Q54	♣KQ543		♥AKJ2	♣J2	♥Q54	♣KQ543

Opener (1)	Responder	Opener (2)	Responder
1spade	1NT	1spade	1NT
3hearts	3spades	3hearts	3spades
4hearts	Pass	4spades	Pass

Opener	(3)		Responder		Opener	(4)		Responder
♠AK432	♦32	♠5	♦JT54		♠AK432	♦-	♠5	♦JT54
♥AK32	♣AJ	♥Q54	♣KQ654		♥AK32	♣JT32	♥Q54	♣KQ654

Opener (3)	Responder	Opener (4)	Responder
1spade	1NT	1spade	1NT
3hearts	3spades	3hearts	3spades
3NT	Pass	4clubs	6clubs

Opener	(5)		Responder		Opener	(6)		Responder
♠AKQ5432	♦2	♠6	♦6543		♠AK432	♦2	♠6	♦6543
♥2	♣A432	♥Q43	♣KQ765		♥AK2	♣A432	♥Q43	♣KQ765

Opener (5)	Responder	Opener (6)	Responder
1spade	1NT	1spade	1NT
3clubs	4clubs	3clubs	4clubs
4spades	Pass	4hearts	6clubs

In examples (1) through (4), responder bids three spades as a waiting bid for lack of a clear-cut bid. In example (1), opener bids four hearts showing five hearts and the 5-3 heart fit is found. In example (2), opener, holding six spades, bids four spades. The 6-1 spade fit is as good as any. In example (3), opener with 5-4-2-2 bids three notrump. Three notrump will always make at least ten tricks. In example (4), opener bids four clubs showing five spades, four hearts and four clubs, and a good six-club contract is reached.

In examples (5) and (6), opener jumps to three clubs, game forcing, over responder's forcing notrump. Responder with good club support raises to four clubs. Since opener might want to play in four spades, responder is barred from jumping to five clubs. In example (5), opener bids four spades, showing a self-sufficient spade suit, and responder passes. Opener can very easily have only three clubs. In example (6), opener shows his heart fragment and responder jumps to six clubs. Opener should have at least three of the five keys to make a slam try by bidding four hearts.

5.18 -- THREE NOTRUMP JUMP IN FORCING AUCTIONS SHOWS 15-17 HCPS.

Opener	(1)		Responder		Opener	(2)		Responder	
♠KQJ32	♦32		♠A4	♦AQ54	♠KQJ32	♦32		♠A4	♦AQ54
♥AKJ2	♣K2		♥654	♣AQT3	♥AK32	♣K2		♥654	♣AQT3

Opener (1)	Responder	Opener (2)	Responder
1spade	2clubs	1spade	2clubs
2hearts	3NT	2hearts	3NT
6NT	Pass	4NT	6NT

Opener	(3)		Responder		Opener	(4)		Responder	
♠KQ432	♦J2		♠A5	♦Q43	♠KQ432	♦2		♠A5	♦Q43
♥AK32	♣32		♥654	♣AQJ65	♥AK32	♣432		♥654	♣AQJ65

Opener (3)	Responder	Opener (4)	Responder
1spade	2clubs	1spade	2clubs
2hearts	2NT	2hearts	2NT
3NT	Pass	3clubs	3spades
		4spades	

If two notrump is forcing, a jump to three notrump by opener or
responder shows the values of a strong notrump. Showing 15-17 HCPs
makes it easier for partner with 16 or 17 HCPs to bid a slam.

In examples (1) and (2), responder jumps to three notrump over
opener's two-heart rebid, showing 15-17 HCPs. In example (1), opener
with 17 HCPs bids six notrump. In example (2), opener with a good 16
HCPs invites. If responder bids only two notrump, in order to get to
six notrump either opener or responder has to bid four notrump
invitational and risk playing opposite a hand that will produce only
nine tricks. Just take away an ace from either hand and see how often
examples (1) and (2) will produce only nine tricks.

Responder has to be able to bid two notrump followed by three
notrump to show doubt about playing in notrump. If responder has only
a partial stopper in the unbid suit, for instance Qxx, responder can
hardly commit the hand to three notrump. Responder has to rebid two
notrump to allow opener to finish describing his hand. If opener
shows shortness in responder's Qxx suit, the hand belongs in a suit.

In examples (3) and (4), responder bids two clubs followed by two
notrump. In example (3), opener with 2-2 in the minors bids three
notrump, which is a reasonable contract. In example (4), opener bids
three clubs showing diamond shortness, and three notrump is avoided.

CHAPTER 6 - THIRD AND FOURTH SEAT MAJOR OPENERS

6.1 -- IN THIRD OR FOURTH SEAT, YOU MAY OPEN A STRONG FOUR-CARD MAJOR.

Holding a minimum opening bid, opener may open a strong four-card major in third or fourth seat. If opener is strong enough to possibly have a game, opener, playing a five-card major system, should open only five-card majors. Opening four-card majors in a five-card major system works if you are planning to take only one bid, which means you have to be able to pass any non-forcing bid partner makes. If opener opens a four-card major, responder is going to compete higher than the Law of Total Tricks allows. ♠Q32♥AKQ2♦J32♣432 is a hand which can be opened one heart in third or fourth seat. In third seat, 5-3-3-2 nine to twelve point hands with at least one defensive trick should be opened at the one-level rather than the two-level unless all the strength is in the five-card suit. You don't want to end up playing a 5-1 fit at the two-level when you're very likely to have a better fit. Having at least one defensive trick will save you in case partner makes a penalty double. If you open light in first or second seat, you don't have to open as light in third or fourth seat.

6.2 -- BY PASSED HAND, TWO CLUBS IS THREE-CARD REVERSE DRURY, TWO DIAMONDS IS FOUR-CARD REVERSE DRURY.

By a passed hand, two clubs by responder is three-card Drury, showing ten or more support points with three-card support for opener's major. Two diamonds by responder is four-card Drury, showing ten or more support points with at least four-card support. If opener doesn't think he can make game opposite a passed hand, opener rebids his major. If opener has enough to make game or wants to gamble on making game, opener jumps to four-of-his-major. Over two clubs, opener bids two diamonds as an artificial game or slam try. Over opener's two-diamond bid, if responder has a minimum Drury bid, responder signs-off in two-of-opener's-major. With 13 or 14 HCPs, opener can encourage and can still play at the two-level opposite a bad ten-point three-card raise.

After opening one spade, opener can bid two hearts, forcing for one round, showing at least four hearts. Four-four heart fits usually play better than 5-3 or even 5-4 spade fits. After Drury, a jump to three-of-opener's-major by opener or responder is game forcing and allows for possible slam cuebidding.

Opener	(1)	Responder		Opener	(2)	Responder	
♠KQ432	♦J32	♠J65	♦A54	♠KQT32	♦KJ32	♠J65	♦A54
♥AJ2	♣J2	♥6543	♣AQ3	♥A2	♣J2	♥6543	♣AQ3
-		Pass		-		Pass	
1spade		2clubs		1spade		2clubs	
2spades		Pass		4spades		Pass	

Opener	(3)	Responder		Opener	(4)	Responder	
♠Q5432	♦A32	♠KJ6	♦65	♠432	♦432	♠KJ6	♦65
♥A32	♣K2	♥8765	♣AQJ3	♥AK432	♣K2	♥8765	♣AQJ3
-		Pass		-		Pass	
1spade		2clubs		1heart		2diamonds	
2diamonds		3spades		2hearts		Pass	
4spades		Pass					

In examples (1), (2) and (3), responder, who is a passed hand, bids two clubs, showing exactly three spades and at least ten support points. In example (1), opener is not interested in game opposite a passed hand and rebids two spades. In example (2), opener has enough to make four spades a good gamble. In example (3), opener has enough to think about game and bids two diamonds. Responder, with sound values and good trumps, jumps to three spades, forcing, which allows opener to cuebid if he's interested in slam. Opener, only interested in game, signs-off in four spades. In example (4), responder shows at least four hearts and at least ten support points. Opener, with a minimum, signs-off in two hearts.

6.3 -- TWO HEARTS, THREE CLUBS AND THREE DIAMONDS BY PASSED HAND ARE NATURAL, CONSTRUCTIVE, BUT NON-FORCING.

Since two clubs and two diamonds by passed hand are conventional major-suit raises, responder's jump to three-of-a-minor is natural and shows approximately eight to eleven HCPs with at least a six-card suit. A two-heart response to one spade is non-forcing and shows eight to eleven HCPs with at least five hearts. If responder has six hearts, there is some reason why he didn't open two hearts. Responder can't have support for opener's major.

New suits by opener are forcing. If opener rebids his major, that is invitational but non-forcing.

114

6.4 -- ONE NOTRUMP IS SEMI-FORCING BY PASSED HAND AND CAN HAVE UP TO 12 HCPS.

Opener	(1)	Responder		Opener	(2)	Responder
♠KQ432 ♦432		♠J5 ♦A765		♠KQ432 ♦432		♠J5 ♦A765
♥AQ2 ♣J2		♥6543 ♣AQ3		♥AQ2 ♣K2		♥6543 ♣AQ3
-		Pass		-		Pass
1spade		1NT		1spade		1NT
Pass				2diamonds		2NT
				3NT		Pass

One notrump response to one-of-a-major by passed-hand is semi-forcing, denies three of opener's major and shows six or more HCPs. Since one notrump can be passed, responder has to raise with all hands containing three-card support. The upper limit of one notrump varies on how light responder opens. Opener with a light or minimum balanced hand can pass one notrump. With 14 or more HCPs, opener treats one notrump as forcing and can bid a three-card minor. I think it's right for responder to bid one notrump with all balanced passed hands, even with 12 HCPs. Once in a while, responder will play one notrump with his 11 or 12 opposite opener's 13 and game makes. More often, responder will be in one notrump +90 or the opponents will balance and go for a number.

In examples (1) and (2), responder, who is a passed hand, bids one notrump with his 11 HCPs. In example (1), opener with a minimum opener passes one notrump. Responder hopes an opponent balances. What contract would you like to be playing with 12 balanced HCPs opposite 11 balanced HCPs? I would like to be playing one notrump. In example (2), opener, who has extras, treats the one notrump as forcing and bids his three-card diamond suit. Responder rebids two notrump showing 11 HCPs and opener raises to three notrump.

6.5 -- TWO NOTRUMP BY PASSED HAND IS FOUR-CARD UNBALANCED LIMIT RAISE.

Responder's jump to two notrump shows a good passed hand, at least four-card support for opener, with an outside singleton. Opener rebids three-of-his major with ten or fewer points denying interest in game. With an opening bid without slam interest, opener jumps to game. If opener wants to make a game try or a slam try and needs to know where responder's singleton is, opener bids three clubs asking responder to bid his shortness.

1.	2.	3.	4.	5.	6.
1♠ 2NT	1♥ 2NT	1♠ 2NT	1♥ 2NT	1♠ 2NT	1♥ 2NT
3♣ 3♦	3♣ 3♦	3♣ 3♥	3♣ 3♠	3♣ 3♠	3♣ 3♥

Above are examples of the six possible passed-hand singleton sequences where responder bids two notrump and opener bids three clubs asking for responder's singleton. Auctions (1) and (2) show a singleton diamond, where ♠KQ76♥KQ32♦2♣6543 is an example of responder's hand. Auction (3) shows a singleton heart, where ♠AJ432♥2♦432♣KQ43 is an example of responder's hand. Auction (4) shows a singleton spade, where ♠2♥AJ432♦432♣KQ43 is an example of responder's hand. Auctions (5) and (6) show a singleton club, where ♠QJ32♥AK32♦5432♣2 is an example of responder's hand.

If opener bids three clubs and then bids three-of-his-major, that's a sign-off. Opener has wasted values opposite responder's singleton. However, if the opening bid is one heart, responder answers three spades to show spade shortness. Therefore, after a one-heart opener, opener can bid three clubs only if he is willing to be in game opposite spade shortness.

Opener	(1)		Responder		Opener	(2)		Responder	
♠KQ432	♦432		♠A765	♦A765	♠KQ432	♦KQJ		♠A765	♦A765
♥A32	♣J2		♥4	♣Q543	♥A32	♣K2		♥4	♣Q543
-			Pass		-			Pass	
1spade			2NT		1spade			2NT	
3spades			Pass		3clubs			3hearts	
					4NT			5hearts	
					6spades			Pass	

In examples (1) and (2), responder bids two notrump showing at least four spades with a maximum passed hand and unspecified shortness. In example (1), opener bids three spades showing ten or fewer HCPs. Responder passes. In example (2), opener, interested in slam, bids three clubs asking. Responder answers three hearts showing heart shortness. Opener bids keycard and bids six spades.

116

6.6 -- ONE HEART - THREE SPADES, ONE SPADE - THREE NOTRUMP BY PASSED HAND SHOWS A FOUR-CARD RAISE WITH A VOID (NEXT BID ASKS).

```
    1.          2.          3.          4.          5.          6.
┌─────────┐ ┌─────────┐ ┌─────────┐ ┌─────────┐ ┌─────────┐ ┌─────────┐
│1♥   3♠  │ │1♠   3NT │ │1♥   3♠  │ │1♠   3NT │ │1♥   3♠  │ │1♠   3NT │
│3NT  4♦  │ │4♣   4♦  │ │3NT  4♥  │ │4♣   4♥  │ │3NT  4♣  │ │4♣   4♠  │
└─────────┘ └─────────┘ └─────────┘ └─────────┘ └─────────┘ └─────────┘
```

♠KJ76♥K5432♦-♣6543   ♠-♥AJ432♦5432♣K543   ♠QJ32♥AJ432♦5432♣-

One heart -- three spades and one spade -- three notrump by a passed hand show at least four-card trump support with an unspecified void. Opener, if interested, asks with the next step. Above are examples of the six possible void sequences. Auctions (1) and (2) show a void in diamonds. Auctions (3) and (4) show a void in the other major. Auctions (5) and (6) show a void in clubs. The hands are examples of responder's passed-hand three-notrump response to a one-heart opener.

Opener	(1)	Responder		Opener	(2)	Responder	
♠KQ432	♦J432	♠AJ876	♦-	♠5432	♦AKJ	♠-	♦Q543
♥AQ2	♣2	♥K876	♣6543	♥A5432	♣2	♥K9876	♣A543

Opener (1)	Responder	Opener (2)	Responder
-	Pass	-	Pass
1spade	3NT	1heart	3spades
4clubs	4diamonds	3NT	4hearts
4hearts	5hearts	4NT	5spades
6spades	Pass	6diamonds	7hearts

In examples (1) and (2), responder shows an unspecified void. In example (1), opener asks with four clubs. Responder makes opener happy by answering four diamonds, showing a void in diamonds. Opener needs extras and bids four hearts, the Last Train. Responder, with a fifth trump, shows his heart values and opener bids a slam. In example (2), opener is not strong enough to open Flannery in third seat. Over three spades, opener bids three notrump asking. Opener's hand improves when responder bids four hearts showing a spade void. Opener keycards. Responder answers five spades showing two keycards with the queen or extra length. Responder knows that he has at least a ten-card heart fit. Opener bids six diamonds, asking responder to bid seven hearts if responder has third-round diamond control. Responder holds the queen of diamonds and bids seven hearts.

CHAPTER 7 - RESPONSE TO MAJOR OPENERS IN COMPETITION

7.1 -- AFTER AN OVERCALL, TWO NOTRUMP SHOWS A GAME-FORCING FOUR-CARD RAISE. CUEBID IS ANY LIMIT RAISE OR FORCING THREE-CARD RAISE.

Opener	(1)	Responder		Opener	(2)	Responder	
♠32	♦AQJ4	♠AQJ	♦32	♠32	♦AQJ4	♠AQJ	♦32
♥AKJ65	♣Q3	♥Q432	♣KJT2	♥K8765	♣Q3	♥Q432	♣KJT2

Open	Over	Resp	Advnc	Open	Over	Resp	Advnc
1♥	1♠	2NT	Pass	1♥	1♠	2NT	3♠
3♥	Pass	3♠	Pass	4♥	Pass	Pass	Pass
4♦	Pass	4NT	Pass				
5♣	Pass	6♥	Pass				

After one heart -- one spade, one-of-a-major -- two-of-a-minor, one spade -- two hearts or a Michaels major-suit cuebid, responder's two notrump is Jacoby, showing at least four-card support for opener's major with game-forcing values. One heart -- two spades is an exception and is explained in examples (7) and (8) below. Opener responds to Jacoby after an overcall by ignoring the overcall (see section 5.10). Opener jumps to game with a balanced minimum, bids a short suit at the three-level, etc. If advancer bids, opener still follows section 5.10. Opener jumps to game with a balanced minimum, passes with extras without a control and bids with extras with a control in the opponent's suit.

In examples (1) and (2), after overcaller bids one spade, responder jumps to two notrump, Jacoby, showing a game-forcing four-card heart raise. In example (1), opener rebids three hearts, showing a balanced hand with at least 16 HCPs. Responder, knowing that his AQJ of spades are very likely worth three tricks, cuebids his ace of spades. Opener cuebids his ace of diamonds. Responder can count 12 tricks if opener has the ace-king of hearts, the ace of diamonds and one more honor -- five heart tricks, three spade tricks and either two diamond tricks, a diamond ruff and one club trick, or three club tricks and one diamond trick. Responder bids keycard, finds one keycard is missing and bids six hearts. In example (2), opener bids four hearts showing a minimum opener without shortness.

Opener	(3)	Responder		Opener	(4)	Responder	
♠AJ2	♦432	♠543	♦AQJ5	♠AQ2	♦432	♠543	♦AQJ5
♥AK432	♣32	♥Q65	♣KJT	♥AK432	♣32	♥Q65	♣Q54

Open	Over	Resp	Advnc	Open	Over	Resp	Advnc
1♥	1♠	2♠	Pass	1♥	2♣	3♣	Pass
3♥	Pass	4♥	All Pass	3♦	Pass	3♥	All Pass

Opener	(5)	Responder		Opener	(6)	Responder	
♠AK432	♦AQ2	♠QJ65	♦6543	♠AK432	♦AQ2	♠QJ5	♦KJ543
♥432	♣32	♥AK5	♣54	♥432	♣32	♥AK5	♣A4

Open	Over	Resp	Advnc	Open	Over	Resp	Advnc
1♠	2♣	3♣	Pass	1♠	2♣	3♣	Pass
3♦	Pass	3♠	Pass	3♦	Pass	4NT	Pass
Pass	Pass			5♣	Pass	6♦	Pass
				7♦	Pass	7NT	Pass

If responder's two notrump is Jacoby showing a forcing raise, then responder's cuebid shows either a limit raise with three or four-card support, or a three-card forcing raise. RESPONDER WITH AT LEAST THREE-CARD SUPPORT SETS TRUMPS IMMEDIATELY SO THAT LEVEL BECOMES THE ONLY CONSIDERATION. Over responder's cuebid, opener signs-off with no interest in game opposite a limit raise, bids an in-between suit as a game try opposite a possible limit raise and cuebids with slam interest. Opener jumps to game with enough to accept a limit raise.

In example (3), responder with a three-card game-forcing heart raise cuebids two spades. Opener, facing a possible limit raise, signs-off in three hearts. Responder, with an opening bid, raises to game. In example (4), responder has a weak three-card limit raise. Opener makes an artificial game try and responder signs-off in three hearts. Three diamonds is artificial since it's the only call between three clubs and three hearts. In example (5), responder, with a four-card limit raise, cuebids three clubs. Opener with a sound minimum makes a game try with three diamonds. Opener may choose either red suit as a natural game try. Responder, with a minimum limit-raise, signs-off in three spades. In example (6), responder has a three-card forcing spade raise and SETS SPADES AS TRUMPS BY CUEBIDDING. Opener bids three diamonds, a game or slam try. Responder bids keycard and opener shows three keycards. Responder jumps to six diamonds asking opener to bid seven with third-round diamond control. Opener with the queen bids seven diamonds and responder bids seven notrump.

Once responder bids four notrump keycard for spades, spades or notrump are the only possible strains. Over five clubs, five diamonds asks for the queen and five notrump asks for specific kings. Therefore, all other non-spade bids ask for third-round control.

Opener	(7)		Responder	Opener	(8)		Responder
♠AQ2	♦432	♠543	♦AQJ5	♠AQ2	♦432	♠543	♦AQJ5
♥AK432	♣32	♥Q65	♣KJT	♥AK432	♣32	♥Q65	♣Q54

Open	Over	Resp	Advnc	Open	Over	Resp	Advnc
1♥	2♠	3♠	Pass	1♥	2♠	2NT	Pass
4♥	Pass	Pass	Pass	3♥	Pass	Pass	Pass

Opener	(9)		Responder	Opener	(10)		Responder
♠AK432	♦AKQ	♠QJ65	♦2	♠AK432	♦AKQ	♠65	♦432
♥432	♣32	♥AKQ65	♣654	♥432	♣32	♥AKJT765	♣4

Open	Over	Resp	Advnc	Open	Over	Resp	Advnc
1♠	2♣	4♦	Pass	1♠	2♣	4♥	Pass
4♠	Pass	Pass	Pass	5♥	Pass	6♥	Pass

After one heart -- two spades, a three-spade cuebid is higher than three hearts and therefore can't show a limit raise. Three spades therefore shows a forcing heart raise and two notrump shows a limit raise. In examples (7) and (8), overcaller bids two spades. In example (7), responder bids three spades showing a forcing heart raise. In example (8), responder bids two notrump showing a limit raise in hearts. Opener with his queen of spades very likely to be worthless, signs-off in three hearts.

Responder has other ways to show support for opener's major. Responder's jump to four-of-a-minor or responder's jump in overcaller's suit are splinter bids and show shortness with four-card game-forcing values. However, in competition, all jumps to game are natural and are not splinter bids.

In example (9), responder jumps to four diamonds, showing four-card spade support and diamond shortness, with game-forcing values. Opener with diamond wastage and no club control signs-off in four spades. In example (10), responder jumps to four hearts showing a long heart suit with no aces or kings on the outside. Opener bids five hearts, asking responder to bid six hearts with first or second-round club control. Responder bids six hearts.

7.2 -- ONE SPADE - TWO DIAMONDS - TWO SPADES - THREE DIAMONDS - THREE HEARTS IS AN ARTIFICIAL GAME TRY.

Opener	(1)	Responder		Opener	(2)	Responder	
♠AK5432	♦32	♠QJ6	♦A54	♠AK5432	♦32	♠QJ6	♦A54
♥32	♣AK2	♥87654	♣Q4	♥32	♣K32	♥87654	♣Q4

Open	Over	Resp	Advnc	Open	Over	Resp	Advnc
1♠	2♦	2♠	3♦	1♠	2♦	2♠	3♦
3♥	Pass	4♥	Pass	3♠	Pass	Pass	Pass
4♠	Pass	Pass	Pass				

According to the Law of Total Tricks, with a nine-card fit, it's very important to be able to compete at the three-level without the risk of ending up at the four-level. After one spade -- two diamonds -- two spades -- three diamonds, opener has to be able to bid three spades and play in only three spades every time opener holds six spades or, sometimes, when short in diamonds. Since three spades by opener is not a game try, three hearts, an artificial bid, is opener's only game try. If there is no room to make a game try, opener has to make the final decision. Competing is more important then being able to make a game try. The more room there is between opponent's suit and opener's suit, the more natural opener's game try is.

If opener has extra values with length in the opponent's suit, length being at least three, opener can make a cooperative double. Responder with three-card support for opener's major passes opener's cooperative double with at least two cards in the opponent's suit. If responder has four-card support for opener's major or a singleton or void in the opponent's suit, responder signs-off with a minimum and jumps to game with a maximum.

In example (1), opener with a 6-2-2-3 14-count, wants to make a game try over advancer's three diamonds. Opener bids three hearts, an artificial game try, and responder with a maximum raise, bids four hearts just in case opener has hearts. Opener corrects to four spades. If responder has a minimum hand with five hearts, responder must sign-off in three spades. In example (2), opener with six spades wants to play in three spades without the risk of getting to game. OPENER BIDS THREE SPADES, WHICH SAYS, I DON'T CARE HOW GOOD YOUR TWO-SPADE RAISE IS, I WANT TO PLAY IN THREE SPADES. RESPONDER IS BARRED FROM BIDDING FOUR SPADES. The more responder has, the better chance opener has to make three spades. Responder, even with a maximum raise, trusts opener and passes three spades.

7.3 -- REBIDS AFTER AN OPPONENT BALANCES.

Opener	(1)	Responder		Opener	(2)	Responder	
♠AQ432	♦32	♠K765	♦654	♠AQ432	♦32	♠765	♦QJT654
♥32	♣AQJ2	♥7654	♣K3	♥32	♣AQJ2	♥54	♣K3

Open	Over	Resp	Advnc	Open	Over	Resp	Advnc
1♠	Pass	2♠	Pass	1♠	Pass	2♠	Pass
Pass	Dbl	3♠	Pass	Pass	Dbl	3♦	Pass
Pass	Pass			Pass	Pass		

Once it goes one-of-a-major -- pass -- two-of-a-major -- pass -- pass, and an opponent balances, neither opener or responder can make a game try. Any new suit by responder is a six-card or longer suit and a suggestion of a possible better trump fit. Any new suit by opener is a four-card or longer suit and a suggestion of a possible better trump fit. Four-four fits play better than 5-3 fits. All doubles and redoubles are penalty orientated. If an opponent bids a suit at the three-level and you have four of them, a penalty double will usually be well rewarded. In passout seat, after partner has had a chance to bid three-of-the-major with shortness in opponent's suit or with an extra trump, a penalty double of a three-level bid with three cards in the opponent's suit and a maximum will usually be well rewarded.

IF RESPONDER HAS FOUR-CARD SUPPORT, RESPONDER BIDS THREE-OF-OPENER'S-MAJOR WITHOUT THINKING, AND OPENER PASSES WITHOUT THINKING. IF OPENER HAS A SIX-CARD MAJOR, OPENER BIDS THREE-OF-HIS-MAJOR WITHOUT THINKING, AND RESPONDER PASSES WITHOUT THINKING. TRUMPS NOT HCPS IS THE ONLY CONCERN.

In examples (1) and (2), overcaller, knowing the opponents are in at least an eight-card spade fit, balances with a takeout double. In example (1), responder with four-card spade support bids three spades and opener passes. Responder looks at his four-card spade support, not at his six-only HCPs. In example (2), responder bids his six-card diamond suit and opener passes. Since three spades has no play, three diamonds is responder's best chance for a plus score.

7.4 -- PREEMPTIVE JUMP RAISES (ONE SPADE - TWO CLUBS - THREE SPADES).

Opener	(1)	Responder		Opener	(2)	Responder	
♠AK765	♦65	♠QJ32	♦432	♠AK7654	♦5	♠QJ32	♦432
♥76	♣AK32	♥5432	♣QJ	♥76	♣A432	♥5432	♣QJ

Open	Over	Resp	Advnc	Open	Over	Resp	Advnc
1♠	2♦	3♠	Pass	1♠	2♦	3♠	4♦
Pass	Pass			4♠	Pass	Pass	Pass

Opener	(3)	Responder		Opener	(4)	Responder	
♠AK987	♦KJ5	♠65432	♦432	♠AK987	♦KJ5	♠65432	♦32
♥5	♣T432	♥432	♣QJ	♥5	♣T432	♥QJ32	♣QJ

Open	Over	Resp	Advnc	Open	Over	Resp	Advnc
1♠	2♦	3♠	Pass	1♠	2♦	3♠	Pass
Pass	Pass			Pass	Pass		

Responder's jump to three-of-opener's-major after an overcall is preemptive, shows four-card support with the lower end of values for a single raise. With five-card support, responder usually jumps to the four-level, but there are some 5-3-3-2 hands that are so bad that a jump to the three-level is high enough. Especially vulnerable, responder might have five-card support for his three-level jump. With a sound four-card raise, where responder will accept a game try, responder raises to the two-level.

In examples (1) and (2), responder has a preemptive jump to three spades. In example (1), opener, not expecting much, passes three spades. In example (2), opener with a sixth spade, bids four spades over advancer's four diamonds. The Law says four spades should be a good result over four diamonds. In examples (3) and (4), responder with five spades still bids only three spades. In example (3), responder is very weak and is 5-3-3-2. The chances are very likely that four spades will get doubled and go down at least two tricks, which will usually be a bad result. In example (4), responder has queens and jacks which will very likely take tricks on defense and not on offense. The opponents will be very unlikely to be able to take ten tricks.

7.5 -- NEW SUITS AT THE FOUR-LEVEL IN COMPETITION ARE NOT SLAM TRIES.

Opener	(1)		Responder		Opener	(2)		Responder	
♠2	♦AK432		♠543	♦QJ65	♠2	♦AK432		♠543	♦65
♥AK432	♣32		♥QJ65	♣54	♥AK432	♣32		♥QJ65	♣QJ54

Open	Over	Resp	Advnc	Open	Over	Resp	Advnc
1♥	1♠	3♥	3♠	1♥	1♠	3♥	3♠
4♦	4♠	5♥	Pass	4♦	4♠	Dbl	Pass

In competitive auctions such as, one heart -- one spade -- two hearts -- three spades, opener sometimes would like help in deciding what to do if the opponents bid over four-of-opener's-major. Opener, therefore, bids a new suit at the four-level over advancer's bid, setting up a forcing situation, showing a five-card or longer suit and inviting responder's input if an opponent bids over four-of-opener's-major. Bidding a new suit is not a slam try, it just sets up a force and shows values in that suit. Once opener bids a new suit showing extra distribution, it doesn't make sense to let the opponents play undoubled. Since opener expects to take at least nine tricks, opener should be able to either set the opponents or take a cheap save. If opener bids four-of-his-major directly, opener doesn't set up a force, and the opponents can play undoubled. Responder doubles the opponents only if he has defense.

In examples (1) and (2), responder jumps to three hearts, showing a bad hand with at least four hearts. Opener bids four diamonds showing a diamond suit, inviting responder's input if the opponents bid over four hearts. Bidding four diamonds sets up a force. In example (1), after overcaller bids four spades, responder, holding four diamonds, carries on with five hearts. In example (2), responder with only two diamonds and possible defensive tricks in clubs, doubles four spades. If responder doesn't know what to do, he can pass the decision to opener. In passout seat responder must do something.

CHAPTER 8 - MINOR SUIT OPENERS

8.1 -- OPEN ONE CLUB WITH 3-3 IN MINORS.   OPEN EITHER MINOR WITH 4-4 IN MINORS.

Opener	(1)	Responder		Opener	(2)	Responder	
♠AKQ	♦Q432	♠432	♦5	♠AKQ	♦Q432	♠432	♦5
♥32	♣Q432	♥Q54	♣KJ8765	♥32	♣Q432	♥Q54	♣KJ8765
1diamond		1NT		1club		3clubs	

With 3-3 in the minors, opener always opens one club. By always opening one club with 3-3, opener makes his one-diamond opener show four except when exactly 4-4-3-2.   I open one club even with ♠A432♥432♦AKQ♣432.

With 4-4 in the minors, opener opens either minor. Opener opens one club if he can rebid one notrump or can rebid one spade. With strong clubs and weak diamonds, I open one club. Opening one club makes it easier to get to either minor. Since you like to have at least five diamonds and at least four clubs to open one diamond and rebid two clubs, opening one diamond planning on rebidding two clubs with 4-4 in the minors is bad bidding. Only with strong diamonds and weak clubs do I open one diamond.

With 5-4 in the minors, opener always opens his five-card minor. Opener might have to rebid one notrump with a singleton, might have to raise responder with three-card support or might have to rebid his five-card minor. If opener ends up playing in a minor, opener will always end up in his best fit.

In examples (1) and (2), opener plans on opening one-of-a-minor and rebidding one notrump over responder's probable one-of-a-major response. In example (1), opener opens one diamond and responder is forced to bid one notrump. One notrump will usually go down at least three tricks. In example (2), opener opens one club and responder raises clubs. Three clubs should make.

8.2 -- ONE CLUB - ONE NOTRUMP = 8-10 HCPS.

If responder does not have a four-card major, responder has to choose between responding one diamond or one notrump. If responder has a choice, with 8-10 HCPs responder responds one notrump. With 6-7 HCPs, responder responds one diamond.

8.3 -- INVERTED MINOR RAISES 10+ HCPs (OFF IN COMPETITION AND BY PASSED HAND).

1.	2.	3.	4.	5.	6.
1♣ 2♣ 2NT	1♣ 2♣ 2♦	1♣ 2♣ 2maj	1♣ 2♣ 3♣	1♣ 2♣ 3any	1♣ 2♣ 3NT
1♦ 2♦ 2NT	1♦ 2♦ 3♣	1♦ 2♦ 2maj	1♦ 2♦ 3♦	1♦ 2♦ 3maj	1♦ 2♦ 3NT
11-13 Bal N.F.	13-14 Bal or 14+ unbal	14+ Unbal Natural	11-13 Unbal N.F.	14+ Unbal Splinter	18-19 Bal

By an unpassed hand, one club -- two clubs or one diamond -- two diamonds, Inverted Minors, shows at least four-card support, usually five, with at least ten HCPs, and no four-card major. With a balanced hand and exactly ten HCPs and only four-card support, responder bids one notrump. Responder's hand is unlimited and denies a four-card major. A passed hand minor raise shows 6-11 HCPs.

Opener rebids three notrump to show a balanced 18-19 HCPs (auction 6). With 11-14 balanced, opener splits the weak notrump range by bidding two notrump (auction 1), non-forcing, with the lower end (11 to a bad 13) and bidding the other minor (auction 2), forcing to three notrump or four-of-the-minor, and possibly artificial, with the higher end (a good 13 or 14). Stoppers are unimportant. Opener doesn't worry about stoppers after one notrump -- three notrump, so why worry when the auction goes one diamond -- two diamonds -- two notrump -- three notrump. Even if there is an unstopped suit, the opening leader has to find it and it could be in his partner's hand.

Since the other minor (auction 2) is a two-way bid, either a balanced 13-14 HCPs or a second suit, opener must bid notrump at his next opportunity with the balanced hand type. With an unbalanced hand and extra values, opener bids a four-card suit (auction 3) which is forcing to three notrump or four-of-a-minor. Except for the balanced 13-14 HCPs discussed above, unless opener is exactly 4-4-4-1 or 4-4-3-2 with concentrated strength in the two four-card suits, opener has at least five of his minor if he bids a new suit. With an unbalanced hand and a minimum, opener rebids three-of-his-minor (auction 4). All jumps into new suits after the raise are splinter bids (auction 5).

126

Opener (1)	Responder	Opener (2)	Responder
♠432 ♦432	♠765 ♦AKQ	♠AK2 ♦432	♠765 ♦AKQ
♥AJ2 ♣AK32	♥K3 ♣QJ654	♥AJ2 ♣AK32	♥K3 ♣QJ654
1club	2clubs	1club	2clubs
2NT	3NT	3NT	6NT

Opener (3)	Responder	Opener (4)	Responder
♠A432 ♦32	♠65 ♦AK54	♠AK32 ♦32	♠65 ♦AK54
♥32 ♣AQJ32	♥54 ♣K7654	♥32 ♣AQJ32	♥A4 ♣K7654
1club	2clubs	1club	2clubs
3clubs	Pass	2spades	3diamonds
		3spades	4NT
		5spades	5NT
		6clubs	Pass

In examples (1) through (4), responder raises to two clubs, showing at least ten points and at least four clubs. In example (1), opener with a balanced minimum bids two notrump, non-forcing, showing 11-13 HCPs. Responder raises to three notrump. Responder, with the same hand minus the diamond ace, raises to two clubs, but retreats to three clubs. Even though the spade suit is unstopped, the opponent's are unlikely to be able to cash five spade tricks. In example (2), opener jumps to three notrump showing a balanced hand stronger than an opening notrump. Responder with 15 HCPs and a five-card suit raises to six notrump. In example (3), opener with an unbalanced minimum rebids three clubs. Opener is not strong enough to bid two spades. Responder, with a minimum raise, passes three clubs. In example (4), opener bids two spades, showing a sound opener with four spades and five or more clubs. Responder bids three diamonds showing diamond values. Opener rebids three spades, denying heart values. Responder, knowing that opener has four good spades and five good clubs, bids RKC. Opener shows two keycards and the queen of clubs. Responder, with all six keys accounted for, bids five notrump telling opener that he can bid seven clubs if opener can count 13 tricks. Opposite an unlimited partner, five notrump does not ask for specific kings. The only time opener bids above six clubs is if opener thinks he can make seven clubs. Opener, with a minimum two-spade response, signs-off in six clubs. If opener holds ♠AKQJ♥2♦32♣AQ5432, he bids seven clubs over five notrump.

Opener	(5)	Responder		Opener	(6)	Responder	
♠A2	♦AK2	♠K3	♦J43	♠A	♦AKQ2	♠K3	♦J43
♥432	♣QJ432	♥A65	♣AK876	♥32	♣QJ5432	♥A65	♣AK876

Opener	Responder		Opener	Responder
1club	2clubs		1club	2clubs
2diamonds	3NT		2diamonds	3NT
Pass			4diamonds	4hearts
			4NT	5clubs
			5NT	6spades
			7clubs	Pass

Opener	(7)	Responder		Opener	(8)	Responder	
♠A2	♦AK2	♠54	♦Q43	♠32	♦K2	♠54	♦Q43
♥432	♣QJ432	♥Q65	♣AK765	♥AKJ2	♣QJ432	♥Q65	♣AK765

Opener	Responder		Opener	Responder
1club	2clubs		1club	2clubs
2diamonds	3clubs		2hearts	3clubs
3NT	Pass		3diamonds	3hearts
			4hearts	Pass

In example (5), opener bids two diamonds, showing a maximum weak notrump or a club-diamond hand. Two diamonds is forcing to three notrump or four-of-a-minor. Responder jumps to three notrump. In all auctions where two notrump is forcing, and after two diamonds two notrump is forcing, responder's jump to three notrump shows the values of a strong notrump. In example (6), opener bids two diamonds, intending to show an unbalanced hand with clubs and diamonds. Opener shouldn't splinter with two small hearts. Over responder's three-notrump bid showing a strong notrump, opener bids four diamonds, showing an unbalanced hand. After responder cuebids four hearts, opener bids four notrump, RKC. Responder shows three keycards. Opener asks for kings (responder's hand is limited) and responder shows the spade king. Opener bids seven clubs. In example (7), opener bids two diamonds, intending to show a game-forcing weak notrump. Responder marks time with three clubs, and opener bids three notrump showing a maximum weak notrump. In example (8), opener bids two hearts, usually showing at least five clubs, exactly four hearts and a sound opener. Only if opener is 4-4-4-1 or 4-4-3-2 with concentrated values can opener have only four clubs. Responder bids three clubs, showing a minimum. Opener bids three diamonds showing diamond values. Responder shows heart values. Opener tries four hearts and responder passes. With two small spades opposite two small spades, three notrump is avoided.

8.4 -- JUMP RAISES ARE PREEMPTIVE.

All jump raises of minor suits to the three-level and the four-level are preemptive in competition as well as not in competition, and by passed hand. Responder tries to have five-card support for a three-level jump and six-card support for a four-level jump, but there are situations where responder has to jump to the three-level with only four-card support. With a singleton in a major, for example, responder, knowing that the opponents have at least an eight-card fit, jumps to the three-level with four-card support. With 8-10 HCPs, responder bids one notrump.

8.5 -- DOUBLE JUMP SHIFTS ARE SPLINTERS.

Opener	(1)	Responder		Opener	(2)	Responder	
♠KQJ	♦432	♠2	♦A765	♠KQJ	♦432	♠A32	♦AQJ5
♥432	♣KQJ2	♥AK5	♣A6543	♥432	♣KQJ2	♥5	♣A6543

Opener	Responder		Opener	Responder
1club	3spades		1club	3hearts
3NT	Pass		3spades	4diamonds
			5clubs	Pass

Double jump shifts, one club -- three spades, for instance, are splinters showing five-card support, usually, shortness in the bid suit, and values in unbid suits, with some slam interest. Responder denies a four-card major. If opener is not interested in slam, opener bids three notrump with at least one stopper in the splinter suit, and bids no higher than four of his minor without a stopper. With slam interest and more than a minimum, opener cuebids higher than four of his minor.

If the splinter gets doubled, opener bids three notrump with two stoppers and no slam interest, passes with one stopper and no slam interest and redoubles with the ace with some slam interest.

In example (1), responder bids three spades showing spade shortness, club support and a mild slam try. Opener with two spade stoppers bids three notrump. Opener does not worry about stoppers in unbid suits since responder promises values in all of the unbid suits. In example (2), responder shows heart shortness. Opener with no wasted heart honors bids three spades showing some slam interest. Responder bids four diamonds. Opener, with a minimum weak notrump, limits his hand by not cuebidding above four clubs.

129

8.6 -- TWO NOTRUMP RESPONSE = 12-15. THREE NOTRUMP RESPONSE = 15+-17. TWO NOTRUMP FOLLOWED BY FOUR NOTRUMP = 18-19.

Opener	(1)	Responder		Opener	(2)	Responder	
♠2	♦AK32	♠A43	♦QJ4	♠KQJ2	♦K32	♠A43	♦AQ4
♥Q32	♣KQJ32	♥AK4	♣7654	♥2	♣KQJ32	♥A54	♣7654

Opener (1)	Responder	Opener (2)	Responder
1club	2NT	1club	2NT
3diamonds	3hearts	3spades	4clubs
4diamonds	4spades	4diamonds	4NT
6clubs	Pass	5diamonds	6clubs

One-of-a-minor -- two notrump shows 12 to a bad 15 HCPs, a balanced hand without a four-card major, stoppers in unbid suits, and is game-forcing. Getting to three notrump with 12 or even 11 HCPs opposite 12 HCPs is not the end of the world. Sometimes three notrump is cold and sometimes the opponents misdefend. One-of-a-minor -- three notrump shows a good 15 to 17 HCPs. Playing two notrump forcing allows exploration of other strains.

In examples (1) and (2), responder jumps to two notrump showing a balanced hand with 12-15 HCPs. In example (1), opener bids three diamonds, showing an unbalanced hand. With a singleton spade, and knowing responder has at most three spades, opener is not sure three notrump will be the best contract. Responder bids three hearts showing strong hearts and weak spades. With strong hearts and strong spades, responder bids three notrump. Opener, afraid of spades, bids four diamonds. With a weaker hand, opener slows the auction down by bidding four clubs. When responder cuebids the ace of spades, opener jumps to six clubs. Opposite likely shortness, the four-spade cuebid shows first-round control. In example (2), opener bids three spades, showing an unbalanced hand with clubs and spades. With three aces, responder supports clubs. When opener shows a diamond fragment, and therefore heart shortness, responder jumps to six clubs. It's nice to be in six clubs making six, when players who respond three notrump go minus.

Opener (3)		Responder		Opener (4)		Responder	
♠2	♦A32	♠Q43	♦KQJ6	♠2	♦A5432	♠Q43	♦KQJ6
♥K32	♣KQJ432	♥AQ4	♣765	♥K32	♣KQJ2	♥AQ4	♣765

Opener (3)	Responder	Opener (4)	Responder
1club	2NT	1diamond	2NT
3clubs	3diamonds	3clubs	3diamonds
3hearts	4clubs	3hearts	4diamonds
5clubs	Pass	5diamonds	Pass

Opener (5)		Responder		Opener (6)		Responder	
♠32	♦AK2	♠A65	♦QJ3	♠432	♦AK2	♠A65	♦QJ3
♥Q32	♣KQ432	♥AK5	♣AJ65	♥432	♣KQ32	♥AK5	♣AJ65

Opener (5)	Responder	Opener (6)	Responder
1club	2NT	1club	2NT
3NT	4NT	3NT	4NT
6NT	Pass	Pass	

In examples (3) and (4), opener is worried about the spade suit. Opener bids three clubs showing an unbalanced hand. Responder bids three diamonds showing diamond values with weakness in one of the majors. Opener bids three hearts showing heart values and therefore weak spades. If opener doesn't have spade help, responder bypasses three notrump and tries for five-of-a-minor. In example (3), responder supports clubs and opener raises to five clubs. In example (4), responder supports diamonds and opener raises to five diamonds.

Responder shows a 4-3-3-3 hand with 18-19 HCPs by jumping to two notrump and then bidding again over opener's three-notrump sign-off. One-of-either-minor -- two notrump -- three notrump -- four clubs shows 18 HCPs with exactly four clubs and one-of-either-minor -- two notrump -- three notrump -- four notrump shows 19 HCPs with exactly four clubs. One-of-either-minor -- two notrump -- three notrump -- four diamonds shows 18-19 HCPs with exactly four diamonds. One-of-either-minor -- two notrump -- three notrump -- four-of-either-major shows 18-19 HCPs with a very weak four-card major. In examples (5) and (6), responder shows a balanced 19 HCPs with exactly four clubs by responding two notrump and then bidding four notrump. In example (5), opener bids six notrump. In example (6), opener passes four notrump.

8.7 -- RESPONDER BIDS SUITS UP THE LINE BUT CAN DECIDE TO BYPASS A DIAMOND SUIT.

When faced with a choice between bidding one diamond or one-of-a-major, responder bids one diamond if his diamonds are better or longer than his major. With AKxx of diamonds and Jxxx of hearts or spades, responder bids one diamond. With Kxxxx of diamonds and Axxx of hearts or spades, responder bids one diamond. If diamonds and hearts are equal, it is reasonable to bid one heart. If there is a diamond fit and responder bids one heart, the diamond fit can be lost. However, if there is a major-suit fit and responder bids one diamond, the major-suit fit will not be lost. If responder holding Jxxx of hearts and AKxx of diamonds ends up playing a 4-3 fit, the diamond fit will probably play better than the heart fit. With a very weak response, ♠xxxx♥Axxx♦xxxx♣x for instance, respond one diamond and pass opener's rebid.

8.8 -- OPENER REBIDS ONE SPADE EVEN WITH 4-3-3-3.

If responder bids up the line, opener has to bid his four-card suits up the line even over a one-diamond response. Therefore, failure to bid one-of-a-major can cause opener to miss his 4-4 major-suit fit when responder has a weak four-card major. If opener denies holding a four-card major whenever opener rebids one notrump, responder does not have to check back and give the opponents vital information which can help their defense.

If opener always rebids one-of-a-major whenever he has four, even 4-3-3-3, whenever responder has a choice between rebidding one notrump and supporting opener's minor, responder has to rebid one notrump. Responder, holding 6-10 HCPs, has to rebid one notrump with unbalanced hands as well as balanced hands. Responder holding ♠5♥Q5432♦KJ543♣32 or ♠5♥Q5432♦KJ5432♣2 after one club -- one heart -- one spade, has to rebid one notrump since two diamonds is game-forcing and two hearts shows six. If responder rebids two hearts, he deserves to find opener with a singleton heart. If opener holding ♠AKQ2♥JT6♦Q32♣Q65, doesn't prefer hearts, responder will be down at least one in one notrump instead of +140 in two hearts. If responder has only four hearts, two hearts in the 4-3 could play better than one notrump. Since opener has to give responder a preference whenever opener has three-card support, it follows that opener's preference of responder's suit shows nothing extra. If opener always gives a preference, even when 4-3-3-3, sometimes opener will be wrong, but more often opener will be right.

132

8.9 -- ONE CLUB - ONE SPADE - TWO CLUBS - TWO HEARTS (NON-FORCING). ONE CLUB - ONE SPADE - TWO CLUBS - TWO DIAMONDS FORCING.

After one club -- one spade -- two clubs, responder can bid two diamonds, new minor forcing. This allows responder to bid two hearts with weak hands that contains both majors. After one diamond -- one spade -- two diamonds, it's inconvenient to bid three clubs to force with major-suit two-suiters, therefore two hearts has to be natural and forcing for one round. After one diamond -- one spade -- two clubs, two hearts is fourth suit, forcing to game.

8.10 -- ONE CLUB - ONE DIAMOND - ONE HEART. TWO SPADES SHOWS FOUR SPADES AND 15+ HCPS. ONE SPADE IS EITHER FOURTH SUIT GAME FORCING OR NATURAL.

After one club -- one diamond -- one heart, responder bids one spade, natural, holding a six-point hand holding four spades and four or more diamonds. Responder also bids one spade, fourth-suit game forcing without four spades, holding a game-forcing hand with club support, a game-forcing diamond hand, a game-forcing heart hand or a game-forcing notrump hand. Responder's jump to two spades shows at least 15 HCPs with four or more diamonds and four spades. Opener responds to one spade the same as opener responds to one club -- one spade. Opener raises to two spades with 11-14 points and four-card spade support. Opener bids one notrump with a weak notrump without four spades and jumps to two notrump with 18-19 HCPs. Opener bids two clubs with a minimum opener and at least five clubs or opener supports diamonds with an unbalanced hand with at least three diamonds.

If opener bids one notrump showing a weak notrump, responder bids two clubs, non-forcing, with ♠A432♥-♦A5432♣5432, or two diamonds, non-forcing, with ♠A432♥2♦K65432♣32. Two notrump is invitational and all other bids are game forcing.

Since responder does not have to have four spades, opener, holding four spades, cannot bid spades above the three-level. Instead of jumping to three or four spades, opener bids two hearts, artificial, to show a hand with 15 or more points and four-card spade support. Over two hearts, responder bids two spades to show a hand not interested in game opposite a 15-point spade raise. Responder jumps to four spades to show a hand interested in game but not interested in slam opposite a 19-point spade raise. Responder jumps to three spades on all other hands containing four spades. Any non-spade bid by responder over two hearts is natural and game forcing, and denies holding four spades.

Opener (1)	Responder		Opener (2)	Responder	
♠Q876 ♦5	♠5432 ♦KQ432		♠Q876 ♦5	♠AK32 ♦AQ432	
♥KJ43 ♣AKQJ	♥32 ♣32		♥KJ43 ♣AKQJ	♥Q2 ♣32	
1club	1diamond		1club	1diamond	
1heart	1spade		1heart	1spade	
2hearts	2spades		2hearts	3spades	
Pass			4spades	4NT	
			5diamonds	5hearts	
			6clubs	6spades	

Opener (3)	Responder		Opener (4)	Responder	
♠A765 ♦2	♠432 ♦AKQJ		♠Q765 ♦2	♠432 ♦AKQJ	
♥KJ32 ♣AKQJ	♥AQ ♣5432		♥KJ32 ♣AKQJ	♥AQ ♣5432	
1club	1diamond		1club	1diamond	
1heart	1spade		1heart	1spade	
2hearts	3clubs		2hearts	3clubs	
3spades	4diamonds		3NT	Pass	
4hearts	4NT				
5clubs	5diamonds				
5hearts	7clubs				

In examples (1) through (4), opener rebids two hearts as an artificial bid to show four spades and at least 15 HCPs. In example (1), responder bids two spades and opener passes. On bad days two spades goes down one. In example (2), responder bids three spades, setting spades as trumps and allowing opener to show extra values. Opener raises to four spades showing only enough strength to raise a one-spade response to three spades. Responder bids keycard and signs-off in six spades. If opener shows extra values by cuebidding over three spades, responder can try six notrump. In examples (3) and (4), responder shows a game-forcing hand with club support without four spades by bidding three clubs. In example (3), opener cuebids three spades showing extra values. After two more cuebids, responder bids keycard and bids five diamonds asking for the club queen. Opener shows the club queen and heart king by bidding five hearts. Responder bids seven clubs. This system is not designed to find out about the jacks needed to make seven notrump. In example (4), since opener doesn't cuebid, responder passes opener's three-notrump bid. Note that if responder has to bid four clubs over a standard jump to three spades to show club support, he will get too high.

134

8.11 -- FOURTH SUIT IS GAME FORCING. JUMP PREFERENCES AND JUMP REBIDS ARE INVITATIONAL.

Opener	(1)	Responder		Opener	(2)	Responder	
♠AK32	♦Q32	♠QJ4	♦4	♠AK32	♦Q32	♠QJ4	♦4
♥32	♣AJT2	♥KQJ654	♣K43	♥32	♣AJT2	♥KQJ654	♣543

Opener (1)	Responder	Opener (2)	Responder
1club	1heart	1club	1heart
1spade	2diamonds	1spade	3hearts
2NT	3hearts	4hearts	Pass
4clubs	4hearts		

Except for one club -- one diamond -- one heart -- one spade, responder's fourth-suit rebid is game forcing and can be artificial. Since all direct jump preferences and jump rebids by responder in non-game-forcing sequences are invitational, the only way for responder to create a force is to bid fourth suit or new minor. With a game-forcing hand and support for one of opener's suits, responder has to bid fourth suit or new minor first and then support. With a game-forcing hand and a strong suit of his own, responder has to bid fourth-suit or new minor first and then rebid his suit. FOURTH-SUIT ARTIFICIAL AND FORCING DOES NOT APPLY IF A GAME FORCE HAS ALREADY BEEN ESTABLISHED.

In example (1), responder has a game-forcing hand with six hearts. Over opener's one-spade rebid, responder bids two diamonds, fourth-suit game forcing. Opener's rebids are natural over the fourth-suit. With three-card heart support, opener supports hearts. With a stopper in the fourth suit, opener bids two notrump. With five or more clubs, opener rebids his clubs. Opener raises the fourth suit with four-card support and a good hand. If opener has nothing better to say, opener rebids his spades. Over opener's natural two-notrump bid, responder rebids his hearts asking for two-card support. Two-card support is the best support possible once opener denies three-card support with his two-notrump rebid. Opener with two-card support and a sound opener cuebids on the way to four hearts. Four clubs cannot be a real suit since responder is interested in hearts, not clubs. Opener raises directly to four hearts with a minimum and two-card support, and rebids three notrump with a singleton heart. Responder, with a minimum game force, signs-off in four hearts. In example (2), responder has an invitational-to-game hand with six hearts. Over opener's one-spade rebid, responder jumps to three hearts. Opener with a sound weak notrump accepts the invitation.

IN-1.	IN-2.	IN-3.	IN-4.	IN-5.	IN-6.	IN-7.
1♣ 1♥	1♣ 1♥	1♣ 1♥	1♣ 1♥	1♣ 1♥	1♣ 1♥	1♣ 1♥
1♠ 3♣	1♠ 3♥	1♠ 3♠	1NT 3♣	1NT 3♦	1NT 3♥	1♠ 2NT

IN-8.	IN-9.	IN-10.	IN-11.	IN-12.	IN-13.	IN-14.
1♣ 1♥	1♣ 1♥	1♣ 1♠	1♣ 1♠	1♦ 1♥	1♦ 1♥	1♦ 1♥
2♣ 3♣	2♣ 3♥	1NT 3♥	2♣ 3♠	1♠ 3♦	1♠ 3♥	1♠ 3♠

IN-15.	IN-16.	IN-17.	IN-18.	IN-19.	IN-20.	IN-21.
1♦ 1♥	1♦ 1♥	1♦ 1♥	1♦ 1♥	1♦ 1♠	1♦ 1♠	1♦ 1♠
1NT 3♦	1NT 3♥	1♠ 2NT	2♦ 3♥	1NT 3♦	1NT 3♥	2♦ 3♠

Sequences (IN-1) through (IN-21) are all invitational sequences. Opener, with a minimum, can pass responder's last bid. Responder shows a six-card or longer suit when he jumps in his suit. Responder shows four-card support when he supports opener's suit.

F-1.	F-2.	F-3.	F-4.	F-5.	F-6.	F-7.
1♣ 1♥	1♣ 1♥	1♣ 1♥	1♣ 1♥	1♣ 1♥	1♣ 1♥	1♣ 1♥
1♠ 2♦	1♠ 2♦	1♠ 2♦	1NT 2♦	1NT 2♦	1NT 2♦	1♠ 2♦
Any 3♣	Any 3♥	Any 3♠	Any 3♣	Any 3♦	Any 3♥	Any 2NT

F-8.	F-9.	F-10.	F-11.	F-12.	F-13.	F-14.
1♣ 1♥	1♣ 1♥	1♣ 1♠	1♣ 1♠	1♦ 1♥	1♦ 1♥	1♦ 1♥
2♣ 2♦	2♣ 2♦	1NT 2♦	2♣ 2♦	1♠ 2♣	1♠ 2♣	1♠ 2♣
Any 3♣	Any 3♥	Any 3♥	Any 3♠	Any 3♦	Any 3♥	Any 2♠

F-15.	F-16.	F-17.	F-18.	F-19.	F-20.	F-21.
1♦ 1♥	1♦ 1♥	1♦ 1♥	1♦ 1♥	1♦ 1♠	1♦ 1♠	1♦ 1♠
1NT 2♣	1NT 2♣	1♠ 2♣	2♦ 2♠	1NT 2♣	1NT 2♣	2♦ 2♥
Any 3♦	Any 3♥	Any 2NT	Any 3♥	Any 3♦	Any 3♥	Any 3♠

Sequences (F-1) through (F-21) are all game-forcing sequences. Opener must keep bidding until game is reached. Sequence (F-1) is the way responder changes sequence (IN-1) from an invitational sequence to a forcing sequence. Sequences (F-2) through (F-21) similarly match sequences (IN-2) through (IN-21). In the forcing sequences, after opener's ANY bid, responder supports opener as cheaply as possible.

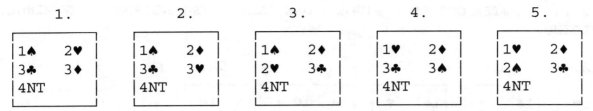

	1.			2.			3.			4.			5.	
1♠	2♥		1♠	2♦		1♠	2♦		1♥	2♦		1♥	2♦
3♣	3♦		3♣	3♥		2♥	3♣		3♣	3♠		2♠	3♣
4NT			4NT			4NT			4NT			4NT	

Opener's jump to four notrump after a three-level fourth-suit call is natural and shows extra strength. In the above auctions, four notrump is natural. Four notrump is only RKC if a trump suit has been established. If opener has four-card support for responder's fourth suit, opener is void in responder's first-bid suit and you don't bid Blackwood with a void.

Opener	(1)	Responder		Opener	(2)	Responder	

♠AK432 ♦32   ♠65   ♦AQ54   ♠AK432 ♦32   ♠65   ♦AQ654

   ♥A2 ♣AK32   ♥KQJT3 ♣Q4   ♥A2 ♣AK32   ♥KQJ3 ♣54

1spade	2hearts		1spade	2diamonds
3clubs	3diamonds		3clubs	3hearts
4NT	6NT		4NT	Pass

In examples (1) and (2), opener rebids three clubs showing extra values. Responder bids the fourth suit, which in this case has to be natural and forcing since he is already in a game-forcing auction and doesn't have to invent a bid to create a force. Opener, with 18 HCPs, jumps to four notrump. With the same hand without the king of clubs, opener bids only three notrump. In example (1), responder with a balanced 14 accepts the notrump slam try. In example (2), responder with a balanced 12 rejects.

8.12 -- JUMPS TO THREE CLUBS AND THREE DIAMONDS ARE WEAK.

	1.			2.			3.			4.			5.			6.	
1♦	1♥		1♦	1♥		1♦	1♠		1♥	1♠		1♥	1♠		1♥	1♠
1♠	3♣		1NT	3♣		1NT	3♣		1NT	3♣		1NT	3♦		2♣	3♦

All of these auctions are sign-offs and show weak hands with a six-card minor and only a four-card major. Responder does not want a preference.

8.13 -- AFTER ONE-OF-A-MINOR - ONE HEART - ONE NOTRUMP, NEW MINOR IS FORCING.

1A.	2A.	3A.	4A.	5A.
1♣ 1♥ 1NT 2♦ 2♠ 2NT	1♣ 1♥ 1NT 2♦ 2♠ 3♣	1♣ 1♥ 1NT 2♦ 2♠ 3♦	1♣ 1♥ 1NT 2♦ 2♠ 3♥	1♣ 1♥ 1NT 2♦ 2♠ 3NT

1B.	2B.	3B.	4B.	5B.
1♦ 1♥ 1NT 2♣ 2♠ 2NT	1♦ 1♥ 1NT 2♣ 2♠ 3♣	1♦ 1♥ 1NT 2♣ 2♠ 3♦	1♦ 1♥ 1NT 2♣ 2♠ 3♥	1♦ 1♥ 1NT 2♣ 2♠ 3NT

After one-of-a-minor -- one heart -- one notrump, two-of-the-other-minor by responder is artificial, asks opener to describe his hand and shows at least game-invitational values. Responder uses new-minor-forcing to find three-card support for hearts, to show game-forcing support for opener's minor and to show a game-forcing six-card heart suit. If opener never bypasses a four-card spade suit, and if responder always forces with two spades whenever responder has four spades, responder's new-minor after a one-heart response will never be looking for spade support. OVER ONE-OF-A-MINOR -- ONE HEART -- ONE NOTRUMP -- NEW MINOR, OPENER'S FIRST DUTY IS TO BID TWO SPADES, ARTIFICIAL, WITH ALL MAXIMUMS TO SET A GAME-FORCING AUCTION AND ALLOW RESPONDER TO FURTHER DESCRIBE HIS HAND. Over two spades, responder bids two notrump to show exactly five hearts, and three hearts to show six or more hearts. Three-of-either-minor is natural and denies five hearts except in auction (3A), where responder must have five hearts to bid hearts and then bid diamonds.

In column (1), responder shows a game-forcing hand with five hearts. Responder wants to play in hearts if opener has three-card support. In column (2), responder shows at least a mild slam try in clubs with only four hearts. In column (3), responder shows at least a mild slam try in diamonds. In auction (3A), responder has five hearts. In auction (3B), responder has only four hearts. In column (4), responder shows a game-forcing hand with six or more hearts. Responder wants opener to raise hearts with two-card support. In column (5), responder shows a game-forcing hand with five hearts offering opener, if he has three-card heart support, a choice between three notrump and four hearts.

	1.	2.	3.	4.	5.	6.
A.	1♣ 1♥ 1NT 2♦ 2♥ 3♠	1♣ 1♥ 1NT 2♦ 2♥ 3♣	1♣ 1♥ 1NT 2♦ 2♥ 3♦	1♣ 1♥ 1NT 2♦ 2♥ 2♠	1♣ 1♥ 1NT 2♦ 2♥ 3NT	1♣ 1♥ 1NT 2♦ 2♥ 3♥
B.	1♦ 1♥ 1NT 2♣ 2♥ 3♠	1♦ 1♥ 1NT 2♣ 2♥ 3♣	1♦ 1♥ 1NT 2♣ 2♥ 3♦	1♦ 1♥ 1NT 2♣ 2♥ 2♠	1♦ 1♥ 1NT 2♣ 2♥ 3NT	1♦ 1♥ 1NT 2♣ 2♥ 3♥

After one-of-a-minor -- one heart -- one notrump -- new minor, if opener has a minimum notrump rebid, opener shows three-card heart support by bidding two hearts. Remember, if opener has a maximum notrump rebid, opener bids two spades, artificial, over responder's new minor force.

In row A, opener opens one club and bids one notrump over responder's one-heart response. Opener denies holding four spades. Responder bids two diamonds, new minor forcing, and opener bids two hearts showing exactly three hearts and a minimum notrump rebid. In row B, opener opens one diamond and bids one notrump over responder's one-heart response. Opener denies holding four spades. Responder bids two clubs, new minor forcing, and opener bids two hearts showing exactly three hearts and a minimum notrump rebid.

In column (1), responder bids three spades, a heart slam try with undisclosed shortness. Opener bids three notrump if he wants to ask. Responder answers four clubs showing club shortness, four diamonds showing diamond shortness, four hearts showing spade shortness with only a mild slam try, and four spades to show spade shortness with enough strength to force to the five-level. In column (2), responder bids three clubs, showing at least a mild slam try in clubs with only four hearts. In column (3), responder bids three diamonds, showing at least a mild slam try in diamonds with only four hearts. In column (4), responder bids two spades, artificial, showing a game-forcing hand with at least five hearts. In column (5), responder bids three notrump showing a game-forcing hand with exactly five hearts, offering opener a choice between three notrump and four hearts. Opener has three hearts in this auction, so responder is willing to miss the 5-3 heart fit. In column (6), responder bids three hearts showing a strongly invitational hand with exactly five hearts.

	2.	3.	4.	5.	6.
C.	1♣ 1♥ 1NT 2♦ 2NT 3♣	1♣ 1♥ 1NT 2♦ 2NT 3♦	1♣ 1♥ 1NT 2♦ 2NT 3♥	1♣ 1♥ 1NT 2♦ 2NT 3NT	1♣ 1♥ 1NT 2♦ 2NT Pas
D.	1♦ 1♥ 1NT 2♣ 2♦ 3♣	1♦ 1♥ 1NT 2♣ 2♦ 3♦	1♦ 1♥ 1NT 2♣ 2♦ 3♥	1♦ 1♥ 1NT 2♣ 2♦ 3NT	1♦ 1♥ 1NT 2♣ 2♦ 2♥

If opener has a minimum notrump rebid, opener denies three-card heart support by bidding two diamonds if two clubs is new minor or by bidding two notrump if two diamonds is new minor. If opener never bids three clubs over new minor, responder will be able to bid three clubs to show a club slam try. Remember, if opener has a maximum notrump rebid, opener bids two spades, artificial, over responder's new-minor-force.

In row C, opener bids one club and bids one notrump over responder's one-heart response. Responder bids two diamonds, new-minor-forcing, and opener bids two notrump showing fewer than three hearts and a minimum notrump rebid. In row D, opener bids one diamond and bids one notrump over responder's one-heart response. Responder bids two clubs, new-minor-forcing, and opener bids two diamonds showing fewer than three hearts and a minimum notrump rebid.

In column (2), responder bids three clubs, showing at least a mild slam try in clubs. In column (3), responder bids three diamonds, showing at least a mild slam try in diamonds. In columns (2) and (3), responder can have five hearts. Since opener has denied holding three hearts, responder is looking elsewhere for a fit. In column (4), responder bids three hearts, showing a game-forcing hand with at least six hearts. Opener raises to four hearts with two hearts and a bad hand for slam, and cuebids with two hearts and a good hand for slam. In column (5), responder signs-off in three notrump. All responder wanted was three-card heart support. In column (6), responder shows an invitational hand with exactly five hearts.

Opener	(1)		Responder	
♠KQ2	♦432		♠43	♦A65
♥A32	♣QJ32		♥K7654	♣A65

1club	1heart
1NT	2diamonds
2hearts	Pass

Opener	(2)		Responder	
♠KQ2	♦432		♠43	♦A65
♥A2	♣QJ432		♥K7654	♣A65

1club	1heart
1NT	2diamonds
2NT	Pass

Opener	(3)		Responder	
♠KQ2	♦432		♠A43	♦5
♥A32	♣QJ32		♥KQ654	♣AK54

1club	1heart
1NT	2diamonds
2hearts	3spades
3NT	4diamonds
4NT	5clubs
5diamonds	6hearts
Pass	

Opener	(4)		Responder	
♠KQ2	♦432		♠A3	♦A65
♥A32	♣QJ32		♥KQ65	♣AK54

1club	1heart
1NT	2diamonds
2hearts	3clubs
3hearts	4NT
5diamonds	6clubs
Pass	

In examples (1) and (2), responder bids two diamonds, new minor, looking for three-card heart support. In example (1), opener bids two hearts, showing three-card heart support and a minimum. Responder, at the bottom of his invitation, passes two hearts. In example (2), opener bids two notrump, showing a minimum and denying three-card heart support. Responder with an invitational hand passes two notrump. In example (3), responder bids two diamonds looking for three-card heart support. Opener bids two hearts showing a minimum hand with three-card heart support. Responder jumps to three spades showing a slam try with at least five hearts with unspecified shortness. Opener bids three notrump asking, and responder shows diamond shortness. If responder is void in diamonds, responder still bids four diamonds showing diamond shortness, but shows the void during RKC (see section 25.6). Opener with three little diamonds bids keycard, checks to make sure the queen of trumps is present and bids a slam. Responder does not show the king of clubs because opener's hand is limited. In example (4), responder bids two diamonds new minor, in this case looking for a club slam. Opener bids two hearts showing a minimum with three hearts. Responder bids three clubs showing a club slam try and denying five hearts. Opener cuebids the ace of hearts showing some slam interest. Responder bids keycard and signs-off in six clubs.

141

Opener	(5)	Responder		Opener	(6)	Responder
♠KQ2 ♦KQ432	♠43 ♦A65		♠KQ2 ♦KQ32	♠43 ♦J65
♥A2 ♣432	♥K6543 ♣A65		♥A32 ♣432	♥KQ654 ♣AK5

Opener	Responder		Opener	Responder
1diamond	1heart		1diamond	1heart
1NT	2clubs		1NT	2clubs
2spades	2NT		2spades	2NT
3diamonds	3NT		3hearts	4hearts
			Pass	

Opener	(7)	Responder		Opener	(8)	Responder
♠KQ2 ♦KQ432	♠43 ♦A65		♠KQ2 ♦KQ32	♠A3 ♦J65
♥A2 ♣432	♥KQ7654 ♣A5		♥A32 ♣432	♥KQ654 ♣AK5

Opener	Responder		Opener	Responder
1diamond	1heart		1diamond	1heart
1NT	2clubs		1NT	2clubs
2spades	3hearts		2spades	2NT
3spades	4clubs		3hearts	3spades
4diamonds	4NT		4diamonds	4NT
5diamonds	6hearts		5diamonds	6hearts

In examples (5) through (8), responder has five or more hearts with at least invitational values. Responder bids two clubs, new-minor, and opener bids two spades showing a maximum weak notrump and creating a game force. In example (5), responder bids two notrump, forcing, showing exactly five hearts. Opener with only two hearts has a choice. With 3-2-5-3 distribution opener bids three diamonds showing five diamonds and denying three-card heart support, just in case responder is interested in a diamond slam. With 3-2-4-4 distribution opener raises two notrump to three notrump. Responder, interested in playing in four hearts if opener has three, signs-off in three notrump. In example (6), over two notrump showing five hearts, opener bids three hearts setting heart as trumps. Responder with a minimum game force raises to four hearts. In example (7), responder bids three hearts showing a six-card heart suit with game-forcing values. With just invitational values, responder jumps to three hearts directly over one notrump. After three cuebids, responder bids keycard and signs-off in six hearts. In example (8), responder bids two notrump showing a five-card heart suit with game-forcing values. Opener bids three hearts setting hearts as trumps. After two cuebids, responder bids keycard and signs-off in six hearts.

8.14 -- AFTER ONE-DIAMOND - ONE SPADE - ONE NOTRUMP, TWO CLUBS IS NEW-MINOR FORCING.

After one diamond -- one spade -- one notrump, two clubs by responder is artificial, asks opener to describe his hand and shows at least game-invitational values. Responder bids new minor for only two purposes; to check for an eight-card or longer major-suit fit, or to make a slam try in either minor. Over two clubs new-minor forcing, opener bids two hearts with four hearts. If opener does not have four hearts, opener bids two spades with three-card spade support. Otherwise, opener bids two diamonds with a minimum or two notrump with a maximum. Bidding two diamonds with a minimum allows responder to play in two-of-a-major with a distributional invitational hand, or in two notrump with a balanced invitational hand.

	1.	2.	3.	4.	5.	6.	7.
A.	1♦ 1♠	1♦ 1♠	1♦ 1♠	1♦ 1♠	1♦ 1♠	1♦ 1♠	1♦ 1♠
	1NT 2♣	1NT 2♣	1NT 2♣	1NT 2♣	1NT 2♣	1NT 2♣	1NT 2♣
	2♦ 2♥	2♦ 2♠	2♦ 2NT	2♥ 2♠	2♥ 2NT	2♥ 3♥	2♠ 3♠

All of the above auctions are invitational. Auctions (1) and (6) show five spades and at least four hearts. Auctions (2), (3), (4) and (5) show five spades with fewer than four hearts. Auction (7) shows five spades saying nothing about hearts. In auctions (1), (2) and (4), responder would rather play in a suit contract then a notrump contract. In auctions (3) and (5), responder would rather play in notrump then a seven-card major-suit fit.

	1.	2.	3.	4.	5.	6.	7.
B.	1♦ 1♠	1♦ 1♠	1♦ 1♠	1♦ 1♠	1♦ 1♠	1♦ 1♠	1♦ 1♠
	1NT 2♣	1NT 2♣	1NT 2♣	1NT 2♣	1NT 2♣	1NT 2♣	1NT 2♣
	2♦ 3any	2♥ 3♣	2♥ 3♦	2♥ 3♠	2♠ 3♣	2♠ 3♦	2♠ 3♥

All of the above auctions are game forcing. New minor followed by three-of-a-minor is a natural slam try. New minor followed by a jump to three hearts shows a game-forcing hand with at least 5-5 in the majors. New minor followed by a jump to three spades shows a game-forcing hand with at least six spades. A jump to four clubs is an artificial slam try supporting opener's last bid suit.

143

Opener (1)		Responder		Opener (2)		Responder	
♠K2	♦KQ432	♠J7654	♦A65	♠K32	♦KQ32	♠J7654	♦A65
♥A32	♣432	♥65	♣KQJ	♥A432	♣32	♥65	♣KQJ

Opener (1)	Responder	Opener (2)	Responder
1diamond	1spade	1diamond	1spade
1NT	2clubs	1NT	2clubs
2diamonds	2NT	2hearts	2spades
Pass		Pass	

Opener (3)		Responder		Opener (4)		Responder	
♠K2	♦QJ32	♠AQ6543	♦AK	♠K2	♦Q432	♠AQ6543	♦AK
♥AJ32	♣J32	♥KQ4	♣54	♥AJ32	♣KJ2	♥KQ4	♣54

Opener (3)	Responder	Opener (4)	Responder
1diamond	1spade	1diamond	1spade
1NT	2clubs	1NT	2clubs
2hearts	3spades	2hearts	3spades
4spades	Pass	4clubs	4NT
		5hearts	6NT

In examples (1) and (2), responder has an invitational hand with five spades. In example (1), over two clubs new minor, opener bids two diamonds showing a minimum weak notrump without three spades and without four hearts. Responder, with weak spades, chooses to play two notrump rather than two spades. In example (2), responder bids two clubs, new minor, and follows with two spades, showing five spades and invitational values. Opener's two-heart bid shows four hearts but says nothing about strength and says nothing about possible three-card spade support. If opener has a minimum weak notrump, opener passes two spades with three-card support or bids two notrump with two-card support. Opener with a maximum weak notrump bids three notrump with two-card spade support and raises spades with three-card spade support. In examples (3) and (4), opener shows four hearts over responder's new minor. Responder jumps to three spades, showing a game-forcing hand with at least six spades. In example (3), opener raises to four spades, showing a minimum four-spade bid. Since opener fails to cuebid, responder passes four spades. In example (4), opener shows club values on the way to four spades, showing a good four-spade bid. Responder bids keycard and bids six notrump. Since opener has a maximum weak notrump, the only loser in both six spades and six notrump figures to be the missing keycard. Six notrump making six scores more than six spades making six, the opponents won't be able to get a ruff and clubs will be protected.

144

Opener	(5)	Responder	
♠J32 ♦Q432		♠AQ54 ♦AK65	
♥A32 ♣KQ2		♥KQ4 ♣43	

Opener	Responder
1diamond	1spade
1NT	2clubs
2spades	3diamonds
3NT	Pass

Opener	(6)	Responder	
♠J32 ♦Q432		♠AQ54 ♦AK65	
♥A32 ♣AK2		♥KQ4 ♣43	

Opener	Responder
1diamond	1spade
1NT	2clubs
2spades	3diamonds
3hearts	3spades
4clubs	4NT
5spades	6diamonds

Opener	(7)	Responder	
♠K32 ♦AJ32		♠AJ654 ♦KQ4	
♥A432 ♣32		♥65 ♣A54	

Opener	Responder
1diamond	1spade
1NT	2clubs
2hearts	3NT
4spades	Pass

Opener	(8)	Responder	
♠K32 ♦AJ32		♠AQ654 ♦4	
♥A432 ♣32		♥KQJ65 ♣KQ	

Opener	Responder
1diamond	1spade
1NT	2clubs
2hearts	4clubs
4diamonds	4NT
5hearts	6hearts

In examples (5) and (6), opener bids two spades showing three-card spade support. Two spades says nothing about strength and denies holding four hearts. Responder bids three diamonds showing a diamond slam try and denying holding five spades. If responder has five spades with the intention of playing in spades, he jumps to four clubs, artificial, setting spades as trumps. Since responder did not set spades as trumps, any further spade bids are interpreted as cuebids. In example (5), opener with a minimum bids three notrump. In example (6), opener with a maximum cuebids three hearts. After two cuebids, responder bids keycard and bids six diamonds. In example (7), opener has a minimum notrump rebid with three spades and four hearts. Opener bids two hearts over two clubs, new minor, showing four hearts, saying nothing about spades. Responder jumps to three notrump showing five spades. Opener corrects to four spades with three-card spade support. Since responder does not have a slam try in a minor and does not have four-card heart support, the only reason responder bid two clubs was in hopes of finding three-card spade support. In example (8), responder jumps to four clubs over two hearts, an artificial bid, showing a heart slam try. Opener with two aces and the valuable king of spades encourages with four diamonds, the Last Train. Responder bids keycard and bids six hearts.

8.15 -- AFTER ONE CLUB - ONE SPADE - ONE NOTRUMP, TWO DIAMONDS IS NEW MINOR FORCING.

After one club -- one spade -- one notrump, two diamonds by responder is artificial, asks opener to describe his hand and shows at least game-invitational values. Remember, responder bids new minor for only two purposes; to check for an eight-card or longer major-suit fit or to make a slam try in either minor. Over two diamonds new minor forcing, opener bids two hearts with four hearts. If opener does not have four hearts, opener bids two spades with three-card spade support. Otherwise, opener bids two notrump with a minimum or three clubs with a maximum.

1.	2.	3.	4.	5.	6.
1♣ 1♠	1♣ 1♠	1♣ 1♠	1♣ 1♠	1♣ 1♠	1♣ 1♠
1NT 2♦	1NT 2♦	1NT 2♦	1NT 2♦	1NT 3♦	1NT 3♥
2♥ 2♠	2♥ 3♥	2♠ 3♠	2NT Pas		

All of the above auctions are invitational. Auction (1) shows five spades with fewer than four hearts. Auction (2) shows an invitational hand with five spades and at least four hearts. Auction (3) shows an invitational hand with five spades, saying nothing about hearts. Auction (4) shows an invitational hand with five spades and maybe four hearts. Auction (5) shows an invitational hand with five spades and five diamonds. Auction (6) shows an invitational hand with five spades and five hearts.

1.	2.	3.	4.	5.	6.	7.
1♣ 1♠	1♣ 1♠	1♣ 1♠	1♣ 1♠	1♣ 1♠	1♣ 1♠	1♣ 1♠
1NT 2♦	1NT 2♦	1NT 2♦	1NT 2♦	1NT 2♦	1NT 2♦	1NT 2♦
2♥ 3♣	2♥ 3♦	2♥ 3♠	2♠ 3♣	2♠ 3♦	2NT 3♥	3♣ 3♥

All of the above auctions are game forcing. Auctions (1) and (4) are club slam tries. In auction (1), responder can still have five spades. Auctions (2) and (5) are diamond slam tries. Responder has five spades and at least four diamonds. Auction (3) shows a game-forcing hand with at least six spades. Auctions (6) and (7) show a game-forcing hand with at least 5-5 in the majors. If opener bids a major in response to two diamonds, responder jumps to four clubs as an artificial slam try in that major.

Opener	(1)	Responder		Opener	(2)	Responder	
♠J32 ♦K2		♠AKQ54 ♦Q3		♠J32 ♦K2		♠AKQ54 ♦Q3	
♥KQJ ♣K5432		♥54 ♣AQJ6		♥AK32 ♣K432		♥54 ♣AQJ6	

Opener (1)	Responder	Opener (2)	Responder
1club	1spade	1club	1spade
1NT	2diamonds	1NT	2diamonds
2spades	4clubs	2hearts	3clubs
4spades	Pass	3spades	4diamonds
		4hearts	4NT
		5diamonds	6spades

Opener (3)	Responder	Opener (4)	Responder
♠32 ♦K32	♠AKQ54 ♦Q54	♠32 ♦K32	♠AKQ54 ♦Q54
♥AQ2 ♣QJ432	♥43 ♣765	♥AQ2 ♣KQ432	♥43 ♣765

Opener (3)	Responder	Opener (4)	Responder
1club	1spade	1club	1spade
1NT	2diamonds	1NT	2diamonds
2NT	Pass	3clubs	3NT

Over two diamonds, new minor, opener with four hearts bids two hearts. If opener does not have four hearts, opener bids two spades with three-card spade support. Otherwise opener bids two notrump with a minimum and three clubs with a maximum.

In examples (1) and (2), responder bids two diamonds new minor forcing. In example (1), opener with three-card spade support and fewer than four hearts bids two spades. Responder jumps to four clubs, artificial, showing a spade slam try. Opener with no aces and weak spades signs-off in four spades. In example (2), opener's first priority is to bid two hearts with four hearts. Two hearts does not promise or deny three spades. Responder bids three clubs showing a game-forcing club hand, saying nothing about spade length. Opener bids three spades showing three-card spade support. Responder bids four diamonds showing a spade slam try. Three notrump or four clubs sets clubs as trumps and denies holding five spades. Opener with a maximum but only one keycard bids four hearts the only call between four diamonds and four spades. Four hearts encourages responder to bid keycard and bid six spades.

In example (3), opener bids two notrump showing a minimum without either three spades or four hearts. Responder passes. In example (4), opener bids three clubs showing a maximum without either three spades or four hearts. Responder bids three notrump.

Opener	(5)	Responder		Opener	(6)	Responder	
♠J32	♦K2	♠AKQ4	♦43	♠J32	♦K2	♠AKQ4	♦43
♥KQJ	♣K5432	♥54	♣AQ876	♥AK32	♣K432	♥54	♣AQ876

Opener (5)	Responder	Opener (6)	Responder
1club	1spade	1club	1spade
1NT	2diamonds	1NT	2diamonds
2spades	3clubs	2hearts	3clubs
3diamonds	3spades	3spades	3NT
3NT	Pass	4diamonds	6clubs

Opener	(7)	Responder		Opener	(8)	Responder	
♠32	♦K32	♠AKQ54	♦AQ654	♠32	♦KJ2	♠AKQ54	♦AQ654
♥KQJ	♣K5432	♥65	♣6	♥A432	♣AQ32	♥65	♣6

Opener (7)	Responder	Opener (8)	Responder
1club	1spade	1club	1spade
1NT	2diamonds	1NT	2diamonds
2NT	3diamonds	2hearts	3diamonds
3NT	Pass	3hearts	4NT
		5clubs	6diamonds

In example (5), responder bids new minor and then bids three clubs to show a club slam try with only four spades. If responder has five spades, he jumps to four clubs or four spades. Opener encourages mildly with three diamonds and then follows with three notrump. In example (6), since responder can still have five spades, opener has to bid three spades with three-card spade support. Responder bids three notrump denying five spades and showing only a mild club slam try. Four clubs shows a stronger club slam try. Opener with a maximum in both high cards and controls encourages with four diamonds. Since opener has to have at least two keycards to bid four diamonds, responder jumps directly to six clubs.

In examples (7) and (8), responder bids new minor followed by three diamonds showing a slam try with at least five spades and at least four diamonds. Over one club, responder always bids one diamond with a game-forcing hand with 4-4 in diamonds and spades. Therefore, when responder bids spades and then bids diamonds, he shows at least five spades. In example (7), opener with a minimum and only one keycard, signs-off in three notrump. In example (8), opener has good cards for a diamond slam, especially if responder has five diamonds. Opener bids three hearts encouraging responder to bid keycard and bid six diamonds.

```
Opener     (9)     Responder        Opener     (10)    Responder

♠32    ♦K32        ♠AKQ54   ♦4       ♠32    ♦K32        ♠87654   ♦4
   ♥KQJ  ♣K5432       ♥32   ♣J9876      ♥KQJ  ♣K5432       ♥A2   ♣AQ876

1club              1spade            1club              1spade
1NT                2diamonds         1NT                3clubs
2NT                ????              Pass
```

What does responder bid with a five-card major, support for opener's club suit, and exactly invitational values? Two diamonds new minor, checking for three-card spade support is very awkward, since opener bids two notrump if he doesn't have either three spades or four hearts. In example (9), what is responder going to bid over two notrump? Three clubs and three spades are game forcing. The answer is, if the major is strong, forget clubs. If the major is weak, forget the major. Responder over one notrump should have bid three spades invitational, treating his five-card spade suit as a six-card spade suit. In example (10), responder invites in clubs treating his five-card spade suit as a four-card suit.

After one heart -- one spade -- one notrump, two clubs is new minor and two diamonds is natural and non-forcing. Two clubs followed by a two-level bid is invitational. Two clubs followed by a three-level bid is forcing.

```
    1.        2.        3.        4.        5.        6.        7.

┌─────────┐┌─────────┐┌─────────┐┌─────────┐┌─────────┐┌─────────┐┌─────────┐
│1♣   1♥  ││1♣   1♠  ││1♣   1♠  ││1♦   1♠  ││1♦   1♠  ││1♥   1♠  ││1♥   1♠  │
│1NT  2♣  ││1NT  2♣  ││1NT  2♥  ││1NT  2♦  ││1NT  2♥  ││1NT  2♦  ││1NT  2♥  │
└─────────┘└─────────┘└─────────┘└─────────┘└─────────┘└─────────┘└─────────┘
```

In the above auctions, the last call by responder is non-forcing. Opener can correct to responder's first bid suit, but can raise only if his hand reevaluates to 17 points.

Opener	(11)	Responder		Opener	(12)	Responder	
♠32 ♦QJ2		♠AKQ54	♦3	♠32 ♦QJ2		♠AKQ54	♦3
♥KQJ ♣QJ432		♥65432	♣65	♥KQJ ♣QJ432		♥A5432	♣65

Opener (11)	Responder		Opener (12)	Responder
1club	1spade		1club	1spade
1NT	3hearts		1NT	2diamonds
Pass			2NT	3hearts
			4hearts	Pass

One-of-a-minor -- one spade -- one notrump -- three hearts is 5-5 invitational. With a minimum, opener passes three hearts with better hearts, bids three spades with better spades. With a maximum, opener bids four spades with better spades or bids four hearts with better hearts.

With a forcing hand and 5-5 in the majors, responder starts with new minor. If opener bids a major, responder jumps to game with a minimum game force or jumps to four clubs with a slam try. If opener bids two diamonds or two notrump denying three spades and denying four hearts, responder bids three hearts looking for a 5-3 heart fit.

In example (11), responder jumps to three hearts showing 5-5 in the majors with invitational values. Opener with a minimum and wasted cards in the minors passes three hearts. In example (12), responder bids two diamonds new minor and opener bids two notrump showing a minimum weak notrump with fewer than three spades and fewer than four hearts. Responder bids three hearts showing at least five hearts with game-forcing values. Since opener denies four hearts, three hearts must show five. Opener raises to four hearts showing three hearts and a bad hand for slam. If opener has three hearts and a good hand for slam, opener bids four clubs. With 2-2 in the majors, opener bids three notrump.

8.16 -- ONE DIAMOND - TWO CLUBS IS GAME FORCING EXCEPT ONE AUCTION; ONE DIAMOND - TWO CLUBS - TWO DIAMONDS - TWO NOTRUMP.

Opener	(1)	Responder		Opener	(2)	Responder	
♠K32	♦KQ32	♠654	♦54	♠K32	♦KQ32	♠654	♦54
♥A432	♣32	♥KJ5	♣AK654	♥A432	♣Q2	♥KJ5	♣AK654

Opener (1)	Responder	Opener (2)	Responder
1diamond	2clubs	1diamond	2clubs
2diamonds	2NT	2NT	3NT

One diamond -- two clubs, is game forcing except for one diamond -- two clubs -- two diamonds -- two notrump. Two clubs followed by two notrump, responder's only non game-forcing sequence, shows a five-card club suit with 11 HCPs. With 11 HCPs and only four clubs, responder bids one notrump, an underbid, or two notrump forcing, an overbid. If opener has the bottom of a weak notrump, 11 to a bad 13, and wants to play in two notrump opposite 11 HCPs, opener must rebid two diamonds. Opener's two-diamond rebid therefore might be a waiting bid, and opener might have only three diamonds. With the top of a weak notrump, opener bids two notrump, game forcing. Opener can also bid two notrump with 18-19 planning on raising three notrump to four notrump. Opener needs a game-forcing hand to raise two clubs to three clubs.

In examples (1) and (2), responder bids two clubs, planning on bidding two notrump, invitational. In example (1), opener with a minimum weak notrump rebids two diamonds, allowing responder to bid two notrump. Opener passes responder's non-forcing two-notrump bid. In example (2), opener has a maximum weak notrump and bids two notrump, which is forcing to game. Responder raises to three notrump.

If opener bids two-of-a-major, opener shows enough strength to force to game, four cards in the major and at worst 4-4-4-1 distribution. Opener will usually have five diamonds. Opener's jump to three-of-either-major is a splinter, showing four-card club support, at least a sound opening bid, and shortness in the bid major.

Responder's jump to three clubs over one diamond shows an invitational club hand, a six-card or longer club suit with 9-12 HCPs. AKQxxx of clubs with nothing outside is a three-club jump. All bids by opener over three clubs are forcing to game.

8.17 -- GAME TRIES.

Opener's Hand	1. 1♣ 1♥ 2♥ 3♣	2. 1♣ 1♥ 2♥ 2NT	3. 1♣ 1♥ 2♥ 3♥	4. 1♣ 1♥ 2♥ 2♠	5. 1♣ 1♥ 2♥ 3♦
AA. ♠2♥A32♦A432♣K5432	Pass	3♣	Pass	2NT	3♥
BB. ♠32♥A32♦5432♣AKJ2	Pass	Pass	Pass	2NT	3♥
CC. ♠2♥A32♦AK32♣K5432	3♦	3♦	4♥	3NT	4♦
DD. ♠32♥A432♦A32♣K432	3♥	3♥	Pass	3♥	3♥
EE. ♠32♥AK32♦A32♣K432	4♥	4♥	4♥	4♣	4♣

Opener can raise responder's one-level response with only three-card support if opener has a ruffing value. Opener bids a four-card spade suit rather than raising with only three hearts. Over opener's raise, responder has two questions. Does opener have a minimum or maximum, and does opener have three-card support or four-card support? To solve these problems, responder has available four game tries; three-of-opener's-minor (auction 1), two notrump (auction 2), three-of-responder's-major (auction 3) and a new suit (auctions 4 & 5). Hands AA through EE represent the five types of hands opener might have to raise responder's one-heart response to two hearts. Hands AA, BB and CC are minimum, middle and maximum hands with three-card support. Hands DD and EE are minimum and maximum hands with four-card support. Under every box is opener's response to responder's game try. When opener raises with only three-card support, opener tries to make a descriptive bid denying four-card heart support. If opener raises with four-card support, opener always bids some number of hearts showing responder that he has four of them.

In auctions (1) and (2), responder's three clubs and two notrump are non-forcing game tries. Opener is allowed to pass with a minimum with three hearts. In auction (3), responder is showing at least five hearts and is asking opener to bid four hearts with a maximum. Auctions (4) and (5) are new-suit game or slam tries. If you have a choice use auction (4), not auction (5), since auction (4) allows opener to show where his values are.

A jump to three notrump by responder is choice of games. If opener has three-card support, opener passes three notrump. If opener has four-card support, opener can pass three notrump if he's 4-3-3-3.

Over help-suit game tries, which can be help-suit slam tries, opener bids four clubs, artificial, to show four-card support with slam going values as in auctions (4) and (5).

8.18 -- FIT JUMPS BY PASSED HAND.

Opener	(1)	Responder		Opener	(2)	Responder	
♠AJ32	♦AQ432	♠5	♦K765	♠A432	♦AQ32	♠5	♦K765
♥2	♣432	♥K8765	♣A65	♥432	♣32	♥K8765	♣A65
-		Pass		-		Pass	
1diamond		2hearts		1diamond		2hearts	
3diamonds		Pass		Pass			

Opener	(3)	Responder		Opener	(4)	Responder	
♠AK2	♦AQ32	♠QJ654	♦K765	♠AK32	♦AQ432	♠QJ654	♦K765
♥432	♣432	♥A65	♣5	♥2	♣432	♥A65	♣5
-		Pass		-		Pass	
1diamond		2spades		1diamond		2spades	
4spades		Pass		4hearts		4NT	
				5clubs		6spades	

A jump shift by a passed-hand shows a five or six-card suit, at least four-card support for opener's suit, and close to opening bid strength. If you don't have at least nine cards in the two suits, you shouldn't jump shift. Responder shows a six-card suit by rebidding it if given the opportunity. With a light opener, opener passes the jump shift with three-card support or signs-off in the opening-bid-suit. A jump to three-of-a-minor over one-of-a-major is not a fit jump since two-of-either-minor is Drury. Three-of-a-minor shows a six-card or longer suit and 8-11 HCPs, with most of the strength in the suit.

In examples (1) and (2), responder, who is a passed hand, shows at least five hearts, at least four diamonds and around ten points. In example (1), opener with a minimum opening bid without a heart fit, signs-off in three diamonds. In example (2), opener with a light opener and three-card heart support passes two hearts. In examples (3) and (4), responder shows at least five spades, at least four diamonds and around ten points. In example (3), opener with all of his honors in spades and diamonds jumps to four spades. Opener probably passes a one-spade response and the great game is missed. In example (4), opener, knowing that a slam is possible, jumps to four hearts, a splinter bid, showing a spade fit with heart shortness. Responder keycards in spades, finds three keycards and bids six spades.

8.19 -- JUMP-SHIFT REBID BY OPENER IS 100% GAME FORCING.

Opener	(1)		Responder	
♠32	♦AKQ32		♠654	♦4
♥32	♣AKQ2		♥KQJ654	♣J43

Opener	(2)		Responder	
♠32	♦AKQ32		♠QJ54	♦54
♥32	♣AKQ2		♥KQJ54	♣43

Opener (1)	Responder
1diamond	1heart
3clubs	3hearts
4hearts	Pass

Opener (2)	Responder
1diamond	1heart
3clubs	3spades
3NT	Pass

Opener	(3)		Responder	
♠32	♦AKQ32		♠KQJ4	♦54
♥32	♣AKQ2		♥QJT4	♣543

Opener	(4)		Responder	
♠32	♦AKQ32		♠KQJ4	♦J4
♥32	♣AKQ2		♥KQJ4	♣J43

Opener (3)	Responder
1diamond	1heart
3clubs	3NT
Pass	

Opener (4)	Responder
1diamond	1heart
3clubs	4NT
Pass	

A jump shift by opener is a commitment that he will not pass any non-game bid by responder. Responder passes short of game only if he doesn't have his first response. One diamond -- one-of-a-major -- three clubs is therefore forcing to three notrump, four-of-a-major or five-of-a-minor. If responder rebids his major, he shows a six-card suit or a five-card suit that can play opposite a doubleton. If responder bids the other major it's natural, and opener supports responder's first major with three-card support. If responder bids three notrump, responder really wants to play three notrump. If responder wants to show good support for one of opener's minors, responder raises to four clubs or jumps to four diamonds. Since opener holding a game-forcing diamond hand has to jump-shift into clubs to create a force, responder can't insist on clubs as the trump suit without at least five.

In example (1), responder rebids three hearts showing a six-card heart suit. Opener raises to four hearts with two-card heart support. In example (2), responder wants to play three notrump unless opener has three-card heart support. Responder bids three spades natural and opener bids three notrump. In example (3), responder bids three notrump which says he has no interest in any other strain. In example (4), responder jumps to four notrump, natural and invitational. To bid keycard responder has to set trumps first.

Opener	(5)	Responder		Opener	(6)	Responder	
♠2 ♦AK432		♠543 ♦5		♠2 ♦AK432		♠543 ♦5	
♥KJ2 ♣AK32		♥A6543 ♣QJ65		♥K2 ♣AK432		♥A6543 ♣QJ65	

Opener (5)	Responder	Opener (6)	Responder
1diamond	1heart	1diamond	1heart
3clubs	3diamonds	3clubs	3diamonds
3hearts	4hearts	4clubs	4hearts
Pass		4NT	5diamonds
		6clubs	Pass

Opener	(7)	Responder		Opener	(8)	Responder	
♠2 ♦AK432		♠543 ♦QJ65		♠2 ♦AK432		♠543 ♦Q5	
♥KJ2 ♣AK32		♥AQ43 ♣QJ		♥KJ2 ♣AK32		♥AQ43 ♣QJ54	

Opener (7)	Responder	Opener (8)	Responder
1diamond	1heart	1diamond	1heart
3clubs	4diamonds	3clubs	4clubs
4spades	4NT	4spades	4NT
5clubs	6diamonds	5clubs	6clubs

Responder bids three diamonds as a waiting bid unless he has something positive to say. Over three diamonds, opener bids three hearts with three-card heart support, bids three notrump with spades stopped, bids three spades to suggest playing three notrump if responder has help in spades, and bids four-of-a-minor otherwise.

In examples (5) and (6), responder has no clear bid over three clubs. Responder can't rebid his hearts because that shows a six-card suit. Responder can't raise clubs because he might belong in three notrump. Therefore, responder bids three diamonds, the waiting bid. In example (5), opener shows his three-card heart support and responder raises to four hearts. In example (6), opener rebids his five-card club suit. If responder doesn't want to play three notrump, opener with a stiff spade can afford to bid above three notrump. Over four clubs, responder first duty is to set trumps. Four diamonds sets diamonds as trumps. Any other bid suggests clubs as trumps. In example (6), responder bids four hearts, setting clubs as trumps. If responder wants to play in hearts, he rebids three hearts. Opener bids four notrump keycard for clubs and then bids six clubs. In example (7), responder jumps to four diamonds, setting diamonds as trumps. In example (8), responder bids four clubs, suggesting clubs as trumps. Opener with only three of the six keys needs responder to have at least two keys for slam to have play. Opener cuebids, and responder with two keys bids keycard.

8.20 -- TWO NOTRUMP JUMP REBID SHOWS 18-19 HCPS. THREE CLUBS CAN BE SIGN-OFF.

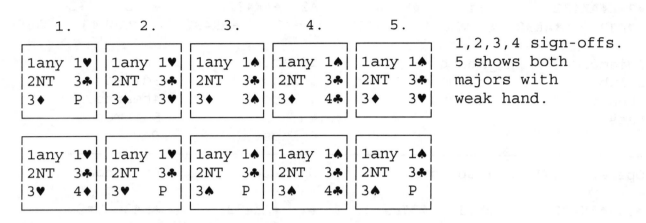

1.	2.	3.	4.	5.
1any 1♥	1any 1♥	1any 1♠	1any 1♠	1any 1♠
2NT 3♣	2NT 3♣	2NT 3♣	2NT 3♣	2NT 3♣
3♦ P	3♦ 3♥	3♦ 3♠	3♦ 4♣	3♦ 3♥

1,2,3,4 sign-offs. 5 shows both majors with weak hand.

1any 1♥	1any 1♥	1any 1♠	1any 1♠	1any 1♠
2NT 3♣	2NT 3♣	2NT 3♣	2NT 3♣	2NT 3♣
3♥ 4♦	3♥ P	3♠ P	3♠ 4♣	3♠ P

Opener's jump rebid of two notrump shows 18-19 HCPs. If responder has an unbalanced hand with fewer than six HCPs and wants to sign-off below game, responder starts with three clubs. Over three clubs, opener bids three diamonds with two of responder's major. With three-card support, opener bids three-of-responder's major. However, if opener has three spades and four hearts, opener bids three hearts over three clubs.

With a diamond sign-off, responder passes three diamonds, or bids four diamonds over three-of-a-major, auction (1). Responder rebids three-of-his-original-major to sign-off in his original major, auctions (2) and (3). Auction (4) is the way responder signs-off in four clubs. Auction (5) is the way responder shows a sign-off with five spades and four or more hearts. Opener bids three spades if his spades are equal to or longer than his hearts. Opener passes three hearts only if his hearts are longer than his spades. If responder has a weak hand with four spades and five hearts, he can't offer opener a choice of majors but signs-off in three hearts, auction (2).

Three clubs is not only used to start sign-off auctions, it is also used to start choice-of-game auctions. If responder has only one major and wants to offer opener a choice between three notrump and four-of-his-major, responder starts with three clubs. If opener bids three diamonds denying three-card support, responder signs-off in three notrump. If opener bids three-of-responder's major, responder can either sign-off in four-of-his-major or can bid three notrump offering opener choice of games. Opener passes three notrump with a 4-3-3-3 hand and bids four-of-responder's-major with 4-4-3-2 or 5-3-3-2 hands. Opener can show a slam-going hand by bidding four clubs, artificial.

156

Opener	(1)		Responder			Opener	(2)		Responder	
♠AK	♦A32		♠QJ5432	♦J4		♠AK	♦A32		♠QJ432	♦54
♥KJ32	♣K432		♥654	♣65		♥KJ32	♣K432		♥7654	♣65

Opener (1)	Responder	Opener (2)	Responder
1club	1spade	1club	1spade
2NT	3clubs	2NT	3clubs
3diamonds	3spades	3diamonds	3hearts

Opener	(3)		Responder			Opener	(4)		Responder	
♠KJ2	♦KJ2		♠A54	♦7654		♠KJ32	♦A32		♠A54	♦7654
♥AK2	♣KJ32		♥QJ543	♣5		♥AK	♣A432		♥QJ543	♣5

Opener (3)	Responder	Opener (4)	Responder
1club	1heart	1club	1heart
2NT	3clubs	2NT	3clubs
3hearts	4hearts	3diamonds	3NT

Opener	(5)		Responder			Opener	(6)		Responder	
♠AKJ	♦A32		♠76543	♦KQ4		♠AK	♦A32		♠76543	♦KQ4
♥JT2	♣AQT2		♥AQ4	♣J5		♥KJ32	♣A432		♥AQ4	♣J5

Opener (5)	Responder	Opener (6)	Responder
1club	1spade	1club	1spade
2NT	3clubs	2NT	3clubs
3spades	3NT	3diamonds	3NT

In examples (1) and (2), responder wants to play in three-of-a-major. In example (1), responder bids three spades, non-forcing, over opener's three-diamond call, and opener passes. Responder shows a weak hand with at least five spades. In example (2), responder, having already bid one spade, bids three hearts over opener's three-diamond call, showing a weak hand with at least five spades and at least four hearts. Opener passes three hearts.

In examples (3) through (6), responder wants to play in either four-of-his-major or three notrump. In example (3), opener bids three hearts showing three-card heart support, and responder, with an unbalanced hand, bids four hearts. In example (4), opener bids three diamonds, denying three-card support, so responder signs-off in three notrump. In example (5), opener bids three spades, showing three-card spade support, and responder bids three notrump, offering opener a choice between three notrump and four spades. Opener with a 4-3-3-3 hand, passes three notrump. In example (6), opener denies three-card spade support so responder signs-off in three notrump.

Opener	(7)	Responder		Opener	(8)	Responder	
♠K2 ♦AJ32		♠QJ43 ♦K4		♠K2 ♦AJ32		♠QJ43 ♦K4	
♥KJ2 ♣AK32		♥Q6543 ♣54		♥KJ2 ♣AK32		♥Q543 ♣654	

Opener	Responder	Opener	Responder
1diamond	1heart	1diamond	1heart
2NT	3clubs	2NT	3spades
3hearts	3spades	3NT	Pass
4hearts	Pass		

Opener	(9)	Responder		Opener	(10)	Responder	
♠K32 ♦AJ32		♠QJ65 ♦K4		♠K432 ♦AJ2		♠QJ65 ♦K4	
♥KJ2 ♣AK2		♥Q543 ♣543		♥KJ2 ♣AK2		♥Q543 ♣543	

Opener	Responder	Opener	Responder
1diamond	1heart	1diamond	1heart
2NT	3spades	2NT	3spades
3NT	Pass	4clubs	4spades

Responder, having responded one heart, needs to be able to show opener five hearts and four spades as well as four hearts and four spades. With five hearts and four spades, responder bids three clubs and then bids three spades, a game-forcing reverse. Over three spades showing four spades and five hearts, opener looks at his hearts and his spades. Opener raises spades with four spades, bids four hearts with three hearts, or bids three notrump with fewer than four spades and fewer than three hearts.

With 4-4 in the majors, responder bids three spades directly over two notrump. Over three spades, opener looks only at his spades. With four spades, opener bids four spades or bids four clubs, an artificial slam try. With fewer than four spades, opener bids three notrump. Hearts are never in the picture.

In examples (7) through (10), responder bids one heart and over opener's jump-rebid of two notrump, wants to show four spades. In example (7), responder bids three clubs and then bids three spades, a game-forcing reverse, showing four spades and five hearts. Opener with three-card heart support bids four hearts. In example (8), responder bids three spades directly, showing four spades and only four hearts. Opener bids three notrump. In examples (9) and (10), responder bids three spades directly showing 4-4 in the majors. Opener does not think about playing in hearts. In example (9), opener, holding three spades, bids three notrump. In example (10), opener bids four clubs, artificial, showing a good four-spade bid.

Opener	(11)	Responder		Opener	(12)	Responder	
♠K2	♦A32	♠QJ543	♦54	♠K2	♦A32	♠QJ543	♦54
♥KJ2	♣AK432	♥A543	♣65	♥KJ2	♣AK432	♥A6543	♣5

Opener (11)	Responder	Opener (12)	Responder
1club	1spade	1club	1spade
2NT	3hearts	2NT	3hearts
3spades	3NT	3spades	4hearts
Pass		Pass	

Opener	(13)	Responder		Opener	(14)	Responder	
♠K2	♦AK2	♠AQJ543	♦43	♠K2	♦KQJ	♠AQJ543	♦43
♥Q32	♣AK432	♥K54	♣65	♥QJ2	♣KQJ32	♥K54	♣65

Opener (13)	Responder	Opener (14)	Responder
1club	1spade	1club	1spade
2NT	3spades	2NT	3spades
4clubs	4NT	4spades	Pass
5clubs	6spades		

Any auction that doesn't start with three clubs is game forcing. If responder rebids his major he shows a six-card major. If responder bids one spade and then bids three hearts, responder shows at least five spades and at least four hearts. Opener bids three notrump with 2-2 in the majors. With four hearts, opener bids four hearts with a minimum and four clubs, artificial, with a slam try. With three spades, opener bids four spades with a minimum and four diamonds, artificial, with a slam try. With three hearts, opener bids three spades, waiting, allowing responder to show how many hearts and spades he has. If responder has six spades and four hearts, responder raises to four spades. If responder has five hearts, responder bids four hearts. If responder has five spades and only four hearts, responder bids three notrump.

In examples (11) and (12), responder bids three hearts showing a game-forcing hand with at least five spades and at least four hearts. Opener bids three spades, allowing responder to finish describing his hand. In example (11), responder bids three notrump showing 5-4 in the majors and opener passes. In example (12), responder bids four hearts, showing 5-5 in the majors, and opener passes. In examples (13) and (14), responder bids three spades, showing a game-forcing hand with at least six spades. In example (13), opener bids four clubs, artificial, showing a good hand for slam. Responder bids keycard and bids six spades. In example (14), opener raises to four spades denying slam values.

Opener (15)	Responder	Opener (16)	Responder
♠KQ2 ♦A32	♠A6543 ♦KQ4	♠KQ ♦A32	♠A6543 ♦KQ4
♥K32 ♣AK32	♥Q5 ♣Q54	♥K432 ♣AK32	♥Q5 ♣Q54

Opener (15)	Responder	Opener (16)	Responder
1club	1spade	1club	1spade
2NT	3diamonds	2NT	3diamonds
3spades	4spades	3NT	Pass
4NT	5diamonds		
6NT	Pass		

THREE DIAMONDS BY AN UNPASSED HAND IS AN ARTIFICIAL SLAM TRY. Responder uses three diamonds to explore for slam in his major or in either minor. Since responder can rebid his major to show at least six or can bid the other major with slam going hands as well as game-going hands, three diamonds denies holding a six-card major and denies holding four cards in the other major. Over three diamonds, opener first duty is to show three-card support for responder's major. If opener does not have three-card support, opener rebids a five-card minor by bidding the other major. Since three diamonds denies the other major, the other major becomes a surrogate for opener's minor. Otherwise, opener bids three notrump and waits for responder to make the next move.

By a passed hand, three diamonds is forcing attempting to find an eight-card major-suit fit. If opener has four of the other major, opener bids three-of-the-other-major. If opener does not have four of the other major but has three of responder's major, opener bids three-of-responder's-major. If opener does not have four of the other major and does not have three of responder's major, opener bids three notrump.

In examples (15) and (16), responder wants to make a slam try if opener has three spades or five clubs. In example (15), opener shows three-card spade support. Responder raises to four spades showing a slammish hand with five spades. If responder is interested only in game, he bids three clubs followed by three notrump instead. Opener bids keycard and bids six notrump when missing one keycard. In example (16), opener's three-notrump bid denies three spades and denies five clubs. Without a good fit, responder passes.

Opener	(17)	Responder		

♠KQ2 ◆A32   ♠A654 ◆K54
  ♥K32 ♣AK32   ♥A5 ♣Q654

Opener	Responder
1club	1spade
2NT	3diamonds
3spades	3NT
4NT	5spades
6clubs	Pass

Opener	(18)	Responder		

♠KQ2 ◆QJ2   ♠A654 ◆K54
  ♥QJ32 ♣AK2   ♥A5 ♣Q654

Opener	Responder
1club	1spade
2NT	3diamonds
3spades	3NT
Pass	

Opener	(19)	Responder		

♠KJ ◆A5432   ♠A543 ◆K6
  ♥K2 ♣AK32   ♥A3 ♣QJ654

Opener	Responder
1diamond	1spade
2NT	3diamonds
3hearts	4clubs
4diamonds	4hearts
4NT	5spades
5NT	6diamonds
7clubs	Pass

Opener	(20)	Responder		

♠KJ ◆A5432   ♠A432 ◆K76
  ♥K2 ♣AK32   ♥A3 ♣QJ54

Opener	Responder
1diamond	1spade
2NT	3diamonds
3hearts	4diamonds
4NT	5clubs
5hearts	6NT

In examples (17) and (18), responder bids three diamonds and follows with three notrump. Since responder did not raise spades, he must not be interested in playing a 5-3 spade fit and, therefore, must be mildly interested in playing six clubs. If responder is strongly interested in playing six clubs, responder bids four clubs over three spades. In example (17), opener has good controls as well as good clubs and bids four notrump RKC for clubs. Three notrump limited responder's hand so opener does not try for seven. In example (18), opener with a minimum and bad controls, passes three notrump.

In examples (19) and (20), opener bids three hearts, the diamond surrogate, showing a five-card diamond suit and fewer than three spades. In example (19), responder bids four clubs showing a club slam try. Opener, who has good controls as well as good clubs, cuebids and then bids keycard. Holding all the keycards, opener bids five notrump. Responder shows the king of diamonds and opener bids seven clubs. In example (20), responder bids four diamonds setting diamonds as trumps. Opener bids RKC and then asks for the queen. Responder bids six notrump denying the queen but showing extra strength. If you're going to lose only one trick, you might as well lose it in six notrump.

8.21 -- THREE NOTRUMP JUMP REBID SHOWS A LONG MINOR SUIT.

Opener	(1)	Responder		Opener	(2)	Responder	
♠2	♦AKJ5432	♠KJ6543	♦Q	♠2	♦AKJ5432	♠AJ543	♦Q
♥KQ2	♣A2	♥A43	♣543	♥KQ2	♣A2	♥A543	♣KQ3

Opener (1)	Responder	Opener (2)	Responder
1diamond	1spade	1diamond	1spade
3NT	Pass	3NT	4diamonds
		4NT	5spades
		5NT	6clubs
		7NT	Pass

After one-of-a-minor -- one-of-a-suit, opener's jump to three notrump shows a solid or semi-solid seven-card or longer minor with the unbid suits at least partially stopped. Opener expects to make three notrump with very little help from responder. Since opener has the unbid suits at least partially stopped, opener usually has shortness in responder's suit. Opener can have as little as ♠2♥J32♦A2♣AKQ5432 to open one club and jump to three notrump after a one-spade response. Opening one-of-a-minor and jumping to three-of-the-same-minor shows a six-card suit with 16-18 HCPs. Opener needs help from responder to make game and help getting to the best game. If opener has a suit oriented hand or does not have one of the unbid suits at least partially stopped, opener can jump shift to three clubs after opening one diamond or reverse into diamonds after opening one club. After a two-level response, jumping to three notrump is different and shows 15-17 HCPs.

In examples (1) and (2), opener jumps to three notrump showing a good hand with a long diamond suit and the unbid suits at least partially stopped. Opener could be weaker. In example (1), responder passes three notrump, since opener is very likely short in spades. In example (2), responder bids four diamonds, setting diamonds as trumps and showing slam values. Opener bids four notrump and finds responder with two keycards and the diamond queen. Opener bids five notrump and finds responder with the club king, which is enough to bid seven notrump.

CHAPTER 9 - TWO-CLUB OPENER

9.1 -- STRONG AND ARTIFICIAL.

If opener is balanced, two clubs shows at least 22 HCPs. Most two-club openers are balanced or semi-balanced hands. If opener has a spade suit, opener needs only eight and a half tricks plus at least two defensive tricks. If opener has a heart suit, opener needs at least nine tricks. If opener has a minor one or two-suiter, opener needs at least nine tricks if he can play three notrump. With an unbalanced minor one or two-suiter, opener needs at least ten tricks. With a spade one-suiter, opener strives to open two clubs. Opening two clubs and being able to rebid two spades keeps the auction low and allows responder to show where his values are. Opener tries to avoid opening two clubs with two-suited hands. Opener may never get a chance to show his second suit, especially if there's competition. Playing control responses, opener tries to avoid opening two clubs with a void. If opener has game in hand with more than 15 HCPs, even with a void or two-suiter, opener should open two clubs to avoid being passed out at the one-level. The lower the rank of the opening bid and the fewer the high-card points, the greater the chance that either partner will keep the auction open or the opponents will overcall or balance.

	Two-club openers	One-level openers	Four-level openers
1.	♠AKJT432♥AK32♦3♣2	♠AKJT432♥AK2♦432♣-	♠AKQJ432♥432♦432♣-
2.	♠AKQJ432♥A432♦2♣2	♠AKQJ432♥QJ32♦2♣2	♠AKQJT65432♥2♦2♣2
3.	♠AKQJ2♥AK432♦A2♣2	♠AK432♥AK432♦32♣2	
4.	♠AK2♥AKQJ432♦32♣	♠A32♥AKQJ432♦32♣2	♠432♥AKQJ432♦32♣2
5.	♠2♥2♦AKQJ432♣AKQJ	♠2♥2♦AKQJ4♣AKQJ32	
6.	♠AKQJ32♥AKQJ32♦2♣-	♠AK5432♥AK5432♦2♣-	
7.	♠AKQ432♥2♦AKQ432♣-	♠AK5432♥2♦AK5432♣-	

9.2 -- CONTROL RESPONSES.

Opener	(1)		Responder			Opener	(2)		Responder	
♠AKQJ432	♦AK		♠5	♦5432		♠AKQJ432	♦AK		♠5	♦QJ2
	♥AQ2	♣2	♥K543	♣A543			♥AKQ	♣2	♥J76543	♣543

Opener		Responder		Opener		Responder
2clubs		2spades		2clubs		2diamonds
7NT		Pass		6spades		Pass

Opener	(3)		Responder			Opener	(4)		Responder	
♠AKQJ432	♦2		♠-	♦QJ3		♠AKQJ432	♦2		♠-	♦QJ3
	♥2	♣AKQJ	♥AKQ876543	♣2			♥2	♣AKQJ	♥KQJ876543	♣2

Opener		Responder		Opener		Responder
2clubs		2NT		2clubs		2diamonds
6spades		Pass		4spades		Pass

An ace is two controls and a king is one control. Two diamonds shows zero or one control, no aces and at most one king. Two hearts shows two controls, one ace or two kings. Two spades shows three controls other than an ace-king in the same suit. Two notrump shows an ace-king in the same suit. Three clubs shows four controls. Three diamonds shows five or more controls. Three hearts shows a sound 6-3-2-2 weak-two in spades, and three spades shows a sound weak-two in hearts. All responses higher than two diamonds are game forcing.

If overcaller bids anything below two notrump, responder uses DOPI. Responder doubles or redoubles with zero controls, passes with one, bids the next suit with two, etc.[5]

In example (1), responder's two spades shows three controls but not an ace-king in the same suit. Opener bids seven notrump, knowing that responder must have the ace of clubs and the king of hearts. In example (2), opener knows that the ace of clubs is missing so opener jumps directly to six spades. In example (3), opener knows that responder has either the AK of diamonds or the AK of hearts. Opener jumps to six spades ending the auction. In example (4), opener knows from responder's two-diamond response that two aces are missing. Opener jumps to four spades ending the auction.

---

[5] If you do not like control responses, I recommend playing two diamonds as negative, not waiting. Responder bids two notrump with eight or more HCPs and a balanced hand. Responder bids any five-card suit holding seven or more points.

What should your thought process be holding ♠AQJT32♥AKQ2♦A2♣2 if you open two clubs and responder makes various control responses?

Two diamonds showing zero or one controls. Responder can have at most one king so you'll always be off the ace of clubs. Unless responder has at least four hearts and the king of spades, slam is very unlikely. Rebid two spades and then bid hearts. Let responder take control if he has a freak.

Two hearts showing two controls. If responder has the ace of clubs, six spades will be on a spade and possible diamond finesse. If responder has four or five hearts, six hearts will be at worst on a spade finesse. If responder has two kings instead of one ace, at least one of them will be working. Six spades will not be a good contract unless partner holds both the diamond king and the spade king. Six hearts will be a good contract opposite the king of spades. Rebid two spades and then bid hearts. If responder bids or supports hearts, bid a slam. If responder raises spades, cuebid four clubs. If responder cuebids four diamonds over four clubs, bid keycard. Otherwise sign-off in four spades.

Two spades showing either the three missing kings or the ace of clubs and either the spade king or diamond king. Six spades should be cold. Unless responder freely bids hearts, seven hearts will be impossible to reach. Rebid three spades and then bid four hearts.

Two notrump showing the ace-king of clubs. Six spades or six hearts should be cold. Rebid three spades followed by six spades unless responder bids hearts.

Three clubs showing the ace of clubs and two of the three missing kings. If responder has the king of spades, seven spades or seven notrump should be cold. If responder is missing the king of spades, six notrump should be cold. Bid spades, followed by RKC. If responder shows two keycards, bid seven notrump.

Three diamonds showing the ace of clubs and the three missing kings. Bid seven notrump.

9.3 -- CHEAPER MINOR IS SECOND NEGATIVE.

Opener	(1)		Responder		Opener	(2)		Responder	
♠AKQJ32	♦AK2		♠7654	♦543	♠AKQJ32	♦AK2		♠7654	♦543
	♥A	♣JT2	♥432	♣543		♥A	♣JT2	♥QJ2	♣Q43

Opener (1)	Responder	Opener (2)	Responder
2clubs	2diamonds	2clubs	2diamonds
2spades	3clubs	2spades	4spades
3spades	Pass	Pass	

Opener	(3)		Responder		Opener	(4)		Responder	
♠AKQJ32	♦AK2		♠7654	♦QJ43	♠AKQJ32	♦AK2		♠54	♦QJ43
	♥A	♣JT2	♥QJ32	♣3		♥A	♣JT2	♥QJ32	♣KQ3

Opener (3)	Responder	Opener (4)	Responder
2clubs	2diamonds	2clubs	2diamonds
2spades	4clubs	2spades	2NT
6spades	Pass	3spades	4clubs
		6spades	Pass

Over opener's rebid, responder bids his cheaper minor, an artificial second negative, to show a hand bad enough to want to play in a partscore opposite an eight-and-a-half trick hand. If opener rebids his suit after the second negative, responder is allowed to pass. After two clubs -- two diamonds -- three clubs, three diamonds is the second negative. Since we're playing Kokish (see section 9.4), two clubs -- two diamonds -- three hearts is forcing while two clubs -- two diamonds -- two hearts -- two spades -- three hearts, is passable. If responder raises opener's major directly to game, he shows four trumps but denies an ace, king, singleton or void. However, responder with ♠J432♥432♦432♣432 bids three clubs, second negative, first and then bids three spades.

Examples (1) through (4) represent responder's wide strength range in response to opener's two-spade rebid after showing zero or one control. In example (1), responder bids three clubs, second negative. Opener, with only nine tricks, rebids three spades, and responder passes. In example (2), responder has some values and jumps to four spades, showing four trumps with some queens and jacks. In example (3), responder splinters over two spades showing spade support with club shortness. Opener jumps to six spades. In example (4), responder bids two notrump, showing values. Responder cuebids his club king and opener bids six spades.

9.4 -- KOKISH AFTER TWO CLUBS - TWO DIAMONDS.

Opener	(1)	Responder		Opener	(2)	Responder	
♠AKQ7	♦AQJ	♠65432	♦32	♠A	♦A4	♠65432	♦32
♥AK5	♣A54	♥J432	♣32	♥AKQ765	♣AK54	♥J432	♣32

Opener (1)	Responder	Opener (2)	Responder
2clubs	2diamonds	2clubs	2diamonds
2hearts	2spades	2hearts	2spades
2NT	3clubs	3clubs	4hearts
3spades	4spades	5clubs	6hearts

Opener	(3)	Responder		Opener	(4)	Responder	
♠A7	♦AKQJ765	♠65432	♦432	♠A7	♦A5	♠65432	♦432
♥A5	♣K5	♥32	♣432	♥AKQ765	♣K65	♥32	♣432

Opener (3)	Responder	Opener (4)	Responder
2clubs	2diamonds	2clubs	2diamonds
3NT	Pass	2hearts	2spades
		3hearts	Pass

After two clubs -- two diamonds, opener bids two hearts, Kokish, forcing responder to bid two spades. If opener then rebids two notrump, opener shows a game-forcing balanced hand with at least 24 HCPs. Opener can have 36 HCPs. Responder treats the two-notrump rebid as a two-notrump opener and uses Chapter Three responses. If opener bids anything other than two notrump, it is natural and the two-heart rebid becomes natural also.

In examples (1) and (2), opener bids two hearts, showing either a balanced monster or an unbalanced heart hand. Responder bids two spades asking. In example (1), opener rebids two notrump, showing a balanced monster. Responder bids three clubs, Stayman, and raises three spades to four spades. If opener bids three diamonds denying a four-card major, responder bids three hearts, Smolen, showing exactly four hearts and five or more spades. In example (2), over responder's two-spade ask, opener rebids three clubs, showing clubs and also showing that two hearts was natural. Responder jumps to four hearts, showing four hearts with no outside aces, kings, singletons or voids. Opener tries again with five clubs, hoping for third-round control, and responder, knowing that his doubleton is working, jumps to six hearts. In example (3), opener bids three notrump, which shows a long minor, not 25-27 HCPs. Unless responder has his own self-sufficient suit, he is expected to pass. In example (4), opener with only eight sure tricks gives responder a chance to stop short of game.

9.5 -- AFTER ALL TWO NOTRUMP REBIDS BY OPENER, PLAY AS TWO NOTRUMP OPENER.

After two clubs -- two any -- two notrump or two clubs -- two diamonds -- two hearts -- two spades -- two notrump, if playing Kokish, treat the two-notrump rebid as a two-notrump opener and use your two-notrump opening system. After any response higher than two diamonds, a two-notrump rebid is forcing and unlimited. Opener can have up to 33 HCPs to rebid two notrump after a positive response.

9.6 -- AFTER TWO CLUBS - TWO NOTRUMP, THREE CLUBS = BALANCED HAND AND ASKS FOR SUITS UP THE LINE.

Opener (1)	Responder	Opener (2)	Responder
♠QJ65 ♦A54	♠AK432 ♦32	♠QJ65 ♦A54	♠AK2 ♦32
♥AK ♣AKQ6	♥432 ♣432	♥AK ♣AKQ6	♥5432 ♣5432
2clubs	2NT	2clubs	2NT
3clubs	3spades	3clubs	3diamonds
6spades	Pass	3spades	4clubs
		6clubs	Pass

When responder responds two notrump to two clubs, it takes away opener's two-notrump rebid. Opener bids three clubs, which takes the place of the two-notrump rebid, and starts Stayman-like auctions. Responder bids a five-card suit if he has one. With no five-card suits, responder bids three diamonds. Four-card suits follow up the line.

In examples (1) and (2), responder bids two notrump showing an AK in the same suit, and opener bids three clubs, asking responder to describe his hand. In example (1), responder bids three spades showing a five-card suit headed by the AK, and opener raises to six spades. Opener knows that responder has an AK in the same suit and that it can only be in spades. In example (2), responder bids three diamonds denying a five-card suit. Opener bids three spades showing four spades and denying four hearts. Responder bids four clubs, and opener raises to slam.

168

CHAPTER 10 - TWO-DIAMOND OPENER

10.1 -- FLANNERY.

Opening two diamonds shows four spades, five hearts and 11-15 HCPs. Opener can also have four spades and six hearts or a minimum hand with five spades and six hearts. Opener should not count Qx, Jx or stiff king in order to get to 11 HCPs. In third or fourth seat, opener should have enough strength, at least 13 HCPs if 4-5-2-2, so that if responder makes an invitational bid, at least nine tricks will be available. With a light opener opposite a passed hand, open one heart. Drury will keep you at the two-level.

10.2 -- TWO NOTRUMP RESPONSE, INVITATIONAL OR BETTER.

Opener (1)		Responder		Opener (2)		Responder	
♠A876	♦K4	♠5432	♦A32	♠A876	♦KQ4	♠5432	♦A32
♥A7654	♣54	♥KQ32	♣32	♥A7654	♣4	♥KQ32	♣32

Opener (1)	Responder	Opener (2)	Responder
2diamonds	2NT	2diamonds	2NT
3hearts	Pass	3diamonds	3hearts
		4hearts	Pass

Responder bids two notrump, invitational or better, asking opener to describe his hand. Opener bids three clubs with three or four clubs. I have never seen jumping to four clubs with four spades, five hearts and four clubs work out well. Opener bids three diamonds with three or four diamonds. Opener bids three hearts with 2-2 in the minors and a minimum two-diamond opener. Opener bids three spades, forcing, with four spades and six hearts. Opener bids three notrump with 2-2 in the minors and a maximum two-diamond opener. Opener bids four hearts with five spades and six hearts. If opener bids three-of-a-minor, then three-of-a-major by responder is invitational. Opener should realize that his minor shortness has not made responder's hand any better.

In example (1), opener bids three hearts, showing a minimum hand with 2-2 in the minors. Responder passes three hearts. Responder would have bid game if opener had rebid three clubs. In example (2), responder wants opener to bid game with a maximum. Over responder's two-notrump ask, opener shows club shortness with his three-diamond bid. Responder bids three hearts, invitational, setting hearts as trumps. Holding two clubs opposite shortness is not a great fit. Opener, with a maximum, bids game.

10.3 -- THREE DIAMONDS IS A SLAM TRY.

Opener	(1)	Responder		Opener	(2)	Responder	
♠AQJ2	♦K32	♠K543	♦54	♠AQJ2	♦A32	♠K543	♦54
♥J5432	♣2	♥KQ6	♣AKQJ	♥J5432	♣2	♥KQ6	♣AKQJ

Opener	Responder	Opener	Responder
2diamonds	3diamonds	2diamonds	3diamonds
3hearts	3spades	3hearts	3spades
4spades	Pass	4diamonds	4hearts
		4NT	5hearts
		6spades	Pass

Opener	(3)	Responder		Opener	(4)	Responder	
♠AQ32	♦K32	♠K54	♦Q4	♠AQ32	♦A32	♠K54	♦Q4
♥Q5432	♣2	♥KJ76	♣AQJ3	♥A5432	♣2	♥KJ76	♣AQJ3

Opener	Responder	Opener	Responder
2diamonds	3diamonds	2diamonds	3diamonds
3hearts	4hearts	3hearts	4hearts
Pass		4NT	5hearts
		6hearts	Pass

Three diamonds is a slam try and forces opener to bid three hearts. Over three hearts, responder bids three spades, setting spades as trumps. Any bid by responder other than three spades is a cuebid and sets hearts as trumps. Over three hearts, three notrump by responder is a spade cuebid in support of hearts, and four notrump is RKC for hearts. If responder bids three diamonds and then bids four of a major, he is making a very mild slam try.

In examples (1) and (2), responder bids three diamonds, forcing opener to bid three hearts. Responder bids three spades, a slam try, with spades as the trump suit. In example (1), when opener can't cuebid a red ace, responder settles for game. In example (2), opener cuebids the diamond ace. Over four diamonds, responder, needing a little extra, bids four hearts, the Last Train. If responder needs a lot of extras, he bids four spades. Remember, responder has already made a slam try when he bid three diamonds. Opener with good trumps bids keycard for spades, and bids six spades. In examples (3) and (4), responder raises three hearts to four hearts to show a very mild heart slam try. In example (3), opener with a minimum passes four hearts. In example (4), opener with a super maximum bids keycard and bids six hearts.

Opener	(5)	Responder		Opener	(6)	Responder	
♠AQJ2	♦K32	♠K43	♦54	♠AQJ2	♦A32	♠K43	♦54
♥J5432	♣2	♥KQ76	♣AKQJ	♥A5432	♣2	♥KQ76	♣AKQJ

Opener (5)	Responder	Opener (6)	Responder
2diamonds	3diamonds	2diamonds	3diamonds
3hearts	4clubs	3hearts	4clubs
4hearts	Pass	4spades	4NT
		5clubs	5spades
		6spades	7NT

In examples (5) and (6), responder cuebids four clubs, setting hearts as trumps. In example (5), opener, with a minimum, signs-off in four hearts. Since opener does not have enough strength to at least make a try with four diamonds, responder passes four hearts. Four diamonds is not a slam commitment, just a slam try. Opener with a little extra, can bid four diamonds, and then pass four hearts. In example (6), opener, who wants to tell rather then ask, cuebids four spades. Responder bids RKC and finds opener with three keycards. With all six keys present, responder bids five spades asking for third-round spade control. Four clubs set hearts as trumps, so five spades is not a sign-off. Opener bids six spades, forcing to seven hearts, showing third and fourth-round control. With only third-round control, opener bids seven hearts. Responder counts 14 tricks and bids seven notrump.

Why does five spades by responder ask opener to bid seven with third-round spade control? All bids have specific meanings over five clubs. Five diamonds asks for the heart queen. Five hearts is a sign-off if opener has zero keycards and forcing if opener has three keycards. Five notrump shows all the keycards and asks for specific kings. Therefore, all other bids below slam are grand slam tries showing all the keycards and asking opener to bid seven with third-round control in that suit. Six clubs over five clubs is a grand slam try showing AK432 of clubs. Over six clubs, opener is supposed to sign-off in six hearts with three small clubs, bid seven hearts with a doubleton club and raise to seven clubs with the queen of clubs knowing that the clubs will run in notrump.

10.4 -- OVER DOUBLE, PASS SHOWS DIAMONDS AND REDOUBLE IS CHOICE OF MAJORS.

Opener	(1)	Responder		Opener	(2)	Responder	
♠8765	♦K5	♠432	♦A432	♠AKJT	♦K5	♠432	♦A432
♥AKJT9	♣65	♥32	♣J432	♥87654	♣65	♥32	♣J432

Open	Over	Resp	Advnc	Open	Over	Resp	Advnc
2♦	Dbl	Rdbl	Pass	2♦	Dbl	Rdbl	Pass
2♥	Pass	Pass	Pass	2♠	Pass	Pass	Pass

Opener	(3)	Responder		Opener	(4)	Responder	
♠7654	♦K5	♠32	♦JT9432	♠7654	♦K5	♠32	♦JT98
♥AKJT9	♣65	♥2	♣J432	♥AKJT9	♣65	♥2	♣JT9432

Open	Over	Resp	Advnc	Open	Over	Resp	Advnc
2♦	Dbl	Pass	Pass	2♦	Dbl	3♣	Pass
Pass				Pass			

A popular interpretation of the double of two diamonds is to show a strong balanced hand, saying nothing about diamonds. If responder has three hearts or four spades, responder has no problem over two-diamonds doubled. How does responder with two hearts and three spades play in opener's stronger major? Responder redoubles two-diamonds doubled requesting opener to bid his better major. How does responder with five or six diamonds play in two-diamonds doubled? Responder passes two-diamonds doubled to suggest playing two-diamonds doubled. If the best result responder can get is playing two-diamonds doubled taking six tricks, why does responder have to be minus 600 in two-diamonds redoubled when responder can be minus 300 in two-diamonds doubled? If responder has a good hand, responder ignores the double and bids two notrump as a game try or three diamonds as a slam try. If responder has four-card heart support or five-card spade support with a weak hand, responder jumps to the three-level.

In examples (1) and (2), responder wants to play in opener's better major. Responder redoubles to get opener to choose. In example (1), opener chooses hearts. In example (2), opener chooses spades. In example (3), responder wants to play in diamonds. Responder passes two-diamonds doubled, indicating willingness to play in diamonds. In example (4), responder bids three clubs to play.

10.5 -- THREE CLUBS NON-FORCING WITH OR WITHOUT COMPETITION.

Responder bids three clubs to play in three clubs. If responder wants to play in diamonds, he passes two diamonds.

10.6 -- THREE-OF-A-MAJOR IS NON-INVITATIONAL AND JUST PROMISES NINE-CARD FIT.

Opener	(1)	Responder		Opener	(2)	Responder	
♠AQJ2	♦32	♠K43	♦54	♠AQJ2	♦A32	♠K43	♦54
♥A5432	♣32	♥K876	♣7654	♥A5432	♣2	♥K876	♣7654
2diamonds		3hearts		2diamonds		3hearts	
Pass				4hearts		Pass	

Opener	(3)	Responder		Opener	(4)	Responder	
♠AQJ2	♦32	♠K6543	♦K54	♠AQJ2	♦A32	♠K6543	♦K54
♥A5432	♣32	♥76	♣654	♥A5432	♣2	♥76	♣654
2diamonds		3spades		2diamonds		3spades	
Pass				4spades		Pass	

A jump to three spades by responder shows five-card spade support, and a jump to three hearts shows four-card heart support, both with around six points. This follows the Law of Total Tricks and gets you directly to the three-level when holding a nine-card fit. If responder holds queens and jacks in the minors he doesn't have to bid three-of-a-major just because he has a nine-card fit. Opener bids game if all he needs are trumps and one outside honor.

In examples (1) and (2), responder jumps to three hearts showing four hearts and around six points. In example (1), opener with a minimum, passes three hearts. If three hearts goes down, the opponents should make three-of-a-minor. In example (2), opener raises to four hearts. If responder's hearts solidify opener's hearts, four hearts from opener's viewpoint will be at worst on a spade finesse. In examples (3) and (4), responder jumps to three spades showing five spades and around six points. In example (3), opener, with a minimum, passes three spades. If three spades goes down, the opponents should make three-of-a-minor. In example (4), opener raises to four spades. From opener's viewpoint, he has good chances to take ten tricks, especially if responder happens to be short in hearts.

173

10.7 -- JUMP TO FOUR-OF-A-MINOR IS RKC IN CORRESPONDING MAJOR.

Opener	(1)	Responder		Opener	(2)	Responder	
♠5432	♦K2	♠A6	♦A3	♠5432	♦K2	♠QJT9	♦AQJ
♥AKJT9	♣32	♥Q432	♣AKQJT	♥AKJT9	♣32	♥2	♣AKQJT

2diamonds	4clubs	
4spades	5clubs	
5diamonds	7NT	

2diamonds	4diamonds
4spades	Pass

Opener	(3)	Responder		Opener	(4)	Responder	
♠Q432	♦2	♠AK	♦43	♠Q432	♦2	♠KJT9	♦543
♥AKQJ9	♣432	♥5432	♣AKQJT	♥AKQJ9	♣432	♥2	♣AKQJT

2diamonds	2NT
3clubs	4clubs
4hearts	4NT
5spades	6hearts

2diamonds	2NT
3clubs	4diamonds
4spades	Pass

A jump to four clubs is RKC for hearts and a jump to four diamonds is RKC for spades. In competition, however, a jump to four-of-a-minor is a transfer to the corresponding major. Four clubs transfers to four hearts and four diamonds transfers to four spades. Two notrump followed by four clubs is a heart slam try and two notrump followed by four diamonds is a spade slam try.

In example (1), responder bids four clubs, RKC for hearts. Opener answers four spades, showing two keycards without the queen. Responder bids five clubs asking for specific kings. When opener shows the diamond king, responder counts 13 tricks and bids seven notrump. In example (2), responder bids four diamonds, RKC for spades. When opener shows only one keycard, responder knows that two keycards are missing and passes four spades.

In examples (3) and (4), responder bids two notrump asking opener to describe his hand. When opener shows a singleton diamond, responder has thoughts of slam. In example (3), opener bids four clubs setting hearts as trumps and then bids four notrump keycard for hearts. Opener shows two keycards and the heart queen. Responder bids six hearts. In example (4), responder bids four diamonds setting spades as trumps. Opener with a minimum and bad trumps signs-off in four spades and responder passes.

174

10.8 -- ONE HEART - ONE SPADE DOES NOT PROMISE FIVE, BUT OPENER CAN RAISE FREELY WITH ONLY THREE SPADES.

Opener	(1)	Responder		Opener	(2)	Responder	
♠K2 ♦K32		♠AQ54 ♦Q654		♠K32 ♦K32		♠AQ54 ♦Q654	
♥QJT32 ♣K32		♥4 ♣Q654		♥QJT32 ♣K2		♥4 ♣Q654	
1heart		1spade		1heart		1spade	
1NT		Pass		2spades		Pass	

Even when playing Flannery, it is often correct to bid a four-card spade suit over opener's one-heart bid. Responding one spade allows opener to rebid one notrump with a balanced hand, thus making opener's two-of-a-minor rebid show four. Hands with 4-1-4-4 distribution containing fewer than 11 points are good candidates for a one-spade response in a four-card suit. Opener raises freely with three-card support, playing responder for five. Responder knows that he's in a 4-3 fit.

In examples (1) and (2), responder bids one spade to avoid playing a 4-3 minor-suit fit. If opener bids two-of-a-minor over one spade, it shows at least four. In example (1), opener rebids one notrump and the 4-3 club fit is avoided. In example (2), two spades is the same 4-3 fit as two diamonds would have been had responder bid one notrump forcing.

Responder, holding three or more hearts, does not bid one spade unless he has a self-sufficient spade suit. Bidding one spade and then later supporting hearts lets opener believe that responder has only two-card heart support. The auction one heart -- one spade -- two clubs -- two hearts, is a misfit auction. Holding three or more hearts forget the spade suit.

After one heart -- one spade, opener with a 19-point hand with five hearts and four spades can jump to four spades with 4-5-2-2. If opener has an unbalanced hand with five or more hearts and four spades, opener can show his strength and shortness by jumping to four-of-his-short-suit. However, if opener has a game-forcing hand with only three spades, jumping to four spades or four-of-a-minor can be a disaster if responder has only four spades. Since opener can't have a natural jump to three notrump over a one-spade response, opener's jump to three notrump shows a game-forcing three-card spade raise. Responder with only four spades passes three notrump.

175

10.9 -- DEFENSE OVER OPPONENT'S FLANNERY.

Overcaller (1)		Advancer		Overcaller (2)		Advancer	
♠AQ2	♦KJT2	♠JT3	♦Q43	♠AQ2	♦KJT2	♠JT3	♦Q3
♥AQ2	♣J32	♥JT3	♣A654	♥AQ2	♣J32	♥JT3	♣AQT54

Open	Over	Resp	Advnc	Open	Over	Resp	Advnc
2♦	Dbl	2♥	Dbl	2♦	Dbl	2♥	3♥
Pass	Pass	Pass		3NT	Pass	Pass	Pass

Overcaller (3)		Advancer		Overcaller (4)		Advancer	
♠A432	♦AK32	♠8765	♦5	♠A2	♦AK432	♠8765	♦5
♥2	♣KQ32	♥6543	♣AJ65	♥2	♣KQ432	♥6543	♣AJ65

Open	Over	Resp	Advnc	Open	Over	Resp	Advnc
2♦	2♥	Pass	2♠	2♦	2NT	Pass	3♣
Pass	Pass	Pass		Pass	4♣	Pass	5♣

Double shows a balanced hand with 15 or more HCPs and at least one stopper in each major. Two hearts is takeout for clubs, diamonds and spades. Two spades is natural and non-forcing. Two notrump shows both minors. Three-of-either-minor is natural and non-forcing. A jump to three hearts asks advancer to bid three notrump with a heart stopper and shows a solid minor. A jump to three spades is natural and shows more offensive strength than a simple two-spade overcall.

After double of two diamonds, advancer's double of responder's preference is for penalties. Advancer assumes that overcaller has at least three cards in each major. Therefore advancer doubles with three-card holdings on hands suitable for defense, knowing the opponents are at best in a seven-card fit. With a hand suitable for offense, such as one with a long minor, advancer bids three notrump or cuebids three hearts asking overcaller to bid three notrump. Two notrump by advancer is choice of minors.

In example (1), advancer holding three hearts and a balanced hand doubles two hearts for penalties. In example (2), advancer with a five-card club suit bids three hearts, leading to three notrump. In example (3), overcaller bids two hearts, takeout for three suits. Advancer bids his four-card spade suit. In example (4), overcaller bids two notrump showing both minors. Advancer bids his four-card club suit.

176

CHAPTER 11 - WEAK-TWO MAJOR OPENER

11.1 -- 5-11 HCPS.

Constructive	Semi-constructive	Destructive
♠AKJT32♥32♦32♣432	♠AJ5432♥32♦32♣432	♠AJT32♥32♦32♣5432
♠AJT432♥Q432♦2♣32	♠KJ5432♥32♦32♣432	♠KQJ32♥32♦32♣5432
♠AQT932♥K2♦32♣432	♠AQ5432♥32♦32♣432	♠AQJ32♥32♦32♣5432
♠KJT432♥A432♦2♣32	♠KJT432♥32♦32♣432	♠KJT32♥32♦32♣J432
♠QJT432♥K2♦32♣Q32	♠QJT432♥5432♦2♣32	♠QJT32♥Q2♦32♣5432
♠KQJT98♥K2♦32♣432	♠AKJT9♥32♦5432♣32	♠KQT92♥32♦32♣5432

You and your partner have to decide whether your weak two-bids are constructive, semi-constructive or destructive. Constructive means that you have two of the top three or three of the top five honors, a six-card suit and at least seven HCPs. Semi-constructive means that you are 95% to have a six-card suit. If you happen to have a five-card suit, you are non-vulnerable and the suit is very strong. Destructive means that non-vulnerable you are equally likely to have a five-card suit as well as a six-card suit. If you open a five-card weak-two, you must have at least five HCPs. If you open a six-card weak-two, you can have as little as three HCPs. A six-card suit headed by the QJT looks like a semi-constructive weak-two bid.

The more weak-two bids I open, the more pressure I put on my opponents. I like my two bids to show five or six-card suits non-vulnerable, and usually six-card suits vulnerable. I like my suits to have more values in the suit than outside. I don't like opening a weak two-bid with 6-5 or 5-5 distribution. It doesn't bother me to open a weak-two with an outside four-card major. Holding only five cards, I like the suit to be a lead director. KQJ32 of spades and out is a perfect five-card weak-two. You want partner to lead a spade and you want to disrupt the opponents. You would be worried that partner might have ♠Axx if you didn't open two spades with KQJxx and the auction went one notrump -- pass -- three notrump. In third seat, even constructive bidders can be more flexible; however, if it looks like an opening bid, open at the one-level.

Above are examples of constructive, semi-constructive and destructive weak two-spade openers. If you're playing destructive weak-two bids, partner expects you to have at least a sound semi-constructive weak-two bid vulnerable.

11.2 -- TWO NOTRUMP IS MODIFIED OGUST FOR FIVE-CARD WEAK-TWOS.

Opener	(1)	Responder		Opener	(2)	Responder
♠KJT432 ♦32		♠Q876 ♦KQJ4		♠AK5432 ♦32		♠Q876 ♦KQJ4
♥32 ♣432		♥AK4 ♣65		♥32 ♣432		♥AK4 ♣65

Opener	Responder		Opener	Responder
2spades	2NT		2spades	2NT
3hearts	3spades		3spades	4spades
Pass			Pass	

Opener	(3)	Responder		Opener	(4)	Responder
♠KJT32 ♦432		♠Q654 ♦KQJ5		♠AKJ32 ♦32		♠Q654 ♦KQJ5
♥32 ♣J32		♥AK4 ♣76		♥32 ♣5432		♥AK4 ♣76

Opener	Responder		Opener	Responder
2spades	2NT		2spades	2NT
3clubs	3spades		3diamonds	4spades

If opener can have a five-card suit, two notrump by responder is Modified Ogust and asks opener to describe his hand. Opener bids three clubs to show a five-card suit and a minimum. Opener bids three diamonds to show a five-card suit and a maximum. Opener bids three hearts to show a six-card suit and a minimum. Opener bids three spades to show a six-card suit and a maximum. Opener bids three notrump to show a solid five-card suit, usually AKQxx. A new suit by responder after bidding two notrump is natural and forcing. If responder bids two notrump and then three notrump, opener with a distributional hand can correct three notrump to four-of-his-major. Only if responder jumps directly to three notrump over opener's weak-two is opener barred from correcting to four-of-his-major.

In examples (1) through (4), responder has enough to invite game and bids two notrump, Modified Ogust, asking opener to describe his hand. In example (1), opener shows a minimum with a six-card suit and responder signs-off in three spades. Two notrump followed by three spades is invitational and opener can raise to game. Since two notrump can be a slam try as well as a game try, opener with a minimum two-spade opener and 6-4 distribution can bid three hearts rejecting a possible slam try. If responder now bids three spades showing a game try, opener can accept. In example (2), opener shows a maximum with a six-card suit and responder raises to game. In example (3), opener shows a minimum and a five-card suit and responder signs-off in three spades. In example (4), opener shows a maximum with a five-card suit and responder jumps to four spades.

Opener	(5)		Responder		Opener	(6)		Responder	
♠AKJ32	♦432		♠Q4	♦KQT5	♠AKJ32	♦32		♠Q4	♦KQT5
♥32	♣432		♥AK765	♣A5		♥432	♣432	♥AK765	♣A5

Opener (5)	Responder	Opener (6)	Responder
2spades	2NT	2spades	2NT
3diamonds	3hearts	3diamonds	3hearts
3spades	4spades	4hearts	Pass

Opener	(7)		Responder		Opener	(8)		Responder	
♠AJT32	♦J32		♠Q4	♦KQT4	♠AJT32	♦J32		♠Q4	♦KQT4
♥32	♣K32		♥AK654	♣A5		♥Q2	♣432	♥AK654	♣A5

Opener (7)	Responder	Opener (8)	Responder
2spades	2NT	2spades	2NT
3diamonds	3hearts	3diamonds	3hearts
3NT	Pass	4hearts	Pass

Over opener's three-club or three-diamond response showing a five-card weak-two, responder's new-suit bids are forcing and ask opener for support. If opener has three-card support, opener raises. Without three-card support, opener has to choose between bidding three notrump, raising on a doubleton or rebidding his major. With outside honors, opener bids three notrump. With a strong five-card suit, opener rebids it. With honor doubleton, opener raises.

In examples (5) through (8), opener bids three diamonds showing only five spades but a maximum weak-two. With 18 HCPs opposite a maximum weak-two, opener has enough strength to force to game. The question is which game. In example (5), opener rebids three spades showing a strong five-card suit. Responder raises to game. In example (6), opener with three-card heart support raises to four hearts. In example (7), opener with honors in the minors bids three notrump. In example (8), opener with honor doubleton of hearts raises to four hearts. In the above examples, if opener bids three clubs over two notrump showing only five spades and a minimum weak-two, responder with only 18 HCPs opposite opener's five HCPs does not have enough strength to force to game and has to sign-off in three spades.

11.3 -- TWO NOTRUMP IS OGUST FOR SIX-CARD WEAK TWOS.

Opener	(1)		Responder			Opener	(2)		Responder	
♠KJT432	♦32		♠Q76	♦KQJ54		♠AK5432	♦32		♠Q76	♦KQJ54
♥32	♣432		♥AK4	♣65		♥32	♣432		♥AK4	♣65

Opener (1)	Responder	Opener (2)	Responder
2spades	2NT	2spades	2NT
3clubs	3spades	3diamonds	4spades
Pass		Pass	

Opener	(3)		Responder			Opener	(4)		Responder	
♠KJT432	♦32		♠Q876	♦A54		♠AK5432	♦32		♠Q876	♦A54
♥32	♣KQ2		♥A54	♣A54		♥32	♣Q32		♥A54	♣A54

Opener (3)	Responder	Opener (4)	Responder
2spades	2NT	2spades	2NT
3hearts	4spades	3spades	3NT
Pass		Pass	

If opener must have a six-card suit, then two notrump by responder is Regular Ogust and asks opener to describe his hand. Opener bids three clubs to show a bad suit and a minimum. Opener bids three diamonds to show a good suit and a minimum. Opener bids three hearts to show a bad suit and a maximum. Opener bids three spades to show a good suit and a maximum. Opener bids three notrump to show a super maximum, usually AKJTxx. A good suit is one with two of the top three honors. A minimum or maximum is based in part on the vulnerability.

In examples (1) through (4), responder has enough to invite game and bids two notrump Regular Ogust. In example (1), opener shows a weak suit and a bad hand and responder signs-off in three spades. Two notrump followed by three spades is an invitational sequence and opener can raise to game. In example (2), opener shows a good suit with two of the top three honors but a minimum hand, and responder bids game. In example (3), opener shows a bad suit but a maximum weak-two, and responder jumps to four spades. In example (4), opener shows a good suit and a maximum. Responder can count nine sure tricks and bids three notrump. Opener with a distributional hand can correct three notrump to four spades. ONLY IF RESPONDER JUMPS DIRECTLY TO THREE NOTRUMP OVER OPENER'S WEAK-TWO IS OPENER BARRED FROM CORRECTING TO FOUR-OF-HIS-MAJOR.

11.4 -- NEW SUITS ARE NON-FORCING.

Opener	(1)		Responder		Opener	(2)		Responder	
♠K32	♦2		♠AJT	♦AKQT43	♠K32	♦2		♠AQJT54	♦AJT
♥AT9432	♣432		♥5	♣765	♥AT9432	♣432		♥5	♣765

Opener	Responder
2hearts	3diamonds
Pass	

Opener	Responder
2hearts	2spades
3spades	4spades

Opener	(3)		Responder		Opener	(4)		Responder	
♠2	♦432		♠AQJT4	♦AJT	♠K32	♦2		♠AQJT4	♦AJT
♥AQ9432	♣432		♥5	♣AK65	♥AT9432	♣432		♥5	♣AK65

Opener	Responder
2hearts	2NT
3hearts	3spades
3NT	Pass

Opener	Responder
2hearts	2NT
3hearts	3spades
4spades	Pass

If opener can have a five-card suit or a weak six-card suit, responder can easily want to improve the contract. New suits by responder are non-forcing. Opener can raise with a good supporting hand. Opening semi-constructive and destructive weak-twos gains in competitive auctions but loses in constructive auctions. However, there are more competitive auctions.

In examples (1) and (2), responder knows that his suit is as least as good opener's suit. In example (1), responder bids three diamonds to play. Three diamonds will usually play better than two hearts, and if the opponents compete, a diamond lead will be ensured. In example (2), responder wants to play in spades. Opener has the perfect hand to raise, three-card trump support, a side singleton and the ace of the weak-two suit. In examples (3) and (4), responder has enough to force to game opposite a weak-two. Responder bids two notrump and follows with three spades, forcing, to offer opener a choice between three notrump, four spades and four hearts. Opener bids four hearts if he can play opposite a singleton. Otherwise, opener chooses between four spades and three notrump. In example (3), opener with a singleton spade bids three notrump. In example (4), opener bids four spades.

11.5 -- MCCABE AFTER TAKEOUT DOUBLES OR TWO-SPADE OVERCALL.

Opener	(1)		Responder			Opener	(2)		Responder	

♠AQJ432 ♦2   ♠765 ♦543   ♠AQJ432 ♦2   ♠5 ♦AQJ6543
　　♥32 ♣J432   ♥54 ♣AKQ65   　♥32 ♣J432   ♥A54   ♣65

Open	Over	Resp	Advnc		Open	Over	Resp	Advnc
2♠	Dbl	3♣	4♥		2♠	Dbl	2NT	Pass
4♠	Dbl	Pass	Pass		3♣	Pass	3♦	Pass
Pass					Pass	Pass		

In competition, Mccabe is the way responder invites game, signs-off in three-of-a-new-suit or makes a lead director. After a takeout double of two-of-a-major or a two-spade overcall of two hearts, two notrump by responder forces opener to bid three clubs. Over three clubs, responder returns to opener's major, inviting opener to bid game with a maximum. With a non-forcing club one-suiter, responder passes three clubs. With a non-forcing diamond one-suiter, responder corrects three clubs to three diamonds. With a non-forcing heart one-suiter, responder corrects three clubs to three hearts.

All direct bids by responder are forcing for one round, show support for opener's major and show values in the bid suit. Two spades -- double -- three clubs, shows spade support and club values, not necessarily club length. Responder's clubs can be AKx.

In example (1), responder wants to raise opener's two spades to three spades and also get a club lead if the opponents play in a red suit or notrump. A direct three clubs over overcaller's takeout double shows a raise to three spades with club values. Over four hearts, opener with four-card club support is allowed to bid again and bids four spades. The two-suited fit is found. If opener has fewer than four clubs, opener passes four hearts and leads a club. In example (2), responder wants to play in three diamonds. Since a direct three diamonds shows spade support, responder bids two notrump, forcing opener to bid three clubs. Over three clubs, responder bids three diamonds to play.

Chapter 12 - OTHER CONVENTIONAL CALLS

12.1 -- STRONG JUMPS SHIFTS AT TWO-LEVEL BY UNPASSED HAND.

Opener	(1)	Responder		Opener	(2)	Responder	
♠2	♦432	♠AKQJ65	♦A65	♠432	♦2	♠AKQJ65	♦A65
♥AKQJ32	♣432	♥5	♣A65	♥AK9432	♣KQJ	♥5	♣A65

Opener (1)	Responder	Opener (2)	Responder
1heart	2spades	1heart	2spades
4hearts	7NT	4diamonds	4NT
		5diamonds	5NT
		6clubs	7spades

Jump shifts at the two-level are strong by unpassed hand, but fit-showing by passed hand (see section 8.18). Responder jump shifts with three types of hands. Type 1 is a one-suiter which is very likely to be the trump suit, for instance examples (1) through (4). If responder jump shifts and then jumps to game, he shows a solid seven or eight-card suit with no outside aces or kings. Type 2 is a two-suiter with at least four-card support for opener's suit, for instance, examples (5) and (6). Type 3 is a semi-balanced hand. A five-card major with 17-19 HCPs where responder jumps in his suit and then bids three notrump, for instance examples (7) and (8). Responder shouldn't jump shift with a two-suited hand without a fit. Holding ♠AKQJ4♥AKQ32♦2♣32 responder bids one spade over opener's minor-suit opening. Responder needs to be able to show both of his suits.

Over responder's jump shift, opener raises with three to an honor or any four-card support. If opener has three-card or better support with a singleton or void in another suit, opener splinters. Since opener does not have to worry about finding a fit in a third suit, a new-suit bid shows concentration of values, not necessarily length. Opener bids a three-card AKx suit or AKQ suit. If opener rebids his suit, it shows a strong but not necessarily solid suit. Opener jumps in his suit to show a solid six-card or longer suit. Opener does not rebid weak suits. If opener has nothing else to bid, opener bids notrump.

In example (1), opener jumps to four hearts showing solid hearts. Responder counts 14 tricks and bids seven notrump. In example (2), opener jumps to four diamonds showing spade support, a sound opening and diamond shortness. Responder bids RKC and opener shows one keycard and the club king. Responder bids seven spades.

Opener (3)		Responder	
♠4 ♦A65		♠AKQJ32 ♦432	
♥A543 ♣KQJ54		♥2 ♣A32	
1club	2spades		
3clubs	3spades		
4diamonds	4NT		
5hearts	7NT		

Opener (4)		Responder	
♠54 ♦KQJ		♠AKQJ32 ♦432	
♥QJ3 ♣K7654		♥2 ♣A32	
1club	2spades		
2NT	3spades		
4spades	Pass		

Opener (5)		Responder	
♠J4 ♦A43		♠AKQ32 ♦2	
♥AQ43 ♣QJ76		♥K2 ♣A5432	
1club	2spades		
2NT	3clubs		
4NT	5hearts		
6clubs	Pass		

Opener (6)		Responder	
♠54 ♦KQJ		♠AKQ32 ♦2	
♥QJ3 ♣QJ876		♥K2 ♣A5432	
1club	2spades		
2NT	3clubs		
3NT	Pass		

Opener (7)		Responder	
♠J4 ♦A43		♠AKQ32 ♦KQ2	
♥AJ54 ♣KJ43		♥K32 ♣Q2	
1club	2spades		
2NT	3NT		
4NT	6NT		

Opener (8)		Responder	
♠J4 ♦A43		♠AKQ32 ♦KQ2	
♥QJ54 ♣KJ43		♥K32 ♣Q2	
1club	2spades		
2NT	3NT		
Pass			

In example (3), opener rebids three clubs showing a good club suit. KQJxx is opener's minimum club holding. When responder rebids his spades showing a strong one-suiter, opener cuebids his ace of diamonds. Four-of-a-red suit is a cuebid in support of spades. Responder no longer worried about diamonds, bids keycard for spades, counts 13 tricks and bids seven notrump. In example (4), opener bids two notrump showing a balanced hand. When responder rebids his spades, opener with nothing to cuebid raises to four spades. If opener can't cuebid, there must be two aces missing, so responder passes four spades. In examples (5) and (6), responder shows a fit with opener by jumping to two spades and then supporting clubs. In example (5), opener with controls bids RKC for clubs and bids a slam. In example (6), opener with a minimum, signs-off in three notrump. In examples (7) and (8), responder shows a strong balanced hand with a five-card spade suit. In example (7), opener with extras bids four notrump. In example (8), opener with a minimum passes three notrump.

12.2 -- WEAK JUMPS SHIFTS IN COMPETITION AT TWO AND THREE-LEVEL.

Opener	(1)		Responder		Opener	(2)		Responder	
♠KQ	♦AKQ32		♠432	♦654	♠KQ	♦AKQ32		♠AJT932	♦654
♥32	♣5432		♥KQJ654	♣6	♥32	♣A432		♥654	♣6

Open	Over	Resp	Advnc		Open	Over	Resp	Advnc
1♦	2♣	3♥	Pass		1♦	2♣	3♠	Pass
Pass	Pass				4♠	Pass	Pass	Pass

Opener	(3)		Responder		Opener	(4)		Responder	
♠AK	♦AKQ2		♠J65432	♦3	♠AK	♦AKQ2		♠432	♦3
♥32	♣QJ432		♥654	♣765	♥32	♣QJ432		♥QJT654	♣765

Open	Over	Resp	Advnc		Open	Over	Resp	Advnc
1♣	1♦	2♠	Pass		1♣	1♦	2♥	Pass
Pass	Pass				Pass	Pass		

Responder's jump to the three-level in competition, one spade -- two clubs -- three-of-a-red-suit for instance, is like a semi-constructive weak-two bid. The jump is not forcing and shows a good six-card suit with not enough strength to make a free bid. Ten points is responder's maximum.

In example (1), responder jumps to three hearts showing a six-card heart suit with not enough strength to bid two hearts. Responder, short in clubs, can't pass two clubs and wait for opener to reopen, because opener is very likely to be long in clubs and short in hearts and will likely pass out two clubs. Opener with a minimum passes three hearts. In example (2), responder jumps to three spades with a minimum weak jump-shift. Opener with extra values raises to four spades.

Responder's jump to the two-level in competition, one club -- one diamond -- two-of-a-major, for instance, is very weak and shows a six-card suit with five or fewer points. With more than five points, responder bids his suit at the one-level.

In examples (3) and (4), responder jumps to two-of-a-major showing a six-card suit with 0-5 HCPs. Opener passes two-of-a-major, expecting to lose at least four tricks. Responder can't have enough strength to make game since he didn't bid one-of-a-major.

12.3 -- UNUSUAL OVER UNUSUAL

Opener	(1)	Responder		Opener	(2)	Responder	
♠AK2 ♦32		♠43 ♦KQJ654		♠AK2 ♦32		♠43 ♦KQJ654	
♥Q32 ♣K5432		♥AK4 ♣76		♥Q32 ♣K5432		♥654 ♣76	

Open	Over	Resp	Advnc	Open	Over	Resp	Advnc
1♣	2♣	2♠	Pass	1♣	2♣	2♦	Pass
2NT	Pass	3NT	Pass	Pass	Pass		

If overcaller makes any bid which promises two specific suits, such as Michaels, Unusual Notrump, Landy or Cappelletti-two-diamonds over a one-notrump opener, responder uses UNUSUAL OVER UNUSUAL to describe his hand. Suppose overcaller bids two clubs, a Michaels cuebid promising both majors. Responder bids two hearts, the lower of overcaller's two suits, to show clubs, the lower of responder's possible two suits. Responder has at least four clubs and at least game invitational values. Responder bids two spades, the higher of overcaller's two suits, to show diamonds the higher of responder's possible two suits. Responder has at least five diamonds and at least game invitational values. Two diamonds and three clubs by responder are natural and show less than invitational values.

If the opening bid is one-of-a-minor, responder needs at least four cards to support opener's minor, either weak or strong. If the opening bid is one-of-a-major, responder needs at least three cards to support opener's major. Responder always needs at least five cards to show a limit raise or better in an unbid suit. Responder needs at least six cards to make a non-forcing bid in the unbid suit. After bidding UNUSUAL OVER UNUSUAL, responder with invitational values can pass any minimum response by opener.

In examples (1) and (2), overcaller bids two clubs showing both majors. In example (1), responder bids two spades, the higher of overcaller's two suits to show a limit raise or better in diamonds, the higher of responder's two suits. Since diamonds is an unbid suit, responder needs at least five diamonds to bid two spades. Opener bids two notrump, non-forcing, showing values in the opponent's suits, and responder with extras raises to game. In example (2), responder bids two diamonds, non-forcing. Since diamonds is an unbid suit, responder needs at least six diamonds to make a non-forcing two-diamond bid. Opener assumes responder has a semi-constructive weak two-diamond opener. With another ace, responder bids two spades to show diamonds with at least limit-raise strength.

186

Opener   (3)   Responder   Opener   (4)   Responder

Opener (3)		Responder			Opener (4)		Responder	
♠432	♦A32	♠KQJ765	♦54		♠432	♦A32	♠KQJ765	♦54
♥AKQJ2	♣J2	♥43	♣543		♥AKQJ2	♣J2	♥43	♣A43

Open	Over	Resp	Advnc		Open	Over	Resp	Advnc
1♥	2NT	3♠	Pass		1♥	2NT	3♦	Pass
Pass	Pass				4♠	Pass	Pass	Pass

In examples (3) and (4), overcaller bids two notrump showing both minors. In example (3), responder bids three spades, non-forcing. Opener assumes responder has a semi-constructive weak two-spade opener. With another ace, responder has enough to bid three diamonds. In example (4), responder bids three diamonds, the higher of overcaller's suits, showing at least five spades and at least ten points. Opener with 15 HCPs and three spades jumps to four spades.

Auction		1. Weak raise in opener's suit 6-10		2. Limit raise in opener's suit 10+		3. Non forcing 6-10		4. Strength in unbid suit 10+	
		Bid	#cards	Bid	#cards	Bid	#cards	Bid	#cards
1♣	2NT (♦,♥)	3♣	♣♣♣♣	3♦	♣♣♣♣	3♠	♠♠♠♠♠♠	3♥	♠♠♠♠♠
1♦	2NT (♣,♥)	3♦	♦♦♦♦	3♣	♦♦♦♦	3♠	♠♠♠♠♠♠	3♥	♠♠♠♠♠
1♥	2NT (♣,♦)	3♥	♥♥♥	3♣	♥♥♥	3♠	♠♠♠♠♠♠	3♦	♠♠♠♠♠
1♠	2NT (♣,♦)	3♠	♠♠♠	3♦	♠♠♠	3♥	♥♥♥♥♥♥	3♣	♥♥♥♥♥
1♣	2♣ (♥,♠)	3♣	♣♣♣♣	2♥	♣♣♣♣	2♦	♦♦♦♦♦♦	2♠	♦♦♦♦♦
1♦	2♦ (♥,♠)	3♦	♦♦♦♦	2♠	♦♦♦♦	3♣	♣♣♣♣♣	2♥	♣♣♣♣

The above chart shows the four unusual notrump auctions and the two Michaels auctions where overcaller shows two specific suits. Column (1) shows responder's 6-10 simple raise of opener's suit and the minimum number of cards promised. Column (2) shows a limit raise or better of opener's suit and the minimum number of cards promised. In columns (1) and (2), responder promises at least three cards if the opening bid is a major and at least four cards if the opening bid is a minor. Column (3) shows responder's non-forcing call in the unbid suit and the number of cards promised. Responder promises at least a six-card suit. Column (4) shows at least limit raise values in the unbid suit and the minimum length promised. Responder promises at least a five-card suit.

12.4 -- MATHE OVER FORCING CLUB.

Overcaller	(1)	Advancer			Overcaller	(2)	Advancer	

```
♠2      ♦432         ♠J543  ♦A65      ♠2      ♦432         ♠J543  ♦A65
♥AQ32   ♣KQ432       ♥K654  ♣65       ♥AQ32   ♣KQ432       ♥K654  ♣65
```

Open	Over	Resp	Advnc		Open	Over	Resp	Advnc
1♣	Pass	1♦	Pass		1♣	Pass	1♦	Pass
1NT	Dbl	Pass	2♦		1♠	Dbl	2♠	3♥
Pass	2♥	Pass	Pass		Pass	Pass	Pass	

Over opponent's forcing club, if it shows at least 16 HCPs, double shows at least 5-4 in the majors, one notrump shows at least 5-4 in the minors, and all other bids are natural. Over one club -- pass -- one diamond or any artificial response, double shows at least 5-4 in the majors, one notrump shows at least 5-4 in the minors, two clubs and two diamonds are both natural. If the opponent's one-club opener can be a minimum opening bid, treat it as a standard club opener (double is takeout for all three suits with an emphasis on the majors, one notrump overcall is 15-18 and two clubs is Michaels).

After a one-club opener which shows at least 16 HCPs, overcaller and advancer treat opener's first rebid and responder's first rebid as if it is the opening bid and the first response. After one club -- pass -- one diamond -- pass -- one notrump, forget the one-club and the one-diamond bid and use chapter 17 defenses against the one notrump bid. After one club -- pass -- one diamond -- pass -- one spade, forget the one-club and the one-diamond bid and bid over a one-spade opener.

In examples (1) and (2), opener opens a forcing club showing at least 16 HCPs. In example (1), opener rebids one notrump. Overcaller doubles one notrump showing a four-card major and a longer minor (see 17.4). Advancer bids two diamonds asking overcaller to bid his major, and overcaller bids two hearts. In example (2), opener rebids one spade. Overcaller doubles one spade for takeout. After responder raises to two spades, advancer bids three hearts, ending the auction. Both one club and one diamond are ignored.

12.5 -- CAPPELLETTI OVER OPPONENT'S ONE-NOTRUMP OVERCALL.

Opener	(1)	Responder		Opener	(2)	Responder	
♠A32 ♦32		♠4 ♦Q654		♠A32 ♦AJ32		♠4 ♦Q654	
♥K32 ♣KQ432		♥QJ654 ♣765		♥2 ♣KQ432		♥QJ654 ♣765	

Open	Over	Resp	Advnc	Open	Over	Resp	Advnc
1♣	1NT	2♥	Pass	1♣	1NT	2♥	Pass
Pass	Pass			2NT	Pass	3♦	Pass

Opener	(3)	Responder		Opener	(4)	Responder	
♠A32 ♦32		♠4 ♦AKJ654		♠A32 ♦32		♠4 ♦AKJ654	
♥K32 ♣KQ432		♥Q654 ♣76		♥2 ♣AKJ5432		♥Q654 ♣76	

Open	Over	Resp	Advnc	Open	Over	Resp	Advnc
1♣	1NT	2♣	Pass	1♣	1NT	2♣	Pass
2♦	Pass	Pass	Pass	Pass	Pass		

When opener opens one-of-a-minor and overcaller bids one notrump, responder bids two clubs showing an unspecified one-suiter, bids two diamonds showing both majors, and bids two-of-a-major showing a major-minor two-suiter. If responder wants to support opener's clubs, responder supports at the three-level. If responder wants to support opener's diamonds, responder bids two clubs and passes opener's two-diamond ask.

Over responder's two clubs showing an unspecified one-suiter, opener bids two diamonds asking for responder's suit. Over responder's two-of-a-major showing a major-minor two-suiter, opener bids two notrump to ask for responder's minor.

In examples (1) and (2), responder bids two hearts showing hearts and a minor. Responder bids because he has an unbalanced hand and opener can't be broke. In example (1), opener has three-card heart support and passes two hearts. In example (2), opener with only one heart bids two notrump, asking for responder's minor, and responder bids three diamonds, ending the auction. In examples (3) and (4), responder, knowing that the opponents have at least an eight-card spade fit, decides to play two diamonds rather then double and defend. Responder bids two clubs showing an unspecified one-suiter expecting to pass opener's two-diamond ask. In example (3), opener bids two diamonds and responder passes. In example (4), opener with seven clubs passes two clubs.

12.6 -- REVERSES.

Opener (1)	Responder	Opener (2)	Responder
♠2 ♦AKJ2	♠A543 ♦6543	♠2 ♦AKJ2	♠A543 ♦6543
♥432 ♣AKJ32	♥Q65 ♣54	♥A32 ♣AKJ32	♥Q65 ♣54

1club	1spade	1club	1spade
2diamonds	2NT	2diamonds	2NT
3clubs	3diamonds	3hearts	3NT

Reverses by opener are forcing, and promise a rebid unless responder jumps to game. Opener shows at least 15 points in high-cards and distribution. Opener's first suit is never shorter than his second suit. Only when opener is 4-4-4-1, can the suit lengths be equal. Sometimes opener has to reverse into a three-card suit to create a force.

If responder has a hand where he wants to stop short of game opposite a minimum reverse, responder bids two notrump or rebids his five-card or longer major. Opener with a minimum reverse then rebids his first-bid suit or two notrump, and responder either passes two notrump or corrects to one of opener's suits. If opener has a game-forcing reverse, he bids higher than his first-bid suit.

In examples (1) and (2), opener bids one club and then bids two diamonds showing clubs, usually at least five, diamonds, usually four, and at least 15 points. Responder with only six HCPs wants to play in three diamonds if opener has a minimum reverse. Responder bids two notrump asking opener to rebid his first-bid suit with a minimum. In example (1), opener rebids three clubs and responder bids three diamonds to play. In example (2), over responder's two notrump, which is the beginning of a possible sign-off, opener with game-forcing values bids higher than three clubs, his first-bid suit. Responder, forced to game, bids three notrump.

With a game-forcing hand and only a four-card major, responder raises opener's second suit, directly prefers opener's first suit or makes a natural bid in the fourth suit. With a five-card major, responder rebids his major first and then supports opener at the four-level or bids the fourth suit. With a six-card or longer major, responder jumps to three-of-his-major. Responder bids two notrump and then three notrump with eight to twelve HCPs, and jumps to three notrump with 13-14.

190

Opener	(3)		Responder		Opener	(4)		Responder	
♠2	♦AKJ2		♠AK543	♦Q3	♠2	♦AKJ2		♠A543	♦Q43
♥432	♣AKJ32		♥A5	♣Q654	♥432	♣AKJ32		♥KQ	♣Q654

Opener (3)	Responder	Opener (4)	Responder
1club	1spade	1club	1spade
2diamonds	2spades	2diamonds	3clubs
3clubs	4clubs	3diamonds	4NT
4diamonds	7clubs	5clubs	6clubs

Opener	(5)		Responder		Opener	(6)		Responder	
♠432	♦AKJ2		♠A8765	♦43	♠32	♦AKJ2		♠A8765	♦43
♥2	♣AKJ32		♥Q54	♣Q54	♥32	♣AKJ32		♥Q54	♣Q54

Opener (5)	Responder	Opener (6)	Responder
1club	1spade	1club	1spade
2diamonds	2spades	2diamonds	2spades
4hearts	4spades	3clubs	3NT

In example (3), responder has five spades and therefore rebids two spades. Opener, treating two spades as a start of a possible sign-off, rebids three clubs. Responder sets clubs as trumps with his game-forcing four-club bid. Over opener's four-diamond cuebid, responder bids seven clubs. In example (4), responder bids three clubs, showing club support with game-forcing values. When opener fails to bid three notrump, thereby showing concentrated values in the minors, responder bids keycard and bids six clubs.

When responder rebids his suit showing at least five and opener has three-card support, opener shows it by jumping to the four-level. In example (5), opener shows three-card spade support and heart shortness by jumping to four hearts. With a balanced three-card raise, ♠KQ2♥32♦A32♣AKQ32 for instance, opener jumps to four spades. With three-card support for responder's major, opener jumps to the four-level even with a minimum. It's more important to show your distribution than your strength.

Opener with a minimum reverse and fewer than three spades has a choice between two notrump and three clubs, depending upon his distribution and heart strength. With a maximum reverse, opener has a choice between three spades showing a two-card raise, three diamonds, three hearts or three notrump, depending upon his distribution and heart strength. In example (6), opener shows a minimum hand by bidding three clubs. Responder with only five spades and a heart stopper bids three notrump.

12.7 -- SPLINTERS BY OPENER.

1.

```
| 1club      1heart |
| 3spades           |
```

♠2♥AK32♦A32♣AK432
♠2♥AQ32♦K32♣AK432

2.

```
| 1club      1heart |
| 4diamonds         |
```

♠AK2♥A432♦2♣AQ432
♠AJ2♥A432♦2♣AK432

3.

```
| 1diamond   1heart |
| 4clubs            |
```

♠AQ32♥A432♦AK32♣2
♠A432♥AK32♦A5432♣-

4.

```
| 1diamond   1heart |
| 3spades           |
```

♠2♥AK32♦AJ432♣AK2
♠2♥A432♦AJ432♣AK2

5.

```
| 1club      1spade |
| 4hearts           |
```

♠AQ32♥2♦KJ2♣AK432
♠AQ32♥2♦AJ2♣AQ432

6.

```
| 1club      1spade |
| 4diamonds         |
```

♠AQ32♥A432♦2♣AQ32
♠A432♥AQ32♦-♣AQ432

7.

```
| 1diamond   1spade |
| 4hearts           |
```

♠AJ32♥2♦AJ432♣AK2
♠AQ32♥2♦A5432♣AK2

8.

```
| 1diamond   1spade |
| 4clubs            |
```

♠AJ32♥A32♦AKJ32♣2
♠AK32♥A32♦AKJ32♣2

9.

```
| 1heart     1spade |
| 4clubs            |
```

♠AK32♥AK432♦A32♣2
♠AQ32♥AQJ432♦KQ♣2

Auctions (1) through (9), are splinter bids. They show four-card
support for responder's major, a singleton or void in the bid-suit and
enough strength to jump to game. Opener can splinter with a singleton
ace. With 4-4-4-1 distribution, opener needs at least 16 HCPs. With
4-5-3-1 distribution, opener needs only 15 HCPs. Auctions (2), (5),
(6) and (7) show stronger hands since a mini-splinter (see next page)
is available. Under each box are examples of opener's hand in the
auction shown.

11.

```
| 1♣         1♥ |
| 3♦            |
```

♠AQ2 ♥A432 ♦2 ♣A5432
♠AQ2 ♥AKQ2 ♦2 ♣AK432

12.

```
| 1♣         1♠ |
| 3♦            |
```

♠AQ32 ♥A32 ♦2 ♣A5432
♠AK32 ♥A32 ♦2 ♣AKQ32

13.

```
| 1♣         1♠ |
| 3♥            |
```

♠AQ32 ♥2 ♦KJ2 ♣A5432
♠AK32 ♥2 ♦KQ2 ♣AKQ32

14.

```
| 1♦         1♠ |
| 3♥            |
```

♠AJ32 ♥2 ♦AJ432 ♣A32
♠AKQ2 ♥2 ♦AKJ32 ♣A32

Jump reverses, auctions (11) through (14) are either mini-splinters or maxi-splinters. They show four-card support for responder's major, shortness in the bid-suit and enough strength to jump to three-of-responder's-major, or enough strength to jump to five-of-responder's-major. If responder has a very weak hand, responder signs-off in three-of-his-major.

The first example under each box is an example of a weak mini-splinter. Opener will pass responder's three-of-a-major sign-off. The second example under each box is an example of a strong mini-splinter. Opener will raise responder's three-of-a-major sign-off to game and will bid again over responder's four-of-a-major sign-off.

15.

```
| 1♣      1major |
| 4♣            |
```

♠32 ♥AK32 ♦2 ♣AKJ432
♠AQ32 ♥32 ♦2 ♣AKQ432

16.

```
| 1♦      1major |
| 4♦            |
```

♠2 ♥AQ32 ♦AKQ432 ♣32
♠AK32 ♥32 ♦AKQ432 ♣2

Auctions (15) and (16) show 6-4 hands with four-card support for responder's major, a solid or one loser six-card or longer minor, and enough strength to jump to game. Opener should splinter with a bad six-card minor. Under each box are two examples of opener's hand in the auction.

12.8 -- PENALTY PASSES AFTER REDOUBLES.

Advancer (1) | **Overcaller**

♠A65 ♦765 ♥65 ♣KJT43   ♠K432 ♦K432 ♥A432 ♣2

Open	Advnc	Resp	Over
3♣	Pass	Pass	Dbl
Rdbl	Pass	Pass	Pass

Advancer (2) | **Overcaller**

♠765 ♦765 ♥765 ♣6543   ♠K432 ♦K432 ♥A432 ♣2

Open	Advnc	Resp	Over
3♣	Pass	Pass	Dbl
Rdbl	3♦	Dbl	Pass

Advancer (3) | **Overcaller**

♠A65 ♦A65 ♥65 ♣KJT43   ♠K432 ♦K432 ♥A432 ♣2

Open	Advnc	Resp	Over
1♣	Pass	Pass	Dbl
Rdbl	Pass	Pass	Pass

Advancer (4) | **Overcaller**

♠A65 ♦A65 ♥765 ♣6543   ♠K432 ♦K432 ♥A432 ♣2

Open	Advnc	Resp	Over
1♣	Pass	Pass	Dbl
Rdbl	1♦	2♣	Pass

Advancer holds ♠A2♥432♦432♣KQT98. Opener, advancer's RHO, opens three clubs and it goes pass -- pass -- double. It doesn't take a world champion to pass overcaller's takeout double for penalties. If advancer holds ♠432♥432♦432♣5432 instead, advancer might pass three-clubs doubled or advancer might bid three diamonds. The point is that advancer has to make a decision, and one of advancer's decisions is to pass overcaller's double for penalties. A redouble by opener shouldn't change anything. Advancer still has to be able to make a penalty pass. Anytime advancer is sitting behind opener, advancer's pass of opener's redouble is for penalties. Overcaller must pass.

In examples (1) and (2), overcaller, sitting in front of opener, doubles for takeout. In example (1), advancer holding KJT43 of clubs is happy to convert overcaller's double to penalties. For some reason, opener redoubles. Overcaller trusts advancer and passes three-clubs redoubled. In example (2), advancer cannot pass three-clubs redoubled since that would show willingness to defend. Advancer bids three diamonds, hoping for the best. In examples (3) and (4), overcaller, in passout seat, doubles one club for takeout, and opener redoubles. In example (3), advancer, planning on passing one club doubled, passes one club redoubled for penalties. Overcaller passes also. In example (4), since advancer can't pass opener's redouble, advancer has to bid his three-card diamond suit.

```
        5.                6.                  7.                    8.
  ┌─────────────────┐ ┌─────────────────────┐ ┌────────────────────┐ ┌─────────────────────┐
  │ 2♣ Dbl Rdbl P   │ │ 1NT Dbl Rdbl P      │ │ 1♣   P   3♣   P    │ │ 1NT  P   2NT  P     │
  └─────────────────┘ └─────────────────────┘ │ P   Dbl  Rdbl  P   │ │ P    Dbl  Rdbl  P   │
                                              └────────────────────┘ └─────────────────────┘
```

If advancer is sitting in front of opener, the story is
different. If a suit has not been raised, penalty passes start with
two clubs. In auction (5), advancer's pass is for penalties. In
auction (6), advancer's pass is not for penalties. If a suit has been
raised, penalty passes start with three clubs. In auction (7),
advancer's last pass is for penalties. In auction (8), advancer's
last pass is not for penalties.

Overcaller   (9)   Advancer   Overcaller   (10)   Advancer

♠A432   ♦A432   ♠K65   ♦KQ5   ♠A432   ♦A432   ♠K65   ♦765
   ♥2   ♣KQ32   ♥KJT43 ♣54   ♥2   ♣KQ32   ♥6543   ♣654

Open	Over	Resp	Advnc		Open	Over	Resp	Advnc
------	------	------	-------		------	------	------	-------
2♥	Dbl	Rdbl	Pass		2♥	Dbl	Rdbl	2♠
Pass	Pass				Pass	Pass	3♥	Pass

───

Overcaller   (11)   Advancer   Overcaller   (12)   Advancer

♠AK32   ♦AK32   ♠654   ♦Q54   ♠AK32   ♦AK32   ♠Q54   ♦654
   ♥2   ♣KQ32   ♥KQJT   ♣654   ♥2   ♣KQ32   ♥543   ♣7654

Open	Over	Resp	Advnc		Open	Over	Resp	Advnc
------	------	------	-------		------	------	------	-------
2♥	Dbl	3♥	Pass		2♥	Dbl	3♥	Pass
Pass	Dbl	Rdbl	Pass		Pass	Dbl	Rdbl	3♠
Pass	Pass				Pass	Pass	Pass	

In examples (9) and (10), overcaller doubles two hearts for
takeout and responder redoubles. In example (9), advancer passes two
hearts redoubled showing that he would have passed two hearts doubled.
Overcaller trusts advancer and passes also. In example (10), advancer
can't pass two hearts redoubled, so he has to bid his three-card spade
suit. In examples (11) and (12), overcaller doubles two hearts and
then three hearts for takeout. In example (11), advancer passes three
hearts redoubled for penalties. In example (12), advancer can't pass
three hearts redoubled, so he bids his three-card spade suit.

195

12.9 -- JUMP CUEBIDS.

Overcaller (1)		Advancer	
♠32 ♦A2		♠KQ54 ♦6543	
♥32 ♣AKQJ432		♥KJ4 ♣65	

Open	Over	Resp	Advnc
1♥	3♥	Pass	3NT
Pass	Pass	Pass	

Overcaller (2)		Advancer	
♠32 ♦A2		♠AK54 ♦KQJ43	
♥32 ♣AKQJ432		♥654 ♣5	

Open	Over	Resp	Advnc
1♥	3♥	Pass	5♣
Pass	Pass	Pass	

Overcaller (3)		Advancer	
♠K2 ♦A2		♠AQJ654 ♦54	
♥32 ♣AKQJ432		♥654 ♣76	

Open	Over	Resp	Advnc
1♥	3♥	Pass	3♠
Pass	4♠	Pass	Pass

Overcaller (4)		Advancer	
♠32 ♦32		♠AK54 ♦KQJ54	
♥K2 ♣KQJ5432		♥654 ♣6	

Open	Over	Resp	Advnc
1♣	3♣	Pass	Pass
Pass			

One-of-a-major -- three-of-the-same-major by overcaller asks advancer to bid three notrump with a stopper in opener's major. Overcaller is supposed to have a solid seven or eight-card minor with outside strength. Overcaller treats AKJxxxxx as solid. If advancer doesn't have a stopper in opener's major, advancer makes the cheapest bid he is willing to be passed in. If advancer is weak, he bids four clubs.

One-of-a-minor -- three-of-the-same-minor by overcaller is natural, wide ranged, and is more preemptive than constructive. Passing and bidding later shows a better hand.

In example (1), overcaller, with eight tricks, wants to get to three notrump if advancer has a heart stopper. Advancer with a heart stopper bids three notrump. In examples (2) and (3), advancer does not have a heart stopper, so advancer can't bid three notrump. In example (2), advancer with an opening bid jumps to five clubs, pass or correct. In example (3), advancer bids his six-card spade suit and overcaller raises to game. In example (4), overcaller jumps to three clubs, showing clubs.

12.10 -- TWO NOTRUMP FOR TAKEOUT.

Opener (1)		Responder	
♠32 ♦AK32		♠AJ54 ♦Q4	
♥32 ♣AJ432		♥654 ♣8765	

Open	Over	Resp	Advnc
1♣	1♥	Dbl	2♥
2NT	Pass	3♣	Pass

Opener (2)		Responder	
♠32 ♦AK32		♠KQ4 ♦Q7654	
♥32 ♣AJ432		♥Q54 ♣65	

Open	Advnc	Resp	Over
1♣	Pass	1NT	2♥
2NT	Pass	3♦	Pass

Opener (3)		Responder	
♠432 ♦KQ32		♠J5 ♦A54	
♥AQ32 ♣32		♥54 ♣KQ7654	

Open	Over	Resp	Advnc
-	-	Pass	Pass
1♦	1♠	2♣	2♠
Pass	Pass	2NT	Pass
3♣	Pass	Pass	Pass

Opener (4)		Responder	
♠32 ♦KQJ32		♠J65 ♦A54	
♥AQ32 ♣32		♥54 ♣KQ654	

Open	Over	Resp	Advnc
-	-	Pass	Pass
1♦	1♠	2♣	2♠
2NT	Pass	3♦	Pass
Pass	Pass		

Unless two notrump shows a strong notrump or is conventional, all non-jump two-notrump calls, when an opponent has made the last bid, are choice of suits and usually choice of partscores. The logic of the situation tells which two suits are in play. If two notrump is for takeout, with a natural two-notrump bid you just have to bid three notrump and test the opponent's defense. I will be happy if I never play in two notrump.

In example (1), responder doubles overcaller's one-heart bid showing four spades and support for one of the minors. After advancer raises hearts, opener wants to play in three-of-a-minor. Opener bids two notrump, choice of minors, and responder bids three clubs. In example (2), opener knows that responder has a four-card minor since responder never bypasses a major to respond one notrump. Over two hearts, opener bids two notrump, choice of minors, and finds his diamond fit. In example (3), responder, assuming the opponents have an eight-card spade fit, wants to compete at the three-level. Responder bids two notrump hoping to find an eight-card minor-suit fit. Opener bids three clubs since responder can't have four diamonds, and the 6-2 club fit is found. In example (4), opener knows the opponents probably have an eight-card fit. Opener bids two notrump hoping for either a 5-3 diamond fit or a 6-2 club fit.

Opener	(5)		Responder		Opener	(6)		Responder	
♠2	♦AK5432		♠KQ543	♦Q6	♠2	♦AK432		♠KQ543	♦Q6
♥32	♣AK32		♥654	♣765	♥32	♣AK432		♥654	♣765

Open	Over	Resp	Advnc		Open	Over	Resp	Advnc
1♦	1♥	1♠	2♥		1♦	1♥	1♠	2♥
2NT	Pass	3♦	Pass		3♣	Pass	Pass	Pass

Opener	(7)		Responder		Opener	(8)		Responder	
♠432	♦AK2		♠65	♦543	♠432	♦AK2		♠65	♦543
♥32	♣AK432		♥KQJ654	♣65	♥32	♣AK432		♥AKQJ54	♣65

Open	Advnc	Resp	Over		Open	Advnc	Resp	Over
1♣	Pass	1♥	2♠		1♣	Pass	1♥	2♠
Pass	Pass	3♥	Pass		Pass	Pass	2NT	Pass
Pass	Pass				3♣	Pass	3♥	Pass
					4♥	Pass	Pass	Pass

Two notrump for takeout can differentiate between suit lengths. Going through two notrump shows two suits, but the first suit is at least two cards longer than the second. When in doubt, responder chooses opener's first bid suit.

In examples (5) and (6), opener has ten cards in the minors and wants to show them over advancer's two-heart raise. In example (5), opener bids two notrump, for takeout, which in this case shows six diamonds and only four clubs. Responder with two diamonds and only three clubs chooses diamonds. In example (6), opener bids three clubs, showing that clubs are equal to diamonds or at worst only one card shorter than diamonds. Responder with more clubs than diamonds chooses clubs.

When responder has the highest suit, two notrump for takeout can sometimes differentiate between whether a call is just competitive or is invitational. In examples (7) and (8), responder has a rebiddable heart suit. In example (7), responder bids three hearts competitively directly over two spades. Example (8) shows how responder uses two notrump for takeout to invite. Over two notrump, opener assumes responder is showing both minors and chooses his five-card club suit. When responder corrects three clubs to three hearts, opener with good controls raises the invitational three-heart bid to game.

12.11 -- LAST TRAIN.

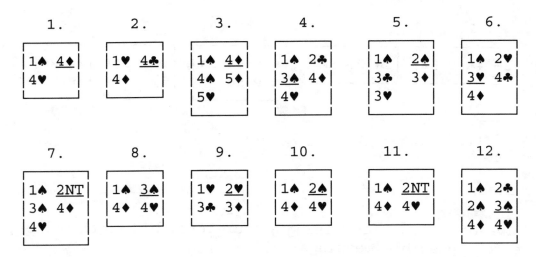

1.
| 1♠ | 4♦ |
| 4♥ | |

2.
| 1♥ | 4♣ |
| 4♦ | |

3.
1♠	4♦
4♠	5♦
5♥	

4.
1♠	2♣
3♠	4♦
4♥	

5.
1♠	2♠
3♣	3♦
3♥	

6.
1♠	2♥
3♥	4♣
4♦	

7.
1♠	2NT
3♠	4♦
4♥	

8.
| 1♠ | 3♠ |
| 4♦ | 4♥ |

9.
| 1♥ | 2♥ |
| 3♣ | 3♦ |

10.
| 1♠ | 2♠ |
| 4♦ | 4♥ |

11.
| 1♠ | 2NT |
| 4♦ | 4♥ |

12.
1♠	2♣
2♠	3♠
4♦	4♥

There are many auctions after a fit[6] has been found, for instance, auction (1), where there is only one call between responder's last call, four diamonds, which is a splinter bid, and opener's sign-off, four spades. If four hearts in this auction has to show first-round heart control, there will be many hands where opener wants to show extra values but will be unable to if he lacks the ace of hearts. Therefore, four hearts becomes the Last Train, and says nothing about hearts, but says opener's interested in slam but doesn't quite have enough to commit the hand to the five-level. If this is a pure point count auction, bidding four spades shows 12-14, bidding four hearts, the Last Train, shows 15-17 and bidding above four spades shows 18 or more. Last Train is used in any auction after a fit has been found, including game tries, slam tries and grand slam tries, where there is only one call between partner's last call and your sign-off.

In auctions (1) through (7), opener's last call is the Last Train, an artificial call showing extra values but saying nothing about that specific suit. In auctions (8) through (12), responder's last call is the Last Train, an artificial call showing extra values but saying nothing about that specific suit. Overcaller and advancer can also use the Last Train. Numerous examples of Last Train auctions are shown throughout this book.

---

[6]The underlined call sets trumps.

12.12 -- SLAM TRIES.

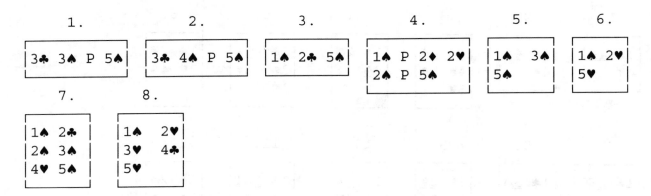

Jumps to five-of-a-major or raising a four-level bid to the five-level can have four possible meanings:

1 - Bid a slam if you have extra values. In auctions (1) and (2), advancer bids five spades asking overcaller to bid six with extra values. Five spades is the only way advancer can set spades as trumps and show extra strength. The only way five spades can logically ask for a club control is if advancer is solid in diamonds, hearts and spades. Not very likely.

2 - Bid a slam if you don't have two quick losers in the opponent's suit. In auctions (3) and (4), responder jumps to five-of-opener's-major, asking opener to bid a slam with first or second-round control in overcaller's suit. Here, there's plenty of room to set trumps and have a constructive auction looking for extra values.

3 - Bid a slam if you have good trumps. In auctions (5) and (6), opener asks responder to bid a slam with good trumps. Here the opponents are silent and there's plenty of room to set trumps and have a constructive auction looking for extra values.

4 - Bid a slam if you have first or second-round control in the unbid suit. In auctions (7) and (8), since diamonds have not been bid, five-of-the-major asks partner to bid slam with a diamond control.

In meanings two and four, partner is asking you to bid a slam with first or second-round control. Without first or second-round control, you pass partner's five-level bid. A five-notrump response shows the king which needs protecting. If you have first-round control, seven is a possibility. You can show first-round control by cuebidding anything below six of the trump suit.

Direct seat takeout doubles can be made with as few as ten HCPs if overcaller is 4-4-4-1 with a singleton in opener's suit. With 4-4-3-2, overcaller has at least 12 HCPs. Overcaller's takeout double promises at least three cards in any unbid major, or a hand worth at least 20 points.

Overcaller (1)		Advancer		Overcaller (2)		Advancer	
♠KQ32 ♦A432		♠A7654 ♦K5		♠KQ2 ♦A432		♠A7654 ♦K5	
♥Q32 ♣32		♥J65 ♣654		♥Q432 ♣32		♥J65 ♣654	

Open	Over	Resp	Advnc	Open	Over	Resp	Advnc
1♣	Dbl	Pass	1♠	1♣	Dbl	Pass	1♠
2♣	2♠	Pass	Pass	2♣	Pass	Pass	2♠
3♣	Pass	Pass	3♠	3♣	Pass	Pass	Dbl

OVERCALLER DOES NOT SHOW EXTRA VALUES RAISING ADVANCER'S ONE-LEVEL-RESPONSE-TO-HIS-TAKEOUT-DOUBLE TO THE TWO-LEVEL IF RIGHT HAND OPPONENT COMPETES. Overcaller just shows four-card support. Overcaller can have the worst takeout double ever made, but if he has four-card support for advancer, he must raise to the two-level if RHO competes. Raising shows extra strength only if RHO passes.

In example (1), overcaller's two-spade bid shows four spades but does not show extra values. When opener competes to three clubs, advancer, knowing that overcaller has four spades, bids three spades. In example (2), overcaller has three spades and passes two clubs. This time when opener competes to three clubs, advancer doubles, knowing that overcaller has three spades and guessing that the opponents are in an eight-card club fit.

After making a takeout double, if overcaller does not support advancer directly, OVERCALLER DENIES FOUR-CARD SUPPORT. Cuebids deny four-card support. If overcaller has four-card support and is interested in slam, he jumps in opener's suit.

If overcaller doubles opener after advancer has made a bid, it's a strength-showing double, showing at least 17 HCPs with at least two cards in the opponent's suit. Advancer assumes overcaller has exactly two. Overcaller denies four-card support for advancer's suit.

Overcaller (3)   Advancer   Overcaller (4)   Advancer

♠KQ2 ♦AQ32   ♠A6543 ♦54   ♠KQ2 ♦AQ32   ♠A543 ♦54
  ♥KQ32 ♣K2   ♥J54 ♣543   ♥KQ32 ♣K2   ♥J54 ♣6543

Open	Over	Resp	Advnc
1♣	Dbl	Pass	1♠
2♣	Dbl	Pass	3♠
Pass	4♠	Pass	

Open	Over	Resp	Advnc
1♣	Dbl	Pass	1♠
2♣	Dbl	Pass	Pass
Pass			

Overcaller (5)   Advancer   Overcaller (6)   Advancer

♠- ♦K432   ♠KJ32 ♦Q65   ♠- ♦KJ32   ♠KJ32 ♦Q65
  ♥K5432 ♣AJ32   ♥J76 ♣654   ♥AKT932 ♣KQ2   ♥J76 ♣654

Open	Over	Resp	Advnc
1♠	Dbl	Pass	1NT
Pass	2♥	Pass	Pass
Pass	Pass		

Open	Over	Resp	Advnc
1♠	Dbl	Pass	1NT
Pass	3♥	Pass	4♥
Pass			

In examples (3) and (4), overcaller, whose hand is too strong for a one-notrump overcall, doubles one club. Overcaller then doubles two clubs showing extra strength, at least 17 HCPs, with at least two clubs and fewer than four spades. A third club would be a bonus. In example (3), advancer with extra strength and extra spade length jumps to three spades. In example (4), advancer holds four clubs and only four spades, and converts overcaller's double to penalties.

If advancer bids one notrump in response to a takeout double, advancer shows a balanced hand with 6-11 HCPs. If overcaller has made a light distributional takeout double with a five-card suit, it is usually better to play in that suit. Therefore, overcaller's two-level rebid shows a minimum and jumping shows extra values.

In example (5), overcaller with a bad heart suit and only 11 HCPs correctly decides to double rather than overcall two hearts. Over one notrump, overcaller, with a void, bids two hearts, attempting to play in a suit contract. Two hearts does not show extra values in this sequence. Two-of-a-minor by overcaller shows the same type of hand but with a five or six-card minor. Advancer, with three hearts, passes two hearts. In example (6), overcaller has a very good heart hand. Over one notrump showing values, overcaller jumps to three hearts to show a game-forcing six-card heart suit. If overcaller has only five hearts, overcaller cuebids and then bids hearts, offering more of a choice.

202

Advancer's cuebid in response to a takeout double promises a rebid opposite a non-game bid. Most of advancer's cuebids start choice-of-game auctions. Advancer's cuebid does not promise a four-card major. Advancer can have a game-forcing hand in a minor and be looking for notrump. If advancer has a five-card or longer major and opening-bid values, advancer makes the auction simple by jumping to game. If advancer cuebids a minor and corrects hearts to spades, advancer is showing four spades and four or more of the other minor.

Over advancer's cuebid, overcaller's first duty is to bid his cheaper four-card major. If overcaller does not bid a major, he denies holding a four-card major. If overcaller does not have a four-card major, overcaller bids notrump with a stopper in the opponent's suit or bids a minor suit. If opener doubles advancer's cuebid, overcaller bids a four-card major if he has one. If overcaller does not have a four-card major, overcaller passes opener's double or bids a minor. The rule is that majors are bid before minors by both overcaller and advancer.

Overcaller (3)		Advancer		Overcaller (4)		Advancer	
♠AJ32	♦65432	♠KQ54	♦AK	♠AJ32	♦65432	♠KQ	♦AKQ7
♥K32	♣A	♥Q654	♣432	♥K32	♣A	♥Q654	♣432

Open	Over	Resp	Advnc	Open	Over	Resp	Advnc
1♣	Dbl	Pass	2♣	1♣	Dbl	Pass	2♣
3♣	Pass	Pass	3♥	3♣	Pass	Pass	3♥
Pass	3♠	Pass	4♠	Pass	3♠	Pass	4♦
Pass	Pass	Pass		Pass	5♦	Pass	Pass

In examples (3) and (4), advancer has enough strength for game but does not know which suit to play game in. Advancer therefore cuebids offering overcaller a choice of strains. Over opener's three-club bid, overcaller passes, showing a minimum takeout double. Passing allows advancer to double three clubs with a balanced hand. In example (3), advancer bids three hearts showing a four-card heart suit. Overcaller with only three hearts corrects to three spades and advancer raises to game. Overcaller knows that if advancer has a five-card heart suit, advancer doesn't cuebid but jumps directly to four hearts. The 4-4 fit is found. In example (4), advancer bids three hearts showing a four-card heart suit. Overcaller with only three hearts corrects to three spades. Advancer bids four diamonds, and overcaller raises to five. The bad 4-3 heart fit is avoided.

13.2 -- EQUAL-LEVEL CONVERSION.

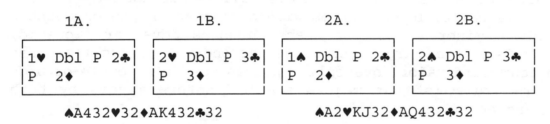

1A.	1B.	2A.	2B.
1♥ Dbl P 2♣	2♥ Dbl P 3♣	1♠ Dbl P 2♣	2♠ Dbl P 3♣
P 2♦	P 3♦	P 2♦	P 3♦

♠A432♥32♦AK432♣32   ♠A2♥KJ32♦AQ432♣32

Equal-level conversion shows four cards in the highest unbid suit and five or more cards in the bid suit, but does not promise extra values. The above four types of auctions are the only equal-level conversion auctions. They can occur after a one, two, three or four-level takeout double. Since overcaller can double one heart and correct two clubs to two diamonds with only 11 HCPs, overcaller has to jump to three diamonds to show a 17-point takeout double. Doubling and bidding spades is never an equal-level conversion and always shows at least 17 points.

In auctions (1A) and (1B), overcaller shows a minimum takeout double with four spades and five or more diamonds by correcting clubs to diamonds at the cheapest level. If advancer bids four clubs, overcaller has to bid four diamonds. If advancer jumps to five clubs, overcaller passes and hopes advancer has his own suit. With four spades and five diamonds, overcaller does not have to overcall two diamonds and risk missing a possible spade fit. In auctions (2A) and (2B), overcaller shows a minimum takeout double with four hearts and five or more diamonds by correcting clubs to diamonds at the cheapest level. With four hearts and five diamonds, overcaller does not have to overcall two diamonds and risk missing a possible heart fit.

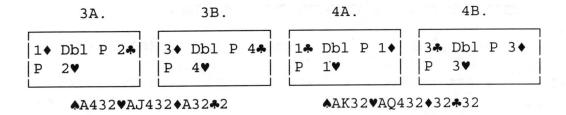

3A.	3B.	4A.	4B.
1♦ Dbl P 2♣ P 2♥	3♦ Dbl P 4♣ P 4♥	1♣ Dbl P 1♦ P 1♥	3♣ Dbl P 3♦ P 3♥

♠A432♥AJ432♦A32♣2   ♠AK32♥AQ432♦32♣32

In auctions (3A) and (3B), overcaller shows a minimum takeout double with four spades and five or more hearts by correcting clubs to hearts at the cheapest level. Overcaller does not have to overcall one heart and risk missing a possible spade fit. In auctions (4A) and (4B), overcaller shows a minimum takeout double with four spades and five or more hearts by correcting diamonds to hearts at the cheapest level.

Overcaller (1) Advancer   Overcaller (2) Advancer

♠32 ♦AQ432 ♠54 ♦K65   ♠32 ♦AQ432 ♠54 ♦K65
 ♥AK32 ♣32 ♥654 ♣KQ654   ♥AK32 ♣32 ♥654 ♣KQ654

Open	Over	Resp	Advnc	Open	Over	Resp	Advnc
1♠	Dbl	2♠	3♣	2♠	Dbl	3♠	4♣
Pass	3♦	Pass	Pass	Pass	4♦	Pass	Pass

Overcaller (3) Advancer   Overcaller (4) Advancer

♠AK32 ♦AQ432 ♠76 ♦K65   ♠AK5432 ♦AQJ2 ♠76 ♦K65
 ♥32 ♣32 ♥654 ♣KJ654   ♥2 ♣A2 ♥654 ♣KJ654

Open	Over	Resp	Advnc	Open	Over	Resp	Advnc
1♥	Dbl	2♥	3♣	1♥	Dbl	2♥	3♣
Pass	3♦	Pass	Pass	Pass	3♠	Pass	4♠

In example (1), overcaller doubles one spade, hoping advancer bids hearts. Over advancer's three-club bid, overcaller bids three diamonds, showing a minimum hand with four hearts and five or more diamonds. If example (2), overcaller doubles two spades with a similar hand. Overcaller corrects four clubs to four diamonds, showing a minimum hand with four hearts and five or more diamonds. In example (3), overcaller's diamond bid is the typical equal-level conversion showing a minimum takeout double with four spades and five or more diamonds. Example (4) is **not** an equal-level conversion auction. Overcaller shows a very good spade hand. Doubling and bidding the highest unbid suit always shows a strong hand.

13.3 -- NEGATIVE DOUBLES THROUGH THREE SPADES.

Opener	(1)	Responder		Opener	(2)	Responder	
♠AJ32	♦32	♠K654	♦654	♠AJ32	♦32	♠KQ54	♦AQ4
♥432	♣AK32	♥KQ65	♣54	♥432	♣AK32	♥KQJ5	♣54

Open	Over	Resp	Advnc	Open	Over	Resp	Advnc
1♣	1♦	Dbl	2♦	1♣	1♦	Dbl	2♦
2♠	Pass	Pass	Pass	2♠	Pass	3♦	Pass
				3♥	Pass	4NT	Pass
				5♥	Pass	6♠	Pass

Over one club -- one diamond, responder's negative double shows at least 4-4 in the majors with 5-25 HCPs. With more than eight cards in the majors, responder has to make a bid assuming advancer is going to jump to three diamonds. With longer spades, responder bids one spade if he has at least 11 points, which will allow him to bid a forcing three hearts over advancer's likely three-diamond call. With longer hearts, responder needs to be stronger to bid one heart, since his next call will have to be three spades, a reverse. With a weak hand and at least nine cards in the majors, responder doubles first and then bids three-of-his-longer-major over advancer's anticipated three-diamond call. IF RESPONDER HAS ONLY ONE MAJOR, RESPONDER BIDS ONE-OF-A-MAJOR EVEN IF IT'S ONLY A FOUR-CARD SUIT.

Over responder's negative double of one diamond, opener bids one-of-a-major with 11-14 support points, two-of-a-major with 15-16 support points, three-of-a-major with 17-18 support points and four-of-a-major with 19+ support points. Opener cuebids, setting up a game force and then describes his hand, with jump-shift values holding a four-card major or holding a minor one-suiter. A jump to four diamonds shows 4-4 in the majors and diamond shortness with game-forcing values. If opener does not have a four-card major, opener rebids assuming responder bid one-of-a-major. If advancer raises diamonds to the two or three-level, opener does not show extra values bidding a four-card major.

In examples (1) and (2), responder doubles one diamond showing at least 4-4 in the majors. Opener bids two spades over two diamonds which doesn't show extras. In example (1), responder passes two spades. With 10-11 points, responder raises to the three-level. In example (2), responder cuebids showing a slam try. Opener bids three hearts showing a sound two-spade bid. Responder bids keycard and bids six spades.

Opener	(3)	Responder		Opener	(4)	Responder	

♠2	♦AJ32	♠K543	♦KQ54	♠2	♦AJ32	♠AK43	♦KQ54
♥432	♣AK432	♥765	♣65	♥432	♣AK432	♥5	♣QJ65

Open	Over	Resp	Advnc	Open	Over	Resp	Advnc
1♣	1♥	Dbl	Pass	1♣	1♥	Dbl	Pass
2♦	Pass	Pass	Pass	2♦	Pass	4♥	Pass
				4NT	Pass	5♠	Pass
				6♦	Pass	Pass	Pass

Over one-of-a-minor -- one heart, responder's negative double shows exactly four spades and support for one of the minors with 5-25 HCPs. With five or more spades, responder bids one spade.

Over responder's negative double of one heart, opener holding four spades bids one spade with 11-14 support points, two spades with 15-16 support points, three spades with 17-18 support points and four spades with 19-20 support points. After opening one diamond, opener rebids two clubs with 11-14 support points, three clubs with 15-16 support points, and cuebids with stronger minor two-suiters. After opening one club, opener rebids two diamonds with 11-14 support points, three diamonds with 15-16 support points, and cuebids with stronger minor two-suiters. With jump-shift values holding four spades or holding a minor one or two-suiter, opener cuebids, setting up a game force, and then describes his hand. A jump to four hearts shows four spades and heart shortness with game-forcing values. A one-notrump rebid shows 11-14 HCPs and a two-notrump jump rebid shows 18-19 HCPs. If advancer raises hearts to the two or three-level, opener does not show extra values bidding spades.

In examples (3) and (4), responder doubles one heart showing four spades and support for a minor. Opener with 12 HCPs and four diamonds, bids two diamonds. Two diamonds is not a reverse. In example (3), responder passes two diamonds. In example (4), responder jumps to four hearts showing four diamonds, heart shortness and enough strength to make a slam try opposite a 11-14 two-diamond rebid. Opener, with a sound two-diamond bid, bids keycard and bids six diamonds.

In examples (3) and (4), if advancer raises to two hearts, opener bids two notrump for takeout (see 12.10), letting responder bid his minor at the three-level. Remember, responder's double of one heart promises only one minor.

Opener	(5)	Responder		Opener	(6)	Responder	
♠32	♦AJ432	♠54	♦KQ65	♠32	♦AJ432	♠54	♦K65
♥32	♣AK32	♥K654	♣654	♥32	♣AK32	♥K654	♣QJ54

Open	Over	Resp	Advnc	Open	Over	Resp	Advnc
1♦	1♠	Dbl	2♠	1♦	1♠	Dbl	2♠
3♣	Pass	3♦	Pass	3♣	Pass	Pass	Pass

Over one-of-a-minor -- one spade, responder's negative double shows four hearts with 6-25 HCPs, or five hearts and 6-10 HCPs. Responder usually has support for one of the minors. With five or more hearts and more than ten HCPs, responder is strong enough to make a free bid of two hearts. With six hearts and 6-10 HCPs, responder makes a weak jump shift.

Over responder's negative double of one spade, opener holding four hearts bids two hearts with 11-14 support points, three hearts with 15-16 support points, or four hearts with 17-18 support points, and cuebids with stronger hands. After opening one diamond, opener rebids two clubs with 11-14 support points, three clubs with 15-16 support points, and cuebids with stronger minor two-suiters. After opening one club, opener rebids two diamonds with 11-14 support points, three diamonds with 15-16 support points and cuebids with stronger minor two-suiters. With jump-shift values holding four hearts or holding a minor one or two-suiter, opener cuebids, setting up a game force, and then describes his hand. A jump to three spades shows four hearts and spade shortness with game-forcing values. If advancer raises spades to the two-level, opener does not show extra values bidding three hearts. If opener has a good three-heart bid, he bids two notrump for takeout and follows with three hearts.

In examples (5) and (6), responder doubles one spade, showing four hearts and support for a minor. In example (5), responder corrects three clubs to three diamonds. In example (6), responder passes three clubs. Two notrump for takeout can be used by opener to show both minors if the opening bid was one club or opener has six diamonds and four clubs.

Over one heart -- one spade, responder's negative double shows both minors with 6-25 HCPs. Opener rebids two-of-a-minor with 11-14 support points, three-of-a-minor with 15-16 support points and cuebids with stronger heart-minor two-suiters.

Opener	(7)	Responder		Opener	(8)	Responder	
♠AJ32 ♦AK32		♠54 ♦QJ54		♠AJ32 ♦AK32		♠KQ54 ♦QJ54	
♥432 ♣32		♥KQ76 ♣654		♥5432 ♣2		♥76 ♣654	

Open	Over	Resp	Advnc	Open	Over	Resp	Advnc
1♦	2♣	Dbl	Pass	1♦	2♣	Dbl	Pass
2♠	Pass	3♦	Pass	2♥	Pass	2♠	Pass

Over one diamond -- two clubs, responder's negative double shows 6-25 HCPs but guarantees only one four-card major. Responder has either both majors or one major and diamonds. If opener has 4-4 in the majors and a minimum, opener bids hearts first, allowing responder to correct to spades with spades and diamonds. With a stronger hand and 4-4 in the majors, opener cuebids if possible to make sure that the 4-4 is found. If advancer raises clubs, opener does not show extra values bidding a four-card major.

In examples (7) and (8), responder makes a negative double with only one major and diamond support. In example (7), responder with hearts and diamonds corrects two spades to three diamonds. In example (8), responder corrects two hearts to two spades, showing spades and diamonds. If responder has a weak hand with at least six spades, he has to make a weak-jump shift. If opener does not want to play in two spades, he bids three diamonds.

Over one heart -- two-of-either-minor, responder's negative double shows either five spades or a four-card spade suit that can play opposite three-card support and support for the unbid minor. Playing Flannery, opener does not usually have a four-card spade suit. Having denied holding a four-card spade suit, opener can freely bid a three-card spade suit.

Over any other two-level or three-level overcall, responder's negative double shows the two unbid suits. Over one-of-a-minor -- two-of-the-same-minor or one-of-a-minor -- three-of-the-same-minor, if natural, responder's negative double shows both majors.

13.4 -- RESPONSIVE DOUBLES THROUGH THREE SPADES.

Overcaller	(1)	Advancer		Overcaller	(2)	Advancer	
♠Q2	♦KJ432	♠AJ43	♦65	♠Q2	♦KJ432	♠AK543	♦5
♥KQ32	♣32	♥A654	♣654	♥KQ32	♣32	♥JT654	♣54

Open	Over	Resp	Advnc	Open	Over	Resp	Advnc
1♣	1♦	2♣	Dbl	1♣	1♦	1NT	Dbl
Pass	2♥	Pass	Pass	Pass	2♥	Pass	Pass
Pass				Pass			

Overcaller	(3)	Advancer		Overcaller	(4)	Advancer	
♠AK32	♦AJ32	♠54	♦7654	♠AK32	♦AJ32	♠7654	♦K54
♥32	♣Q32	♥K54	♣AJ54	♥Q32	♣32	♥AJ54	♣54

Open	Over	Resp	Advnc	Open	Over	Resp	Advnc
1♥	Dbl	2♥	Dbl	1♣	Dbl	3♣	Dbl
Pass	3♦	Pass	Pass	Pass	3♠	Pass	Pass

After a one-level overcall, advancer's double of responder's single or double raise is responsive and shows the two unbid suits, (example 1). After a one-level overcall or a takeout double, advancer's double of responder's one-notrump response is responsive and shows the two unbid suits (example 2). After a takeout double of a major, advancer's double of responder's single or double raise is responsive and shows both minors, since advancer can easily bid the unbid major (example 3). After a takeout double of a minor, advancer's double of responder's single or double raise is responsive and shows both majors (example 4). The strength of a responsive double ranges from enough to take one bid to enough to force to game.

In example (1), advancer doubles two clubs, showing hearts and spades. In example (2), advancer doubles one notrump, showing hearts and spades. Overcaller bids two hearts and the 5-4 heart fit is found. Since responder's one notrump is a free bid, a penalty double is unlikely to do much damage. What happens more frequently is that advancer has the two unbid suits and has to guess which suit to bid. In this example, if double isn't responsive, advancer would have to guess which major to bid, and might guess wrong and bid spades. In example (3), advancer doubles two hearts, showing both minors. By using the responsive double, advancer plays in his 4-4 diamond fit, rather then guessing which minor to play in. In example (4), advancer doubles three clubs, showing both majors. The 4-4 spade fit is found.

13.5 -- SNAP-DRAGON DOUBLES.

Overcaller (1)		Advancer	
♠Q ♦Q5432		♠J432 ♦AKJ	
♥K7 ♣A6543		♥65432 ♣2	

Open	Over	Resp	Advnc
1♣	1♦	1♠	Dbl
2♠	Pass	Pass	3♦

Overcaller (2)		Advancer	
♠Q ♦Q5432		♠J432 ♦K76	
♥K7 ♣A6543		♥AQJ32 ♣2	

Open	Over	Resp	Advnc
1♣	1♦	1♠	2♥
2♠	Pass	Pass	3♦

Overcaller (3)		Advancer	
♠432 ♦J32		♠8765 ♦KQ654	
♥AQ432 ♣K2		♥K5 ♣43	

Open	Over	Resp	Advnc
1♣	1♥	1♠	Dbl
2♣	2♦	3♣	3♦

Overcaller (4)		Advancer	
♠432 ♦J32		♠8765 ♦AKQ54	
♥AQ432 ♣K2		♥K5 ♣43	

Open	Over	Resp	Advnc
1♣	1♥	1♠	2♦
3♣	3♦	Pass	Pass

Advancer's Snap-Dragon double of responder's third-suit bid, after an overcall, shows the fourth suit with tolerance for overcaller's suit. Advancer doubles with a hand not suitable to make a free bid in the fourth suit. After one club -- one diamond -- one spade (the third suit), advancer's double shows hearts (the fourth suit), usually at least five, diamond tolerance and a hand not suitable to bid two hearts. The hearts are not strong enough or the hand is not strong enough to make a free two-heart bid. After one club -- one diamond -- one heart, advancer doubles to show four spades and bids one spade to show at least five spades. With a penalty double of the third suit, advancer has to wait for the opponents to get higher before doubling or for overcaller to reopen with a double. Why tell the opponents, who are in a forcing auction, that they are in trouble. Let them get higher before you apply the ax.

In example (1), advancer doubles one spade, showing a heart suit with tolerance for diamonds. In this case, advancer with great diamond support and weak hearts, doesn't want to play in hearts unless overcaller bids them freely. In example (2), advancer has a good heart suit and enough strength to make a free two-heart bid. In example (3), advancer's double of one spade shows at least five diamonds. Overcaller, with only two clubs, competes by bidding two diamonds. Over three clubs, advancer with honors in both red suits, bids three diamonds. In example (4), advancer has enough strength and a good enough suit to bid two diamonds freely.

Overcaller (5)   Advancer

♠432   ♦J32   ♠KQ765   ♦654
    ♥AQ432 ♣K2   ♥K5   ♣543

Open	Over	Resp	Advnc
1♦	1♥	2♣	Dbl
3♣	Pass	Pass	Pass

Overcaller (6)   Advancer

♠432   ♦J32   ♠KQJ765   ♦654
    ♥AQ432 ♣K2   ♥K5   ♣43

Open	Over	Resp	Advnc
1♦	1♥	2♣	2♠
3♣	3♠	Pass	Pass

Overcaller (7)   Advancer

♠AQ432   ♦J32   ♠K5   ♦654
    ♥432   ♣K2   ♥AQ765   ♣543

Open	Over	Resp	Advnc
1♣	1♠	2♦	Dbl
3♣	Pass	Pass	Pass

Overcaller (8)   Advancer

♠AQ432   ♦J32   ♠K5   ♦654
    ♥432   ♣K2   ♥AQJ765 ♣43

Open	Over	Resp	Advnc
1♣	1♠	2♦	2♥
3♣	3♥	Pass	Pass

In example (5), advancer doubles two clubs, showing a spade suit and tolerance for hearts, with a hand that is not able to bid either two hearts or two spades. Tolerance is usually two-card support. Advancer doesn't have three hearts so he can't raise hearts, and bidding two spades shows a better spade suit. Since advancer does not promise six spades, overcaller is not able to bid three spades over three clubs with only three-card support. In example (6), advancer with six spades is able to bid two-non-forcing spades. Since advancer usually has six or a very strong five-card suit for his two-spade free bid, overcaller is able to compete to three spades over three clubs with three-card spade support. In example (7), advancer doubles two diamonds, showing a heart suit and tolerance for spades, with a hand that is not able to bid either two hearts or two spades. Since advancer does not promise six hearts, overcaller is not able to bid three hearts over three clubs with only three-card support. In example (8), advancer with six hearts is able to bid two non-forcing hearts. Since advancer usually has six hearts for his two-heart free bid, overcaller is able to compete to three hearts over three clubs with three-card heart support.

13.6 -- SUPPORT DOUBLES AND REDOUBLES.

Opener	(1)	Responder		Opener	(2)	Responder	
♠AQ32 ♦432		♠K7654 ♦765		♠AQ2 ♦432		♠K7654 ♦765	
♥K2 ♣K432		♥Q43 ♣A6		♥K2 ♣K5432		♥Q43 ♣A6	

Open	Advnc	Resp	Over	Open	Over	Resp	Advnc
1♣	Pass	1♠	2♥	1♣	1♥	1♠	2♥
2♠	3♥	3♠	Pass	Dbl	Pass	2♠	Pass
Pass	Pass			Pass	3♥	Dbl	

A SUPPORT DOUBLE AND REDOUBLE ARE MADE BY THE OPENING BIDDER AND ONLY BY THE OPENING BIDDER AND SHOW THREE-CARD SUPPORT. When opener can raise responder's one-level response to the two-level after an intervening bid by RHO, a direct raise shows 11-14 points with four-card support, and double or redouble shows an unlimited hand with three-card support. Doubles of natural bids, cuebids and one-notrump are all support doubles. If opener has a choice between bidding a four-card major at the one-level or making a support double or redouble, opener bids the four-card major. Holding four spades, opener always bids one spade rather then raise responder's diamonds or hearts with only three-card support. Opener, holding three-card support, does not have to show his support. Opener might rebid a seven-card suit rather then show support. I have found that if I have three-card support, it usually works out better to show the support rather then passing, even if I don't have the values for my previous bids. There is one exception to double showing three-card support. If responder responds one diamond and he can have a weak hand with four hearts, then opener's double of a one-spade overcall shows four hearts rather than three diamonds. This allows responder to respond one diamond with good diamonds and bad hearts and not lose the heart suit.

In example (1), opener raises to two spades, showing a minimum raise with four-card support. Over advancer's three-heart bid, responder, knowing that he has a nine-card spade fit, confidently bids three spades. In example (2), opener has a minimum three-card raise to two spades, which opener shows by doubling two hearts and passing responder's two-spade rebid. This time, when overcaller bids three hearts, responder doubles, knowing that he has only an eight-card spade fit. Responder's two-spade rebid does not promise five spades. If responder is 4-3-3-3 for example, he has to bid something over two-hearts doubled.

213

Opener	(3)	Responder	
♠AJ2 ♦32		♠KQ543 ♦A65	
♥K2 ♣AKQJ32		♥543 ♣65	

Open	Advnc	Resp	Over
1♣	Pass	1♠	2♣
Dbl	Pass	2♠	Pass
3♥	Pass	4♦	Pass
4NT	Pass	5♠	Pass
6NT	Pass	Pass	Pass

Opener	(4)	Responder	
♠AJ2 ♦432		♠KQ543 ♦A65	
♥K2 ♣AJ432		♥543 ♣65	

Open	Advnc	Resp	Over
1♣	Pass	1♠	Dbl
Rdbl	Pass	2♠	Pass
Pass	Pass		

Opener	(5)	Responder	
♠A32 ♦32		♠654 ♦AK765	
♥K432 ♣AQ32		♥8765 ♣4	

Open	Advnc	Resp	Over
1♣	Pass	1♦	1♠
Dbl	Pass	2♥	Pass
Pass	Pass		

Opener	(6)	Responder	
♠A2 ♦432		♠654 ♦AK765	
♥K432 ♣AQ32		♥8765 ♣4	

Open	Advnc	Resp	Over
1♣	Pass	1♦	1♥
Dbl	Pass	2♦	Pass
Pass			

In example (3), opener doubles two clubs, alerted as Michaels, showing exactly three spades with unlimited values. This time opener has a very strong hand. It doesn't matter whether two clubs is natural or Michaels. If overcaller had bid one notrump, opener's double would still be a support double. Opener then bids three hearts over responder's sign-off, showing more than a minimum support double. Responder with a maximum sign-off cuebids four diamonds on the way to four spades. Opener bids RKC, finds out responder has two keycards and the spade queen and jumps to six notrump, protecting the heart king. In example (4), opener redoubles overcaller's take-out double to show a three-card spade raise. Responder signs-off in two spades and opener passes showing a minimum opener. Example (5) is the only exception. Opener's double of one spade shows four hearts with not enough strength to bid two hearts, not three-card diamond support. In example (6), opener doubles one heart, which shows exactly three diamonds and denies four spades. If opener has four spades and three diamonds, opener bids one spade and supports diamonds later. A direct diamond raise shows four. If opener has ♠KJ10♥KJ10♦432♣AQ32, opener can rebid one notrump rather than making a support double.

13.7 -- EXTRA STRENGTH DOUBLES.

Opener	(1)	Responder		Opener	(2)	Responder	
♠A2 ♦432		♠KQ543 ♦A76		♠A2 ♦5432		♠KQ543 ♦A76	
♥AQJ2 ♣K432		♥54 ♣Q65		♥32 ♣AK432		♥54 ♣Q65	

Open	Advnc	Resp	Over	Open	Advnc	Resp	Over
1♣	Pass	1♠	2♥	1♣	Pass	1♠	2♥
Pass	Pass	Dbl	Pass	Pass	Pass	Dbl	Pass
Pass	Pass			3♣	Pass	Pass	Pass

Opener	(3)	Responder		Opener	(4)	Responder	
♠Q65 ♦KQ765		♠AK432 ♦432		♠Q ♦KQ765		♠AK432 ♦432	
♥K3 ♣KJ4		♥Q2 ♣Q32		♥K43 ♣KJ54		♥Q2 ♣Q32	

Open	Over	Resp	Advnc	Open	Over	Resp	Advnc
1♦	1♥	1♠	3♥	1♦	1♥	1♠	3♥
Pass	Pass	Dbl	Pass	Pass	Pass	Dbl	Pass
3♠	Pass			Pass	Pass		

There are situations where double shows extra-strength rather than be a penalty double. Usually, doubler has two cards in the opponent's suit. All low-level non-conventional doubles should be for takeout. In example (1), opener, who is playing support doubles, cannot double two hearts for penalties, so opener has to pass. Responder, who is in passout seat, doubles showing extra strength, usually with fewer than three hearts and support for whatever opener bids. Responder would be happy if opener passes his double for penalties. In this case, opener passes for penalties. Playing support doubles, opener can still penalize overcaller. In example (2), opener pulls responder's extra-strength double to three clubs.

In examples (3) and (4), responder's double of three hearts shows values. It's very unlikely when a suit has been bid and raised to have a clear-cut penalty double. Responder is more likely to have a hand similar to examples (3) and (4), where responder has too much strength to sell out, but doesn't have a clear-cut action. Responder can support whatever opener does. In example (3), holding three-card spade support, opener bids three spades. In example (4), holding one spade and three hearts, opener passes responder's extra-strength double for penalties. In example (3), three spades is very likely to make. In example (4), three-hearts doubled is very likely to go down.

CHAPTER 14 - NOTRUMP OVERCALLS

14.1 -- DIRECT ONE NOTRUMP OVERCALL 15-18 HCPS.

1.

```
| 1♠ 1NT P 2♥ |
| P  2♠  P 3♣ |
```

2.

```
| 1♠ 1NT P 2♥ |
| P  2♠  P 3♦ |
```

3.

```
| 1♠ 1NT P 2♥ |
| P  2♠  P 3♥ |
```

4.

```
| 1♠ 1NT P 2♥ |
| P  2♠  P 2NT |
```

5.

```
| 1♠ 1NT P 2♥ |
| P  2♠  P 3♠ |
```

6.

```
| 1♠ 1NT P 2♥ |
| P  2♠  P 4♥ |
```

7.

```
| 1♠ 1NT P 2♥ |
| P  2♠  P  P |
```

8.

```
| 1♠ 1NT P 4♥ |
| P  4♠  P  P |
```

A one-notrump overcall shows 15-18 HCPs with a stopper in opener's suit. Usually overcaller has a balanced hand. However, there are some unbalanced hands with suits that are not good enough to overcall at the two-level and that can best be described by overcalling one notrump. Advancer ignores the opening bid and uses all conventions in chapters one and two; Jacoby, Four-suit Transfers, Lebensohl, Texas etc. If responder bids over overcaller's notrump, advancer ignores the opening bid and plays "system on" over responder's bid. All Lebensohl bids are directed towards responder's suit, since overcaller has already promised a stopper in opener's suit. However, all doubles of bid-and-raised-suits are responsive.

If advancer transfers into opener's suit, overcaller is required to accept the transfer. If advancer is weak and wants to play in the opponent's suit, he passes. All other bids by advancer after transferring into opener's suit are natural, game-forcing, and show a singleton or void in opponent's suit.

In auction (1), advancer shows a game-forcing hand, a club suit, and spade shortness. In auction (2), advancer shows a game-forcing hand, a diamond suit, and spade shortness. In auction (3), advancer shows a game-forcing hand, five hearts, and spade shortness. In auction (4), advancer shows a game-forcing hand, both minors, and spade shortness. In auction (5), advancer shows a game-forcing hand, a four-card heart suit, and spade shortness. In auction (6), advancer shows a slam try, at least six hearts, and spade shortness. In auction (7), advancer wants to play in two spades. In auction (8), advancer wants to play in four spades. Advancer can use similar auctions after one club, one diamond or one-heart openers.

Overcaller	(1)	Advancer	

♠JT ♦AQ32   ♠KQ432 ♦654
  ♥AT9 ♣KQJ2   ♥J2 ♣A43

Open	Over	Resp	Advnc
1♥	1NT	Pass	2♥
Pass	2♠	Pass	3NT
Pass	Pass	Pass	

Overcaller	(2)	Advancer	

♠JT ♦AQ32   ♠KQ432 ♦654
  ♥AT9 ♣KQJ2   ♥2 ♣A543

Open	Over	Resp	Advnc
1♥	1NT	Pass	2♦
Pass	2♥	Pass	2♠
Pass	3♣	Pass	4♣
Pass	4NT	Pass	5♦
Pass	6♣	Pass	Pass

Overcaller	(3)	Advancer	

♠A5 ♦A765   ♠432 ♦32
  ♥AK65 ♣Q65   ♥432 ♣KJ432

Open	Over	Resp	Advnc
1♣	1NT	Dbl	Rdbl
Pass	2♣	Pass	Pass
Pass			

Overcaller	(4)	Advancer	

♠A5 ♦A765   ♠432 ♦KJ432
  ♥AK65 ♣Q65   ♥432 ♣32

Open	Over	Resp	Advnc
1♣	1NT	Dbl	Rdbl
Pass	2♣	Pass	2♦
Pass	Pass		

In example (1), advancer has a normal Jacoby transfer sequence showing five spades with game-forcing values. Overcaller with only two spades passes three notrump. In example (2), advancer transfers to two hearts and then bids two spades, showing five spades and game-forcing values with shortness in hearts. Overcaller, with a maximum notrump and only one heart stopper, bids three clubs, showing a club suit. With two heart stoppers, overcaller bids two notrump. When advancer raises clubs, overcaller bids keycard and bids six clubs. Since three notrump goes down on a heart lead, even getting to five clubs is a good result.

In examples (3) and (4), advancer wants to play in two-of-a-minor after responder doubles overcaller's one notrump for penalties. After responder's penalty double, advancer redoubles, forcing overcaller to bid two clubs. Advancer passes two clubs with a club suit and corrects to two diamonds with a diamond suit. In example (3), advancer passes overcaller's forced two-club bid. In example (4), advancer corrects two clubs to two diamonds.

14.2 -- BALANCING ONE NOTRUMP 11-14 NON-VULNERABLE, 14-16 VULNERABLE.

Advancer (1)		Overcaller		Advancer (2)		Overcaller	
	Vul				Vul		
♠A43 ♦543		♠K2 ♦AQJ2		♠6543 ♦43		♠K2 ♦AQJ2	
♥Q4 ♣KJT65		♥K32 ♣Q432		♥QJ654 ♣K5		♥K32 ♣Q432	

Open	Advnc	Resp	Over	Open	Advnc	Resp	Over
1♦	Pass	Pass	1NT	1♦	Pass	Pass	1NT
Pass	2♣	Pass	2♦	Pass	2♣	Pass	2♦
Pass	2NT	Pass	3NT	Pass	2♥	Pass	Pass

Advancer (3)		Overcaller		Advancer (4)		Overcaller	
	Non-vul				Non-vul		
♠A54 ♦43		♠Q32 ♦AQ2		♠A54 ♦KJT543		♠Q32 ♦AQ2	
♥43 ♣KJT876		♥KJ2 ♣5432		♥43 ♣76		♥KJ2 ♣5432	

Open	Advnc	Resp	Over	Open	Advnc	Resp	Over
1♥	Pass	Pass	1NT	1♥	Pass	Pass	1NT
Pass	2♠	Pass	3♣	Pass	2NT	Pass	3♦
Pass	Pass	Pass		Pass	Pass		

If overcaller has a balanced hand or a hand where advancer's response to a takeout double can prove embarrassing, and chooses to bid in balancing seat, overcaller's best call is usually one notrump. Stoppers in opener's suit, especially if it's a minor, are not as important as for a direct one-notrump overcall. Overcaller can be outside the above ranges but will know what advancer expects if advancer invites. Advancer responds the same as section 14.1, Stayman, Jacoby, Texas, etc.

In examples (1) and (2), overcaller, who is vulnerable, balances with one notrump, showing 14-16 HCPs. In example (1), advancer bids two clubs followed by two notrump, inviting overcaller to bid three notrump with a maximum. Two clubs followed by two notrump does not promise a four-card major and is the way advancer invites in notrump. In example (2), advancer bids two clubs followed by two hearts to show a weak hand with both majors. In examples (3) and (4), overcaller, who is non-vulnerable, balances with one notrump showing 11-14 HCPs. In example (3), advancer bids two spades transfer to clubs, and overcaller bids three clubs. In example (4), advancer bids two notrump transfer to diamonds. Even though overcaller has a good diamond fit, overcaller has a minimum with no outside aces and bids three-diamonds, denying, rather than three-clubs, accepting.

218

14.3 -- BALANCING TWO-NOTRUMP JUMP 19-21 HCPS. DOUBLE FOLLOWED BY TWO NOTRUMP 17-18 VULNERABLE, 15-18 NON-VULNERABLE.

Advancer   (1)   Overcaller   Advancer   (2)   Overcaller

♠543   ♦43   ♠K2 ♦AQJ2   ♠6543   ♦43   ♠K2 ♦AQJ2
  ♥QJ7654 ♣K4   ♥K32 ♣AQ32   ♥QJ654 ♣K4   ♥K32 ♣AQ32

Open	Advnc	Resp	Over
1♠	Pass	Pass	2NT
Pass	4♦	Pass	4♥
Pass	Pass	Pass	

Open	Advnc	Resp	Over
1♣	Pass	Pass	2NT
Pass	3♣	Pass	3♦
Pass	3♠	Pass	4♥

Advancer   (3)   Overcaller   Advancer   (4)   Overcaller

♠A54 ♦432   ♠Q32 ♦AQJ   ♠654 ♦K65432   ♠Q32 ♦AQJ
  ♥43   ♣KJT65   ♥KJ2 ♣A432   ♥43   ♣65   ♥KJ2 ♣A432

Open	Advnc	Resp	Over
1♥	Pass	Pass	Dbl
Pass	2♣	Pass	2NT
Pass	3NT	Pass	

Open	Advnc	Resp	Over
1♥	Pass	Pass	Dbl
Pass	2♦	Pass	2NT
Pass	3♦	Pass	Pass

A balancing two-notrump jump shows a balanced 19-21 HCPs. Advancer uses conventions in Chapter Three (two-notrump opener).

In examples (1) and (2), overcaller jumps to two notrump, showing a balanced hand with 19-21 HCPs. In example (1), advancer bids four diamonds, a Texas transfer, and overcaller bids four hearts. In example (2), advancer bids three clubs, Stayman, and overcaller bids three diamonds, denying a four-card major. Advancer bids three spades, Smolen, showing exactly four spades and five or more hearts. Overcaller bids four hearts, ending the auction.

Double followed by two notrump is 17-18 vulnerable and 15-18 non-vulnerable. All of advancer's bids are natural. In examples (3) and (4), overcaller doubles and then bids two notrump, showing the middle range between a balancing one notrump and a balancing two notrump. In example (3), advancer raises to three notrump. In example (4), advancer signs-off in three diamonds.

CHAPTER 15 - UNUSUAL NOTRUMP

Overcaller (1)	Advancer		Overcaller (2)	Advancer	
♠- ♦AJT432	♠5432	♦65	♠- ♦AJT43	♠5432	♦65
♥K2 ♣AQT32	♥A6543	♣J5	♥K2 ♣AQT432	♥A6543	♣J5

Open	Over	Resp	Advnc	Open	Over	Resp	Advnc
1♠	2NT	4♠	Pass	1♠	2NT	4♠	Pass
Pass	4NT	Pass	5♦	Pass	5♣	Dbl	Pass
Dbl	Pass	Pass	Pass	Pass			

Overcaller (3)	Advancer		Overcaller (4)	Advancer	
♠2 ♦KQJ32	♠QJ43	♦65	♠2 ♦AK432	♠QJ43	♦65
♥KQJ32 ♣32	♥54	♣87654	♥AQJ32 ♣32	♥54	♣87654

Open	Over	Resp	Advnc	Open	Over	Resp	Advnc
1♣	2NT	4♠	Pass	1♣	2NT	4♠	Pass
Pass	Pass			Pass	Dbl	All Pass	

A jump to two notrump shows at least 5-5 in the two lowest unbid suits, any strength. Usually, overcaller has some 5-5 ten-count, and two notrump says it all. If overcaller has extra length or extra strength, overcaller can bid again. In competition, if overcaller has a good defensive hand, he doubles. If overcaller has extra length, and overcaller's lower suit is equal to or longer than his higher suit, overcaller bids his lower suit. If overcaller's higher suit is longer, overcaller bids notrump again.

In example (1), overcaller with six diamonds and five clubs bids two notrump. Over four spades, overcaller decides to bid again and bids four notrump, suggesting longer diamonds, and advancer with 2-2 in the minors bids five diamonds. In example (2), overcaller with six clubs and five diamonds bids two notrump. Over four spades, overcaller bids five clubs, suggesting clubs are equal to or longer than diamonds. Advancer with 2-2 in the minors chooses clubs. In examples (3) and (4), overcaller jumps to two notrump showing diamonds and hearts. In example (3), overcaller has an average two-notrump bid so he passes four spades. In example (4), overcaller has extra values and wants to bid again. With good defensive values, rather then bidding four notrump and forcing his side to declare, overcaller doubles to give advancer a choice. Advancer with four spades and only 2-2 in the red suits, is happy to pass the double.

16.1 -- CAN BE LIGHT.

At the one-level in direct seat, I overcall anytime I have a five-card suit with at least eight HCPs. This overcall is not meant to be a lead-directing overcall, but is designed to allow advancer to raise to the two-level with three-card support and the three-level with four-card support. The Law of Total Tricks protects overcaller. ♠K2♥65432♦QJ32♣K2 is an example of a hand which I overcall one heart. A one-level overcall can be a very good hand. I overcall one heart holding ♠-♥AKQJ4♦32♣AKQJ32 to avoid having to correct four spades to five hearts. At the two-level, overcaller needs a good suit and a good hand. To overcall at the two-level with a five-card suit, you should have at least an opening bid with a suit headed by two of the top three or three of the top five honors. With a six-card suit, you don't need quite as much.

16.2 -- JUMP RAISE PREEMPTIVE.

Overcaller (1)   Advancer   Overcaller (2)   Advancer

♠K2   ♦KQ32   ♠6543   ♦654   ♠K2   ♦KQ32   ♠543   ♦J654
  ♥65432   ♣32   ♥KJ87   ♣54   ♥65432   ♣32   ♥QJ87   ♣54

Open	Over	Resp	Advnc	Open	Over	Resp	Advnc
1♣	1♥	Dbl	3♥	1♣	1♥	1♠	3♥

Overcaller (3)   Advancer   Overcaller (4)   Advancer

♠AJ432   ♦QJ2   ♠KQ65   ♦76543   ♠AJ432   ♦QJ2   ♠QJ65   ♦76543
  ♥432   ♣32   ♥65   ♣54   ♥432   ♣32   ♥J5   ♣54

Open	Over	Resp	Advnc	Open	Over	Resp	Advnc
1♣	1♠	Dbl	3♠	1♣	1♠	2♥	3♠

After an overcall, advancer's jump raise is preemptive, showing four-card support with fewer than seven points. The jump raise makes the opponents continue their auction at the three or four-level. As long as the overcall is a five-card suit, the Law protects the raise. In examples (1) through (4), advancer's jump raise to the three-level forces the opponents, who have 27-28 HCPs between them, to guess where they belong. If the overcaller is a passed hand, advancer may jump raise with any hand containing four-card support.

16.3 -- JUMP CUEBID SHOWS 7-9 HCPS WITH FOUR-CARD SUPPORT.

Overcaller	(1)	Advancer	
♠K2 ♦KQ32		♠A543 ♦654	
♥65432 ♣32		♥K987 ♣54	

Open	Over	Resp	Advnc
1♣	1♥	Dbl	3♣
Pass	3♥	Pass	Pass

Overcaller	(2)	Advancer	
♠K2 ♦KQ32		♠Q543 ♦654	
♥65432 ♣32		♥AK87 ♣54	

Open	Over	Resp	Advnc
1♣	1♥	Dbl	3♣
Pass	3♥	Pass	Pass

Overcaller	(3)	Advancer	
♠AJ432 ♦AQ2		♠KQ65 ♦543	
♥432 ♣32		♥65 ♣KJ54	

Open	Over	Resp	Advnc
1♦	1♠	Dbl	3♦
Pass	3♠	Pass	Pass

Overcaller	(4)	Advancer	
♠AJ432 ♦AQ2		♠KQ65 ♦543	
♥432 ♣A2		♥65 ♣KJ54	

Open	Over	Resp	Advnc
1♦	1♠	Dbl	3♦
Pass	3♥	Pass	4♠

After an overcall, advancer's jump cuebid is a mixed raise, showing four-card support with seven to nine HCPs. The mixed raise says nothing about distribution. Advancer can be 4-3-3-3. The mixed raise is stronger than a preemptive jump raise and weaker than a limit raise. If overcaller is a passed hand, advancer avoids using the mixed raise. If opener doubles the jump cuebid, overcaller rebids his suit with no game interest. With game interest, overcaller passes, redoubles or bids any in-between suit. At the three-level or higher, returning to the trump suit is weaker than passing a lead-directing double.

In examples (1) and (2), advancer's jump to three clubs shows four-card heart support with seven to nine points. Overcaller signs-off in three hearts. Over three clubs, overcaller can make a game try by bidding three diamonds, a Last-Train artificial game try. If overcaller holds his red-suit losers to two, he makes three hearts. If you can't make three hearts, the opponents probably will be able to make at least three clubs. In examples (3) and (4), advancer jumps to three diamonds showing a mixed raise. In example (3), overcaller with an average overcall, signs-off in three spades. In example (4), overcaller has enough to make a game try. Overcaller bids three hearts, the Last Train, the only call between three diamonds and three spades, as an artificial game try. With a maximum mixed raise, advancer accepts the game try.

16.4 -- NEW SUIT NON-FORCING. JUMP SHIFT INVITATIONAL.

Overcaller (1)   Advancer   Overcaller (2)   Advancer

♠K32 ♦KQ2   ♠AQJ54 ♦543   ♠K32 ♦KQ2   ♠QJ4 ♦AJT543
  ♥65432 ♣32   ♥K7 ♣654   ♥65432 ♣32   ♥K7 ♣54

Open	Over	Resp	Advnc	Open	Over	Resp	Advnc
1♣	1♥	Pass	1♠	1♣	1♥	Pass	2♦
2♣	2♠	3♣	Pass	3♣	3♦	Pass	Pass

Overcaller (3)   Advancer   Overcaller (4)   Advancer

♠AK432 ♦32   ♠65 ♦KQ   ♠AK432 ♦32   ♠65 ♦AKQ654
  ♥432 ♣432   ♥AKQ765 ♣765   ♥432 ♣KJ2   ♥A65 ♣65

Open	Over	Resp	Advnc	Open	Over	Resp	Advnc
1♣	1♠	Pass	3♥	1♣	1♠	Pass	3♦
Pass	Pass	Pass		Pass	3NT	Pass	Pass

Advancer responds as if overcaller has an opening bid, even though overcaller might have only eight points. Overcaller can have a very good hand to overcall at the one-level. A new suit by advancer is non-forcing but shows values. A jump shift is also non-forcing but highly invitational, showing at least a solid or semi-solid six-card suit.

In examples (1) and (2), overcaller with five hearts and eight HCPs overcalls one heart. 65432 is a five-card suit, believe it or not. When advancer raises, overcaller's aggressive action usually wins. In example (1), advancer bids one spade, a typical new-suit non-forcing response to responder's overcall. Overcaller, even though he has a minimum overcall, competes to two spades. In example (2), advancer bids two diamonds. Without the king of hearts, advancer still bids two diamonds. Overcaller, following total-trick concepts rather than point-count concepts, competes to three diamonds. Someone is very likely to have a nine-card minor-suit fit, which makes bidding three diamonds correct according to the Law. IF YOU ARE IN DOUBT ABOUT WHETHER TO COMPETE OR PASS, COMPETE IF YOU ARE SHORT IN THE OPPONENT'S SUIT, PASS IF YOU ARE LONG. In example (3), advancer shows a very good heart hand. Overcaller, with a minimum overcall, passes three hearts. In example (4), advancer has a good diamond suit with an opening hand. Advancer jumps to three diamonds, inviting overcaller to bid with extra values. Overcaller, with a club stopper and some extra values, bids three notrump.

16.5 -- CUEBID IS A LIMIT RAISE OR BETTER OR FORCING HAND WITH OWN SUIT. WHEN HAVING CHOICE OF TWO SUITS TO CUEBID, HIGHER CUEBID SHOWS FOUR-CARD LIMIT RAISE OR BETTER, LOWER CUEBID SHOWS THREE-CARD LIMIT RAISE OR BETTER OR FORCING HAND WITH OWN SUIT.

Overcaller (1)	Advancer	Overcaller (2)	Advancer

♠K2 ♦KQ32	♠A543 ♦A54	♠K2 ♦KQ32	♠A543 ♦A54
♥65432 ♣32	♥QJ7 ♣654	♥65432 ♣32	♥QJ87 ♣54

Open	Over	Resp	Advnc	Open	Over	Resp	Advnc
1♣	1♥	Dbl	Rdbl	1♣	1♥	1NT	2NT
2♣	Pass	Pass	2♥	3♣	3♥	Pass	Pass
Pass	Pass	3♣	Pass	Pass			

Advancer's cuebid shows at least ten support points. The cuebid shows either a limit raise or better with support for overcaller's suit, or a hand without support with game-forcing values. If advancer has two suits to cuebid, the higher cuebid shows a limit raise or better with at least four-card support for overcaller's suit. The lower cuebid denies four-card support. Over a negative double, cuebid shows a limit raise or better with at least four-card support, and redouble shows at least ten points denying four-card support. If responder bids one notrump, a two-notrump cuebid by advancer shows a limit raise or better with at least four-card support, and a cuebid denies four-card support.

In example (1), advancer redoubles, showing either a three-card limit raise or better in hearts, or a game-forcing diamond or spade hand. Sometimes advancer has to redouble with only two-card heart support. Advancer bids two clubs to show four-card heart support with at least limit raise values. Since overcaller doesn't have six hearts and advancer doesn't have four hearts, they sell out to three clubs. In example (2), advancer cuebids two notrump, showing four-card heart support with at least limit raise values. With only three-card heart support and limit raise values, advancer cuebids two clubs. With a nine-card fit, overcaller competes to three hearts. Overcaller bids three diamonds, artificial, if he wants to invite game.

16.6 -- WHEN CUEBID GETS DOUBLED, PASS SHOWS WEAKNESS, REBIDDING SUIT SHOWS A SIX-CARD SUIT, NOT EXTRA VALUES, IN-BETWEEN SUIT IS CONSTRUCTIVE AND MAY BE ARTIFICIAL.

Overcaller (1)		Advancer		Overcaller (2)		Advancer	
♠K32	♦KQ2	♠AQ54	♦A43	♠K32	♦KQ2	♠AQ54	♦A43
♥65432	♣32	♥KJ7	♣654	♥A5432	♣32	♥KJ7	♣654

Open	Over	Resp	Advnc	Open	Over	Resp	Advnc
1♣	1♥	Pass	2♣	1♣	1♥	Pass	2♣
Dbl	Pass	Pass	2♥	Dbl	2♦	Pass	4♥

Overcaller (3)		Advancer		Overcaller (4)		Advancer	
♠K32	♦KQ2	♠A654	♦A43	♠K32	♦KQ2	♠A654	♦A43
♥765432	♣2	♥KJ8	♣654	♥A5432	♣32	♥K98	♣654

Open	Over	Resp	Advnc	Open	Over	Resp	Advnc
1♣	1♥	Pass	2♣	1♣	1♥	Pass	2♣
Dbl	2♥	3♣	3♥	Dbl	2♦	Pass	2♥

When advancer cuebids in response to an overcall and opener doubles, overcaller is not forced to bid. Overcaller passes the double with a minimum overcall and a five-card suit. Overcaller rebids the suit to show a minimum overcall with a six-card suit. It is very important for overcaller to show how many trumps he has. Overcaller bids any in-between suit or redoubles to show interest in game.

In example (1), overcaller passes two-clubs doubled to show a weak five-card overcall. Since overcaller passed two-clubs doubled, advancer bids only two hearts, ending the auction. In example (2), overcaller shows at least a minimum opening bid with his artificial two-diamond Last Train bid. Advancer with a sound opening bid jumps to four hearts. If overcaller wants to be in game opposite a hand with limit raise strength, he bids higher than two-of-his-suit. A jump to three hearts shows a game-forcing hand with a six-card suit. In example (3), overcaller bids two hearts, showing a six-card suit. Overcaller doesn't show extra values, just an extra heart. Advancer with a minimum opening bid passes two hearts, but with a nine-card fit competes to three hearts over three clubs. In example (4), overcaller bids two diamonds, an artificial game try. With only a limit raise, responder signs-off in two hearts, ending the auction.

16.7 -- ADVANCER'S PASSED HAND JUMP TO TWO NOTRUMP SHOWS FOUR-CARD SUPPORT. CUEBID SHOWS THREE-CARD SUPPORT.

Overcaller (1)		Advancer		Overcaller (2)		Advancer	
♠K2	♦KQ2	♠AQJ4	♦543	♠K32	♦KQ2	♠AQJ4	♦543
♥765432	♣32	♥KJ8	♣654	♥AQ432	♣32	♥KJ8	♣654

Open	Over	Resp	Advnc	Open	Over	Resp	Advnc
-	-	-	Pass	-	-	-	Pass
1♣	1♥	Pass	2♣	1♣	1♥	Pass	2♣
Dbl	2♥	Pass	Pass	Dbl	2♦	Pass	4♥

Overcaller (3)		Advancer		Overcaller (4)		Advancer	
♠K32	♦KQ2	♠AQJ4	♦43	♠K32	♦AQ2	♠AQJ4	♦43
♥765432	♣2	♥KJ98	♣654	♥A5432	♣32	♥KJ98	♣654

Open	Over	Resp	Advnc	Open	Over	Resp	Advnc
-	-	-	Pass	-	-	-	Pass
1♣	1♥	Pass	2NT	1♣	1♥	Pass	2NT
Pass	3♥	Pass	Pass	Pass	3♦	Pass	4♥
Pass	Pass			Pass	Pass	Pass	

If advancer is a passed hand, advancer can't have enough values to make a natural jump to two notrump in response to an overcall. Therefore, a jump to two notrump shows a four-card limit raise, and a cuebid shows fewer than four trumps. Usually advancer has three-card support to cuebid, but there are some hands where cuebidding with two-card support best describes his hand.

In examples (1) and (2), advancer, who is a passed hand, cuebids two clubs, showing a three-card or possibly a two-card limit raise in hearts. ♠5432♥KJ♦AQJ2♣432 is an example where advancer cuebids with only two-card heart support. In example (1), overcaller, with a minimum overcall but an extra heart, rebids two hearts. In example (2), overcaller has enough to invite. With a sound limit raise, advancer jumps to four hearts. In examples (3) and (4), advancer, who is a passed hand, jumps to two notrump, showing a four-card limit raise in hearts. In example (3), overcaller signs-off in three hearts. In example (4), overcaller makes a game try and advancer accepts. In this case, overcaller has a choice between three clubs and three diamonds as possible game tries and chooses the suit with values.

17.1 -- TWO CLUBS SHOWS BOTH MAJORS.

Overcaller	(1)	Advancer		Overcaller	(2)	Advancer	
♠KQJ32	♦2	♠54	♦KQJ3	♠KQJ32	♦2	♠54	♦KQJ43
♥Q5432	♣32	♥876	♣A654	♥Q5432	♣32	♥76	♣A654

Open	Over	Resp	Advnc	Open	Over	Resp	Advnc
1NT	2♣	Pass	2♥	1NT	2♣	Pass	2♦
Pass	Pass	Pass		Pass	2♥	Pass	Pass

Overcaller	(3)	Advancer		Overcaller	(4)	Advancer	
♠AQJ32	♦2	♠654	♦KQJ	♠AQJ32	♦2	♠54	♦K6543
♥A432	♣432	♥765	♣A765	♥A432	♣432	♥65	♣A765

Open	Over	Resp	Advnc	Open	Over	Resp	Advnc
1NT	2♣	Pass	2♦	1NT	2♣	Pass	2♦
Pass	2♠	Pass	Pass	Pass	2♠	Pass	Pass

Two clubs by overcaller shows at least 4-4 in the majors. Overcaller would like to be 5-5, or better, but usually is 5-4. Anytime overcaller has a singleton he tries to enter the auction. Over two clubs, advancer bids his longer major. If advancer is 2-2 or 3-3 in the majors, advancer bids two diamonds, asking overcaller to bid his longer major. Two diamonds by advancer denies holding a four-card major. Advancer with four-card or longer support for one of overcaller's major, some distribution and a good hand, can jump. REMEMBER, ADVANCER BIDS CONSERVATIVELY AND OVERCALLER WITH DISTRIBUTION BIDS AGGRESSIVELY.

In examples (1) through (4), overcaller bids two clubs showing both majors. In example (1), advancer, with three hearts and two spades, bids two hearts. In example (2), advancer with 2-2 in the majors bids two diamonds, asking overcaller to choose his longer major. Overcaller with 5-5 in the majors bids two hearts. In examples (3) and (4), advancer with equal majors bids two diamonds, asking overcaller to bid his longer major. Overcaller with five spades and four hearts bids two spades. These methods allow you to play in your 5-3 spade fit instead of your 4-3 heart fit in example (3) and your 5-2 spade fit instead of your 4-2 heart fit in example (4).

Overcaller	(5)	Advancer		Overcaller	(6)	Advancer	

Overcaller (5)   **Advancer**   **Overcaller (6)**   **Advancer**

♠AQJ32   ♦32   ♠K7654   ♦A4   ♠AQJ32   ♦32   ♠K54   ♦54
   ♥AQ432   ♣2   ♥65   ♣A543   ♥AQ432   ♣2   ♥65   ♣A76543

Open	Over	Resp	Advnc		Open	Over	Resp	Advnc
1NT	2♣	Pass	3♠		1NT	2♣	Pass	2♠
Pass	4♠	Pass			Pass	3♠	Pass	4♠

Overcaller (7)   **Advancer**   **Overcaller (8)**   **Advancer**

♠AQJ2   ♦65432   ♠543   ♦K87   ♠AQJ2   ♦65432   ♠43   ♦K7
   ♥A432   ♣-   ♥765   ♣A432   ♥A432   ♣-   ♥65   ♣A765432

Open	Over	Resp	Advnc		Open	Over	Resp	Advnc
1NT	2♣	Pass	2♦		1NT	2♣	Pass	Pass
Pass	Pass	Pass			Pass			

In examples (5) and (6), overcaller bids two clubs showing both majors. In example (5), advancer with five-card spade support, two doubletons and two aces, bids three spades invitational. Overcaller, whose hand can be a lot worse, raises to game. In example (6), advancer with 3-2 in the majors bids two spades. Overcaller knows that advancer has more spades than hearts. Since responder passed over two clubs, overcaller places some values as well as support in advancer's hand. With any major suit finesse likely to work, overcaller invites game and advancer accepts.

If advancer does not have four-card or longer support for one of overcaller's majors, other strains can be found. One possibility is that advancer with a long club suit passes two clubs. Another possibility is overcaller has at least four diamonds and passes advancer's two-diamond ask. Advancer can also bid three-of-a-minor which is natural and non-forcing.

In examples (7) and (8), overcaller bids two clubs showing both majors. In example (7), advancer with 3-3 in the majors bids two diamonds, asking overcaller to choose his longer major. With five diamonds and only 4-4 in the majors, overcaller takes a chance and passes two diamonds, hoping that advancer is not 3-3-1-6. In example (8), advancer with seven clubs and only 2-2 in the majors passes two clubs, hoping that overcaller is not 6-6 in the majors.

17.2 -- TWO DIAMONDS SHOWS ONE MAJOR.

Advancer (1)		Overcaller		Advancer (2)		Overcaller	
♠32	♦A432	♠J87654	♦Q65	♠AK32	♦AJ2	♠J87654	♦Q65
♥K432	♣AKQ	♥5	♣654	♥A432	♣32	♥5	♣654

Open	Advnc	Resp	Over	Open	Advnc	Resp	Over
1NT	Pass	Pass	2♦	1NT	Pass	Pass	2♦
Pass	2♠	Pass	Pass	Pass	4♥	Pass	4♠

Two diamonds by overcaller shows a one-suiter in either hearts or spades. Overcaller with a seven-card major suit can bid two diamonds or can bid his suit at the three-level. All major-suit bids by advancer are pass or correct. If advancer has a two-card or more difference in the majors, he bids his shorter major. If advancer is 1-3 he bids the one. If advancer is 2-4 he bids the two. Advancer makes the lowest bid he wants to be passed in. If advancer has four hearts and one spade, advancer assumes that overcaller has spades so advancer bids two spades. Advancer always assumes the worst. If overcaller has spades, he passes. If overcaller happens to have hearts, overcaller corrects to three hearts and advancer will be happy to play the 6-4 heart fit at the three-level. If advancer has his own major, advancer has to bid and rebid it.

In example (1), overcaller in balancing position has six spades and bids two diamonds, showing a heart or spade one-suiter. Overcaller is safe bidding such a weak suit since advancer has to have a strong balanced hand since he passed over one notrump and responder didn't bid. Advancer with four hearts and two spades bids two spades, pass or correct. Overcaller with a spade one-suiter passes. In example (2), advancer in direct seat, decides not to bid two clubs showing both majors with only 4-4. Overcaller in balancing seat bids two diamonds showing a heart or spade one-suiter. Advancer with four-card support for both majors and a possible ruffing value bids four hearts, pass or correct. All major-suit bids by advancer are pass or correct, even jumps to game. Overcaller corrects to four spades.

```
Overcaller  (3)   Advancer              Overcaller  (4)    Advancer

♠AQJ432  ♦432     ♠65   ♦KJ765          ♠AQJ432 ♦432       ♠-       ♦K5
    ♥2   ♣K32     ♥KQ    ♣Q765              ♥2   ♣432      ♥KQJ6543 ♣QJ76

Open    Over    Resp    Advnc             Open    Over    Resp    Advnc
1NT     2♦      Pass    2♥                1NT     2♦      Pass    2♥
Pass    2♠      Pass    Pass              Pass    2♠      Pass    3♥
Pass                                      Pass    Pass    Pass
```

```
Overcaller  (5)   Advancer              Overcaller  (6)    Advancer

♠AQJ432  ♦432     ♠65   ♦K8765          ♠AQJ432 ♦432       ♠765    ♦AK65
    ♥2   ♣K32     ♥KQ    ♣Q654              ♥2   ♣K32       ♥543    ♣Q54

Open    Over    Resp    Advnc             Open    Over    Resp    Advnc
1NT     2♦      Dbl     2♥                1NT     2♦      Dbl     Rdbl
Pass    2♠      3♥      Pass              Pass    2♠      3♥      Pass
Pass    Pass                             Pass    3♠      Pass    Pass
```

In examples (3) and (4), overcaller in direct seat bids two
diamonds, showing a heart or spade one-suiter. In example (3),
advancer with 2-2 in the majors bids two hearts pass or correct.
Overcaller corrects to two spades. In example (4), advancer with a
void in spades wants to play in hearts. Advancer bids two hearts,
pass or correct, and overcaller corrects to two spades. Advancer now
bids three hearts, which is his own suit, and overcaller passes. If
advancer wants to make a game try over two diamonds, he bids two
notrump, which is invitational in whichever major overcaller has.
Remember, advancer bids conservatively and overcaller bids
aggressively.

If responder doubles two diamonds, advancer has three options.
Advancer can pass with diamonds, giving overcaller a choice of playing
two diamonds or two-of-his-major. Advancer can bid a major at any
level, pass or correct, with a weak hand. With 4-4 in the majors and
a weak hand, advancer can bid three hearts. Advancer can redouble
showing a constructive hand with support for both majors, inviting
overcaller to compete at the three-level with a sound overcall.

17.3 -- TWO-OF-MAJOR SHOWS A FIVE-CARD SUIT AND A MINOR -- TWO NOTRUMP ASKS FOR THE MINOR.

Advancer (1)   Overcaller   Advancer (2)   Overcaller

♠432   ♦AK2   ♠AQ765 ♦5   ♠2   ♦K432   ♠AQ765 ♦5
  ♥QJ32 ♣AQ2   ♥876   ♣K654   ♥5432 ♣AQ32   ♥876   ♣K654

Open	Advnc	Resp	Over
1NT	Pass	Pass	2♠
Pass	Pass	Pass	

Open	Advnc	Resp	Over
1NT	Pass	Pass	2♠
Pass	2NT	Pass	3♣
Pass	Pass	Pass	

Two-of-major shows a five-card major and a four-card or longer minor. OVERCALLER BIDS AGGRESSIVELY, ESPECIALLY WITH DISTRIBUTIONAL HANDS, AND ADVANCER BIDS CONSERVATIVELY. Advancer with two or three-card support usually passes two-of-overcaller's-major. If advancer wants to know which minor overcaller has, advancer asks with two notrump. If advancer bids a suit, it's natural, and overcaller is expected to pass.

In example (1), advancer with 16 balanced points is forced by system to pass. Overcaller in balancing seat with five spades and four clubs, bids two spades. This is safe since advancer, who is in direct seat, is marked with strength and therefore has a balanced hand with at least two spades. With a strong unbalanced hand, advancer would have bid. Advancer, holding three spades, conservatively passes. On very bad days, two spades will lose the top two hearts, a heart ruff plus three additional trump tricks and go down one. In example (2), overcaller has five spades and four clubs and bids two spades. Advancer with only one spade bids two notrump, asking overcaller to bid his minor. Overcaller bids three clubs, which advancer passes.

231

Advancer	(3)		Overcaller	Advancer	(4)		Overcaller
♠AJ32	♦A2		♠K7654 ♦Q654	♠32	♦A32		♠K7654 ♦Q654
♥5432	♣AQJ		♥6 ♣543	♥K432	♣AQJ2		♥6 ♣543

Open	Advnc	Resp	Over	Open	Advnc	Resp	Over
1NT	Pass	Pass	2♠	1NT	Pass	Pass	2♠
Pass	4♠	Pass	Pass	Pass	Pass	Pass	

Overcaller	(5)		Advancer	Overcaller	(6)		Advancer
♠2	♦KQ32		♠KQJ654 ♦A54	♠32	♦KQJ32		♠7654 ♦A
♥A5432	♣432		♥6 ♣765	♥A5432	♣2		♥6 ♣KQJ8765

Open	Over	Resp	Advnc	Open	Over	Resp	Advnc
1NT	2♥	Pass	2♠	1NT	2♥	Pass	3♣
Pass	Pass	Pass		Pass	Pass	Pass	

In examples (3) and (4), overcaller in balancing seat with five spades and four diamonds bids two spades. In example (3), advancer with four-card spade support and a ruffing value, and knowing that finesses are going to work, jumps to four spades. Usually you're more likely to go down at the two-level than make game. In example (4), advancer passes two spades, preferring to play the 5-2 spade fit rather than the possible 4-3 club fit. ALWAYS ASSUME THE WORST.

If advancer bids a new suit, it's natural and non-forcing. In examples (5) and (6), overcaller in direct seat with five hearts and a diamond suit bids two hearts. In example (5), advancer bids two spades, his own suit, and overcaller passes. In example (6), advancer knows that overcaller has exactly five hearts, and holding seven clubs, bids three clubs to play. Overcaller trusts advancer and passes three clubs. Overcaller knows that if advancer wanted to hear about his diamonds, advancer would have inquired with two notrump.

17.4 -- DOUBLES OF ALL NOTRUMPS SHOW A FOUR-CARD MAJOR AND A LONGER MINOR OR A MINOR ONE-SUITER OR 19+ BALANCED OR A VERY STRONG MAJOR-MINOR TWO-SUITER. RESPONDER BIDS TWO CLUBS IF HE WANTS TO PLAY IN THE MINOR AND TWO DIAMONDS IF HE WANTS TO PLAY IN THE MAJOR.

Overcaller (1)		Advancer		Overcaller (2)		Advancer	
♠A876 ♦QJ987		♠32 ♦K2		♠A876 ♦QJ987		♠5432 ♦32	
♥654 ♣6		♥QJ32 ♣A5432		♥AK4 ♣6		♥QJ32 ♣Q32	

Open	Over	Resp	Advnc	Open	Over	Resp	Advnc
1NT	Dbl	Pass	2♣	1NT	Dbl	Pass	2♦
Pass	2♦	Pass	Pass	Pass	2♠	Pass	Pass
Pass				Pass			

Double of one notrump in any seat shows a variety of hands, the most common of which is a four-card major and a longer minor. Overcaller doesn't need a strong hand to enter the auction. If overcaller has a singleton, he should attempt to enter the auction. Example (1) is an example of a minimum vulnerable direct seat 4-5 double against a strong notrump. Over weak notrumps, overcaller needs to be stronger since advancer is more likely to try for game or convert the double to penalties. In balancing seat, overcaller can have a lot less. The singleton is important, since most of the opponent's points in that suit will be rendered useless. Over the double, advancer bids two clubs, pass or correct, to play in overcaller's minor and advancer bids two diamonds to play in overcaller's major. Two-of-a-major or three-of-a-minor by advancer is his own long suit.

Examples (1) and (2) show the range of overcaller's strengths. Since overcaller will be very aggressive getting in the auction, advancer should be very conservative. In example (1), advancer has only two spades so he bids two clubs, pass or correct, to play in overcaller's minor. Overcaller corrects to two diamonds. In example (2), advancer with four-card support for both majors bids two diamonds, and overcaller bids two spades. Advancer's worst case two-diamond bid, asking for overcaller's major is 4-3-5-1.

If advancer bids two clubs, pick a minor, and corrects overcaller's two-diamond bid to two hearts, advancer is showing five hearts and three spades, offering overcaller a choice of majors.

Advancer	(3)	Overcaller		Advancer	(4)	Overcaller	
♠A2 ♦A32		♠K765 ♦Q7654		♠432 ♦2		♠AK65 ♦Q7654	
♥A432 ♣A432		♥876 ♣7		♥5432 ♣65432		♥A76 ♣A	

Open	Advnc	Resp	Over	Open	Advnc	Resp	Over
1NT	Pass	Pass	Dbl	1NT	Pass	Pass	Dbl
Pass	2♣	Pass	2♦	Pass	2♦	Pass	2♠
Pass	Pass	Pass		Pass			

Overcaller	(5)	Advancer		Overcaller	(6)	Advancer	
♠QJ54 ♦5		♠32 ♦K432		♠QJ54 ♦5		♠32 ♦32	
♥65 ♣J98765		♥AK32 ♣Q32		♥65 ♣J98765		♥KQJ432 ♣432	

Open	Over	Resp	Advnc	Open	Over	Resp	Advnc
1NT	Dbl	Pass	2♣	1NT	Dbl	Rdbl	2♥
Pass	Pass	Pass		Pass	Pass	3NT	

In examples (3) and (4), overcaller in balancing seat doubles with four spades and five diamonds. Overcaller's double is safe as long as advancer doesn't hang him, since advancer, marked with strength, has to have a balanced hand. In example (3), advancer in direct seat with a balanced 16-point hand was forced by his system to pass. Over overcaller's balancing double, advancer with 4-3 in the minors bids two clubs, pass or correct, and overcaller corrects to two diamonds. In example (4), advancer with a singleton diamond prefers to play a 4-3 spade fit rather than a 5-1 diamond fit, so advancer bids two diamonds. Advancer must always assume the worst when trying to find a fit. Overcaller bids two spades and the 4-3 spade fit is found.

In examples (5) and (6), overcaller in direct seat with four spades and six clubs doubles. You can see how little you need to double with 4-6 distribution. In example (5), advancer with 4-2 in the majors bids two clubs, pass or correct, to play in overcaller's minor, and overcaller passes. In example (6), advancer, with his own suit, bids two hearts, and overcaller passes.

Advancer	(7)	Overcaller		Advancer	(8)	Overcaller	

♠A2　♦432　　　♠K65　♦QJ8765　　　♠A432　♦32　　　♠K65　♦QJ8765

　♥A432　♣A432　　♥765　　♣5　　　　♥A432　♣A32　　♥765　　♣5

Open	Advnc	Resp	Over	Open	Advnc	Resp	Over
1NT	Pass	Pass	Dbl	1NT	Pass	Pass	Dbl
Pass	2♣	Pass	2♦	Pass	2♦	Pass	Pass

Overcaller	(9)	Advancer		Overcaller	(10)	Advancer	

♠QJ5　♦6　　　♠32　♦K5432　　　♠QJ5　♦6　　　♠K432　♦432

　♥654　♣AJ7654　♥AK32　♣Q2　　　♥654　♣AJ7654　♥AK32　♣32

Open	Over	Resp	Advnc	Open	Over	Resp	Advnc
1NT	Dbl	Pass	2♣	1NT	Dbl	Pass	2♦
Pass	Pass	Pass		Pass	3♣	Pass	Pass

Overcaller has two ways to describe a minor one-suiter. One method is to jump directly to the three-level. This has the advantage of avoiding confusion and taking away the two-level from the opponents, but has the disadvantage of getting to the three-level. The second method is to double. If the opponents are silent there is no problem. If advancer bids two clubs asking for overcaller's minor, overcaller passes two clubs if clubs is his minor, and bids two diamonds if diamonds is his minor. If advancer bids two diamonds asking for overcaller's major, overcaller passes two diamonds if diamonds is his minor and bid three clubs if clubs is his minor. If responder competes, advancer has to remember that overcaller does not have to have a four-card major.

In examples (7) and (8), overcaller in passout seat wants to show a diamond one-suiter. The suit is not strong enough to commit the hand to the three-level. Overcaller doubles, showing either a four-card major and a longer minor, or a minor one-suiter. In example (7), advancer bids two clubs, asking for overcaller's minor, and overcaller bids two diamonds. In example (8), advancer bids two diamonds, asking for overcaller's major. Since overcaller has a diamond one-suiter, overcaller passes two diamonds. In examples (9) and (10), overcaller doubles, hoping to play in two clubs. In example (9), advancer bids two clubs to play in overcaller's minor. In example (10), advancer bids two diamonds to play in overcaller's major. Overcaller bids three clubs showing a club one-suiter.

Overcaller (11) Advancer   Overcaller (12) Advancer

♠AKJ76 ♦5   ♠432   ♦432   ♠AKJ76 ♦5   ♠5432   ♦K32
    ♥A6 ♣AKJ65   ♥K432 ♣432   ♥A6 ♣AKJ65   ♥5432   ♣32

Open	Over	Resp	Advnc	Open	Over	Resp	Advnc
1NT	Dbl	Pass	2♣	1NT	Dbl	Pass	2♦
Pass	2♠	Pass	2NT	Pass	4♠	Pass	Pass
Pass	4♠	Pass	Pass	Pass			

    With a very strong major-minor two-suiter, overcaller doubles one notrump. Overcaller doesn't want to bid two-of-a-major and have it go all pass. If overcaller is very strong, he can have a five-card or longer major along with his five-card or longer minor. When advancer bids two clubs, pass or correct to play in overcaller's minor, overcaller bids his major instead. If advancer has anything at all, he should bid over two-of-a-major. Advancer raises with four-card support. With three-card support, advancer bids two notrump. With less than three-card support, advancer bids three-of-a-minor, pass or correct, with a weak hand, or the other major with a game-forcing hand. When advancer bids two diamonds asking overcaller to bid his major, overcaller jumps directly to game, knowing that advancer has support.

    In examples (11) and (12), overcaller doesn't want to bid two spades showing spades and a minor and have it go all pass. Overcaller doubles showing a four-card major and a longer minor. In example (11), advancer with 3-3 in the minors bids two clubs, pass or correct, to play in overcaller's minor. Overcaller shows his strength by bidding two spades. Over a 10-12 notrump, overcaller has to jump to three spades to show this hand. Advancer with three-card spade support bids two notrump. Overcaller, needing only breaks, bids four spades. In example (12), advancer with 4-4 in the majors bids two diamonds, showing at least 4-3 in the majors. Overcaller, knowing advancer has at least three-card spade support, bids four spades.

Overcaller (13)   Advancer   Overcaller (14)   Advancer

♠AKJ54 ♦6   ♠2   ♦5432   ♠AKJ54 ♦6   ♠32   ♦K32
    ♥A6 ♣AKJ76   ♥K432 ♣5432   ♥A6 ♣AKJ76   ♥5432 ♣Q432

Open	Over	Resp	Advnc	Open	Over	Resp	Advnc
1NT	Dbl	Pass	2♣	1NT	Dbl	Pass	2♣
Pass	2♠	Pass	3♣	Pass	2♠	Pass	3♣
Pass	3♥	Pass	5♣	Pass	3♥	Pass	3NT
Pass	Pass	Pass		Pass	Pass	Pass	

In examples (13) and (14), advancer bids two clubs, pass or correct, and overcaller shows his strength by bidding two spades. In example (13), advancer with only one spade bids three clubs, showing fewer than three spades. Overcaller shows his heart fragment, and advancer jumps to five clubs, pass or correct. In example (14), advancer with a stopper in both minors, bids three notrump over three hearts.

Overcaller (15)   Advancer   Overcaller (16)   Advancer

♠AKQ2 ♦AKQ2   ♠43   ♦J43   ♠AKQ2 ♦AKQ2   ♠6543   ♦J43
    ♥Q32 ♣32   ♥KJ654 ♣654   ♥Q32 ♣32   ♥K54 ♣Q54

Open	Over	Resp	Advnc	Open	Over	Resp	Advnc
1NT	Dbl	Pass	2♣	1NT	Dbl	Pass	2♣
Pass	2NT	Pass	3♦	Pass	2NT	Pass	3♣
Pass	3♥	Pass	3NT	Pass	3♠	Pass	4♠
Pass	4♥	Pass	Pass	Pass	Pass	Pass	

Overcaller with a balanced hand containing 19 or more points can double one notrump and then bid two notrump. This occurs more often against weak notrumps. Over advancer's two clubs or two diamonds, overcaller bids two notrump. Treat the two-notrump bid like a two-notrump opener and play whatever you play over a two-notrump opener.

In examples (15) and (16), overcaller, with 20 HCPs, doubles one notrump, planning on bidding two notrump. Advancer with 3-3 in the minors bids two clubs, pass or correct. In example (15), over two notrump, advancer with five hearts transfers to hearts and then offers overcaller a choice by bidding three notrump. Overcaller with three hearts corrects to four hearts. In example (16), over two notrump, advancer bids three clubs, Stayman, and the 4-4 spade fit is found.

17.5 -- IN COMPETITION, DOUBLE OR REDOUBLE SHOWS SUPPORT FOR ANYTHING THAT PARTNER CAN HAVE. NEW SUITS ARE THEREFORE NATURAL.

Overcaller (1) Advancer   Overcaller (2) Advancer

♠KQJ765 ♦Q5   ♠432 ♦K32   ♠KQJ765 ♦Q5   ♠2   ♦432
    ♥7 ♣6543   ♥432 ♣AQJ2   ♥7 ♣6543   ♥65432 ♣AQJ2

Open	Over	Resp	Advnc
1NT	2♦	Dbl	Rdbl
2♥	2♠	3♥	3♠

Open	Over	Resp	Advnc
1NT	2♦	Dbl	2♠
3♥	Pass	3NT	

Overcaller (3) Advancer   Overcaller (4) Advancer

♠KQJ4 ♦87   ♠A32 ♦65432   ♠KQJ4 ♦7   ♠A32 ♦65432
   ♥A6543 ♣54   ♥KQ2 ♣32   ♥AJT3 ♣J654   ♥KQ2 ♣32

Open	Over	Resp	Advnc
1NT	2♣	3♣	Dbl
Pass	3♥	Pass	Pass

Open	Over	Resp	Advnc
1NT	2♣	3♣	Dbl
Pass	Pass	Pass	

Most doubles and redoubles by advancer and overcaller after the original call are for takeout. They can be converted to penalties with a stack. Advancer doubles or redoubles if he has values and if he knows that he has an eight-card fit at the two-level or a nine-card fit at the three-level.

In examples (1) and (2), overcaller bids two diamonds showing an unspecified major, and responder doubles two diamonds. In example (1), advancer redoubles, showing constructive values and promising that a nine-card fit at the three-level exists. Opener bids two hearts and overcaller with 6-4 distribution bids two spades. In example (2), advancer with five hearts and one spade bids two spades, pass or correct. Two spades shows either a weak hand, fewer than three spades or both. Passing two-diamonds doubled shows diamonds. Overcaller passes three hearts knowing that advancer either doesn't have a fit or is weak. In examples (3) and (4), overcaller bids two clubs showing both majors. Responder bids three clubs non-forcing. If three clubs is non-forcing, overcaller can't be broke. Advancer, with only two clubs knows that it is not right to allow the opponents to play their likely nine-card club fit. Rather than trying to guess which major to play in, advancer doubles giving overcaller a choice. In example (3), overcaller bids his five-card heart suit. In example (4), overcaller holding four clubs, passes the double and advancer is surprised.

Overcaller	(5)	Advancer	
♠AQ32	♦2	♠7654	♦A543
♥432	♣K5432	♥65	♣AQ6

Open	Over	Resp	Advnc
1NT	Dbl	2♥	Dbl
Pass	2♠	Pass	Pass

Overcaller	(6)	Advancer	
♠A32	♦2	♠7654	♦A543
♥AQJ2	♣K5432	♥65	♣AQ6

Open	Over	Resp	Advnc
1NT	Dbl	2♥	Dbl
Pass	Pass	Pass	

Overcaller	(7)	Advancer	
♠A432	♦K32	♠8765	♦654
♥2	♣AJ432	♥987	♣AQ5

Open	Over	Resp	Advnc
1NT	Dbl	2♥	Pass
Pass	Dbl	Pass	2♠

Overcaller	(8)	Advancer	
♠A432	♦K32	♠765	♦54
♥2	♣AJ432	♥KQJ98	♣765

Open	Over	Resp	Advnc
1NT	Dbl	2♥	Pass
Pass	Dbl	Pass	Pass

In examples (5) through (8), overcaller doubles one notrump, showing a four-card major and a longer minor or a minor one-suiter, and responder bids two hearts natural. In examples (5) and (6), advancer doubles two hearts, a competitive double, prepared to play in either two spades if overcaller has four spades, three-of-a-minor if overcaller has a minor one-suiter, or two-hearts doubled if overcaller's four-card major is hearts. Advancer should have at least eight points to make a competitive double. In example (5), overcaller bids two spades and the 4-4 fit is found. In example (6), overcaller with four good hearts, passes the competitive double. In example (7), advancer is not strong enough to compete so he passes responder's natural two-heart bid. Overcaller with extra values and shortness in hearts reopens with a double, and advancer bids his four-card spade suit. In example (8), advancer would like to double responder's natural two-heart call for penalties, but his double would be competitive. Advancer passes and overcaller, with shortness in hearts and a reasonable hand, reopens with a double. Advancer is happy to convert to penalties.

A double of two clubs alerted as Stayman, two diamonds alerted as Jacoby, or two hearts alerted as Jacoby shows values. Advancer is prepared to play in one of overcaller's suits. Overcaller passes advancer's double for penalties with length.

17.6 -- DEFENSE AGAINST 10-12 OPENING NOTRUMPS.

Overcaller (1)   Advancer   Overcaller (2)   Advancer

♠AQ32 ♦2   ♠7654 ♦A543   ♠A32 ♦2   ♠7654 ♦AQJ3
  ♥A32 ♣K5432   ♥54 ♣AQ6   ♥AQJ2 ♣K5432   ♥54 ♣AQ6

Open	Over	Resp	Advnc
1NT	Dbl	Pass	Pass
Pass			

Open	Over	Resp	Advnc
1NT	Dbl	2♦	Pass
Pass	Dbl	Pass	Pass

Overcaller (3)   Advancer   Overcaller (4)   Advancer

♠KJ32 ♦KQ2   ♠Q654 ♦A543   ♠KJ32 ♦KQ2   ♠7654 ♦43
  ♥AJ2 ♣K32   ♥43 ♣A54   ♥AJ2 ♣K32   ♥6543 ♣Q54

Open	Over	Resp	Advnc
1NT	Dbl	Pass	Pass
Pass			

Open	Over	Resp	Advnc
1NT	Dbl	Pass	2♦
Pass	2♠	Pass	Pass

Just because you're playing double shows a four-card major and a longer minor doesn't mean that you can't penalize the opponent's 10-12 one-notrump opener. I would rather double a weak notrump with a 4-2-2-5 12-count where I have a good opening lead then with a 4-3-3-3 16-count where I have to guess what to lead. In examples (1) through (4), overcaller doubles opener's 10-12 notrump showing a four-card major and a longer minor, a minor one-suiter, or 17 or more balanced. The weaker the opponent's notrump, the stronger the double should be. Over a strong notrump, overcaller can double with any 4-6 hand, attempting to compete for the part score since he's very unlikely to have a game. However, defending against weak notrumps, overcaller is more likely to have a game. Overcaller wants advancer to know that he has at least 11 HCPs when he enters the auction. In example (1), advancer with ten HCPs passes the double. Advancer knows that overcaller will lead a minor and with Ace, Queen, Ace in the minors, advancer will be happy whichever minor overcaller leads. In example (2), responder bids two diamonds, showing a one-suiter. Since advancer's double is competitive, he has to pass. Overcaller doubles for takeout, and advancer passes for penalties. In examples (3) and (4), overcaller with 17 HCPs gambles that advancer has some strength and can pass the double. Overcaller has to pass if the notrump is stronger or his hand is any weaker. In example (3), advancer with ten HCPs passes the double and overcaller is happy. In example (4), advancer, with a weak hand, bids two diamonds, asking for overcaller's major. At least overcaller has a good resting place.

CHAPTER 18 - JUMP OVERCALLS

18.1 -- DIRECT JUMP OVERCALLS PREEMPTIVE.

Single jump overcalls of opening bids are preemptive and usually show a six-card suit. With a sound six-card suit and less than a sound opening bid, it usually works better to make a jump overcall. If partner is a passed hand, the range is even wider. Over one club, overcalling two diamonds with ♠32♥32♦AKJT32♣Q32 as well as with ♠32♥32♦QJT43♣5432 puts a lot of pressure on the opponents. Over a one-diamond overcall, responder bids one-of-a-major with six points and a four-card major but he can't over a two-diamond overcall. Over one spade, overcalling three hearts with ♠32♥AKJT32♦432♣Q2 as well as with ♠32♥KQJ432♦32♣432 puts pressure on the opponents. After a two-heart overcall, responder can show a simple, limit or forcing spade raise depending on his strength. Over a three-heart overcall, responder can't show both a simple raise and a limit raise.

Jump overcalls over preempts and 11-16 two-level openers are strong, not weak. They show a good suit with around 17 HCPs or eight and half tricks. ♠AKQ432♥2♦AKJ♣432 is jump to three spades over a weak-two heart opener.

18.2 -- PASSOUT SEAT JUMP OVERCALLS INTERMEDIATE.

Advancer	(1)	Overcaller		Advancer	(2)	Overcaller	
♠K54	♦8765	♠32	♦AQ	♠K54	♦8765	♠32	♦AKQ432
♥765	♣AQ5	♥AKQ432	♣432	♥765	♣AQ5	♥A32	♣32

Open	Advnc	Resp	Over	Open	Advnc	Resp	Over
1♠	Pass	Pass	3♥	1♠	Pass	Pass	3♦
Pass	4♥	Pass	Pass	Pass	3NT	Pass	Pass

Single jump overcalls in passout seat are intermediate and show a good six-card suit with a sound opening bid. The suit is at worst a one-loser suit. Intermediate jumps are non-forcing. Double followed by a new suit is stronger. Responses to intermediate jumps are game forcing.

In examples (1) and (2), overcaller in passout seat jumps to the three-level showing a good six-card suit and a sound opening bid. In example (1), advancer raises to four hearts. In example (2), advancer bids three notrump over overcaller's three-diamond jump.

CHAPTER 19 - OVER OPPONENT'S TAKEOUT DOUBLE

19.1 -- NEW SUIT FORCING AT ONE-LEVEL.

At the one-level, unless responder wants to try for penalties, responder ignores overcaller's takeout double. Responder makes the same one-level response he would have made had overcaller passed. Since many players make takeout doubles with only three cards in a major, failure to respond four-card suits up the line can cause responder to miss his eight-card major-suit fit. However, since opener will get another chance to bid, responder doesn't have to bid on garbage just to keep the bidding alive.

19.2 -- WEAK JUMP SHIFTS AT TWO AND THREE-LEVEL. DOUBLE JUMP SHIFTS ARE SPLINTERS.

Over takeout doubles, two-level jump-shifts and a three-heart jump over one spade are weak jump shifts. After one club -- double, bid two spades holding ♠J109432♥2♦K32♣432 or ♠Q109432♥432♦2♣432. After one spade -- double, bid three hearts holding ♠2♥QJ109432♦K2♣432 or ♠2♥QJ1098432♦2♣432

Since one-of-a-major -- double -- two-of-either-minor shows 7-9 HCPs and trump support (see section 19.3), jumps to three-of-either-minor over one-of-a-major -- double are natural and constructive, but non-forcing. Responder has between seven and ten HCPs. After one heart -- double, bid three clubs holding ♠32♥32♦Q32♣KQJ432 or ♠32♥32♦K32♣AJT432.

After one spade -- double, jumps to four clubs, four diamonds or four hearts are splinter bids. After one heart -- double, jumps to three spades, four clubs and four diamonds are splinter bids. Over one diamond -- double, jumps to three hearts, three spades and four clubs are splinter bids. Over one club -- double, jumps to three diamonds, three hearts and three spades are splinter bids. Since jumping in a short suit allows advancer to double, which can help the opponents find a cheap save, responder, in order to splinter, has to have slam aspirations. With a minimum game-forcing hand, responder jumps to two notrump instead (see section 19.4).

19.3 -- ONE-OF-A-MAJOR - DOUBLE - TWO CLUBS IS THREE-CARD RAISE 7-9 HCPS, TWO DIAMONDS IS FOUR-CARD RAISE 7-9 HCPS.

Opener	(1)	Responder		Opener	(2)	Responder	
♠AQ432 ♦Q32		♠K65 ♦J654		♠AQ432 ♦Q32		♠K765 ♦J654	
♥K32 ♣K2		♥54 ♣A543		♥K32 ♣K2		♥54 ♣A43	

Open	Over	Resp	Advnc	Open	Over	Resp	Advnc
1♠	Dbl	2♣	2♥	1♠	Dbl	2♦	2♥
2♠	Pass	Pass	3♥	2♠	Pass	Pass	3♥
Dbl	Pass	Pass	Pass	3♠	Pass	Pass	Pass

Opener	(3)	Responder		Opener	(4)	Responder	
♠AK5432 ♦K32		♠J76 ♦54		♠AK432 ♦K32		♠J76 ♦54	
♥2 ♣AKT		♥J9654 ♣432		♥32 ♣AKT		♥J9654 ♣432	

Open	Over	Resp	Advnc	Open	Over	Resp	Advnc
1♠	Dbl	2♠	3♦	1♠	Dbl	2♠	3♦
3♥	Pass	3♠	Pass	Pass	Pass	Pass	
Pass	Pass						

After one-of-a-major -- double, two clubs shows a three-card raise with 7-9 HCPs, two diamonds shows a four-card raise with 7-9 HCPs. A direct raise shows a three-card raise with 0-6 HCPs.

In example (1), over the takeout double, responder bids two clubs, showing three spades with 7-9 HCPs. When advancer competes with three hearts, opener, with a sound opener and three hearts, doubles. In example (2), over the takeout double, responder bids two diamonds, showing four spades with 7-9 HCPs. Opener competes to three spades, knowing responder has four spades. In examples (3) and (4), responder bids two spades showing a bad raise to two spades. In example (3), opener has six spades so he can compete to the three-level. Opener bids three hearts, an artificial game try (see section 7.2), just in case responder has a maximum bad raise. Responder signs-off in three spades. In example (4), opener knows that he has an eight-card fit and guesses that the opponents are in at best an eight-card diamond fit. Opener follows the Law and passes three diamonds. With a trump lead three spades can very easily be down three.

19.4 -- ONE-OF-ANY-SUIT - DOUBLE - THREE-OF-SAME-SUIT IS A PREEMPTIVE RAISE. ONE-OF-ANY-SUIT - DOUBLE - TWO NOTRUMP IS A LIMIT RAISE OR BETTER. RESPONDER SHOWS AT LEAST FOUR-CARD SUPPORT.

Opener	(1)	Responder		Opener	(2)	Responder	

♠AQ432 ♦Q32   ♠K765 ♦J654   ♠AQ432 ♦Q32   ♠K765 ♦KJ4
    ♥K32 ♣J2   ♥54   ♣543   ♥K32 ♣J2   ♥54   ♣A543

Open	Over	Resp	Advnc	Open	Over	Resp	Advnc
1♠	Dbl	3♠	Pass	1♠	Dbl	2NT	Pass
Pass	Pass			3♠	Pass	Pass	Pass

Opener	(3)	Responder		Opener	(4)	Responder	

♠A432 ♦Q32   ♠65   ♦J654   ♠A432 ♦Q32   ♠5   ♦KJ54
    ♥K32 ♣A32   ♥54   ♣KJ654   ♥K32 ♣A32   ♥654 ♣KJ654

Open	Over	Resp	Advnc	Open	Over	Resp	Advnc
1♣	Dbl	3♣	Pass	1♣	Dbl	2NT	Pass
Pass	Pass			3♣	Pass	Pass	Pass

One-of-a-major -- double -- three-of-the-same-major shows zero to six points with at least four-card support. Usually responder has four-card support, but there are 5-3-3-2 hands that are too weak to jump to the four-level. One-of-a-major -- double -- two notrump shows at least 10 support points with at least four-card support.

In example (1), responder bids three spades showing fewer than seven points with at least four spades. In example (2), responder bids two notrump showing a limit raise or better with at least four spades. Opener has a minimum opener and signs-off in three spades. Three-of-either-red suit is a game or slam try.

One-of-a-minor -- double -- three-of-the-same-minor shows zero to six points with at least five-card support. One-of-a-minor -- double -- two notrump shows a distributional limit raise or better, usually with five-card support. Responder redoubles and supports with ten or more HCPs.

In example (3), responder bids three clubs showing fewer than seven points, usually with five clubs. In example (4), responder bids two notrump showing a distributional limit raise or better, usually with at least five clubs. Opener has a minimum opener and signs-off in three clubs.

19.5 -- REDOUBLE FOLLOWED BY SINGLE RAISE IS A THREE-CARD MAJOR-SUIT LIMIT RAISE OR A FOUR-CARD MINOR-SUIT LIMIT RAISE. REDOUBLE FOLLOWED BY DOUBLE RAISE IS THREE-CARD MAJOR-SUIT FORCING RAISE.

Opener	(1)	Responder		Opener	(2)	Responder	
♠AK5432 ♦32		♠Q76 ♦KJ5		♠AK432 ♦432		♠Q76 ♦KJ5	
♥A32 ♣32		♥654 ♣KQ54		♥A32 ♣32		♥654 ♣KQ54	

Open	Over	Resp	Advnc	Open	Over	Resp	Advnc
1♠	Dbl	Rdbl	2♥	1♠	Dbl	Rdbl	2♥
2♠	Pass	3♠	Pass	Pass	Pass	2♠	Pass

Responder's redouble of a takeout double shows ten or more points. Responder redoubles to show a three-card limit raise or better in opener's major. It's very important for opener to know that responder has only three-card support. Responder also redoubles to show a forcing one-suiter which can't be bid at the one-level, or a four-card limit raise or better in opener's minor with high-card points rather than distribution.

If responder has a three-card limit raise in opener's major, responder supports opener as soon as possible at the lowest possible level. If responder has a three-card forcing raise in opener's major, responder jumps or bids game as soon as possible.

In examples (1) and (2), responder has a three-card limit raise in spades. In example (1), opener bids two spades directly, showing a minimum opener with a six-card spade suit. Responder with a bad three-card limit raise invites and opener rejects. In example (2), responder redoubles and supports at the minimum level to show a three-card limit raise. Opener with a minimum opener passes the three-card limit raise.

If responder has a four-card limit raise in opener's minor, responder redoubles then supports opener as soon as possible at the lowest possible level. If responder has a four-card forcing raise in opener's minor, responder cuebids.

If responder has a one-suiter which can't be bid at the one-level, responder redoubles and then bids his suit at his next opportunity. The only way to show a game-forcing minor one-suiter after a major-suit opener is to redouble and then bid the minor.

Opener	(3)	Responder		Opener	(4)	Responder	
♠AK432	♦32	♠Q65 ♦A54		♠AKJ32	♦32	♠Q65 ♦A54	
♥32	♣AQ32	♥AQ4 ♣JT54		♥32	♣AKQ2	♥AQ4 ♣JT54	

Open	Over	Resp	Advnc		Open	Over	Resp	Advnc
1♠	Dbl	Rdbl	2♦		1♠	Dbl	Rdbl	Pass
Pass	Pass	3♠	Pass		Pass	Any	3♠	Pass
4♠	Pass	Pass	Pass		4♣	Pass	4NT	Pass
					5♣	Pass	5NT	Pass
					6♣	Pass	6♠	Pass

In examples (3) and (4), responder shows a three-card forcing raise by redoubling and jumping in spades. In example (3), opener signs-off in game. In example (4), opener cuebids showing extra values. Responder, knowing that any red-suit finesses will probably work, bids keycard and then bids a slam.

19.6 -- TABLE OF MAJOR-SUIT RAISES, STRENGTH SHOWN, NUMBER OF CARDS PROMISED AND REFERENCE.

1♥ Dbl 2♥	1♠ Dbl 2♠	0-6	3	19.3
2♣	2♣	7-9	3	19.3
Rdbl*	Rdbl*	10+	3	19.5
3♥	3♠	0-6	4	19.4
2♦	2♦	7-9	4	19.3
2NT	2NT	10+	4	19.4

*Followed by support

19.7 -- REDOUBLE OF TAKEOUT DOUBLE FOLLOWED BY DOUBLE IS FOUR-CARD PENALTY DOUBLE.

Responder redoubles to show a four-card penalty double of at least one of takeout doubler's suits. After responder redoubles, opener doubles with at least four cards in the opponent's suit. Responder probably will not pass opener's penalty double with a singleton or void, since the opponents usually will be in at least an eight-card fit. Opener with an unbalanced minimum does not have to pass the redouble. With a minimum, opener rebids a six-card suit or bids a new suit with a weak 5-5.

If the opponents bid Michaels, unusual notrump or any other bid which shows two suits, responder's double has the same meaning as a redouble. Responder can penalize at least one of overcaller's suits.

Opener	(1)	Responder		Opener	(2)	Responder	
♠AK432	♦32	♠5	♦AJ54	♠AK432	♦32	♠65	♦AJ654
♥32	♣AQ32	♥AQ54	♣JT54	♥32	♣AQ32	♥AQ54	♣JT

Open	Over	Resp	Advnc	Open	Over	Resp	Advnc
1♠	Dbl	Rdbl	Any	1♠	Dbl	Rdbl	2♣
Pass	Pass	Dbl	All pass	Dbl	Pass	Pass	Pass

Opener	(3)	Responder		Opener	(4)	Responder	
♠AK432	♦32	♠5	♦AJ54	♠AK432	♦32	♠65	♦AJ654
♥32	♣AQ32	♥AQ54	♣JT54	♥32	♣AQ32	♥AQ54	♣JT

Open	Over	Resp	Advnc	Open	Over	Resp	Advnc
1♠	2NT	Dbl	Any	1♠	2♠	Dbl	2NT
Pass	Pass	Dbl	Pass	Pass	3♣	Pass	Pass
Pass	Pass			Dbl	Pass		

In examples (1) and (2), responder wants to penalize the opponents. In example (1), responder redoubles and then doubles anything the opponents bid. In example (2), responder is able to double the red suits. Responder redoubles, setting up a force. Responder doubles if the opponents bid a red suit and hopes opener can double clubs. Opener, holding four clubs, doubles two clubs. In example (3), responder doubles two notrump and then doubles anything the opponents bid. In example (4), responder doubles two spades, Michaels, setting up a force. Responder will double if the opponents bid either red suit, and hopes opener can double clubs. Opener, holding four clubs, doubles three clubs.

19.8 -- PASS FOLLOWED BY DOUBLE IS COOPERATIVE DOUBLE WITH TEN+ HCPS.

If responder has ten or more HCPs and wants to make a three-card or a weak four-card cooperative penalty double, responder passes and then doubles at his next opportunity. Opener passes responder's one-level cooperative double with three or more cards and removes the double with fewer than three cards in the opponent's suit. This strategy allows you to double the opponents in a seven-card or worse fit at the one-level, and not double them in an eight-card or better fit. At the two-level, opener with extra strength can pass responder's cooperative double with only two cards in the opponent's suit. Sometimes you get a bonus if advancer has to bid a three-card suit and overcaller raises.

Opener	(1)	Responder		Opener	(2)	Responder	
♠AK432 ♦432		♠65 ♦AJ5		♠AK432 ♦32		♠65 ♦AJ5	
♥432 ♣AQ		♥AQ6 ♣JT432		♥5432 ♣AQ		♥AQ6 ♣JT432	

Open	Over	Resp	Advnc	Open	Over	Resp	Advnc
1♠	Dbl	Pass	2♦	1♠	Dbl	Pass	2♦
Pass	Pass	Dbl	Pass	Pass	Pass	Dbl	Pass
Pass	Pass			2♥	Pass	3NT	All pass

Opener	(3)	Responder		Opener	(4)	Responder	
♠AK5432 ♦2		♠76 ♦AJ5		♠AK432 ♦432		♠76 ♦AJ5	
♥432 ♣AQ2		♥AQ5 ♣JT543		♥432 ♣AQ		♥AQ5 ♣JT543	

Open	Over	Resp	Advnc	Open	Over	Resp	Advnc
1♠	2NT	Pass	3♦	1♠	2♠	Pass	2NT
Pass	Pass	Dbl	Pass	Pass	3♦	Dbl	Pass
3♠	Pass	4♠	Pass	Pass	Pass		

In examples (1) through (4), responder, holding three cards in each red suit, wants to make a cooperative double if the opponents bid a red suit or make a penalty double if the opponents play in notrump. The odds are strong that the opponents will not end up in clubs. In example (1), responder passes the takeout double and then doubles two diamonds. Opener with three diamonds is happy to pass the double. In example (2), opener, with only two diamonds, knows the opponents are in an eight-card fit, and pulls the cooperative double to two hearts. Responder jumps to three notrump.

Responder can also make a cooperative double if the opponents bid Michaels or the Unusual Notrump. In example (3), responder passes overcaller's unusual two-notrump bid in order to make a cooperative double of either red suit. Opener, holding only one diamond, knows the opponents are in a nine-card fit and pulls the double to three spades. In example (4), responder passes overcaller's Michael's cuebid in order to make a cooperative double of either red suit. Opener is happy to pass responder's cooperative double.

CHAPTER 20 - OPENING PREEMPTS

20.1 -- LIGHT. CAN BE SIX-CARD SUIT AT THREE-LEVEL.

It is very important for you and your partner to know what type of preempts each of you will make. Preempts are designed to interfere with the opponents. I recommend that they be on the lighter side. They should not be designed for constructive auctions. Three-level minor suit preempts are made on six and seven-card suits non-vulnerable, seven-card suits vulnerable. Non-vulnerable vs vulnerable, ♣QJT543 is a possible three-club first-seat preempt. I would also open three clubs with ♣KQJ5432. Second seat non-vulnerable, I would have at least ♣KQJ432 or a seven-card suit. For every one in twenty hands where opener goes for a number or misses a game, there will be at least five hands where something good happens.

Three-level major-suit preempts are usually made on seven-card suits, since with a six-card suit you can open a weak-two. Six-four hands, which have more playing strength, can be opened at the three-level. In third seat, even sound preemptors can open lighter.

Four-level preempts show eight-card suits vulnerable, strong seven or eight-card suits non-vulnerable. It is not unreasonable to open four hearts holding ♠-♥AKQxxx♦Jxxxxx♣x

In fourth seat any preempt should be close to an opening bid.

20.2 -- CHEAPER MINOR ONLY FORCE OVER THREE-LEVEL PREEMPTS.

Since opening three-level preempts are so bad, responder can have a better suit. If opener opens three clubs, responder wants to play in three spades, not four spades, holding ♠KQJ5432♥A32♦32♣2. Responder is more likely to make three spades than three clubs. Responder will take at least seven tricks in three spades. Who knows how many tricks opener will take in three clubs? Responder wants a spade lead if the opponents bid three notrump, so responder bids three spades.

Responder has to have a way to find out if opener has a good preempt or a bad preempt. Cheaper unbid minor is forcing, and asks opener to describe his hand. Three diamonds is game forcing over a three-club opener and asks opener to bid a three-card major. If opener does not have a three-card major, opener bids three notrump. Over other three-level preempts, four clubs is forcing inviting slam. Opener rebids his suit with a minimum. With a maximum, opener cuebids shortness or bids keycard.

Over four-level major preempts, new suits are cuebids in support of opener's suit.

CHAPTER 21 - CUEBIDS

21.1 -- MICHAELS CUEBID PROMISING AT LEAST 5-5 ANY STRENGTH. MAJOR CUEBID SHOWS OTHER MAJOR AND EITHER MINOR. MINOR CUEBID SHOWS BOTH MAJORS.

Overcaller (1)   Advancer   Overcaller (2)   Advancer

♠KJ432 ♦AJ432   ♠Q5 ♦Q765   ♠AK432 ♦AKQ32   ♠65 ♦J765
    ♥32   ♣2   ♥54   ♣AQ543   ♥32   ♣2   ♥54   ♣76543

Open	Over	Resp	Advnc	Open	Over	Resp	Advnc
1♥	2♥	3♥	4♣	1♥	2♥	3♥	Pass
Pass	4♦	Pass	Pass	4♥	Dbl	Pass	Pass

One-of-a-major -- two-of-a-major, Michaels, shows the other major and a minor, at least 5-5, any strength. The average Michaels is ten HCPs. Over a major cuebid, advancer bids two notrump to ask for overcaller's minor. If advancer bids two notrump and then bids three-of-overcaller's-major, he is making a game try. Three-of-either-minor is natural and non-forcing. If responder raises to three-of-opener's-major, advancer's three notrump by an unpassed hand is natural. By a passed hand, three notrump asks for overcaller's minor. If three notrump is natural, four-of-a-minor or five-of-a-minor by advancer is pass or correct. Four diamonds says pass four diamonds if diamonds is your other suit but bid five clubs if clubs is your other suit. If overcaller raises to four-of-opener's-major, four notrump asks for overcaller's other suit.

If overcaller bids two-hearts Michaels and responder doubles, advancer can pass the double and let overcaller show which is his minor. Overcaller redoubles to show that his minor is clubs, and bids two spades to show that his minor is diamonds. Advancer will thus know overcaller's minor when he has to make a decision of which suit to play in.

In example (1), advancer wants to compete in four-of-overcaller's-minor. Advancer bids four clubs, pass or correct, and overcaller corrects to four diamonds. Three notrump is to play. In example (2), overcaller wants to bid again over four hearts. Overcaller doubles four hearts, showing a good defensive hand. Advancer, hoping overcaller has four tricks, passes.

Overcaller (3)   Advancer   Overcaller (4)   Advancer

♠AKJ32   ♦32   ♠T ♦7654   ♠QJ432   ♦32   ♠T   ♦A654
    ♥AKQ32 ♣A   ♥765 ♣Q6543   ♥QJ432 ♣2   ♥8765 ♣543

Open	Over	Resp	Advnc		Open	Over	Resp	Advnc
1♣	2♣	Pass	2♥		1♣	2♣	Dbl	3♥
Pass	4♣	Pass	4♥		Pass	Pass	3NT	

Overcaller (5)   Advancer   Overcaller (6)   Advancer

♠AQ432   ♦32   ♠65 ♦AK54   ♠QJ432   ♦32   ♠65 ♦AK54
    ♥AQ432 ♣2   ♥K65 ♣Q543   ♥QJ432 ♣2   ♥K65 ♣Q543

Open	Over	Resp	Advnc		Open	Over	Resp	Advnc
1♣	2♣	Pass	3♣		1♣	2♣	Pass	3♣
Pass	3♠	Pass	4♥		Pass	3♦	Pass	3♥

One-of-a-minor -- two-of-a-minor, Michaels, shows both majors, at least 5-5, any strength. Advancer's jump to three-of-a-major shows four-card support with some values. After two-clubs Michaels, two diamonds is natural, three clubs sets hearts as trumps and three diamonds sets spades as trumps. After two-diamonds Michaels, two notrump sets hearts as trumps, three clubs is natural and three diamonds sets spades as trumps. These trump setting bids are invitational to game or better. Overcaller should try to let advancer play the hand in order to protect advancer's minor holdings.

In example (3), over advancer's two-heart sign-off, overcaller jumps in clubs showing a strong hand with club shortness. Advancer signs-off in four hearts. In example (4), overcaller has a sub-minimum Michaels. Advancer jumps to three hearts, showing four-card heart support. If advancer wants to invite in hearts he bids three clubs. In examples (5) and (6), advancer wants to invite in hearts. Advancer bids three clubs, setting hearts as trumps and inviting game. In example (5), overcaller accepts by bidding three spades, the other major, allowing advancer to play four hearts. If opener has the AK of clubs, advancer's queen will stop opener from continuing clubs. In example (6), overcaller rejects by bidding three diamonds. Three diamonds allows advancer to play three hearts, again possibly protecting the queen of clubs.

21.2 -- SANDWICH NOTRUMPS. ONE ANY - PASS - ONE OTHER - ONE NOTRUMP SHOWS AT LEAST 5-5 IN UNBID SUITS ANY STRENGTH. BOTH "CUEBIDS" ARE NATURAL.

Advancer   (1)   Overcaller   Advancer   (2)   Overcaller

♠5   ♦AJ4   ♠KJ432   ♦32   ♠5   ♦654   ♠KJ432   ♦32
 ♥8765 ♣Q6543   ♥AKQ32   ♣A   ♥Q765 ♣76543   ♥KJ432   ♣2

Open	Advnc	Resp	Over
1♣	Pass	1♦	1NT
Dbl	2♥	Pass	4♥

Open	Advnc	Resp	Over
1♣	Pass	1♦	1NT
Dbl	3♥	3NT	Pass

Advancer   (3)   Overcaller   Advancer   (4)   Overcaller

♠76   ♦AK6   ♠K5432   ♦Q5432   ♠AQ65 ♦Q76   ♠KJ432   ♦AJ432
 ♥654 ♣KJ543   ♥32   ♣2   ♥654 ♣AQ3   ♥32   ♣2

Open	Advnc	Resp	Over
1♣	Pass	1♥	1NT
Dbl	2♦	2♥	Pass
Pass	3♦	3♥	Pass

Open	Advnc	Resp	Over
1♣	Pass	1♥	1NT
2♥	3♥	Pass	4♠
Pass	Pass		

One notrump, after both opponents have bid a suit, shows at least 5-5 in the unbid suits any strength. A takeout double shows at most nine cards in the two unbid suits.

In examples (1) and (2), overcaller bids one-sandwich notrump, showing at least 5-5 in the majors. In example (1), when advancer freely bids two hearts over opener's support double, responder raises to game. In example (2), over opener's support double, advancer jumps to three hearts, preemptive, showing four-card heart support. If advancer wants to invite he cuebids clubs to show a limit raise or better in hearts or cuebids diamonds to show a limit raise or better in spades.

In example (3), overcaller bids a sub-minimum sandwich notrump, showing at least 5-5 in diamonds and spades. Over opener's support double showing three-card heart support, advancer bids two diamonds. When two hearts comes back to advancer, he bids three diamonds, refusing to let the opponents play in an eight-card fit at the two-level. He also does not hang overcaller for entering the auction. In example (4), overcaller shows at least 5-5 in spades and diamonds. Advancer with a good hand cuebids three hearts, inviting four spades. Overcaller, whose hand can be a lot worse, bids four spades.

253

Advancer (5)		Overcaller	
♠K654 ♦765		♠32 ♦AKQ	
♥A654 ♣65		♥32 ♣KQJ432	

Open	Advnc	Resp	Over
1♣	Pass	1♦	2♣
Pass	Pass	Pass	

Advancer (6)		Overcaller	
♠K654 ♦765		♠32 ♦KQJ432	
♥A654 ♣65		♥32 ♣A32	

Open	Advnc	Resp	Over
1♣	Pass	1♦	2♦
Pass	Pass	Pass	

Advancer (7)		Overcaller	
♠K654 ♦654		♠32 ♦A32	
♥A65 ♣765		♥32 ♣KQJ432	

Open	Advnc	Resp	Over
1♣	Pass	1♥	2♣
2♥	3♣	Pass	Pass
Pass			

Advancer (8)		Overcaller	
♠K654 ♦654		♠32 ♦A32	
♥A65 ♣765		♥KQJ432 ♣32	

Open	Advnc	Resp	Over
1♣	Pass	1♥	2♥
3♣	3♥	Pass	Pass
Pass			

When two suits have been bid, and overcaller bids opener's suit or responder's suit, it's natural and non-forcing. Overcaller doesn't necessarily show a lot of strength. If only one suit has been bid, however, and overcaller bids opener's suit, it's Michaels. Over one club -- pass -- one notrump, two clubs shows both majors.

In example (5), overcaller bids two clubs, opener's suit, showing clubs. In example (6), overcaller bids two diamonds, responder's suit, showing diamonds. In example (7), overcaller bids two clubs, opener's suit, showing clubs. When opener raises hearts, advancer raises to three clubs. In example (8), overcaller bids two hearts, responder's suit, showing hearts. When opener rebids clubs, advancer raises to three hearts.

CHAPTER 22 - DEFENSE AGAINST PREEMPTS

22.1 -- TAKEOUT DOUBLES THROUGH FOUR SPADES.

All doubles of preempts are takeout doubles in principle. If overcaller is 4-4-4-1, he needs only 11 HCPs to make a takeout double. If overcaller is 4-4-3-2, he needs at least 13 HCPs to make a takeout double. In order to double a preempt, you have to be able to support the pulling of the double, which means you can't double a four-level preempt with AKQJ of trumps and out or double a lower preempt with shortness in unbid majors. The higher the preempt, the more likely it is that the double will be left in. The more balanced advancer is, the more likely it is that he will sit for the double.

Balancing takeout doubles can be a little lighter.

Over a four-spade preempt, four notrump is for takeout showing a two-suiter. If advancer has two four-card or longer suits, advancer bids his cheapest suit. If advancer is 4-3-3-3, advancer bids his four-card suit unless advancer's four-card suit is hearts in which case advancer bids five clubs. With ♠432♥K32♦5432♣432, advancer bids five diamonds. With ♠432♥K432♦432♣432, advancer bids five clubs. If advancer is 5-3-3-2, advancer bids his five-card suit unless advancer's five-card suit is hearts in which case advancer bids his cheaper three-card suit. With ♠432♥K32♦65432♣32, advancer bids five diamonds. With ♠432♥K5432♦432♣32, advancer bids five diamonds. As long as overcaller always corrects five clubs to five diamonds holding both red suits, or corrects five diamonds to five hearts holding clubs and hearts, a disaster will be averted. If advancer is 3-6-2-2 with 2-2 in the minors, advancer has to decide whether to bid five clubs or five hearts depending upon the strength of his heart suit. With ♠432♥K65432♦32♣32, advancer bids five clubs. With ♠432♥KQJ432♦32♣32, advancer bids five hearts.

Over a four-spade preempt, double is for takeout showing a balanced hand, usually a strong notrump. Overcaller expects the double to be left in more often than not. Since advancer is allowed to pull the double, overcaller can't double with just spade values. When in doubt advancer sits for the double with exactly two spades and pulls with shortness. Advancer bids four notrump as choice of suits.

22.2 -- OVER TWO-OF-A-MAJOR, THREE-OF-THAT-MAJOR ASKS FOR STOPPER, NORMALLY WITH A SOLID MINOR. FOUR-OF-A-MINOR SHOWS THAT MINOR AND OTHER MAJOR, AT LEAST 5-5 WITH A REASONABLE OPENING BID.

Overcaller	(1)	Advancer			Overcaller	(2)	Advancer	
♠A2 ♦AKQ5432		♠6543 ♦76			♠A2 ♦AKQ5432		♠KQJ43 ♦76	
♥32 ♣A2		♥K54 ♣K543			♥32 ♣A2		♥654 ♣K43	

Open	Over	Resp	Advnc		Open	Over	Resp	Advnc
2♥	3♥	Pass	3NT		2♥	3♥	Pass	3♠
Pass	Pass	Pass			Pass	4♠		

Advancer	(3)	Overcaller			Advancer	(4)	Overcaller	
♠KQ32 ♦32		♠54 ♦AKQ9876			♠AK2 ♦32		♠54 ♦AKQ9876	
♥QJ2 ♣KQ32		♥65 ♣A5			♥432 ♣JT432		♥65 ♣A5	

Open	Advnc	Resp	Over		Open	Advnc	Resp	Over
2♥	Pass	Pass	3♥		2♥	Pass	Pass	3♥
Pass	3NT	Pass	Pass		Pass	4♣	Pass	4♦

A direct cuebid or a balancing cuebid asks advancer to bid three notrump with a stopper, and shows a solid or nearly solid minor. If advancer does not have a stopper, advancer with a weak hand bids four-of-a-minor, pass or correct. With a game-forcing hand, advancer cuebids, bids five-of-a-minor, pass or correct, or bids a six-card or good five-card major. If the cuebid gets doubled, advancer redoubles with a partial stopper.

In examples (1) and (2), overcaller bids three hearts, asking advancer to bid three notrump with a heart stopper. In example (1), advancer bids three notrump. In example (2), advancer does not have a heart stopper so advancer with five good spades, bids three spades. Overcaller raises to four spades. In examples (3) and (4), overcaller in passout seat bids three hearts, asking advancer to bid three notrump with a heart stopper. In example (3), advancer bids three notrump. In example (4), advancer does not have a heart stopper so advancer bids four clubs pass or correct. Overcaller corrects to four diamonds.

Overcaller (3) Advancer

♠AK432 ♦2   ♠Q65 ♦AQ54
  ♥32 ♣AQ432   ♥654 ♣K65

Open	Over	Resp	Advnc
2♥	2♠	Pass	3♠
Pass	4♠	Pass	

Overcaller (4) Advancer

♠AKJT2 ♦32   ♠Q65 ♦AQ54
  ♥2 ♣AQJ32   ♥654 ♣K65

Open	Over	Resp	Advnc
2♥	4♣	Pass	4♠
Pass	Pass	Pass	

Overcaller (5) Advancer

♠AKJT2 ♦2   ♠Q43 ♦J876
  ♥2 ♣AK5432   ♥Q43 ♣Q76

Open	Over	Resp	Advnc
2♦	4♣	Pass	4♦
Pass	4♠	Pass	Pass

Overcaller (6) Advancer

♠AKJT2 ♦AK5432   ♠Q43 ♦J876
  ♥2 ♣2   ♥Q43 ♣Q76

Open	Over	Resp	Advnc
2♣	4♦	Pass	4♥
Pass	4♠	Pass	Pass

A jump to four-of-a-minor over a major-suit weak-two opener, in direct seat and in balancing seat, shows at least five of that minor and five of the other major. Over a weak two-diamond opener, a jump to four diamonds shows at least 5-5 in the majors, and a jump to four clubs shows at least five clubs and five of an unspecified major. Advancer bids four diamonds to ask for overcaller's major. Over a weak or precision two-club opener, a jump to four clubs shows at least 5-5 in the majors, and a jump to four diamonds shows at least five diamonds and five of an unspecified major. Advancer's bids are pass or correct. Overcaller has to be careful, since jumping to four-of-a-minor does not allow you to play in three notrump.

Example (3) is a two-spade overcall, not a jump to four clubs. Holding two hearts, if advancer has a good hand without at least three spades, three notrump can be where you belong. Advancer invites and overcaller accepts. Example (4) is good example of a four-club jump. Overcaller has spades which will play opposite two little, a singleton heart and extra values. If advancer's spades were Qxxx, he can jump to five spades asking overcaller to bid six with more than a minimum. In example (5), overcaller jumps to four clubs showing at least 5-5 in clubs and an unspecified major. Advancer bids four diamonds, asking overcaller to bid his major. Overcaller bids four spades, ending the auction. In example (6), overcaller jumps to four diamonds showing at least 5-5 in diamonds and an unspecified major. Advancer bids four hearts pass or correct. Overcaller bids four spades, ending the auction.

22.3 -- LEBENSOHL OVER TWO-ANYTHING - DOUBLE - PASS.

Over overcaller's takeout double of a weak-two bid, advancer can show whether a non-jump three-level bid is weak or constructive. A constructive hand contains eight to twelve HCPs. To show a weak hand, advancer bids two notrump, Lebensohl, forcing three clubs, and then passes or bids three-of-a-suit which is lower than opener's suit. To show a constructive hand, advancer directly bids three-of-a-suit which is lower than opener's suit. Two notrump, Lebensohl, followed by three notrump shows doubt. Two notrump followed by a cuebid shows four of the other major and a stopper. A direct three notrump is to play.

Overcaller (1)   Advancer   Overcaller (2)   Advancer

♠32   ♦A432   ♠K54   ♦765   ♠32   ♦A432   ♠K54   ♦765
  ♥AKQ2   ♣K32   ♥43   ♣Q7654   ♥AKQ2   ♣K32   ♥43   ♣AQJ54

Open	Over	Resp	Advnc		Open	Over	Resp	Advnc
2♠	Dbl	Pass	2NT		2♠	Dbl	Pass	3♣
Pass	3♣	Pass	Pass		Pass	3♠	Pass	3NT

Overcaller (3)   Advancer   Overcaller (4)   Advancer

♠32   ♦A432   ♠654   ♦K65   ♠32   ♦A432   ♠654   ♦K65
  ♥AKQ2   ♣K32   ♥J543   ♣Q54   ♥AKQ2   ♣K32   ♥J543   ♣AQJ

Open	Over	Resp	Advnc		Open	Over	Resp	Advnc
2♠	Dbl	Pass	2NT		2♠	Dbl	Pass	3♥
Pass	3♣	Pass	3♥		Pass	4♥	Pass	Pass

In example (1), advancer wants to show a weak hand with clubs. Advancer bids two notrump, forcing three clubs, and then passes. If advancer has a weak diamond or heart hand, advancer corrects three clubs to three-of-a-red-suit. In example (2), advancer bids three clubs directly, showing a constructive hand with clubs. Overcaller bids three spades trying for three notrump, and advancer with a spade stopper bids three notrump. In example (3), advancer bids two notrump forcing three clubs and then bids three hearts. This sequence shows a weak three-heart bid. Overcaller passes three hearts. In example (4), advancer bids a direct three hearts, showing a constructive hand with at least four hearts. Overcaller raises to four hearts. With hearts, advancer's maximum is lower then with a minor.

Overcaller (5)   Advancer

Overcaller		Advancer		
♠32	♦AK32	♠A54	♦Q4	
♥AQ32	♣432	♥K654	♣AQJ6	

Open	Over	Resp	Advnc
2♠	Dbl	Pass	2NT
Pass	3♣	Pass	3♠
Pass	4♥	Pass	Pass

Overcaller (6)   Advancer

Overcaller		Advancer		
♠32	♦AK32	♠A54	♦Q4	
♥AQ2	♣5432	♥K654	♣AQJ6	

Open	Over	Resp	Advnc
2♠	Dbl	Pass	2NT
Pass	3♣	Pass	3♠
Pass	3NT	Pass	Pass

Overcaller (7)   Advancer

Overcaller		Advancer		
♠-	♦AJ32	♠J654	♦K54	
♥AK32	♣65432	♥Q4	♣AKJ7	

Open	Over	Resp	Advnc
2♠	Dbl	Pass	2NT
Pass	3♣	Pass	3NT
Pass	4♣	Pass	5♣

Overcaller (8)   Advancer

Overcaller		Advancer		
♠32	♦AJ2	♠J654	♦K54	
♥AK32	♣5432	♥Q4	♣AKJ7	

Open	Over	Resp	Advnc
2♠	Dbl	Pass	2NT
Pass	3♣	Pass	3NT
Pass			

With four cards in the other major and a stopper in opener's major, advancer gives overcaller a choice between four-of-a-major and three notrump by bidding two notrump and then cuebidding. If overcaller has three cards in the other major, he bids three notrump. If overcaller has four cards in the other major, he normally bids four-of-the-other-major, but can bid three notrump with a balanced hand. If advancer jumps directly to three notrump, he wants to play three notrump, normally ending the auction. However, sometimes advancer has a doubtful stopper in the opponent's suit, such as Jxxx. If advancer bids two notrump, forcing three clubs, and follows with three notrump, advancer wants overcaller to run from three notrump with a void or small singleton in opener's suit. Advancer has to have an alternative strain in order to bid two notrump followed by three notrump.

In examples (5) and (6), advancer wants to play in four hearts only if overcaller has four hearts. Advancer bids two notrump followed by three spades, showing four hearts and a spade stopper. In example (5), overcaller holding four hearts bids four hearts. In example (6), overcaller with only three hearts, bids three notrump. In examples (7) and (8), advancer does not want to play in three notrump if overcaller is void or has a small singleton spade. In example (7), overcaller, void in spades, bids four clubs, and five clubs is reached. In example (8), overcaller, with two little spades, passes three notrump.

22.4 -- CUEBID BY ADVANCER IS CHOICE OF GAMES.

After overcaller's double of a preempt, if advancer has a five-card major and enough to be in game, he bids game. If advancer has enough strength to be in game but advancer is not sure which game, advancer cuebids to get overcaller's help. Choice-of-games cuebids take priority over slam-try cuebids.

Overcaller's first obligation over advancer's three-diamond cuebid of a doubled weak-two diamond opener is to bid three-of-his-lower four-card major. If advancer corrects three hearts to three spades, he shows four spades and a club suit. If advancer corrects three spades to four hearts, he shows four hearts and a club suit.

Overcaller's first obligation over advancer's three-heart cuebid of a doubled weak-two heart opener is to bid three notrump with a heart stopper. If overcaller bids three notrump and advancer then bids four spades, advancer is showing a four-card spade suit and the ability to play five-of-a-minor if overcaller does not have four spades. If overcaller does not have a heart stopper, overcaller bids three spades with a four-card suit, otherwise overcaller bids four-of-his-better-minor.

Overcaller's first obligation over advancer's three-spade cuebid of a doubled weak-two spade opener is to bid three notrump with a spade stopper. If overcaller bids three notrump and advancer then bids four hearts, advancer is showing a four-card heart suit and the ability to play five-of-a-minor if overcaller does not have four hearts. If overcaller does not have a spade stopper, overcaller bids four hearts with a five-card heart suit, otherwise overcaller bids four-of-his-better-minor.

Overcaller's first obligation over advancer's cuebid after a doubled three club or three diamond opener is to bid four-of-his-lower four-card major. If advancer corrects four hearts to four spades, he shows four spades and the unbid minor.

Overcaller (1)		Advancer		Overcaller (2)		Advancer	
♠AQ ♦A432		♠2 ♦K65		♠AQ ♦A432		♠2 ♦K65	
♥Q32 ♣Q432		♥JT54 ♣AKJ65		♥Q32 ♣Q432		♥JT654 ♣AKJ5	

Open	Over	Resp	Advnc	Open	Over	Resp	Advnc
2♠	Dbl	Pass	3♠	2♠	Dbl	Pass	4♥
Pass	3NT	Pass	4♥	Pass	Pass	Pass	
Pass	4NT	Pass	5♣				

Overcaller (3)		Advancer		Overcaller (4)		Advancer	
♠A32 ♦AJ32		♠K54 ♦KQ		♠A32 ♦AJ32		♠K654 ♦KQ	
♥32 ♣K432		♥54 ♣AQT765		♥K2 ♣J432		♥54 ♣AQT65	

Open	Over	Resp	Advnc	Open	Over	Resp	Advnc
2♥	Dbl	Pass	3♥	2♥	Dbl	Pass	3♥
Pass	4♣	Pass	5♣	Pass	3NT	Pass	4♠
Pass	Pass	Pass		Pass	4NT	Pass	Pass

In example (1), advancer wants to be in four hearts only if overcaller has four hearts. Advancer cuebids three spades. When overcaller bids three notrump, advancer then bids four hearts, showing a game-forcing hand with only four hearts and at least a four-card minor. Overcaller with only three hearts runs from four hearts and advancer bids five clubs. In example (2), advancer with five hearts jumps to four hearts, ending the auction. Advancer only cuebids if he has an alternative strain. In example (3), advancer wants to be in three notrump if overcaller has a heart stopper. Advancer cuebids, asking overcaller to bid three notrump with a heart stopper. Overcaller bids four clubs, denying a heart stopper and denying four spades. Advancer raises to five clubs. In example (4), advancer wants to be in four spades only if overcaller has four spades. Advancer cuebids and then bids four spades. Overcaller, with only three spades, runs to four notrump.

CHAPTER 23 - TWO NOTRUMP OVERCALL

23.1 -- TWO NOTRUMP OVER A WEAK-TWO SHOWS 15-18 HCPS.

A two-notrump overcall over a weak-two in either seat shows a strong notrump. Over two notrump, three clubs is Stayman, and Smolen applies if the opening bid is two-of-either-minor. Three diamonds and three hearts are Jacoby transfers. Three spades is minor-suit Stayman. If the weak-two is a major, you do not need to transfer into the opponents major. Therefore a transfer into the opponent's major shows a slam try in one of the minors. Advancer uses Texas transfers if he knows that he wants to play in four-of-a-major.

If responder doubles two notrump, advancer uses the same methods used to escape from one-notrump doubled. Redouble forces three clubs to play in three of either minor. A direct three clubs is Stayman and transfers apply.

If responder raises opener's weak-two, advancer's double is responsive and new suits are forcing. If it goes two clubs(weak or Precision) -- two notrump -- three clubs or two any -- two notrump -- three clubs, then double is Stayman and transfers apply.

CHAPTER 24 - THREE NOTRUMP OVERCALL

24.1 -- THREE NOTRUMP OVER A WEAK-TWO SHOWS 19+ HCPS.

There are two ways to get to three notrump over a weak-two, directly by jumping to three notrump, or indirectly, by doubling and then bidding three notrump. Double followed by three notrump is more flexible. Therefore, if advancer has a five-card or longer major, advancer pulls the indirect three-notrump bid, but sits for the direct three-notrump bid. Over a direct three notrump, four clubs is Stayman, and four diamonds and four hearts are transfers showing a six-card or longer suit. Four spades is a slam try with an emphasis on unbid minors.

24.2 -- THREE NOTRUMP OVER A THREE-BID SHOWS 16+ HCPS.

When the opponents preempt at the three-level and you have a strong notrump, you have to close your eyes and bid three notrump. If partner only has his expected six HCPs, you might go down. Most of the times he'll have more or you'll play the hand double dummy and make contracts that, without the information gained from the preempt, you would never have had a chance to make. Over three notrump, four clubs is Stayman, and four diamonds and four hearts are transfers showing a six-card or longer suit. Four spades is a slam try with an emphasis on unbid minors.

CHAPTER 25 - FOUR NOTRUMP VARIATIONS

25.1 -- ROMAN KEYCARD BLACKWOOD (RKC).

1.	2.	3.	4.	5.	6.	7.
1♠ 2♥	1♠ 2♥	1♠ 2♥	2♣ 2♦	1♠ 2♣	1♣ 2♠	1♣ 2♠
3♥ 3♠	3♠ 4♥	3♣ 3♥	2♠ 3♥	3♣ 3♠	3♣ 3♠	2NT 3♣
4♥ 4NT	4NT	4♣ 4NT	4NT	4♣ 4NT	4♣ 4NT	4♣ 4NT

Roman Keycard Blackwood (RKC) is a variation of standard Blackwood where the king of trumps counts as a fifth ace. Similar to regular Blackwood, RKC's only use is to avoid getting to slam missing two keycards or one keycard and the queen of trumps. IF YOU BID RKC, FIND OUT THAT YOU ARE OFF ONLY ONE KEY AND DON'T BID A SLAM, YOU HAVE MISUSED RKC. Before using RKC, asker must be careful to make sure that there aren't any negative responses above the trump suit. Even after a cuebid auction, four notrump is still RKC and answerer counts all aces, whether cuebid or not.

The responses to RKC are; five clubs shows zero or three keycards, five diamonds shows one or four keycards, five hearts shows two or five keycards without the queen of trumps, and five spades shows two or five keycards with the queen of trumps or WITH AT LEAST TEN TRUMPS PRESENT.

Whether or not four notrump is RKC, and what's the trump suit, cause a lot of problems. The following are rules on what the trump suit is: 1. Highest possible agreed-on trump suit. 2. Jump rebid suits, strong jump-shift suits and strong-two-bid suits. 3. Last natural bid suit unless asker can easily set that suit as trumps. If asker can easily set a suit as trumps but would have difficulty setting another suit, then the other suit is the keycard suit.

In auction (1), spades is the keycard suit since it's the highest possible agreed-on trump suit. In auction (2), spades is the keycard suit since opener jumped in spades. In auction (3), clubs is the keycard suit, since it was the last natural bid suit. In auction (4), spades is the keycard suit since it's a strong-two suit. In auction (5), spades is the keycard suit since it's the highest possible agreed-on trump suit. In auction (6), spades is the keycard suit since it's a jump-shift suit. In auction (7), clubs is the keycard suit since it's an agreed-on trump suit.

8.	8Z.	9.	9Z.	10.	10Z.
1♠　2♣ 2♠　4NT	1♠　2♣ 2♠　3♣ 3♠　4NT	1♠　2♣ 2♥　4NT	1♠　2♣ 2♥　3♣ 3NT　4NT?	1♠　2♥ 2♠　4NT	1♠　2♥ 2♠　3♥ 3♠　4NT?

There are some situations where the last bid suit is not the trump suit. If it's easy for asker to set a suit as trumps and he does not, then four notrump is not RKC for that suit. One-any -- pass -- four notrump, is regular Blackwood, not RKC, since asker can easily set trumps by bidding either Jacoby Two Notrump if the opening bid is a major, or Inverted Minors if the opening bid is a minor.

In auction (8), four notrump should be RKC for clubs, not spades. It's very easy to set spades as trumps by raising to three spades and then bidding RKC. It's almost impossible to set clubs as trumps. In auction (8Z), since spades is the last natural bid suit, most players would interpret four notrump as RKC for spades, not clubs. The only way for responder to bid RKC with clubs as trumps is auction (8). In auction (9), four notrump should be RKC for clubs, not hearts or spades. It's very easy to raise hearts or support spades and then bid RKC, but it's almost impossible to set clubs as trumps and then bid RKC. In auction (9Z), four notrump is natural and five clubs is Gerber, so responder can't bid RKC for clubs. In example (10), four notrump should be RKC for hearts since it's easy to set spades as trumps by bidding three spades and then bidding RKC for spades. In example (10Z), four notrump is RKC for spades, the last bid suit, not for hearts, so example (10) is how you bid RKC for hearts.

If possible, asker should try to avoid situations where he has to play at the five-level. Holding ♠AKQ432♥2♦2♣KQJ32, opposite a three-card forcing raise, cuebid four clubs. If responder can't cuebid a red ace, there is no slam.

25.2 -- QUEEN ASKING - CHEAPEST BID AFTER 0-3 OR 1-4 RESPONSE ASKS FOR THE QUEEN.

1.		2.		3.		4.		5.		6.	
4♠	4NT	4♠	4NT	4♠	4NT	4♠	4NT	4♠	4NT	4♠	4NT
5♣	5♦	5♣	5♦	5♣	5♦	5♦	5♥	5♦	5♥	5♦	5♥
5♠		6♣		6♠		5♠		6♣		6♠	

A five-heart answer denies the queen of trumps or extra length and five spades shows the queen of trumps or extra length. Five clubs and five diamonds neither promise nor deny the queen of trumps. Over five clubs, if asker wants to know if answerer has the queen of trumps, asker bids five diamonds. Answerer signs-off in five-of-the-trump-suit if he does not have the queen of trumps. If answerer has the queen of trumps, he bids his cheapest useful king, or jumps to six of the trump suit if he doesn't have a king. FIVE NOTRUMP SHOWS THE KING OF THE QUEEN-ASKING SUIT AND THE TRUMP QUEEN, so that when the ask is five diamonds, five notrump shows the diamond king. Over five diamonds, with spades as trumps, if asker wants to know if answerer has the queen of trumps, asker bids five hearts. The answers are similar to those over asker's five-diamond ask. IF ANSWERER KNOWS THAT THERE ARE AT LEAST TEN TRUMPS PRESENT, HE SHOWS THE QUEEN.

In auctions (1), (2) and (3), asker bids four notrump RKC for spades, and answerer bids five clubs, showing zero or three keycards. Asker bids five diamonds, asking if answerer has the queen of spades. In auction (1), answerer bids five spades saying, no, I don't have the spade queen. In auction (2), answerer bids six clubs saying, yes, I have the spade queen and I have the club king but I don't have the heart king, since I would have bid five hearts, and I don't have the diamond king, since I would have bid five notrump. In auction (3), answerer bids six spades saying, I have the spade queen, but I don't have any kings.

In auctions (4), (5) and (6), asker bids four notrump, RKC for spades, and answerer bids five diamonds, showing one or four keycards. Asker bids five hearts asking if answerer has the queen of spades. In auction (4), answerer bids five spades saying, no, I don't have the spade queen. In auction (5), answerer bids six clubs saying, yes I have the spade queen and I also have the club king, but I don't have the heart king, since I would have bid five notrump. In auction (6), answerer bids six spades, saying, yes I have the spade queen, but I don't have any kings.

If hearts is the trump suit and the answer is five diamonds, five spades asks for the queen. Since five spades is forcing to slam, asker must be interested in getting to seven if answerer has the queen. If clubs or diamonds is the trump suit and the answer is five diamonds, five hearts asks for the queen. Since five hearts is forcing to slam, asker must be interested in getting to seven if answerer has the queen.

7.	8.	9.	10.	11.	12.
4♠ 4NT	4♠ 4NT	4♠ 4NT	4♥ 4NT	4♥ 4NT	4♥ 4NT
5♣ 5♠	5♣ 5♠	5♣ 5♠	5♣ 5♥	5♣ 5♥	5♣ 5♥
Pass	5NT	6♣	Pass	5♠	6♦

If the asker does not know whether answerer has zero or three keycards, asker signs-off in five-of-the-trump-suit. SIGNING OFF IN FIVE-OF-THE-TRUMP-SUIT IS FORCING IF ANSWERER HAS THREE KEYCARDS, AND NON-FORCING IF ANSWERER HAS ZERO. The only exception is if it is guaranteed from the auction that answerer has to have at least three keycards and it is possible that asker can have zero. If answerer has three keycards, and is going to continue the auction, answerer shows or denies the queen of trumps. The cheapest response denies the queen. With the queen, answerer bids his lowest useful king or bids six-of-the-trump-suit.

In auctions (7) through (12), asker bids four notrump RKC and answerer bids five clubs, showing zero or three keycards. In auctions (7) through (9), asker has a hand where it's possible that answerer has zero keycards, so asker signs-off in five spades. In auction (7), answerer has zero keycards and passes five spades. In auction (8), answerer has three keycards but doesn't have the spade queen, and bids five notrump. In auction (9), answerer has three keycards, the spade queen, and the club king, and bids six clubs. In auctions (10) through (12), asker has a hand where it's possible that answerer has zero keycards, so asker signs-off in five hearts. In auction (10), answerer has zero keycards and passes five hearts. In auction (11), answerer has three keycards but doesn't have the heart queen and bids five spades. In auction (12), answerer has three keycards, the heart queen and the diamond king but not the club king, and bids six diamonds. With three keycards, the heart queen and the spade king, answerer bids five notrump. Remember, five spades denies the heart queen.

268

25.3 -- FOUR NOTRUMP - ANY - FIVE NOTRUMP ASKS FOR SPECIFIC KINGS (PROMISES ALL KEYCARDS).

Opener	(1)	Responder		Opener	(2)	Responder	
♠2	♦K32	♠A543	♦A5	♠2	♦KQJ432	♠A543	♦A5
♥AK432	♣A432	♥QJ65	♣KQ5	♥AK432	♣A	♥QJ65	♣KQ5

Opener (1)	Responder	Opener (2)	Responder
1heart	2NT	1heart	2NT
3spades	4NT	3spades	4NT
5clubs	5NT	5clubs	5NT
6diamonds	7hearts	7NT	Pass

If asker finds two keys are missing, he signs-off at the appropriate level. If all keycards and the trump queen are present, asker can think about seven. If answerer's hand is unlimited, asker must show him that all six keys (four aces, and the KQ of trumps) are present, so that if answerer holds ♠KQJ2♥K2♦KQJ432♣A, he can bid seven notrump. Asker promises all six keys if he bids five notrump. Over five notrump, answerer first tries to count 13 tricks. If answerer counts 13 tricks he bids seven. Otherwise answerer bids his cheapest king below the trump suit, or signs-off in the trump suit. Only if answerer's hand is limited can answerer bid a king above six-of-the-trump-suit. If answerer shows a king and asker bids another suit, he is asking answerer to bid seven if he has the king of the other suit.

If asker is interested in third-round control rather than kings, asker bids that suit at the six-level instead of five notrump. Answerer bids seven-of-the-trump-suit if he has a doubleton or just the queen. With the queen and jack, answerer raises the asking suit.

In examples (1) and (2), responder's two notrump shows a game-forcing heart raise, and opener's three spades shows spade shortness. In example (1), responder bids RKC and opener answers five clubs, showing zero or three keycards. Responder bids five notrump, promising all six keys, and asking for specific kings. Opener answers six diamonds, showing the diamond king and denying the club king. Responder bids seven hearts. In example (2), opener would like to bid keycard himself, but a five-diamond response would not allow opener to ask for the queen and stay out of slam if the queen were missing. Responder bids RKC. Opener answers five clubs showing three keycards. Responder bids five notrump promising all six keys asking for specific kings. Opener counts 13 tricks and bids seven notrump.

Opener	(3)	Responder		Opener	(4)	Responder	
♠2	♦AQJ32	♠AJ43	♦54	♠2	♦AQJ32	♠A43	♦54
♥AQ432	♣A2	♥KJ65	♣QJ3	♥AQ432	♣A2	♥KJ65	♣KQ43

Opener (3)	Responder	Opener (4)	Responder
1heart	2NT	1heart	2NT
4NT	5hearts	4NT	5hearts
5NT	6hearts	5NT	6clubs
Pass		6diamonds	6hearts
		Pass	

Opener	(5)	Responder		Opener	(6)	Responder	
♠2	♦A	♠A543	♦K32	♠2	♦A	♠A543	♦K32
♥AQ5432	♣AK432	♥KJ76	♣65	♥AQ5432	♣AK432	♥K876	♣QJ

Opener (5)	Responder	Opener (6)	Responder
1heart	2NT	1heart	2NT
4NT	5hearts	4NT	5hearts
6clubs	7hearts	6clubs	7clubs
Pass		7NT	Pass

In examples (3) and (4), responder shows four-card heart support with game-forcing values. Opener bids four notrump, RKC for hearts, and responder answers five hearts, showing two keycards without the heart queen. With all six keys present, opener bids five notrump, asking for specific kings and inviting seven. In example (3), responder answers six hearts, denying the club and diamond kings. Unless responder knows for sure that all opener needs to make seven is the king of spades, responder can't show it since it's above six-of-the-trump-suit. Since responder's hand is unlimited, opener holding all the keys has to bid five notrump even though he is not interested in seven, just in case responder can bid seven. In example (4), responder answers six clubs, showing the club king. Opener bids six diamonds, asking responder to bid seven holding the diamond king. Responder answers six hearts, denying the diamond king.

In examples (5) and (6), opener bids six clubs, showing all six keys present, asking for third-round club control and inviting seven. In example (5), responder with a doubleton club, bids seven hearts. With three little clubs, responder signs-off in six hearts. In example (6), responder with the club queen and jack, bids seven clubs and opener bids seven notrump.

25.4 -- DOPI, DEPO.

Opener	(1)	Responder		Opener	(2)	Responder	
♠AK5432 ♦32		♠9876 ♦AKQJ654		♠AK5432 ♦32		♠9876 ♦AKQJ654	
♥432 ♣32		♥5 ♣A		♥32 ♣432		♥5 ♣A	

Open	Over	Resp	Advnc	Open	Over	Resp	Advnc
2♠	4♥	4NT	5♥	2♠	4♥	4NT	6♥
5♠	Pass	6♠	Pass	6♠	Pass	Pass	Pass

If an opponent bids over four notrump, RKC, answerer doubles with zero keycards and passes with one keycard. DOPI (double zero, pass one, bid the next suit with two, skip a step with three) and DEPO (double zero, two or four, pass one or three), have identical answers with zero or one keycard. Using DOPI or DEPO, the queen is ignored. Answerer has two ways to show two keycards, the next higher step or double. **IF ANSWERER CAN POSSIBLY SHOW HIS KEYCARDS USING DOPI, ANSWERER USES DOPI. ONLY IF DOPI WOULD TAKE YOU TO THE SIX-LEVEL AND YOU CAN BE OFF TWO KEYCARDS WOULD YOU USE DEPO.** Answerer always shows two keycards below five-of-the-trump-suit by bidding the next higher step, DOPI. If showing two keycards takes answerer above five-of-the-trump-suit, answerer has to choose between the next higher step and doubling, based on the auction. If answerer doubles to show zero or two, DEPO, asker with three keycards might assume answerer has zero and pass the double. Answerer shows three keycards by either skipping a step, DOPI, or by passing, DEPO. Since holding three keycards is usually enough to bid a small slam, answerer always shows three keycards by skipping a step, DOPI, to avoid ambiguity. If four notrump is doubled, ignore the double.

In examples (1) and (2), responder, opposite a vulnerable weak-two, bids four notrump RKC for spades. In example (1), over advancer's five-heart bid, opener bids five spades, the next higher step, to show two keycards. Opener doubles five hearts to show zero keycards and passes five hearts to show one keycard. In example (2), over advancer's six-heart bid, opener bids six spades, the next higher step, to show two keycards. In this situation, two keycards must be enough to bid a slam. If two keycards are enough to bid a slam, answerer always bids the next higher step, and never doubles. If opener doubles six hearts with zero or two keycards, how can responder know whether opener has the example hand or ♠QJT432♥43♦2♣KQJ2? If advancer sacrifices at seven hearts, opener has to double with zero or two keycards.

271

25.5 -- GRAND SLAM FORCE.

Opener (1)	Responder	Opener (2)	Responder
♠AK5432 ♦32	♠QJ76 ♦-	♠2 ♦432	♠AKQJ876 ♦A5
♥32 ♣432	♥AKQJ876 ♣A5	♥AJ5432 ♣432	♥K876 ♣-

2spades	5NT	2hearts	5NT
7clubs	7spades	6hearts	7hearts

A jump to five notrump when there's an obvious trump suit asks answerer to bid seven clubs with two of the top three trump honors. Always bidding seven clubs allows asker to play in a different strain, or allows answerer's other bids to be attempts to play in seven notrump. If answerer does not have two of the top three trump honors, the more answerer has, based on the auction, the higher answerer bids. Assume spades are trumps. Six spades shows the ace or king with extra length, six hearts shows the ace or king with normal length, six diamonds shows the queen or extra length and six clubs shows less. However, after showing exactly three-card trump support, AJx is the best possible holding not to bid seven, and xxx is the worst possible holding. AJ5432 is the best possible holding not to bid seven if answerer has opened a weak-two, and 76543 is the worst. Opening one spade playing five-card majors, AJxxxx is the best possible holding not to bid seven, and xxxxx is the worst. Deciding how high to bid is relative, based on minimum and maximum possible holdings. If hearts are trumps and answerer doesn't have two of the top three honors, answerer has only three responses. If diamonds are trumps, answerer has only two responses, and if clubs are trumps, answerer has only one response. Answerer has to use his judgement based on the auction as to what are his possible minimum and maximum trump holdings, and grade his responses accordingly.

In examples (1) and (2), responder, with a void, can't bid RKC. In example (1), responder bids five notrump, and opener with ace-king of spades bids seven clubs. Responder corrects seven clubs to either seven hearts or seven spades. In example (2), responder bids five notrump, and opener answers six hearts, showing a six-card suit headed by the ace. Responder bids seven hearts. With AJxxx, opener answers six diamonds, and responder signs-off in six hearts. Without the ace or king of hearts, opener answers six clubs.

272

Opener	(3)	Responder		Opener	(4)	Responder	
♠AKQ432	♦-	♠765	♦AKQ	♠AKQ432	♦-	♠765	♦AKQ
♥K432	♣AK2	♥A8765	♣Q3	♥K432	♣AK2	♥A98765	♣3

Opener	Responder	Opener	Responder
1spade	2hearts	1spade	2hearts
5NT	6diamonds	5NT	6hearts
6hearts	Pass	7hearts	Pass

Opener	(5)	Responder		Opener	(6)	Responder	
♠AQ432	♦-	♠765	♦A32	♠AQ432	♦-	♠K65	♦432
♥-	♣AKQ65432	♥KQ432	♣87	♥-	♣AKQ65432	♥KQ432	♣87

Opener	Responder	Opener	Responder
1spade	2spades	1spade	2spades
5NT	6clubs	5NT	6hearts
Pass		7spades	Pass

In examples (3) and (4), responder bids two hearts showing a minimum of five hearts. Opener bids five notrump, the Grand Slam Force, asking about the quality of responder's hearts. In example (3), responder answers six diamonds, showing the ace or king of hearts, with minimum length. Opener signs-off in six hearts. In example (4), responder answers six hearts, showing the ace or king of hearts with extra length. Opener bids seven hearts, knowing responder has six hearts to the ace. In examples (5) and (6), responder raises spades, showing either a three or four-card raise. Opener bids five notrump, asking about the quality of responder's spades. In example (5), responder answers six clubs, showing the worst possible spade holding. Opener passes six clubs, since six clubs has to be at least as good a contract as six spades and can be a better contract. In example (6), responder answers six hearts showing a top honor with the minimum length. Opener bids seven spades hoping for a 3-2 spade break or dummy having the jack of spades.

25.6 -- VOIDS.

Opener	(1)	Responder		Opener	(2)	Responder	
♠KQJ32	♦AK2	♠-	♦5	♠KQJ32	♦A432	♠A	♦KQJ
♥KQJ2	♣2	♥A76543	♣AKQJ43	♥KQJ2	♣-	♥A76543	♣543

Opener (1)	Responder	Opener (2)	Responder
1spade	2hearts	1spade	2hearts
4NT	6diamonds	4clubs	4NT
7hearts	Pass	6hearts	7hearts

How does answerer show a void along with his keycards? First of all, answerer has to know that his void will be a useful void. When in doubt, answerer just answers aces. Second of all, it is very important for asker to know which suit answerer is void in. In order for asker to know, I use three rules. If an opponent has bid a suit, answerer is void in that suit. If answerer has shown shortness, answerer is void in that suit. Otherwise, answerer is void in asker's first bid suit. Answerer bids five notrump to show zero or three keycards with a void. Answerer bids six clubs to show one or four keycards with a void. Answerer with a useful void bids six diamonds to show two keycards without the queen and bids six hearts to show two keycards with the queen. Answers without a void start at five clubs and end at five spades. Answers with a void start at five notrump and end at six hearts.

In example (1), opener, needing responder to have two keycards for slam to be cold, bids RKC. Responder bids six diamonds, showing two keycards without the heart queen, and a spade void. Responder can show the void in opener's first bid suit since he doesn't need any spade tricks to make six or seven hearts. The only reason responder shows his void in spades is because he is interested in reaching seven hearts opposite two keycards and the heart queen. If responder wants to be in seven hearts opposite two keycards and the queen, opener trusts responder and bids the grand. In example (2), opener jumps to four clubs, showing four-card heart support with club shortness. Over responder's RKC, opener bids six hearts, showing two keycards, the heart queen and a club void. Responder bids seven hearts.

25.7 -- GERBER.

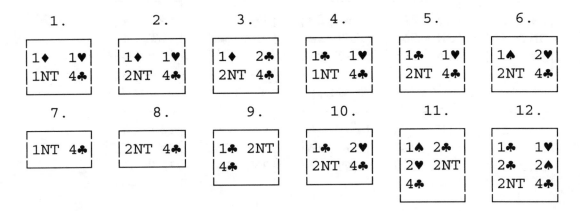

1.	2.	3.	4.	5.	6.
1♦ 1♥	1♦ 1♥	1♦ 2♣	1♣ 1♥	1♣ 1♥	1♠ 2♥
1NT 4♣	2NT 4♣	2NT 4♣	1NT 4♣	2NT 4♣	2NT 4♣

7.	8.	9.	10.	11.	12.
1NT 4♣	2NT 4♣	1♣ 2NT	1♣ 2♥	1♠ 2♣	1♣ 1♥
		4♣	2NT 4♣	2♥ 2NT	2♣ 2♠
				4♣	2NT 4♣

If one notrump or two notrump shows a balanced hand, then a jump to four clubs is Gerber and asks for the number of aces. Gerber has to be a jump. Answerer bids four diamonds to show zero or four aces, four hearts to show one ace, four spades to show two aces and four notrump to show three aces. If all four aces are present, asker can then bid five clubs to ask for the number of kings. Either opener or responder can use Gerber. If a jump to four clubs is Gerber, then a jump to four notrump is natural and invitational.

If overcaller doubles four clubs, ignore the double if you have first or second-round club control. With zero or four aces and a club control bid four diamonds. With one ace and a club control bid four hearts. With two aces and a club control bid four spades. With three aces and a club control bid four notrump. If you don't have first or second-round club control, pass four-clubs doubled. If asker has a club control, asker redoubles to continue ace asking. Any bid by asker other than redouble is a sign-off. If advancer raises to five clubs, asker passes five clubs to ask for aces.

In auctions (1) through (12), one notrump or two notrump is a natural bid; therefore, all four-club jumps are Gerber. A jump to four notrump instead is natural and invitational.

13.		14.		15.		16.		17.		18.	
1♣	1♥	1♦	1♥	1♦	2♣	1♣	2♦	1♠	2♥	1♦	2♦
3NT	5♣	3NT	5♣	3NT	5♣	3NT	5♣	3NT	5♣	3NT	5♣
5♦	5♥	5♥	5♠	5♠	5NT	5NT	6♣				

19.		20.		21.		22.		23.		24.	
1♠	2♣	1♣	1♥	1NT	2♥	2NT	3♣	1♠	2♣	1♣	2♣
2♥	3NT	2♣	2♠	2♠	3♣	3♦	3♠	2♠	2NT	2♥	2NT
5♣		3NT	5♣	3NT	5♣	3NT	5♣	3NT	5♣	3NT	5♣

Over a natural three-notrump bid, a jump to five clubs is Gerber. Answerer bids five diamonds to show zero or four aces, five hearts to show one ace, five spades to show two aces and five notrump to show three aces. The cheapest forcing bid is used to show all the aces and ask for kings.

If overcaller doubles five clubs, ignore the double if you have first or second-round club control. If you don't have first or second-round club control, pass five-clubs doubled. If asker has a club control, asker redoubles to continue ace asking. Any bid by asker other than redouble is a sign-off.

In auctions (13) through (24), three notrump is natural and passable. Therefore five clubs is Gerber and four notrump is natural and invitational. Auction (13) is an example where answerer shows show zero or four aces and asker, with all four aces present, bids five hearts asking for kings. Auction (14) is an example where answerer shows one ace and asker, with all four aces present, bids five spades asking for kings. Auction (15) is an example where answerer shows two aces and asker, with all four aces present, bids five notrump asking for kings. Auction (16) is an example where answerer shows three aces and asker, with all four aces present, bids six clubs asking for kings. Auctions (17) through (24) will continue based upon the number of aces answerer has.

CHAPTER 26 - LEADS AND SIGNALS

26.1 -- AGAINST NOTRUMP:

The following leads are only if you're leading your own suit. If you're leading partner's suit, go to section 26.2 and lead as if against suits. If partner makes a takeout double and you're leading a major, go to section 26.2 also.

Fourth from your longest and strongest from at least the jack. Playing fourth best, partner of the opening leader uses the rule of 11. Partner subtracts the lead from 11 and that's how many cards higher than the opening lead are in partner's hand, dummy's hand, and declarer's hand. If you lead the six and dummy has the Q87, partner with AT32 knows that if the six is fourth best, there are only five (11-6 = 5) cards higher than the six in dummy's hand, declarer's hand and his hand. Since there are three higher in dummy (Q87) and two higher in his hand (A10), declarer should have only small spots, so the ten is the correct play. Partner knows that you have led the six from KJ96.

Second best or fourth best from weaker holdings other than 98(x). Never top. A player led the eight from the 8654 against six notrump, found partner with JT9. Declarer, with AKQ7, made four tricks in that suit. If you always lead second highest even from a doubleton, partner knows that you always have at least one higher spot card. From 8765 lead the seven. From 10876 lead the eight. If you lead the eight from 10876, partner with QJ9 will know that it's safe to continue. Leader should follow with the highest spot if possible.

Lead of the ace asks partner to drop an honor (king, queen or jack) or give count. Lead the ace from AKJ103 to get partner to play the queen or give count. If the 654 is in dummy and partner plays the two showing three, declarer's queen will drop. If partner plays the nine, showing two, you have to get partner in to lead through declarer's queen. Lead the ace from AKQ102 which will tell you if declarer has four to the jack. Lead the ace from AQJ102 with an entry to pick off a possible stiff king or have partner unblock with Kx.

Lead of the king is from KQ(x) or AK(x) (where x represents one or more spot cards) and asks partner to give attitude with an honor. The only time third hand gives count is if it is impossible on the auction for third hand to have an honor. There is a problem whether third hand should encourage with the jack.

If you lead the king and continue with the queen, you are leading a short suit, and you don't want partner to overtake with the ace. If you lead the king and follow with the jack or ten, you want partner to overtake with the ace and return the suit.

Lead of the queen is from QJ(x) or from KQ109(x). If partner leads the queen, you encourage with the king, ace or ten. If partner leads the queen and you have the jack, he is leading from KQ109(x) and wants you to play the jack. If you don't play the jack, you don't have the jack. If partner leads the queen and continues with the jack, he is leading a short suit and he doesn't want you to overtake. If partner leads the queen and continues with ten or lower, he wants you to unblock.

Lead of the jack shows zero or two higher and is from J10(x) or AQJ(x). Leading zero or two higher gives declarer some help, but more importantly, it gives partner help. Defense is the toughest part of the game, and you need all the help you can get. When your partner leads the jack and you have Axx, you know declarer has the KQ and can plan your defense accordingly. Playing standard leads, partner can have KJ10xx, so you have to win the ace and return the suit.

Lead of the ten shows zero or two higher. You lead the ten from 109(x), AK109(x), KJ10(x), AJ10(x) or AQ109(x).

Lead of the nine shows zero or two higher. You lead the nine from 98(x), A109(x), K109(x) or Q109(x).

Lead of the eight is either fourth best from AK98(x), AQ108(x), AQ98(x), KJ98(x) or AJ98(x) or second best from 108(x).

26.2 -- AGAINST SUITS:

The following leads are against suit contracts. You also use the following leads in notrump contracts if you're leading partner's suit or if partner has made a takeout double and you're leading a major.

From three small, lead third best unless you have shown at least three, in which case you lead top. From 987, lead the seven. From 1098 lead the eight. It is very important for partner to be able to distinguish between doubletons and tripletons. From three to an honor, lead third best.

From four small or four to an honor, lead third best and follow with your fourth best. From KJ65, lead the six and follow with the five. Leading third best, partner of the opening leader uses the rule of 12. Partner subtracts the lead from 12 and that's how many cards higher than the opening lead are in partner's hand, dummy's hand, and declarer's hand. If you lead the six and dummy has the Q87, partner with AT92 knows that if the six is third best, there are only six (12-6 = 6) cards higher than the six in dummy's hand, declarer's hand and his hand. Since there are three higher in dummy (Q87) and three higher in his hand (A109), declarer should have only small spots, so the nine is the correct play. Partner knows that you have led the six from KJ6.

From five small or five to an honor, lead fifth best. From Q5432 lead the two. Leading fifth best, partner of the opening leader uses the rule of 10.

From six small or six to an honor, lead third best. From Q65432 lead the five and follow with a suit-preference lower spot in tempo. Partner should be able to distinguish from the auction that your 5-4 is from six rather than from two or four. Leading third best, partner of the opening leader uses the rule of 12.

From seven, lead fifth best. From Q765432, lead the four. Lead seventh best when you have a void and want a ruff.

Lead of the jack shows zero or two higher and is from J10(x) or AQJ(x). The only time you lead the jack from AQJ is if partner doubles a cuebid showing the king.

Lead of the ten shows zero or two higher. Lead the ten from 109(x) only if you can't have a doubleton, or from KJ10(x).

Lead of the nine shows zero or two higher. Lead the nine from K109(x) or Q109(x) or from 98(x) only if you can't have a doubleton.

Lead of the king is from KQ(x) or AK(x). Lead ace from AK(x) if you suspect partner can be void.

Lead of the ace and following with the king shows a doubleton with the desire for a ruff. Partner gives a suit preference signal under the king.

Some players like ace from AK(x). If you want to play ace from AK(x), you should exclude those situations where you are likely to lead an unsupported ace. Against slams, you often lead aces, and you want partner to encourage only if he has the king. If you have AK(x), you want to lead the king so that if Qxx(x) turns up in dummy, partner gives count so you know whether to cash the ace. When you bid a suit and partner supports, you might easily lead an unsupported ace. You want partner to encourage only with the king. If an opponent has shown a two-suiter, you can lead an unsupported ace. Again, you want partner to encourage with the king and not the queen.

Lead queen from AKQ(x) or QJ(x). Leading the queen from AKQ, allows you to use the continuation of the king or ace as suit preference signal.

26.3 -- IN THE MIDDLE OF THE HAND LEAD EITHER ATTITUDE OR THIRD AND FIFTH FOR COUNT AGAINST BOTH SUIT AND NOTRUMP, DEPENDING UPON WHICH IS NECESSARY.

Attitude means that if you lead a low spot, you want partner to return that suit. If you lead a high spot, you want partner to return a different suit. For instance, opening leader defending against a notrump contract gets in again and switches suits. If opening leader switches to a low spot, he doesn't want the opening lead returned. If opening leader switches to a high spot, he wants the opening lead returned. A second example is when you are defending against a suit contract and partner gives you a ruff. If you switch to a low spot, you don't want another ruff. If you switch to a high spot, you want another ruff. A third example is if you are leading a possible singleton and declarer wins the trick. You win the next trick with the ace of trumps and switch. If you switch to a low spot, your opening lead was not a singleton or you do not want a ruff. If you switch to a high spot, your opening lead was a singleton and you want a ruff.

| (1) | (2) |

	(1)		(2)
	North		North
	♠65		♠65
	♥43		♥43
	♦K862		♦K862
West	♣KJ984 East	West	♣KJ984 EAST
♠AJ932	♠1087	♠J9432	♠1087
♥Q872	♥AJ109	♥K872	♥AJ109
♦543	♦J1097	♦Q43	♦J1097
♣A	South ♣103	♣A	South ♣103
	♠KQ4		♠AKQ
	♥K65		♥Q65
	♦AQ		♦A5
	♣Q7652		♣Q7652

In examples (1) and (2), South is declarer in three notrump with the three of spades lead. East plays the spade ten, third hand high, and South wins the king of spades. At trick two South leads a club and West wins the ace. In example (1), West wants East to continue spades so he leads the eight of hearts. In example (2), West wants East to continue hearts, so he leads the two of hearts. In example (1), East wins the ace of hearts and plays back a spade. In example (2), East wins the ace of hearts and plays back a heart.

26.4 -- SMITH VS NOTRUMP

(1)

```
                    North
                    ♠65
                    ♥643
                    ♦A62
West                ♣KQJ54          East
♠AJ932                              ♠1087
♥754                               ♥QJ1098
♦543                               ♦J108
♣102                South           ♣A3
                    ♠KQ4
                    ♥AK
                    ♦KQ97
                    ♣9865
```

(2)

```
                    North
                    ♠65
                    ♥643
                    ♦A62
West                ♣KQJ54          EAST
♠J9432                             ♠1087
♥A54                               ♥QJ1098
♦543                               ♦J108
♣102                South           ♣A3
                    ♠AKQ
                    ♥K7
                    ♦KQ97
                    ♣9876
```

Hi-Lo by either defender in the first suit played by declarer shows positive attitude for the opening lead unless count is important. If it's obvious from trick one that you started with either a singleton or a doubleton in the suit that partner led, then positive attitude can be having one card left, and negative attitude can be that you're void and partner's on his own. Positive attitude can be having led from the AQ and the suit is ready to run, and negative attitude can be having led from the KJ and declarer has one stopper left.

In examples (1) and (2), South is declarer in three notrump with the three of spades lead. East plays the spade ten, third hand high and South wins the king of spades. At trick two South leads the five of clubs. This is where Smith comes in. In example (1), West wants East to continues spades so he plays the ten of clubs, starting a hi-lo. In example (2), West knows from East's play of the ten at trick one that South has the AKQ of spades. West therefore wants a shift and plays the two of clubs starting a lo-hi. In example (1), East leads back the eight of spades and West takes the next four spade tricks. In example (2), East leads back the queen of hearts and the defense takes the next five heart tricks.

```
              (3)                                          (4)
┌─────────────────────────────────┐      ┌─────────────────────────────────┐
│           North                 │      │           North                 │
│           ♠65                   │      │           ♠65                   │
│           ♥K43                  │      │           ♥K43                  │
│           ♦762                  │      │           ♦762                  │
│   West    ♣KQJ94     East       │      │   West    ♣KQJ94     EAST       │
│   ♠A10932            ♠QJ8       │      │   ♠A10932            ♠J84       │
│   ♥Q65              ♥109872     │      │   ♥Q65              ♥A10987     │
│   ♦543              ♦J109       │      │   ♦543              ♦J109       │
│   ♣A2       South    ♣103       │      │   ♣A2       South    ♣103       │
│           ♠K74                  │      │           ♠KQ7                  │
│           ♥AJ                   │      │           ♥J7                   │
│           ♦AKQ8                 │      │           ♦AKQ8                 │
│           ♣8765                 │      │           ♣8765                 │
└─────────────────────────────────┘      └─────────────────────────────────┘
```

In examples (3) and (4), South is declarer in three notrump with the three of spades lead. East plays the spade Jack, third hand high and South wins the king of spades. At trick two South leads the five of clubs and West wins the ace. This is where Smith comes in. In example (3), East wants West to continues spades so he plays the ten of clubs starting a hi-lo. In example (4), East has nothing extra in the spade suit, so he plays the three of clubs starting a lo-hi. In example (3), West leads the ace of spades, East unblocks the queen of spades, and West takes the next four spade tricks. In example (4), West shifts to the six of hearts, East wins the ace and plays back the eight of spades, and the defense takes the next four spade tricks. I don't see how you can get examples (1) through (4) right without playing Smith Echoes or being an exceptional guesser.

```
              (5)                                    (6)

┌─────────────────────────────┐      ┌─────────────────────────────┐
│           North             │      │           North             │
│           ♠5432             │      │           ♠5432             │
│           ♥AK32             │      │           ♥AK32             │
│           ♦Q54              │      │           ♦Q54              │
│  West     ♣K4      East      │      │  West     ♣K4      EAST      │
│  ♠AQ1098           ♠7        │      │  ♠AQ1098           ♠76       │
│  ♥54               ♥QJ109    │      │  ♥54               ♥QJ109    │
│  ♦A32              ♦876      │      │  ♦A32              ♦76       │
│  ♣Q65     South    ♣J10987   │      │  ♣Q65     South    ♣J10987   │
│           ♠KJ6              │      │           ♠KJ               │
│           ♥876             │      │           ♥876             │
│           ♦KJ109           │      │           ♦KJ1098          │
│           ♣A32             │      │           ♣A32             │
└─────────────────────────────┘      └─────────────────────────────┘
```

In examples (5) and (6), South is declarer in three notrump after West overcalls one spade and leads the ten of spades. East plays the spade seven, which is count, since he doesn't have an honor, and South wins the jack of spades. At trick two, South leads the ten of diamonds and West ducks the ace. This is where Smith comes in. In example (5), East started with only one spade, so he wants West to switch; therefore, he plays the six of diamonds starting a lo-hi. In example (6), East started with two spades so he knows it's safe for West to continue spades; therefore, he plays the seven of diamonds, starting a hi-lo. In example (5), West wins the ace of diamonds at trick three, East playing the eight of diamonds, completing the lo-hi. As long as West does not lead a spade, South will have only eight tricks. In example (6), West wins the ace of diamonds at trick three, East playing the six of diamonds, completing the hi-lo. East leads the ace of spades, dropping the king, and runs the spade suit.

```
          (7)                              (8)

+-----------------------------+  +-----------------------------+
|          North              |  |          North              |
|          ♠K8                 |  |          ♠K8                 |
|          ♥K3                 |  |          ♥K3                 |
|          ♦KQJ1076            |  |          ♦KQJ1076            |
| West     ♣Q64      East      |  | West     ♣Q64      EAST      |
| ♠QJ32              ♠7654     |  | ♠J1032             ♠7654     |
| ♥J9762             ♥A10      |  | ♥87642             ♥A10      |
| ♦-                 ♦5432     |  | ♦-                 ♦5432     |
| ♣J1032    South    ♣K85      |  | ♣A1032    South    ♣K85      |
|          ♠A109               |  |          ♠AQ9                |
|          ♥Q854               |  |          ♥QJ95               |
|          ♦A98                |  |          ♦A98                |
|          ♣A97                |  |          ♣J97                |
+-----------------------------+  +-----------------------------+
```

In examples (7) and (8), South is declarer in three notrump after one diamond -- one heart -- two diamonds -- three notrump. West leads the two of spades and North plays the eight. East plays the spade seven, count, since he can't beat the eight, and South wins the nine of spades. At trick two, South leads the five of hearts. This is where Smith comes in. In example (7), West has hearts bottled up and can't stand a club switch, so he wants East to continue spades. West therefore plays the seven of hearts starting a hi-lo. In example (8), West has nothing in hearts and can stand a club switch, so he doesn't care what East does. West therefore plays the two of hearts starting a lo-hi. In example (7), East wins the ace of hearts at trick two, and continues spades holding South to 11 tricks. In example (8), West wins the ace of hearts at trick two and switches to a club, holding South to ten tricks.

26.5 -- SIGNALS.

The basic rule of signaling is that when you are playing high, you always play the highest card you can afford, and when you are playing low, you always play your lowest card. From the 987, you either play the nine to encourage, or the seven to discourage. You never play the eight. Your first signal when partner leads an honor or partner leads a spot card and dummy plays an honor should be attitude. Hi-lo says you like partner's lead or you like the suit you're discarding. Lo-hi says you don't like partner's lead or you don't like the suit you're discarding. You also hi-lo with a doubleton and the ability to ruff, and lo-hi otherwise. If there is a doubleton in dummy and it's possible that you can have a doubleton, you hi-lo if you can overruff and lo-hi otherwise. Your second signal in a suit is current count if that is unknown and can be important. After count and attitude, the rest of your signals are suit preference. If attitude in a suit is obvious, for instance dummy plays the ten and you can't beat it, give current count. If attitude and current count are obvious or unimportant, give suit preference.

Current count is the number of cards you have in the suit at the time you give count. If you lead the ace from A9876 and later you have to give count, discard the nine, showing an even number of cards left. If you lead the ace from A987, discard the seven to show an odd number of cards left.

When partner leads the king, and the queen is in dummy, you normally play hi-lo only with a doubleton and the ability to ruff. At the five-level or higher, however, you hi-lo with any even number amount and lo-hi with any odd number.

The strength of your signal, when you know that you are going to make at least two discards, can help partner. If you have opened two hearts, partner knows that you have values in that suit. Sitting behind declarer with spot cards in dummy, from AQ9832 discard the nine followed by the two, and from KJ9832 discard the three followed by the two.

The order of your signals can make a difference. If you discard a club and then a diamond, the club signal is the stronger signal, and more emphasis should be placed on it.

You don't signal with a card which can cost a trick. If declarer leads the three from the K93, playing the ten from 102 will cost a trick if dummy has Q54 and partner has AJ876.

26.6 -- WHEN CONTINUING, LEAD HIGH FROM EVEN, LOW FROM ODD.

If you win a trick and want to continue the suit with the correct count card, lead the highest card you can afford with an even number of cards left, lead your lowest card with an odd number of cards left. From A98, win the ace and return the nine. From A765, win the ace and return the five. From A9876, win the ace and return the nine. From A98765, win the ace and return the five. Partner should be able to tell the difference between A98 and A9876, or between A765 and A98765. The most difficult problem is what the partner of the opening leader against a notrump contract returns at trick two after winning trick one. If you have to unblock, lead high and hope for the best. If you want partner to continue the suit, leading low works in most situations. World champions have allowed declarer to win a trick with Qx opposite xx.

26.7 -- WHEN SPLITTING, SPLIT LOW FROM TWO HONORS, HIGH FROM THREE OR MORE HONORS.

If you are second to play, and you have touching honors, play the lower honor from two touching honors, and play the highest honor from three or more touching honors. From QJT(x) or KQ(x), split with the queen. Partner should be able to tell the difference. Split with the jack from QJ(x), JT9(x) or KJT9(x). Split with the King from AK(x) or KQJ(x). Split with the ten from the JT(x), KJT(x), or QT98(x). You don't give count when you split.

If you are third to play, and you have touching honors, always play your lowest honor.

26.8 -- FREQUENT SUIT PREFERENCE SIGNALS.

There are frequent situations where the order of the cards you play tells partner which of the two off-suits you are interested in. Assume spades are trumps. Partner leads the nine of hearts, you have the AK432 and dummy has the 876. Partner's nine of hearts is a doubleton and you are going to give him a ruff. If you want partner to return a diamond after he ruffs, play the ace, king and then the four of hearts. Playing the ace first and then the king helps those partners who don't watch spots and who might think the four is a low spot. If you want partner to return a club, play the king, ace and then the two of hearts. If you can stand partner to return either minor, play the ace, king and then the two of hearts. If you can't stand either minor and want partner to make a safe return, play the king, ace and then the three of hearts, and hope partner is watching the spots.

If partner leads an ace or king and there's a singleton in dummy, your signal is a suit preference signal, assuming you have a choice of cards to play and partner knows you have a choice. A high card says lead the highest off-suit. A low card says lead the lowest off-suit. Middle, if partner can read it, says continue. However, in all other situations, the highest card you can afford says continue and all other cards are suit preference signals. Clubs are trumps and partner, who has shown four spades, leads the ten from 10987. Dummy has AK32 and you have QJ654. The queen says continue. The jack says you strongly want a heart shift. The four says you strongly want a diamond shift. The six says you can stand a heart shift and the five says you can stand a diamond shift.

If partner leads the ten, a likely singleton trying for a ruff, and there's KQJ32 in dummy, your play at trick one is a suit preference signal. Play the nine from 9876 to get partner to shift to the higher off-suit. Play the six to get partner to shift to the lower off-suit. If dummy contains the AKQ of the lower off-suit, play the six if you can't stand partner to lead the higher off-suit. Never play the seven or the eight.

If you are leading a suit and you know partner is going to be overruffed, lead the highest spot. You lead the king from AKT432, partner plays the eight, starting a hi-lo, and dummy has the QJ9. If you decide to continue the suit, play the king and then the ten. Partner will know that declarer is going to overruff.

288

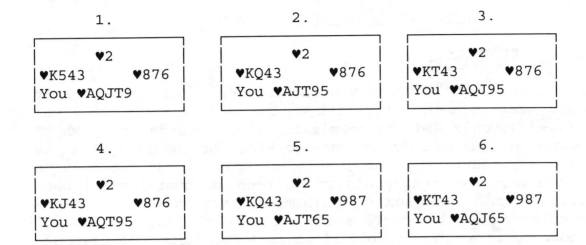

1.
♥2
♥K543   ♥876
You ♥AQJT9

2.
♥2
♥KQ43   ♥876
You ♥AJT95

3.
♥2
♥KT43   ♥876
You ♥AQJ95

4.
♥2
♥KJ43   ♥876
You ♥AQT95

5.
♥2
♥KQ43   ♥987
You ♥AJT65

6.
♥2
♥KT43   ♥987
You ♥AQJ65

There are some situations where it's impossible to tell whether an honor card asks for a high suit or asks for a low suit. In the above situations, spades are trumps. Partner leads the heart two, a singleton, and you win the ace. In all six cases you must return an honor to force declarer to play an honor. If you return the jack, and declarer plays the king, is the jack a middle card, as in example (1), a high card as in examples (2) and (5), or a low card as in examples (3) and (6).

In order for partner to know whether your honor card is suit preference for the high suit or suit preference for the low suit, we will say that the queen and ten are high honors and the jack and nine are low honors. In example (1), the queen or ten asks for diamonds, the jack or nine asks for clubs. In example (2), the ten asks for diamonds, the jack or nine asks for clubs. In example (3) the queen asks for diamonds, the jack asks for clubs. In example (4), the ten asks for diamonds, the nine asks for clubs. In example (5), the ten asks for diamonds, the jack asks for clubs. In example (6), the queen asks for diamonds, the jack asks for clubs.

CHAPTER 27 - ADVANCED METHODS

27.1 -- KICKBACK.

Four notrump, RKC, works very well with spades as trumps. Four notrump, RKC, can be a disaster with clubs as trumps. If partner responds five diamonds and you're missing two keycards, then what? Kickback switches four notrump and one-over-four-of-the-trump-suit as RKC. If one-over-four-of-the-trump-suit is unpassable by a beginning player, or the sequence has been discussed, then one-over-four-of-the-trump-suit is keycard, and four notrump means what one-over-four-of-the-trump-suit means. If hearts are trumps, four spades is keycard and four notrump is a spade cuebid if it is a non-jump. If diamonds are trumps, four hearts is keycard and four notrump is a heart cuebid if it is a non-jump. If clubs are trumps, four diamonds is keycard and four notrump is a diamond cuebid. If four diamonds is keycard, a four-heart response shows zero or three keycards; a four-spade response shows one or four; a four-notrump response shows two without the trump queen; a five-club response shows two with the trump queen; a five-diamond response has the same meaning as if responder answers five notrump to four notrump. If asker bids four hearts, Kickback, and then bids five hearts, it carries the same meaning as four notrump followed by five notrump.

When is one-over-four-of-the-trump-suit Kickback? If opener opens one club, one diamond or one heart making that suit opener's primary suit, and that suit gets supported, then one-over-four-of-that-suit is Kickback, assuming it's forcing. If responder responds two clubs or two diamonds, making that suit responder's primary suit, and that suit gets supported, then one-over-four-of-that-suit is Kickback, assuming it's forcing. If opener's or responder's second bid suit gets supported at the three-level, then one-over-four-of-that-suit is Kickback, assuming it's forcing. If you jump to one-over-four-of-the-trump suit, then that is keycard.

After one heart -- two notrump, showing a forcing heart raise, four spades by either player is keycard for hearts, and four notrump is a spade cuebid. After one spade -- two clubs -- three clubs, four diamonds by either player is keycard for clubs, and four notrump is a diamond cuebid. However, if there are two trump suits, one heart -- two clubs -- three clubs -- three hearts for instance, then the higher suit becomes the keycard suit and one-over-that-suit will be Kickback for only that suit.

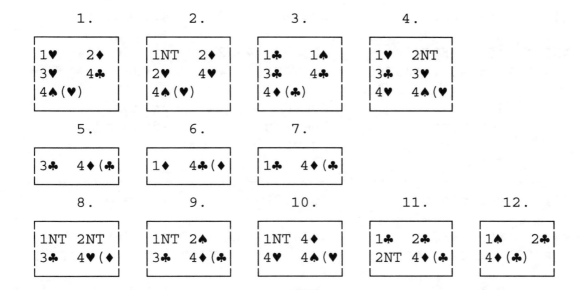

```
   1.              2.              3.              4.
 ┌──────────┐    ┌──────────┐    ┌──────────┐    ┌──────────┐
 │ 1♥   2♦  │    │ 1NT  2♦  │    │ 1♣   1♠  │    │ 1♥   2NT │
 │ 3♥   4♣  │    │ 2♥   4♥  │    │ 3♣   4♣  │    │ 3♣   3♥  │
 │ 4♠(♥)    │    │ 4♠(♥)    │    │ 4♦(♣)    │    │ 4♥   4♠(♥)│
 └──────────┘    └──────────┘    └──────────┘    └──────────┘

        5.              6.              7.
 ┌──────────┐    ┌──────────┐    ┌──────────┐
 │ 3♣   4♦(♣)│    │ 1♦   4♣(♦)│    │ 1♣   4♦(♣)│
 └──────────┘    └──────────┘    └──────────┘

   8.              9.             10.             11.             12.
 ┌──────────┐    ┌──────────┐    ┌──────────┐    ┌──────────┐    ┌──────────┐
 │ 1NT  2NT │    │ 1NT  2♠  │    │ 1NT  4♦  │    │ 1♣   2♣  │    │ 1♠   2♣  │
 │ 3♣   4♥(♦)│    │ 3♣   4♦(♣)│    │ 4♥   4♠(♥)│    │ 2NT  4♦(♣)│    │ 4♦(♣)    │
 └──────────┘    └──────────┘    └──────────┘    └──────────┘    └──────────┘
```

In the above sequences, the last bid is keycard for the trump suit in parenthesis. In auction (1), three hearts sets hearts as trumps, so four spades is keycard. In auction (2), responder's jump to four hearts is a mild slam try and sets hearts as trumps, so four spades is keycard. In auction (3), four clubs sets clubs as trumps, so four diamonds is keycard. In auction (4), two notrump sets hearts as trumps, so four spades is keycard. In auctions (5) and (7), a jump to four diamonds sets clubs as trumps and is keycard. Auction (6) is a specific keycard auction. In auction (8), two notrump, transfer to diamonds, sets diamonds as trumps, so four hearts is keycard. In auction (9), two spades, transfer to clubs, sets clubs as trumps, so four diamonds is keycard. In auction (10), four diamonds sets hearts as trumps, so four spades is keycard. In auction (11), two clubs sets clubs as trumps, so four diamonds is keycard. In auction (12), four diamonds, a jump to one-over-four-of-the-trump-suit, is keycard setting clubs as trumps.

If bidding four diamonds asks for keycards, then a jump to five diamonds is the Grand Slam Force. If bidding four hearts asks for keycards, then a jump to five hearts is the Grand Slam Force. If bidding four spades asks for keycards, then a jump to five spades is the Grand Slam Force.

If overcaller doubles Kickback, ignore the double if you have first or second-round control. If you don't have first or second-round control pass. If asker has a control, asker redoubles to continue ace asking.

Opener	(1)	Responder		Opener	(2)	Responder	
♠AJ432	♦A32	♠5	♦KQJ4	♠KQJ32	♦A32	♠5	♦KQJ4
♥2	♣KQ32	♥J43	♣AJT54	♥2	♣KQ32	♥J43	♣AJT54

Opener (1)	Responder	Opener (2)	Responder
1spade	2clubs	1spade	2clubs
3hearts	4diamonds	3hearts	4diamonds
4hearts	4spades	5clubs	Pass
6clubs	Pass		

Opener	(3)	Responder		Opener	(4)	Responder	
♠AJ432	♦A32	♠5	♦KQJ4	♠AJ432	♦A32	♠5	♦KQJ4
♥A	♣KQ32	♥J32	♣AJT65	♥A	♣K432	♥J32	♣AJT65

Opener (3)	Responder	Opener (4)	Responder
1spade	2clubs	1spade	2clubs
3hearts	4diamonds	3hearts	4diamonds
4spades	5clubs	4spades	5clubs
6clubs	7clubs	5diamonds	6clubs

In examples (1) through (4), responder bids two clubs, setting clubs as his primary suit. Opener supports clubs by splintering in hearts, and responder bids four diamonds, keycard for clubs. Responder's first-bid suit is his primary suit. Unless responder supports one of opener's suits, four diamonds is Kickback once opener supports clubs. If responder supports spades, then spades is the keycard suit and four diamonds is a cuebid in support of spades.

In example (1), opener answers four hearts, showing zero or three keycards. Responder bids four spades asking for the queen, and opener jumps to six clubs, showing the club queen but denying any outside kings. Once responder starts Kickback, four spades is no longer passable. In example (2), opener answers five clubs, showing two keycards and the club queen. Responder, missing two keycards, passes five clubs. If you're not using Kickback, you can easily get to slam off two keycards. In examples (3) and (4), three hearts sets clubs as trumps, and four diamonds is Kickback for clubs. Opener answers four spades, showing one or four keycards. Responder signs-off in five clubs just in case opener has only one keycard. In example (3), opener bids six clubs showing four keycards and the queen of clubs, and denying any kings. Responder, needing to be able to ruff only two hearts in dummy, bids seven clubs. In example (4), opener bids five diamonds showing four keycards rather than one keycard but denying the queen of clubs. Responder, missing the queen of clubs, signs-off in six clubs.

Opener	(5)	Responder		Opener	(6)	Responder	
♠Q32	♦AK2	♠4	♦4	♠AJ2	♦A32	♠4	♦4
♥432	♣K432	♥KQJ5	♣AJ98765	♥432	♣K432	♥KQJ5	♣AJ98765

Opener (5)	Responder	Opener (6)	Responder
1club	1heart	1club	1heart
1NT	2diamonds	1NT	2diamonds
2hearts	3clubs	2hearts	3clubs
3NT	4diamonds	3NT	4diamonds
4NT	5clubs	4hearts	5clubs
Pass		5diamonds	6clubs

Opener	(7)	Responder		Opener	(8)	Responder	
♠KQJ	♦KJ2	♠A	♦AQ54	♠Q32	♦K32	♠A	♦AQ54
♥432	♣Q432	♥KQJ5	♣AJ65	♥A32	♣KQ32	♥KQJ5	♣AJ65

Opener (7)	Responder	Opener (8)	Responder
1club	1heart	1club	1heart
1NT	2diamonds	1NT	2diamonds
2hearts	3clubs	2hearts	3clubs
3NT	4diamonds	3NT	4diamonds
4hearts	4NT	5clubs	5diamonds
Pass		5NT	7clubs

In examples (5) through (8), responder bids three clubs, setting clubs as trumps. Over three notrump, responder bids four diamonds, RKC for clubs. In example (5), opener answers four notrump, showing two keycards without the club queen. Responder missing two keycards signs-off in five clubs. If you're not using Kickback, you can easily get to slam off two keycards. In example (6), opener answers four hearts, showing zero or three keycards. Responder signs-off in five clubs just in case opener has zero. Opener with three keycards bids five diamonds, denying the queen of clubs. Responder signs-off in six clubs. In example (7), opener answers four hearts, showing zero or three keycards. Responder signs-off in four notrump. Since four spades asks for the queen of clubs, four notrump is a sign-off. In example (8), opener answers five clubs, showing two keycards and the queen of clubs. Responder then bids five diamonds, asking for specific kings. Opener answers five notrump, showing the diamond king and denying the heart king and the spade king. Over five diamonds, five hearts would show the heart king and five spades would show the spade king and deny the heart king. Responder bids seven clubs, expecting to ruff a spade in his hand for his 13th trick.

27.2 -- RUSINOW HONOR (SECOND HIGHEST) LEADS VS NOTRUMP.

Your partner leads the king against a notrump contract and you have J82. Does partner have KQ943, and you should encourage with the eight, or does partner have AKT43, and you should discourage with the two? The following lead conventions can be used in order to differentiate between the two holdings. These leads are only on opening lead, and only when you are leading your own suit.

The lead of the ace shows the king and is from AKJ(x) or AK(x) (where x represent one or more spot cards) and asks partner to encourage with the queen.

The lead of the queen shows the king and is from KQ(x), AKQ(x), KQ10(x) or KQJxx(x), and asks partner to encourage with the jack or the ace. If you lead the queen and continue with the king, you are leading a short suit and you don't want partner to overtake. If you lead the queen and continue with a lower honor, you want partner to overtake and return the suit.

The lead of the jack shows the queen and is from QJ(x), KQJx or AQJ(x), and asks partner to encourage with the ten or any higher honor. When you lead the jack from KQJx, it's more important for you to know who has the ten than for partner to know that you have the king, since partner might not think you have the king. If you lead the jack and continue with the queen, you are leading a short suit and you don't want partner to overtake. If you lead the jack and continue with the king or a lower card, you want partner to overtake and return the suit.

The lead of the ten shows the jack and is from J10(x), AJ10(x) or KJ10(x). The lead of the nine shows the ten and is from 109(x), K109(x), Q109(x), AQ109(x), AK109(x) or A109(x). If you lead the ten and continue with the jack, you are leading a short suit.

If you want your partner to unblock or give count, lead the king. The lead of the king is from AKJT(x), AKQ10(x), KQ109(x) or KQTxx(x) and asks partner to play an honor (ace, queen or jack) or give count.

27.3 -- UPSIDE DOWN COUNT AND ATTITUDE SIGNALS.

The concept of upside down signals is very simple. If playing standard signals you start a hi-lo, then with upside down signals you start a lo-hi. If playing standard signals you start a lo-hi, then with upside down signals you start a hi-lo. Suit preference signals and trump echoes don't change when playing upside down signals.

From the 987, you either play the nine to discourage, or the seven to encourage. You never play the eight. Your first signal when unable to play third hand high to partner's lead, or when discarding, should be attitude. Lo-hi says you like partner's lead or you like the suit you're discarding. Hi-lo says you don't like partner's lead or you don't like the suit you're discarding. You also lo-hi with a doubleton and the ability to ruff, and hi-lo otherwise. If there is a doubleton in dummy and it's possible that you can have a doubleton, you lo-hi if you can overruff, and hi-lo otherwise. Your second signal in a suit is current count if that is unknown and can be important. After count and attitude, the rest of your signals are standard suit preference. If attitude in a suit is obvious, for instance dummy plays the ten and you can't beat it, give current upside down count. If attitude and current count are obvious or unimportant, give suit preference.

Current count is the number of cards you have in the suit at the time you give count. If you lead the ace from A9876 and later you have to give count, discard the six, showing an even number of cards left. If you lead the ace from A987, discard the nine to show an odd number of cards left.

When partner leads the king, and the queen is in dummy, you normally play lo-hi only with a doubleton and the ability to ruff. At the five-level or higher, however, you lo-hi with any even number and hi-lo with any odd number.

The strength of your signal, when you know that you are going to make at least two discards, can help partner. If you have opened two hearts, partner knows that you have values in that suit. From AQ9832, discard the two followed by the nine, and from KJ9832 discard the eight followed by the nine. Partner should know that you have lower spot cards.

27.4 -- BART.

Opener	(1)		Responder		Opener	(2)		Responder	
♠AKT98	♦AJT	♠32	♦432		♠AKT98	♦AJT	♠32	♦432	
♥65	♣765	♥AQJ32	♣432		♥65	♣765	♥AQJ432	♣32	

Opener (1)	Responder	Opener (2)	Responder
1spade	1NT	1spade	1NT
2clubs	2diamonds	2clubs	2hearts
2hearts	Pass	2hearts	Pass

Opener	(3)		Responder		Opener	(4)		Responder	
♠A5432	♦432	♠76	♦K65		♠A5432	♦32	♠76	♦K65	
♥2	♣AKQ2	♥QJ543	♣654		♥2	♣AKQ32	♥QJ543	♣654	

Opener (3)	Responder	Opener (4)	Responder
1spade	1NT	1spade	1NT
2clubs	2diamonds	2clubs	2diamonds
2spades	Pass	3clubs	Pass

After one spade -- one notrump -- two clubs -- two hearts, opener with a singleton heart, has a problem deciding whether to pass two hearts or not. Does responder have ♥A5432 or ♥AQJ432? By giving up the natural two-diamond response to two clubs, responder can avoid playing the 5-1 heart fit. Over two clubs, responder bids two hearts showing at least six hearts, and bids two diamonds, Bart, with five hearts. Over responder's two-diamond Bart bid, opener bids two hearts with two or three hearts. If opener has three hearts, the 5-3 heart fit should play very well. If opener has only two hearts, the 5-2 heart fit can play better than the possible 5-2 spade fit.

In examples (1) and (2), responder wants to show opener how many hearts he has. In example (1), responder shows a five-card heart suit by going through two diamonds and passing two hearts. In example (2), responder shows at least six hearts by bidding two hearts directly.

If opener has fewer than two hearts, opener makes his most natural rebid. In examples (3) and (4), responder wants to play in two hearts if opener has at least two hearts. Responder bids two diamonds asking opener to bid two hearts with at least two hearts. Opener has only one heart so he can't bid two hearts. In example (3), opener bids two spades and responder passes. In example (4), opener rebids his five-card club suit which ends the auction.

Opener	(5)		Responder		Opener	(6)		Responder	
♠AKT98	♦AJ	♠32	♦5432		♠AKT98	♦AJ	♠32	♦K432	
♥43	♣KJ65	♥AQJ2	♣432		♥43	♣KJ65	♥AQJ2	♣432	

Opener (5)	Responder	Opener (6)	Responder
1spade	1NT	1spade	1NT
2clubs	2spades	2clubs	2diamonds
Pass		2hearts	2spades
		3NT	Pass

Opener	(7)		Responder		Opener	(8)		Responder	
♠AKT98	♦A65	♠32	♦432		♠AKT98	♦A65	♠32	♦K32	
♥765	♣K4	♥432	♣AQJ32		♥765	♣K4	♥432	♣AQJ32	

Opener (7)	Responder	Opener (8)	Responder
1spade	1NT	1spade	1NT
2clubs	3clubs	2clubs	2diamonds
Pass		2hearts	2NT
		3NT	Pass

Responder can differentiate between a weak or a strong preference to two spades. One spade -- one notrump -- two clubs -- two spades shows two spades with 5-8 HCPs or three spades with 4-7 HCPs. Going through two diamonds and then bidding two spades over two hearts cancels showing five hearts and shows nine or ten HCPs with exactly two spades. In example (5), responder bids two spades directly over two clubs showing fewer than nine HCPs. Opener with only a seven-card spade fit and a maximum of 24 HCPs, passes two spades. In example (6), responder bids two spades after going through two diamonds, showing exactly two spades with nine or ten HCPs. With combined 25 or 26 HCPs, opener jumps to three notrump.

Responder can also differentiate between a weak or a strong raise to three clubs. A direct raise shows a minimum raise to three clubs. Bidding two diamonds and then over two hearts bidding either two notrump or three clubs, cancels showing five hearts and shows the strongest possible non-forcing raise to three clubs. Since opener might have only two clubs, responder bids two notrump with a four or weak five-card raise. With a strong five-card raise or a six-card raise responder bids three clubs. In example (7), responder shows a weak raise by bidding three clubs directly over two clubs and opener passes. In example (8), responder shows a 9-11 club raise by going through two diamonds. Opener with a good 14-count bids three notrump.

Opener	(9)	Responder		Opener	(10)	Responder	
♠A5432 ♦A32		♠6 ♦KQJ654		♠A5432 ♦A32		♠76 ♦KQJ54	
♥A32 ♣32		♥654 ♣654		♥A32 ♣32		♥J7654 ♣4	
1spade		1NT		1spade		1NT	
2clubs		3diamonds		2clubs		2diamonds	
Pass				2hearts		3diamonds	
				3hearts		Pass	

Opener	(11)	Responder		Opener	(12)	Responder	
♠A5432 ♦A32		♠6 ♦KQJ54		♠A5432 ♦A32		♠6 ♦QJ54	
♥A32 ♣32		♥7654 ♣654		♥A32 ♣32		♥QJ54 ♣7654	
1spade		1NT		1spade		1NT	
2clubs		Pass		2clubs		Pass	

What happens if responder has diamonds and wants to play in two diamonds? Responder has to jump to three diamonds over two clubs. In examples (9) and (10), opener with 5-3-3-2 distribution bids two clubs. In example (9), responder bids three diamonds to play. In example (10), responder has hearts and diamonds with a reasonable hand. Responder bids two diamonds and over two hearts bids three diamonds, showing five or more diamonds and exactly five hearts. Opener with three hearts and a minimum, bids three hearts.

Bart works only over a one-spade opening bid and has no effect if responder bids one notrump and then bids two notrump. Bart is so useful that after one spade -- one notrump, opener bids two clubs on a doubleton club instead of two diamonds with 5-3-3-2 hands. This has the advantage of making opener's two-diamond bid natural.

When Bart works, it works well, but you do pay a price. In examples (11) and (12), responder has a singleton spade so he can't bid two spades. In example (11), responder has a choice between passing two clubs and bidding three diamonds. Responder passes two clubs and plays the 3-2 club fit instead of the 5-3 diamond fit. In example (12), responder passes two clubs and plays the 4-2 club fit instead of the 4-3 diamond fit. On better days, opener has a five-card club suit. In spite of these last two examples, I feel the gains of playing Bart far outweigh the losses.

27.5 -- OVER TWO NOTRUMP OPENING, THREE SPADES FORCES THREE NOTRUMP.

Opener (1)	Responder	Opener (2)	Responder
♠AQ3 ♦K65	♠2 ♦AQ432	♠AQ43 ♦K5	♠2 ♦AQ432
♥AK5 ♣KJ65	♥432 ♣A432	♥AK65 ♣KJ5	♥432 ♣A432

Opener (1)	Responder	Opener (2)	Responder
2NT	3spades	2NT	3spades
3NT	4diamonds	3NT	4diamonds
4hearts	4NT	4NT	Pass
5clubs	5diamonds		
6clubs	Pass		

Three spades by responder, asking for four-card minors, is a very simple method. Another method is to play three spades by responder forces opener to bid three notrump. Over three notrump, responder bids <u>four clubs</u> showing both minors, with clubs equal to or longer than diamonds. Four clubs shows five clubs and five diamonds, five clubs and four diamonds or six clubs and five diamonds. Over three notrump, <u>four diamonds</u> by responder shows both minors but diamonds are longer than clubs. Four diamonds shows five diamonds and four clubs or six diamonds and five clubs. Over four clubs or four diamonds, opener bids four hearts to set clubs as trumps, or bids four spades to set diamonds as trumps. <u>Four hearts</u> by responder shows a one-suited club, slam try and <u>four spades</u> shows a one-suited diamond slam try. <u>Four notrump</u> and <u>five notrump</u> by responder over opener's forced three-notrump bid show 4-4 in the minors. Four notrump is invitational to six, and five notrump is invitational to seven.

In examples (1) and (2), three spades by responder forces opener to bid three notrump. In example (1), responder bids four diamonds, showing a minor-suit slam try with at least five diamonds and at least four clubs. Opener bids four hearts setting clubs as trumps. Responder bids four notrump, RKC for clubs. Opener shows three keycards. Responder bids five diamonds asking for the club queen. Opener denies the queen by signing-off in six clubs. In example (2), responder bids four diamonds over opener's forced three-notrump bid, showing a slam try with both minors emphasizing diamonds. Opener with only two diamonds and only three clubs signs-off in four notrump. In example (1), opener made a positive response by setting clubs as trumps so four notrump is keycard. In example (2), there weren't any positive responses, so four notrump is a sign-off.

Opener (3)	Responder	Opener (4)	Responder
♠AK3 ♦K54	♠2 ♦A32	♠AKQ3 ♦KQJ4	♠2 ♦A32
♥AK5 ♣KJ76	♥432 ♣AQ5432	♥KQ5 ♣76	♥432 ♣AQ5432
2NT	3spades	2NT	3spades
3NT	4hearts	3NT	4hearts
4spades	5hearts	4NT	Pass
5spades	6clubs		

Opener (5)	Responder	Opener (6)	Responder
♠AK3 ♦K76	♠2 ♦AQ5432	♠AKQ3 ♦76	♠2 ♦AQ5432
♥AK5 ♣KJ54	♥432 ♣A32	♥KQ5 ♣KQJ4	♥432 ♣A32
2NT	3spades	2NT	3spades
3NT	4spades	3NT	4spades
5clubs	5NT	4NT	Pass
6clubs	6diamonds		

Over opener's forced three-notrump bid, responder bids four hearts to show a club one-suiter, and four spades to show a diamond one-suiter. Over four hearts or four spades, opener with no slam interest, signs-off in four notrump or five of responder's minor. Over four hearts showing clubs, opener bids four spades, keycard for clubs, with a forward-going hand. Over four spades showing diamonds, opener bids five clubs keycard, for diamonds, with a forward-going hand.

In examples (3) and (4), responder bids four hearts over opener's forced three-notrump bid, showing a one-suited club slam try. In example (3), opener with a club fit and three keycards bids four spades, keycard for clubs. Responder answers five hearts, showing two keycards and the club queen. Opener bids five spades, inviting seven, and responder with no extras signs-off in six clubs. In example (4), opener with a minimum and without a fit, signs-off in four notrump. In examples (5) and (6), responder bids four spades to show a diamond one-suiter. In example (5), opener, with a diamond fit and three keycards, bids five clubs, keycard for diamonds. Responder answers five notrump, showing two keycards and the diamond queen. Opener bids six clubs, inviting seven, and responder with no extras signs-off in six diamonds. Since responder's hand is unlimited, opener has to bid six clubs in order to confirm the presence of all six keys. In example (6), opener with a minimum and without a fit, signs-off in four notrump.

CHAPTER 28 - ADVANCED CONCEPTS.

28.1 -- EASTERN CUEBIDS.

Western Cuebids ask opener to bid three notrump with a stopper in the opponent's suit. I hate the term Western Cuebid. I like to describe cuebids as: "Do something intelligent". Usually the intelligent thing is to bid notrump when holding a stopper in the opponent's suit. Sometimes responder has a stopper, wants to play three notrump, but wants the lead to come to opener's hand. When there are two forcing calls available and the forcing call is not needed as natural, the cuebid shows a stopper and the artificial forcing call denies a stopper. Opener assumes that both calls are notrump probes. Eastern Cuebids occur in the following situations - strong minor suit raises and negative doubles of one heart. Minor suit raises deny four-card majors, and the negative double of one heart denies more than four spades.

Opener (1)		Responder		Opener (2)		Responder	
♠Q2	♦A32	♠K43	♦K54	♠Q2	♦A32	♠543	♦K54
♥QJ32	♣A432	♥K4	♣KQ765	♥QJ32	♣A432	♥AK	♣KQ765

Open	Over	Resp	Advnc	Open	Over	Resp	Advnc
1♣	1♠	2♠	Pass	1♣	1♠	2♠	Pass
3♣	Pass	3♠	Pass	3♣	Pass	3♥	Pass
3NT	Pass	Pass	Pass	4♣	Pass	5♣	Pass

In examples (1) and (2), responder bids two spades showing a limit raise or better in clubs. Opener bids three clubs showing a minimum. In example (1), responder has K43 of spades and wants opener to play the hand. Responder bids three spades, the Eastern Cuebid which shows a stopper and opener bids three notrump. Three notrump is very good from opener's side. Played from responder's side, three notrump goes down with a spade lead thru the queen. Since responder's three-spade bid promises a spade stopper, opener bids three notrump no matter what his spade holding is. In example (2), responder has 543 of spades and wants opener to bid three notrump with a spade stopper. Responder bids three hearts asking opener to do something intelligent. Responder can't have four hearts, since he didn't make a negative double. Since three hearts denies a spade stopper, opener bids four clubs and responder raises to five. Over three hearts, opener bids three notrump if he has K2 of spades instead of Q2.

28.2 -- ARTIFICIAL SUPER-ACCEPTS.

Opener bids one notrump, responder transfers to hearts, and opener has four-card heart support. If responder has a close decision whether to try for game after transferring, knowing about the four-card support and where the doubleton is can make a big difference. There are five different hand types that opener would like to be able to show -- doubleton spade, doubleton club, doubleton diamond, a balanced maximum, and a minimum. There are only four bids available: two spades, two notrump, three clubs and three hearts. Three diamonds is not available, since responder has to use it to retransfer. By making two spades do double duty, opener can show all five hand types. Two spades is artificial and shows a doubleton in one of the minors. Two notrump shows a doubleton spade, three clubs shows a balanced maximum and three hearts shows a minimum of some type. Over two spades showing a doubleton in one of the minors, two notrump asks for the doubleton. Three clubs shows a doubleton club, three hearts shows a doubleton diamond. Since opener never bids three diamonds, responder will always be able to bid three diamonds in order to allow opener to play the hand. Three diamonds by responder is a retransfer. Opener can also super-accept over two hearts, transfer to spades. Two notrump shows a doubleton in one of the minors, three clubs shows a doubleton heart, three diamonds shows a balanced maximum, and three spades shows a minimum of some type.

Opener	(1)	Responder		Opener	(2)	Responder	
♠K32	♦AQ32	♠54	♦K4	♠K32	♦32	♠54	♦K4
♥AQJ2	♣32	♥K10987	♣7654	♥AQJ2	♣AQ32	♥K10987	♣7654

Opener (1)	Responder	Opener (2)	Responder
1NT	2diamonds	1NT	2diamonds
2spades	2NT	2spades	2NT
3clubs	3diamonds	3hearts	Pass
3hearts	4hearts		

In examples (1) and (2), opener bids two spades, showing four-card heart support and a doubleton in one of the minors. Responder asks with two notrump. In example (1), opener shows a doubleton club. Responder's holding of four small clubs opposite opener's shortness makes game worth bidding. Responder retransfers with three diamonds and then raises to game. Responder passes if opener bids only two hearts. In example (2), opener shows a doubleton diamond. Responder's holding of two diamonds opposite opener's shortness is a turnoff, so responder passes three hearts. Bidding up to three hearts is reasonable, since the opponents have a nine-card diamond fit.

302

28.3 -- WHEN TRANSFERS GET DOUBLED.

Opener bids one notrump, responder transfers to hearts, and overcaller doubles. Playing Standard American, redouble shows good diamonds and is an attempt to get rich. You won't get rich if the doubler has six winners. Better use of the redouble is to more accurately describe the hand. OPENER PASSES THE DOUBLE TO SHOW EXACTLY TWO HEARTS. After opener passes, responder redoubles with all 0-7 point hands. Responder also redoubles holding a six-card suit, invitational to game or invitational to slam. With a six-card suit and just game interest, responder bids Texas. Responder bids two hearts with a five-card suit and invitational values. Responder might lose by playing the hand from his side, but gains by staying at the two-level. All bids other than two hearts or redouble are game forcing and show exactly five hearts. With balanced hands, responder cuebids denying a diamond stopper, bids two notrump showing one stopper, or bids three notrump showing two stoppers. New suits are natural, show a second suit and are game forcing. After responder redoubles, forcing opener to bid two hearts, responder passes two hearts with 0-7 HCPs, raises with invitational values and makes a mild slam try by bidding four hearts. This also works with spades.

HOLDING FIVE HEARTS, RESPONDER REDOUBLES TO SIGN-OFF OR BIDS TWO HEARTS WITH INVITATIONAL HANDS. ALL OTHER BIDS ARE GAME FORCING.

Opener	(1)	Responder		Opener	(2)	Responder	
♠KJ32	♦Q32	♠654	♦54	♠KJ32	♦Q32	♠Q54	♦54
♥A2	♣AJ32	♥76543	♣654	♥A2	♣AJ32	♥KQ6543	♣54

Open	Advnc	Resp	Over	Open	Advnc	Resp	Over
1NT	Pass	2♦	Dbl	1NT	Pass	2♦	Dbl
Pass	Pass	Redbl	Pass	Pass	Pass	Redbl	Pass
2♥	Pass	Pass	Pass	2♥	Pass	3♥	Pass

In examples (1) and (2), opener passes the double of two diamonds showing exactly two hearts. Responder redoubles forcing opener to bid two hearts. In example (1), responder decides that his hand is not good enough to invite, and passes. In example (2), responder invites and opener declines. This is a six-card invitation. With six-card suits responder has game-invitational values or slam interest. [1]

---

[1] Thanks to Randy Thompson who suggested this

Opener	(3)	Responder		Opener	(4)	Responder	

♠KJ32 ♦432　♠A54 ♦65　　　♠KJ32 ♦432　♠A54 ♦65
　♥A2 ♣AQJ2　♥KQ543 ♣543　　♥A2 ♣AQJ2　♥KQ543 ♣K43

Open	Advnc	Resp	Over	Open	Advnc	Resp	Over
1NT	Pass	2♦	Dbl	1NT	Pass	2♦	Dbl
Pass	Pass	2♥	Pass	Pass	Pass	3♦	Pass
Pass	Pass			3♠	Pass	4♦	Pass
				4♥	Pass	Pass	Pass

In examples (3) and (4), opener passes the double showing exactly two hearts. In example (3), responder bids two hearts showing an invitational hand with exactly five hearts. Opener has a minimum and passes. In example (4), responder has a balanced game-forcing hand with exactly five hearts. Responder cuebids denying a diamond stopper. Opener bids three spades, natural. Responder cuebids, offering opener a choice of majors, and opener chooses hearts.

If opener has at least three hearts, he shows whether he has a minimum or a maximum. Opener bids two hearts with a minimum or redoubles with a maximum. Responder with a weak hand has to bid two hearts and play it. This might wrong-side it, but that is a small price to pay for playing at the two-level. If responder has at least invitational values, he continues by retransferring with 3♦.

Opener	(5)	Responder		Opener	(6)	Responder	

♠KJ32 ♦QJ2　♠Q4 ♦543　　　♠KJ32 ♦AJ2　♠Q4 ♦543
　♥A32 ♣KJ2　♥KQ654 ♣Q43　　♥A32 ♣KJ2　♥KQ654 ♣Q43

Open	Advnc	Resp	Over	Open	Advnc	Resp	Over
1NT	Pass	2♦	Dbl	1NT	Pass	2♦	Dbl
2♥	Pass	Pass	Pass	Redbl	Pass	3♦	Pass
				3♥	Pass	4♥	Pass

In examples (5) and (6), responder transfers to hearts and overcaller doubles. In example (5), opener bids two hearts, showing a minimum with three hearts. Responder has an invitational hand and passes two hearts. In example (6), opener redoubles showing a maximum with three hearts. Responder transfers to hearts and bids game.

OPENER PASSES THE DOUBLE WITH TWO HEARTS. WITH THREE HEARTS, OPENER BIDS TWO HEARTS WITH A MINIMUM AND REDOUBLES WITH A MAX. With four hearts, opener can bid two hearts, redouble, or super-accept.

304

28.4 -- ONE NOTRUMP - THREE CLUBS IS BALANCED PUPPET STAYMAN.

In Washington Standard, three level responses to one notrump are all five-fives. I suggest a better set of responses. Three clubs is Balanced Puppet Stayman. Responder uses Puppet Stayman to check for a five-card major if he has a worthless doubleton and has a good three-card major. Responder also uses Balanced Puppet Stayman with 4333 hands if the four-card suit is a major. Over three clubs, opener bids a five-card major. If opener does not have a five-card major, opener bids three diamonds if he has a four-card major but only if he has an unbalanced hand. If opener is 4333 he bids three notrump. Over three diamonds, responder bids the major he doesn't have, allowing the notrump bidder to play the hand.

Opener	(1)	Responder		Opener	(2)	Responder	
♠54	♦A43	♠32	♦KQJ2	♠KJ4	♦543	♠32	♦KQJ2
♥AQ654	♣AQ4	♥K32	♣KJ32	♥AQ54	♣AQ4	♥K32	♣KJ32

Opener	Responder	Opener	Responder
1NT	3clubs	1NT	3clubs
3hearts	4hearts	3NT	Pass

In examples (1) and (2), responder has two little spades. He bids three clubs, Balanced Puppet Stayman. In example (1), opener has five hearts and bids three hearts. Responder raises to four hearts. In example (2), opener is 4333 and bids three notrump.

Opener	(3)	Responder		Opener	(4)	Responder	
♠J10	♦A654	♠A32	♦K32	♠J109	♦A54	♠A32	♦K32
♥AQ65	♣AQ2	♥K432	♣J109	♥AQ65	♣AQ2	♥K432	♣J109

Opener	Responder	Opener	Responder
1NT	3clubs	1NT	3clubs
3diamonds	3spades	3NT	Pass
4hearts	Pass		

In examples (3) and (4), responder is 4333 but has four hearts. He wants to play in four hearts if opener has five hearts or if opener has four hearts and an unbalanced hand. Responder bids three clubs, Balanced Puppet Stayman. In example (3), opener is 4432 with four hearts. He bids three diamonds showing that he has a four-card major and an unbalanced hand. Responder bids three spades showing four hearts. Opener bids four hearts ending the auction. In example (4), opener is 4333. Opener bids three notrump denying a five-card major and denying a four-card major with an unbalanced hand.

28.5 -- ONE NOTRUMP - THREE HEARTS IS 3-1-5-4 OR 3-1-4-5.

A three-heart response to one notrump shows shortness in hearts and 5-4 in the minors either way, with at least nine HCPs. Over three hearts, when opener is 3-3 in the minors, he bids three spades to learn responder's exact distribution. Opener bids three notrump to play with good hearts. With four little hearts and with nothing else clear to bid, opener bids three notrump, and gambles that the opponent's hearts split 4-4. If opener has a four-card minor, a minimum, and doesn't want to play three notrump, opener bids four-of-that-minor, setting that minor as trumps. Four-of-a-minor is non-forcing. Opener jumps to four spades with five spades or a very good four-card spade suit. If opener wants to be at least in game, and knows which minor he wants to play in, opener bids four hearts RKC for clubs, or four notrump RKC for diamonds.

Over opener's three-spade asking bid, responder transfers into his five-card minor. Three spades is forcing to four-of-responder's-five-card minor. Three notrump by responder shows five clubs, and four clubs shows five diamonds. After responder bids three notrump showing five clubs and opener bids four clubs, responder can pass with a minimum, cuebid, ask for keycards, or sign-off in five clubs. After responder bids four clubs showing five diamonds, and opener bids four diamonds, responder can pass with a minimum, cuebid, ask for keycards, or sign-off in five diamonds. The cheapest forcing bid should be RKC.

Opener	(1)	Responder		Opener	(2)	Responder	
♠KJ5 ♦K54		♠432 ♦AQ32		♠KJ5 ♦K54		♠A32 ♦AQ32	
♥J43 ♣AQJ6		♥2 ♣K5432		♥J43 ♣AQJ6		♥2 ♣K5432	
1NT		3hearts		1NT		3hearts	
4clubs		Pass		4clubs		4diamonds	
				4spades		4NT	
				5diamonds		6clubs	

In examples (1) and (2), responder bids three hearts, showing at least nine HCPs, a singleton heart, and exactly nine minor-suit cards. Opener does not have a heart stopper, and bids four clubs. Four clubs promises at least four clubs, and sets clubs as trumps. In example (1), responder passes four clubs. In example (2), responder bids four diamonds RKC for clubs. Four diamonds is the cheapest forcing bid. Opener shows one keycard and, in response to responder's queen asking bid, bids five diamonds, showing the queen of clubs and the king of diamonds. Responder signs-off in six clubs.

Opener	(3)	Responder		Opener	(4)	Responder	
♠K765	♦KJ5	♠432	♦AQ32	♠K765	♦KJ5	♠QJ2	♦AQ432
♥J43	♣AQJ	♥2	♣K5432	♥J43	♣AQJ	♥2	♣K432

Opener	Responder	Opener	Responder
1NT	3hearts	1NT	3hearts
3spades	3NT	3spades	4clubs
4clubs	Pass	4diamonds	5diamonds

Opener	(5)	Responder		Opener	(6)	Responder	
♠AQ	♦KJ654	♠432	♦AQ32	♠AQJ65	♦K6	♠432	♦AQ32
♥543	♣AQ6	♥2	♣K5432	♥543	♣AQ6	♥2	♣K5432

Opener	Responder	Opener	Responder
1NT	3hearts	1NT	3hearts
4NT	5diamonds	4spades	Pass
6diamonds	Pass		

In examples (3) thru (6), responder bids three hearts, showing heart shortness and exactly nine cards in the minors. In examples (3) and (4), opener does not have a heart stopper and is not sure which minor to set as trumps. Opener bids three spades, asking for responder's five-card minor. In example (3), responder bids three notrump showing five clubs. Opener bids four clubs showing a minimum. Opener denies holding four clubs, since he bid three spades asking for responder's five-card minor. Responder has a minimum and passes four clubs. In example (4), responder bids four clubs, showing five diamonds. Opener bids four diamonds, showing a minimum and only three diamonds. Responder raises to five diamonds. In example (5), opener bids four notrump, RKC for diamonds. Opener should have at least four diamonds. Responder shows one keycard. Opener bids a slam, since all he needs responder to have is the diamond ace and the club king for slam to have play. In example (6), opener jumps to four spades, ending the auction. Opener bids four spades holding five spades, or anytime he has four very good spades. If responder wants to continue, he bids his five-card minor or bids four notrump RKC for spades. Holding ♠K32♥2♦AQJ10♣KJ1098, responder bids five clubs showing a good hand with five clubs, and opener bids six spades.

28.6 -- ONE NOTRUMP - THREE SPADES IS 1-3-5-4 OR 1-3-4-5.

Three spades shows shortness in spades and 5-4 in the minors either way. Over three spades, three notrump is to play. If opener has four small spades, he bids three notrump and gambles that the opposing spades are divided 4-4. Four clubs by opener is semi-natural, and is what opener bids if he doesn't have anything clear to bid. With ♠432♥Q432♦AKQ♣A32, opener has to bid four clubs. Four clubs is forcing to responder's five-card minor. Four diamonds is natural, shows at least four diamonds with a minimum or average hand. Four hearts suggests hearts as trumps, showing five or a very strong four-card suit. If opener wants to be in game and knows which minor he wants to set as trumps, opener bids four spades RKC for clubs, or four notrump RKC for diamonds.

Over opener's three-notrump sign-off, responder bids his four-card minor, Minor-suit Smolen, to show a slam try. Opener can then sign-off in four notrump or cuebid. Over opener's four-club probe, responder passes with five clubs and a minimum, bids four diamonds with five diamonds and a minimum, bids four hearts showing a good hand with five clubs, or bids four spades showing a good hand with five diamonds. Over opener's four-diamond bid, which shows four diamonds and a minimum, responder can pass, raise to game, cuebid, or bid keycard. If responder has too much to pass four hearts, he can bid four spades keycard for hearts. Responder can also transfer into his five-card minor. Four notrump shows a very good club hand and five clubs shows a very good diamond hand.

Opener	(1)	Responder		Opener	(2)	Responder	
♠543	♦KJ5	♠2	♦AQ32	♠543	♦KJ5	♠2	♦AQ432
♥A765	♣AQJ	♥432	♣K5432	♥A765	♣AQJ	♥432	♣K432
1NT		3spades		1NT		3spades	
4clubs		Pass		4clubs		4diamonds	
				Pass			

In examples (1) and (2), responder bids three spades showing a singleton spade, at least nine HCPs, and nine cards in the minors. Opener can't bid three notrump with three small spades, and can't bid four hearts with only one heart honor. Opener's only choice is to probe with four clubs. Four clubs denies good spades and four good hearts. In example (1), responder has a minimum with five clubs, and passes. In example (2), responder bids four diamonds, showing a minimum with five diamonds, ending the auction.

308

Opener	(3)		Responder		Opener	(4)		Responder
♠AKQ4	♦K65		♠2	♦AQ32	♠AKQ4	♦K65		♠2	♦AQJ32
	♥QJ65	♣76	♥432	♣K5432		♥QJ65	♣76	♥432	♣AKQ2

Opener	Responder	Opener	Responder
1NT	3spades	1NT	3spades
3NT	Pass	3NT	4clubs
		4NT	Pass

Opener	(5)		Responder		Opener	(6)		Responder
♠543	♦KJ654		♠2	♦AQ32	♠543	♦K6		♠2	♦AQ32
	♥AQ	♣AQ6	♥432	♣K5432		♥AQJ65	♣AQ6	♥432	♣K5432

Opener	Responder	Opener	Responder
1NT	3spades	1NT	3spades
4NT	5diamonds	4hearts	Pass
6diamonds	Pass		

In examples (3) thru (6), responder shows a spade singleton, at least nine HCPs, and exactly nine minor-suit cards. In examples (3) and (4), opener, holding AKQ of spades, bids three notrump. In example (3), responder passes three notrump. In example (4), responder bids four clubs, showing a slam try with five diamonds. Opener bids four notrump, which is a sign-off, and responder passes. Any bid other than four notrump is a forward-going cuebid. In example (5), opener bids four notrump, RKC for diamonds. Responder shows one keycard. Opener bids a slam, since all opener needs responder to have is the diamond ace and the club king for slam to have play. In example (6), opener bids four hearts and responder passes. If responder has a stronger hand such as ♠2♥K32♦AQJ10♣KJ1098, which is too strong to pass four hearts, responder bids four notrump, showing a good hand with five clubs. If responder makes a move with four notrump, opener bids six hearts.

How do we replace the old 5-5's? Three diamonds still shows a 5-5 minor-suit slam try. With other minor-suited slam tries, such as 6-4 or 5422, see 28.20. To show weak 5-5 minor-suited hands, bid two notrump (transfer to diamonds) and then pass opener's response. Let three diamonds show the diamond pre-acceptance. If opener does not bid a two-card minor, a 5-3 minor suit fit will be found. To show 5-5 in the majors, game forcing, transfer to spades and then bid three hearts. You can't describe invitational 5-5 major-suited hands, so treat those hands as either weak or game forcing.

28.7 -- EXCLUSION ROMAN KEYCARD BLACKWOOD.

Exclusion Roman Keycard Blackwood (ERKCB) is used when asker has a void, wants to bid keycard, but doesn't want answerer to show the ace in the void suit. The answers to ERKCB are similar to the answers to regular Roman Keycard, but the ace of the void suit is not shown. There are two ways to bid ERKCB. ONE METHOD IS TO JUMP TO A NON-PLAYABLE SUIT HIGHER THAN REGULAR KEYCARD. Opener bids one spade and overcaller bids two clubs. Responder's jump to four notrump is Roman Keycard for spades. Responder's jump to five clubs is ERKCB. If you use Kickback, a jump to a non playable suit higher than Kickback is ERKCB. For example, opener bids one club and responder bids two clubs, an Inverted Minor. Four diamonds by opener is Kickback asking for keycards. Four hearts by opener is ERKCB asking for keycards minus the heart ace. Four spades by opener is ERKCB asking for keycards minus the spade ace. Four notrump by opener is ERKCB asking for keycards minus the diamond ace. Using Kickback, four notrump replaces the Kickback suit asking for Keycards minus the Kickback suit. THE SECOND METHOD IS TO SPLINTER AND THEN REPEAT THE SPLINTER. For example, opener bids one spade and responder bids four clubs, splinter, showing a four-card game-forcing hand with club shortness. If responder then bids five clubs, that is ERKCB. Once asker finds out how many keycards answerer has, asker can bid the next higher suit to ask for specific kings. The logic is similar to four notrump followed by five notrump in RKC.

Opener	(1)	Responder		Opener	(2)	Responder	
♠654	♦A2	♠AK32	♦-	♠654	♦A2	♠-	♦KQJ43
♥AQ765	♣Q32	♥K432	♣KJ654	♥AQ765	♣Q32	♥K2	♣AKJ654

1heart		4diamonds	1heart		2clubs
4hearts		5diamonds	3clubs		4spades
5spades		6hearts	5hearts		7clubs

In example (1), responder bids four diamonds showing a game-forcing four-card heart raise with diamond shortness. Opener has a minimum with only two diamonds and bids four hearts. Responder bids five diamonds, Exclusion Roman Keycard Blackwood (ERKCB) for diamonds. Opener bids five spades showing one keycard outside the diamond suit. Responder bids six hearts. In example (2), a jump to four diamonds over three clubs would be Kickback, Roman Keycard Blackwood. Therefore four spades is ERKCB. How many keycards do you have outside the spade suit? Opener bids five hearts showing two keycards and the queen of clubs. Responder bids seven clubs.

28.8 -- SIMPLE TRANSFER ADVANCES.

When overcaller bids one-of-a-major and responder makes a negative double, advancer, by giving up the natural one-notrump advance, can describe many different holdings. STARTING WITH ONE NOTRUMP, ALL CALLS BELOW TWO-OF-OVERCALLER'S SUIT ARE TRANSFERS, either natural or showing a raise in overcaller's suit. The auction starts one club - one spade - double. Redouble by advancer shows a two-card raise with at least ten HCPs. This allows overcaller to compete holding a six-card suit. One notrump, a transfer into opener's club suit, is a three-card limit raise or better. Transfers into opener's minor suit show three-card support, with at least limit-raise values. Two clubs is a transfer to diamonds, showing at least five. Transfers into unbid suits are natural and show at least five. Overcaller accepts the transfer to diamonds, even with shortness, if he would have passed two diamonds. Two diamonds is a transfer to hearts, and shows at least five hearts. Two hearts is a transfer to spades. A transfer into overcaller's major shows a constructive three-card raise, 7-10 support points. Two spades shows a weak three-card raise, 4-6 HCPs. A ten HCP three-card raise can go either way, constructive or limit, based on judgment.

With four-card support, advancer jumps to three-of-overcaller's-major (preemptive) with 0-6 HCPs, or three-of-opener's-minor (mixed-raise) with 7-9 HCPs. Advancer jumps to two notrump with a four-card limit raise or better. The auction starts one club - one spade - double. Three spades shows 0-6, three clubs shows 7-9 and two notrump shows 10+ support points.

Overcaller (1) Advancer   Overcaller (2) Advancer

♠AQ5432 ♦432   ♠K6 ♦8765   ♠AQ5432 ♦432   ♠K76 ♦8765
    ♥K32 ♣2   ♥AQ4 ♣K543   ♥K32 ♣2   ♥AQ4 ♣543

Open	Over	Resp	Advnc	Open	Over	Resp	Advnc
1♣	1♠	Dbl	Redbl	1♣	1♠	Dbl	2♥
2♣	2♠	Pass	Pass	3♣	3♠	Pass	Pass

In examples (1) and (2), opener bids one club, overcaller bids one spade, and responder makes a negative double. In example (1), advancer redoubles showing exactly two spades with at least ten HCPs. Overcaller, with a six-card suit, competes to two spades over opener's two-club bid. In example (2), advancer bids two hearts showing a 7-10 three-card raise. This allows overcaller to follow the Law and bid three spades. Over a 4-6 raise, overcaller sells out to three clubs.

311

Overcaller (3)   Advancer   Overcaller (4)   Advancer

♠AQ432   ♦K432   ♠K765 ♦J765   ♠AQ432   ♦K432   ♠5   ♦765
    ♥K32   ♣2   ♥AQ4   ♣K3   ♥K32   ♣2   ♥A54 ♣QJ10987

Open   Over   Resp   Advnc   Open   Over   Resp   Advnc
1♣   1♠   Dbl   2NT   1♦   1♠   Dbl   1NT
3♣   4♠   Pass   Pass   Pass   2♣   Pass   Pass
Pass   Pass

    In examples (3) and (4), opener bids one-of-a-minor, overcaller bids one spade, and responder makes a negative double. In example (3), advancer bids two notrump, showing a four-card limit raise or better. Overcaller bids game. In example (4), advancer bids one notrump, which is a transfer to clubs. Since overcaller would pass a natural non-forcing two clubs, he bids two clubs ending the auction. If overcaller has ♠AQ432♥K32♦2♣K432, he can jump to four clubs over advancer's club-showing-one-notrump bid.

    Below is a chart of advancer's strength and trump lengths.

Advancer's bid after the negative dbl shows	1♣ - 1♥ Double	1♦ - 1♥ Double	1♣ - 1♠ Double	1♦ - 1♠ Double	1♥ - 1♠ Double
10+ 2-card raise	Redbl	Redbl	Redbl	Redbl	Redbl
10+ 3-card LR+	1NT	2♣	1NT	2♣	2♦
7-10 3-card good raise	2♦	2♦	2♥	2♥	2♥
4-6 3-card bad raise	2♥	2♥	2♠	2♠	2♠
10+ 4-card LR +	2NT	2NT	2NT	2NT	2NT
7-9 4-card mixed raise	3♣	3♦	3♣	3♦	3♥
0-6 4-card preemptive	3♥	3♥	3♠	3♠	3♠
shows at least 5 clubs	--	1NT	--	1NT	1NT
shows at least 5 diam	2♣	--	2♣	--	2♣
shows at least 5 hearts	--	--	2♦	2♦	--

Opener bids one club, overcaller bids one diamond, responder bids one heart, and advancer passes. If opener has three hearts, he would like to make a support double, but he can't double his partner. Playing support raises, opener raises to two hearts. Two hearts shows a three-card raise with 11-14 HCPs. With four hearts and 11-14 HCPs, opener cuebids two diamonds. Two diamonds, a cuebid, shows one of two types of hands: A four-card heart raise with 11-14 HCPs or a game-forcing hand without four hearts. Since a cuebid hand is much stronger than an 11-14 HCP four-card-heart-raise hand, subsequent bids will make the auction clear. Opener never bids again over a sign-off with the 11-14 hand. With four hearts and more than 14 HCPs, opener makes the same bid he would have made had there not been an overcall. Three hearts shows four hearts and 15-17 HCPs. Four hearts shows a stronger four-card raise, and splinters show game-forcing values with shortness in the splinter suit. ♠AQ2♥K2♦32♣AKQ432 is an example of a strong cuebid hand. Opener bids three clubs over responder's two-heart sign-off and responder knows that two diamonds was a game-forcing cuebid. ONLY OPENER CAN MAKE A SUPPORT RAISE. Support raises occur only when overcaller bids a suit, responder bids a suit at the one-level, and advancer passes.

Opener	(1)		Responder		Opener	(2)		Responder	
♠K32	♦32		♠Q54	♦654	♠K2	♦32		♠Q54	♦654
♥Q32	♣AQJ32		♥AJ765	♣54	♥Q432	♣AQJ32		♥AJ765	♣54

Open	Over	Resp	Advnc	Open	Over	Resp	Advnc
1♣	1♦	1♥	Pass	1♣	1♦	1♥	Pass
2♥	3♦	Pass	Pass	2♦	3♦	3♥	Pass

In example (1), opener shows exactly three hearts when he bids two hearts. When overcaller bids three diamonds, responder does not bid three hearts, since he knows that he has only an eight-card heart fit. In example (2), opener bids two diamonds, the two-way cuebid, which usually shows exactly four hearts. Responder bids three hearts, since he knows that he has a nine-card heart fit. Knowing how many trumps partner has helps you follow the Law of Total Tricks.

Suppose in example (2), opener has ♠AK2♥2♦32♣AKQJ432, the strong cuebid hand. Over three hearts, opener bids three spades forcing, denying four-card heart support. Responder bids four diamonds, choice of games, and opener bids five clubs.

Opener can also make a support raise when overcaller makes a takeout double. This time the cheapest reverse is the two-way bid. Opener bids one club, overcaller doubles, responder bids one heart, and advancer passes. Playing support raises, two hearts shows a three-card raise with 11-14 HCPs. Two diamonds, a reverse, shows one of two types of hands: A four-card heart raise with 11-14 HCPs or a reverse.

A reverse in this situation would be like any normal reverse, promising a rebid, and denying four-card heart support. Since a reverse hand is much stronger than a four-card-heart-raise hand, subsequent bids will make the auction clear. Opener never bids again over a sign-off with the 11-14 HCP hand.

Opener	(3)		Responder		Opener	(4)		Responder	
♠A32	♦32		♠Q54	♦654	♠A2	♦32		♠Q54	♦654
♥Q32	♣AQJ32		♥AJ765	♣54	♥Q432	♣AQJ32		♥AJ765	♣54

Open	Over	Resp	Advnc	Open	Over	Resp	Advnc
1♣	Dbl	1♥	Pass	1♣	Dbl	1♥	Pass
2♥	3♦	Pass	Pass	2♦	2♠	3♥	Pass

In example (3), opener shows exactly three hearts when he bids two hearts. When overcaller bids three diamonds, responder does not bid three hearts, since he knows that he has only an eight-card heart fit. In example (4), opener bids two diamonds, the two-way reverse which usually shows exactly four hearts. Responder bids three hearts, since he knows that he has a nine-card heart fit. Knowing how many trumps partner has helps you follow the Law of Total Tricks.

Suppose in example (4), opener has ♠2♥32♦AK32♣AKQJ32, the reverse hand. Over three hearts, opener bids three spades forcing, denying heart support, and showing the reverse hand. Responder bids four clubs, and opener bids five clubs. With everyone bidding, the odds are against opener holding the strong hand type.

How does responder continue after the three-card support raise? If responder has at least five, he invites by raising. If responder has only four, he must be able to sign-off in opener's minor. New suits are natural, and are attempts to get to three notrump.

314

28.10 -- DEFENSE AGAINST WEAK-TWOS.

When opener bids two spades, the 5-5 hearts-and-a-minor-Michaels hand comes up more often than the solid-minor-looking-for-a-stopper hand. If overcaller uses three spades to ask for a stopper, he has to use another method to show 5-5. Jumping to four-of-a-minor shows 5-5 but bypasses three notrump. Overcaller could try three hearts and hope to bid his minor later but three hearts could be a horrible contract. Since the solid-minor hand rarely comes up, three spades by overcaller should be Michaels, showing five hearts and a five-card minor, a hand that, if advancer bids three notrump, overcaller would be happy to pass. Advancer's three-notrump advance is to play. Therefore, all minor bids by advancer are pass or correct. Four diamonds by advancer invites overcaller to pass if diamonds is his minor, and correct to five clubs if clubs is his minor. A jump to four-of-a-minor by overcaller shows that minor and hearts, but with a more extreme hand - 5-6 or 6-6. With these hands, three notrump is unlikely to be where you belong. Four-of-a-minor should be forcing.

Over opener's two spades, a jump to four spades shows both minors, at least 5-5. A jump to four notrump is Blackwood.

If opener bids two hearts, three hearts is Michaels. Four-of-a-minor by overcaller shows an extremely distributional hand, with spades and that minor. Four hearts by overcaller shows both minors, and four notrump is Blackwood. You can use this in both seats.

Overcaller (1)		Advancer			Overcaller	(2)	Advancer	
♠2	♦32	♠KQJ	♦AQJ54		♠-	♦2	♠KQJ	♦AQJ54
♥KQ432	♣AQJ32	♥105	♣1065		♥KQJ432	♣AQJ432	♥105	♣1065

Open	Over	Resp	Advnc		Open	Over	Resp	Advnc
2♠	3♠	Pass	3NT		2♠	4♣	Pass	4♥
Pass	Pass	Pass			Pass	Pass	Pass	

In examples (1) and (2), opener bids two spades. In example (1), overcaller bids three spades, showing five hearts and a five-card minor. Advancer bids three notrump, which is a good contract. If advancer has 543 of spades instead of the KQJ, he bids four clubs, asking overcaller to pass if clubs is his minor. Notice that if overcaller jumps to four clubs, showing clubs and hearts, advancer bids four hearts, which goes down. In example (2), overcaller bids four clubs, showing an extreme club-heart hand. Advancer bids four hearts, which is a good contract.

Overcaller	(3)	Advancer		Overcaller	(4)	Advancer	

♠2 ♦AKQ54   ♠A43   ♦32   ♠2 ♦AKQ7654   ♠A43   ♦32

♥3 ♣AQ5432   ♥QJ1098 ♣J76   ♥3 ♣AKQ2   ♥QJ1098 ♣J76

Open	Over	Resp	Advnc		Open	Over	Resp	Advnc
2♠	4♠	Pass	5♣		2♠	4NT	Pass	5♦
Pass	Pass	Pass			Pass	6♦	Pass	

In examples (3) and (4), opener bids two spades. In example (3), overcaller bids four spades, showing both minors. Advancer bids five clubs, ending the auction. In example (4), overcaller bids four notrump asking for aces. Advancer bids five diamonds, showing one ace. Overcaller bids six diamonds.

28.11 -- TRANSFER LEBENSOHL.

Opener bids one notrump and overcaller bids two-of-either-major. If responder has an invitational or better hand with a five-card major, responder bids three diamonds transferring to the other major. Over two hearts, three clubs shows clubs, three diamonds is a transfer to spades, three hearts is a cuebid and three spades shows diamonds. Over two spades, three clubs shows clubs, three diamonds is a transfer to hearts, three hearts shows diamonds and three spades is a cuebid. Minor-showing bids are game forcing. Other Lebensohl sequences remain the same. Over two diamonds, two notrump shows clubs, three clubs is Stayman, three diamonds transfers to hearts, three hearts transfers to spades and show invitational or better values.

Opener	(1)	Responder		Opener	(2)	Responder	

♠K32 ♦AQJ10   ♠54   ♦654   ♠K32 ♦AQJ10   ♠AQ654 ♦654

♥K32 ♣QJ2   ♥AQ654 ♣K43   ♥K32 ♣QJ2   ♥54 ♣K43

Open	Over	Resp	Advnc		Open	Over	Resp	Advnc
1NT	2♠	3♦	Pass		1NT	2♥	3♦	Pass
4♥	Pass	Pass	Pass		4♠	Pass	Pass	Pass

In example (1), opener bids one notrump and overcaller bids two spades. Responder bids three diamonds, an invitational or better transfer to hearts. Opener, with a maximum, jumps to four hearts. In example (2), opener bids one notrump and overcaller bids two hearts. Responder bids three diamonds, an invitational or better transfer to spades. Opener, with a maximum, jumps to four spades. With a minimum, opener bids three spades and responder passes.

28.12 -- IMPROVED RESPONSES TO MICHAELS.

Over one-of-a-major - two-of-a-major the Michaels cuebid, advancer bids three diamonds to show a limit raise or better in overcaller's major. If advancer has strength and wants to play in overcaller's minor, advancer bids two notrump asking overcaller to bid his minor. Overcaller bids his minor with a weak hand but bids more with a strong hand. If advancer is weak, advancer bids three clubs, pass or correct. Overcaller passes three clubs with clubs or bids three diamonds with diamonds.

Over one-of-a-minor - two-of-a-minor, Michaels, it's very important to set trumps. Advancer bids two notrump to show a limit raise or better in hearts. Advancer bids opener's minor to show a limit raise or better in spades. Jumping to three-of-a-major is a mixed raise with four trumps and 7-9 HCPs.

Overcaller (1) Advancer

♠AQJ32 ♦AQJ32 ♠65   ♦654
   ♥32   ♣2   ♥654 ♣K6543

Open	Over	Resp	Advnc
1♥	2♥	Pass	3♣
Pass	3♦	Pass	Pass

Overcaller (2) Advancer

♠AQJ32 ♦AQJ32 ♠65   ♦K54
   ♥32   ♣2   ♥AQ10 ♣QJ1098

Open	Over	Resp	Advnc
1♥	2♥	Pass	2NT
Pass	3♥	Pass	3NT

Overcaller (3) Advancer

♠AQ432   ♦2   ♠765   ♦A543
   ♥KJ432 ♣32   ♥AQ65 ♣K4

Open	Over	Resp	Advnc
1♣	2♣	Pass	2NT
Pass	3♠	Pass	4♥

Overcaller (4) Advancer

♠AQ432   ♦2   ♠765   ♦Q543
   ♥KJ432 ♣32   ♥AQ65 ♣54

Open	Over	Resp	Advnc
1♣	2♣	Pass	3♥
Pass	Pass	Pass	

In examples (1) and (2), overcaller bids two hearts, showing at least 5-5, spades and a minor. In example (1), advancer bids three clubs, asking overcaller to pass if clubs is his minor, or bid three diamonds if diamonds is his minor. Responder bids three diamonds. In example (2), advancer has a good hand. Advancer bids two notrump, asking for responder's minor. Overcaller also has a good hand and cuebids three hearts. Advancer bids three notrump. In example (3) advancer bids two notrump setting hearts as trumps and inviting game. Overcaller bids three spades, letting advancer play four hearts. In example (4), advancer jumps to three hearts - a mixed raise.

317

28.13 -- TWO-WAY CHECKBACK OVER ONE NOTRUMP.

Two-way checkback is used when opener rebids one notrump.   Two important rules of Two-Way Checkback: IT IS OFF IN COMPETITION AND OFF IF RESPONDER IS A PASSED HAND.   IT IS ON AFTER ONE HEART - ONE SPADE - ONE NOTRUMP AND ONE CLUB - ONE DIAMOND - ONE NOTRUMP.

Two clubs is either a diamond sign-off, any invitational checkback, or a hunt for three-card support. Two diamonds is game-forcing. A jump to three clubs is weak, shows a six-card suit, and demands that opener pass. All other jumps are invitational.

Over two diamonds, which is 100% game forcing, opener's first obligation is to show three-card support for responder's suit. Opener's second obligation is to show an unbid four-card major. Otherwise opener rebids a five-card minor, bids the other minor, or bids two notrump. Opener shouldn't jump. Responder needs the room to describe his hand.

After opener shows three-card support, responder bids three notrump to offer opener a choice between three notrump and four-of-his-major; bids three-of-his-major to initiate slam cuebidding; bids two notrump to allow opener to show four cards in the other major, in order to try to find a 4-4 fit. All other bids by responder are natural and deny holding a five-card major.

Once opener denies three-card support or four cards in the other major, responder rebids his major, looking for two-card support, or bids the other major, looking for three-card support. Any minor bid by responder is natural and shows at least four.

Over two clubs, opener is forced to bid two diamonds, which is how responder gets to play in two diamonds. After opener bids two diamonds, responder bids two-of-either-major to show an unbalanced hand with invitational values. Responder bids two notrump to show a balanced invitational hand with a five-card major. After one club - one spade - one notrump, responder can jump directly to three spades, or can bid two clubs and then jump to three spades. Both are invitational. A direct jump to three spades shows a very good six-card suit. Two clubs followed by three spades shows a six-card suit with scattered honors. Responder can jump directly to three hearts, the other major, or he can bid two clubs, and then jump to three hearts. Both are invitational and show 5-5 in the majors. A direct jump is stronger and shows better suits. Two clubs followed by three hearts shows scattered values.

Opener	(1)	Responder		Opener	(2)	Responder	
♠432	♦KJ2	♠AK765	♦Q43	♠432	♦KJ2	♠AK765	♦43
♥AJ54	♣AJ2	♥KQ2	♣K4	♥AJ54	♣AJ2	♥32	♣KQ43

Opener (1)	Responder	Opener (2)	Responder
1club	1spade	1club	1spade
1NT	2diamonds	1NT	2clubs
2spades	3NT	2diamonds	3NT
Pass		4spades	Pass

Opener	(3)	Responder		Opener	(4)	Responder	
♠Q2	♦A32	♠AKJ54	♦4	♠Q2	♦A32	♠AKJ654	♦K54
♥K32	♣K5432	♥A4	♣AQ876	♥K32	♣K5432	♥A4	♣A6

Opener (3)	Responder	Opener (4)	Responder
1club	1spade	1club	1spade
1NT	2diamonds	1NT	2diamonds
3clubs	4diamonds	3clubs	3spades
4NT	7clubs	4diamonds	4NT
Pass		5diamonds	5hearts
		5NT	6clubs
		7clubs	7spades

In example (1), responder wants to find out if opener has three spades, and then offer him a choice. Responder bids two diamonds, game-forcing checkback. Opener shows three spades. Responder bids three notrump, showing a 5332 hand, giving opener the choice. Opener chooses three notrump. In example (2), responder wants three-card spade support. Responder bids two clubs, followed by three notrump, demanding three-card support. Opener bids four spades. If all responder wants is three-card support, he can bid two-of-his-better-minor to avoid a lead-directing double. Using these methods, the opponents will not know if opener has four of the other major. In examples (3) and (4), opener bids three clubs, showing five clubs and fewer than three spades. In example (3), responder bids four diamonds, RKC for clubs. Opener bids four notrump, showing two keycards without the queen. Responder bids seven clubs. In example (4), responder bids three spades, showing six. Opener bids four diamonds, showing a good hand with two-card spade support. Responder bids RKC and finds out opener has one keycard. Responder asks for the queen, and opener shows the queen of spades and the king of hearts. Responder bids six clubs, asking opener if he has the club king. Opener bids seven clubs, showing the king. Responder bids seven spades. A 4-2 or 3-3 club break will allow declarer to set up a club pitch for his third diamond.

Opener	(5)	Responder	Opener	(6)	Responder
♠432 ♦A32		♠AQJ1098 ♦K54	♠432 ♦A32		♠KJ10987 ♦KJ
♥A32 ♣AJ32		♥54 ♣54	♥A32 ♣AJ32		♥54 ♣K105

Opener	Responder	Opener	Responder
1club	1spade	1club	1spade
1NT	3spades	1NT	2clubs
3NT	Pass	2diamonds	3spades
		4spades	Pass

Opener	(7)	Responder	Opener	(8)	Responder
♠K32 ♦A32		♠AQ654 ♦K54	♠K32 ♦A32		♠AQ654 ♦KQ54
♥Q432 ♣AJ2		♥K765 ♣3	♥Q432 ♣AJ2		♥K5 ♣K3

Opener	Responder	Opener	Responder
1club	1spade	1club	1spade
1NT	2diamonds	1NT	2diamonds
2spades	2NT	2spades	3spades
3hearts	4hearts	4clubs	4diamonds
Pass		4hearts	4NT
		5clubs	6spades

In example (5), responder jumps to three spades showing an invitational hand with a good suit. Opener bids three notrump. If opener has ♠K32♥432♦AJ2♣KQJ2, he knows the heart suit is a problem, and bids four spades. In example (6), responder bids two clubs, and then jumps to three spades, showing a six-card spade suit, an invitational hand, and scattered values. Opener bids four spades. If responder doesn't have a good suit, it will take too much time to set it up. If opener has ♠Q2♥QJ109♦AQ2♣QJ43, he bids three notrump. In examples (7) and (8), responder bids two diamonds, game-forcing checkback. Opener shows three-card spade support. In example (7), responder bids two notrump, a further major-suit probe. Responder could have made another natural bid, so two notrump shows five spades. Opener bids three hearts and responder bids four hearts. That is how the 4-4 heart fit is found. In example (8), responder bids three spades setting spades as trumps. This is a slam try, since responder didn't bid two notrump or four spades. Opener bids four clubs, showing club values, and responder bids four diamonds, showing diamond values. Both aces and kings can be cuebid. Opener bids four hearts, Last Train (page 199), showing extra values. Opener's bad 3433 distribution stops him from bidding keycard over four diamonds. Responder bids four notrump, making sure that there aren't two keycards missing.

320

28.14 -- MOST JUMPS TO FIVE NOTRUMP ARE CHOICE OF SLAMS.

Jumps to five notrump can have four different meanings. One meaning is the Grand Slam Force. The Grand Slam force occurs when there is only one possible trump suit. Any number of hearts - Pass - five notrump is the Grand Slam Force. The Grand Slam Force is rarely used since Roman Keycard Blackwood yields the same result. The second meaning occurs after a natural notrump which shows a specific range. Jumping to five notrump is invitational to seven. One notrump - five notrump for example. With a maximum, the notrump bidder bids seven notrump. With a minimum, he bids six notrump. He can bid suits up the line to try to find a 4-4 fit. The third meaning occurs after a preempt and a three notrump overcall. Jumping to five notrump shows two or three little in the preempt suit, and asks the three-notrump bidder to bid a slam unless there are two top losers in the preempt suit.

The fourth and most frequent used meaning is to offer choice of slams. The five-notrump bidder has enough strength to be in slam, but is not sure which is the best strain. He wants his partner to use his judgment, and choose the slam based upon the previous auction. Extra spots, extra length, extra strength and holding the jack are helpful features responder evaluates when making a choice. Playing in notrump is also one of responder's options.

Opener (1)		Responder		Opener (2)		Responder	
♠K5432	♦A2	♠AQ6	♦K43	♠KJ432	♦A2	♠AQ6	♦K43
♥KJ2	♣432	♥AQ654	♣KQ	♥K32	♣432	♥AQ654	♣KQ

Opener (1)	Responder	Opener (2)	Responder
1spade	2hearts	1spade	2hearts
3hearts	3spades	3hearts	3spades
4diamonds	5NT	4diamonds	5NT
6hearts	Pass	6spades	Pass

In examples (1) and (2), responder knows that he has two 5-3 major-suit fits. Responder knows that opener does not have the ace of clubs since opener did not bid four clubs. Responder, with twenty HCPs, wants to play in a small slam and wants to be in the suit with the most meat in it. Responder bids five notrump, choice of slams. In example (1), opener has the jack of hearts and bids six hearts. In example (2), opener has the jack of spades and bids six spades. The suit with the jack is the better slam, since this suit holding will overcome a possible 4-1 trump break.

321

28.15 -- TRANSFERS AFTER ONE MAJOR - ONE NOTRUMP - TWO NOTRUMP.

After one-of-a-major - one notrump - two notrump, transfers help responder describe more hands. Using transfers it's best to play two notrump as forcing and unlimited, anywhere from a very good seventeen to twenty HCPs. Responder passes two notrump only if he's not close to having a one-notrump response. Opener must accept all transfers, unless he can visualize game opposite a weak hand. Over two notrump, responder's jump to game is a sign-off.

After one heart - one notrump - two notrump, responder's three-clubs is a transfer to diamonds. Three diamonds is a transfer to hearts. Three hearts is not a transfer. Three hearts shows exactly three hearts, 6-7 HCPs, and is invitational. Responder has a 6-7 HCP three-card heart raise. Three spades is a transfer to clubs and shows a weak club hand.

After responder transfers to three diamonds, responder passes with a weak hand or makes a natural bid to show diamonds. If responder has three-card heart support, he transfers to three hearts. Responder passes three hearts with a weak hand; bids three spades, giving opener a choice between three notrump and four hearts; shows a limit raise by bidding a good five-card suit at the four-level; or shows a balanced limit raise by bidding four hearts. If responder has two hearts, he transfers to three hearts and then bids three notrump giving opener a choice between three notrump and four hearts in the 5-2 fit. If responder bids three spades, opener bids four clubs, unless he can visualize game opposite a weak-club hand.

After one-spade - one notrump - two notrump, responder's three-clubs is a transfer to diamonds. Three diamonds is a transfer to hearts. Three hearts is a transfer to spades. Three spades is not a transfer. Three spades shows exactly three spades, 6-7 HCPs, and is invitational. Responder has a 6-7 HCP three-card spade raise.

After responder transfers to three diamonds, responder passes with a weak hand, or makes a natural bid to show diamonds. After responder transfers to three hearts, responder passes with a weak hand, or makes a natural bid to show hearts. If responder has three-card spade support, he transfers to three spades. Responder passes three spades with a bad hand; shows a limit raise by bidding a good five-card suit at the four-level; or shows a balanced limit raise by bidding four spades. If responder has two spades, he transfers to three spades, and then bids three notrump, giving opener a choice between three notrump and four spades in the 5-2 fit.

```
Opener    (1)      Responder          Opener    (2)      Responder

♠AQJ109   ♦A2      ♠K32  ♦Q543        ♠AQJ109   ♦A2      ♠432  ♦K543
     ♥AQ2 ♣Q32        ♥543  ♣654          ♥AQ2 ♣Q32        ♥K43  ♣654

1spade            1NT                 1spade            1NT
2NT               3hearts             2NT               3spades
3spades           Pass                4spades


Opener    (3)      Responder          Opener    (4)      Responder

♠AQJ109   ♦AQ2     ♠2       ♦K543     ♠AQJ109   ♦AQ2     ♠2       ♦K543
     ♥A2  ♣Q32        ♥J109876  ♣54        ♥A2  ♣Q32        ♥KQ1098  ♣J54

1spade            1NT                 1spade            1NT
2NT               3diamonds           2NT               3diamonds
3hearts           Pass                3hearts           3NT


Opener    (5)      Responder          Opener    (6)      Responder

♠AKJ109   ♦A32     ♠Q2  ♦KQJ54        ♠AKJ109   ♦A32     ♠Q32  ♦KQJ54
     ♥32  ♣AQ2        ♥54  ♣J1098          ♥32  ♣AQ2        ♥4       ♣J1098

1spade            1NT                 1spade            1NT
2NT               3hearts             2NT               3hearts
3spades           3NT                 3spades           4diamonds
4spades           Pass                4hearts           4NT
                                      5diamonds         6spades
```

In examples (1) thru (6), responder bids one-notrump forcing, and opener bids two notrump. In example (1), responder forces opener to bid three spades and passes. In example (2), responder bids three spades, invitational, showing 6-7 HCPs with three spades. Opener bids four spades. In examples (3) and (4), responder bids three diamonds, a transfer to hearts. Opener, with the hand from example (1), would jump to four hearts over three diamonds. In example (3), responder passes three hearts. In example (4), responder bids three notrump, showing five hearts, and giving opener a choice. Opener passes three notrump. In examples (5) and (6), responder bids three hearts, forcing opener to bid three spades. In example (5), responder bids three notrump, showing two spades, and offering a choice of games. Opener has two little hearts, very good spades, and chooses the 5-2 spade fit. In example (6), responder bids four diamonds, showing a limit raise in spades with at least five good diamonds. Opener probes with four hearts. Responder bids keycard and then bids six spades.

28.16 -- ARTIFICIAL RESPONSES TO JACOBY TWO NOTRUMP.

OPENER BIDS THREE CLUBS TO SHOW ALL MINIMUM HANDS -- either 11-14 HCPs balanced, or 11-13 HCPs unbalanced. If opener shows a minimum, responder with a minimum knows there's no slam and jumps to game. The opponents will be in the dark about opener's distribution. Opener bids three diamonds to show a balanced hand with at least 15 HCPs. Three hearts shows short clubs with at least 14 HCPs. Three spades shows short diamonds, and three notrump shows shortness in the other major. Four-level bids show at least 14 HCPs with 5-5 distribution. Jumps to game are hands that look like a weak-two -- an 11-13 HCP balanced hand with a six-card suit.

Over opener's minimum-showing three clubs, responder bids three diamonds to ask if opener has shortness. Opener bids three hearts to show a balanced hand with 11-14 HCPs; bids three spades to show short clubs with 11-13 HCPs; bids three notrump to show short diamonds; and bids four clubs to show shortness in the other major. Four diamonds, four hearts, and four spades show 5-5 hands with clubs, diamonds, and hearts with 11-13 HCPs. Over a one-heart opening, you can't show a hand with five spades. All subsequent bids by responder are cuebids.

Opener	(1)	Responder		Opener	(2)	Responder	
♠AQJ109	♦2	♠K432	♦43	♠AQJ109	♦2	♠K432	♦A543
♥A32 ♣5432		♥KQJ4 ♣KJ6		♥A32 ♣5432		♥KQ4 ♣KQ	
1spade		2NT		1spade		2NT	
3clubs		4spades		3clubs		3diamonds	
				3NT		4NT	
				5spades		6spades	

In examples (1) and (2), responder shows a game-forcing four-card spade raise and opener shows an unspecified minimum. In example (1), responder has no slam interest and jumps to game. With a major-suit lead, game will always make. With a diamond lead and continuation, opener can strip the majors and then play clubs. Game could make even if the AQ10 of clubs are offside. If the opponents know about the singleton diamond, they are more likely to get the defense right. In example (2), responder has slam interest, and bids three diamonds, asking for further description. Opener bids three notrump, the third step showing diamond shortness. Responder bids keycard and bids slam. If opener's minor-suit holdings were reversed, he would bid three spades, showing short clubs and responder would sign-off. Shortness opposite shortness diminishes trick-taking potential.

28.17 -- TWO WAY GAME TRIES AFTER A RAISE.

Opener bids one-of-a-major and responder raises. Opener might want to make a long-suit try, or he might want to make a short-suit try. There's a way to do both. After one heart - two hearts, two spades, the next step, is the start of a short-suit game or slam try. Two notrump (spades), three clubs (clubs) and three diamonds (diamonds) are help-suit game or slam tries. After one spade - two spades, two notrump is the start of a short-suit game or slam try. Three clubs, three diamonds and three hearts are natural tries.

Over the short-suit try, responder bids the next step to ask for opener's shortness. When playing many asking bids, it's easier to remember if all responses are up the line. The first step is always clubs. After one heart - two hearts - two spades; two notrump asks for opener's shortness. Three clubs shows short clubs, three diamonds shows short diamonds, and three hearts shows short spades. The next three steps show short-suit slam tries. Three spades shows short clubs, three notrump shows short diamonds and four clubs shows short spades. After one spade - two spades - two notrump; three clubs asks for opener's shortness. Three diamonds shows short clubs, three hearts shows short diamonds, and three spades shows short hearts. The next three steps are short-suit slam tries. Three notrump shows short clubs, four clubs shows short diamonds, and four diamonds shows short hearts. Responder does not have to ask for opener's shortness. With a bad hand, responder signs-off in three-of-opener's-major.

Opener (1)		Responder		Opener (2)		Responder	
♠2	♦A32	♠6543	♦K4	♠2	♦A32	♠6543	♦K4
♥A5432	♣AQJ2	♥J876	♣K54	♥AKQ32	♣AQ32	♥J876	♣K54

Opener (1)	Responder	Opener (2)	Responder
1heart	2hearts	1heart	2hearts
2spades	2NT	2spades	2NT
3hearts	4hearts	4clubs	4diamonds
		6hearts	Pass

In examples (1) and (2), opener bids two spades, starting a short-suit game or slam try. Responder bids two notrump, asking. In example (1), opener bids three hearts, showing a short-suit spade GAME try. Four little opposite a short suit is the best possible holding. If opener bids three diamonds, showing a short-suit diamond game try, responder signs-off. K2 opposite a short suit is a poor holding. In example (2), opener bids four clubs, showing a short-suit spade SLAM try. Responder probes with four diamonds, and opener bids a slam.

28.18 -- ARTIFICIAL TWO-HEART RESPONSE TO MINOR OPENER.

When opener bids one-of-either-minor, responder can show three different hand types, by making two hearts a three-way bid. Two hearts shows one of three hands; a strong jump shift, an invitational 11-12 notrump hand, or a 7-9 mixed raise of opener's minor. A direct two notrump bid by responder shows 13-15 HCPs, and is forcing to game.

Over two hearts, opener bids two spades, asking which hand type responder has. Responder bids two notrump, showing a balanced hand with 11-12 HCPs. Responder bids three-of-opener's-minor to show a mixed raise. All other bids by responder show a strong jump shift in hearts. Over two hearts, opener can bid two notrump, forcing, if he wants notrump played from his side, and would raise an invitational two notrump to three notrump.

Opener	(1)	Responder		Opener	(2)	Responder
♠AQ2 ♦K432		♠J54 ♦AQ765		♠AQ2 ♦K432		♠543 ♦QJ5
♥32 ♣AJ32		♥654 ♣54		♥32 ♣AJ32		♥KQ4 ♣K654
1diamond		2hearts		1diamond		2hearts
2spades		3diamonds		2spades		2NT
Pass				3NT		Pass

Opener	(3)	Responder		Opener	(4)	Responder
♠QJ2 ♦KQ32		♠654 ♦A54		♠A32 ♦KQ32		♠654 ♦A54
♥32 ♣KQ32		♥AKQJ54 ♣A		♥32 ♣KQ32		♥AKQJ54 ♣A
1diamond		2hearts		1diamond		2hearts
2spades		3hearts		2spades		3hearts
3NT		4diamonds		3spades		4spades
4NT		Pass		5clubs		5spades
				7NT		

In examples (1) thru (4), responder bids two hearts, the three-way bid, and opener marks time with two spades. In example (1), responder shows a mixed raise. In example (2), responder shows an invitational balanced hand. In examples (3) and (4), responder shows a strong jump shift. In example (3), opener bids three notrump. Responder tries once more. In example (4), opener bids three spades, showing a good four-heart bid. Responder bids four spades, kickback, and then bids five spades showing that all six keys are present. Opener counts thirteen tricks (6 hearts, 6 minors, 1 spade), and bids seven notrump.

28.19 -- TWO-TIERED SPLINTERS BY OPENER.

Opener bids one-of-a-minor, responder bids one-of-a-major, and opener has four-card support with at least 15 HCPs. There are nine hand types that opener would like to show. Singletons in either unbid suit with 15-17 or 18-20 HCPs; 15-17 2425 raise; game forcing 2425 18-20 raise; game-forcing 18-19 raise; 4-6 raise, and a preemptive raise.

After one club - one heart; opener bids three diamonds holding (A) ♠AK32♥A432♦2♣A432, (B) ♠AK32♥AK32♦2♣A432, (C) ♠2♥A432♦AK2♣A5432 or (D) ♠2♥AK32♦AK2♣A5432 -- the four hand types that contain shortness. (A) and (C) are limit raises, (B) and (D) are game-forcing raises. If responder is interested in slam, he bids three spades to learn opener's shape and strength. Opener's first step (three notrump) shows (B) 18+ HCPs with shortness in the lower unbid suit; the second step (four clubs) shows (D) 18+ with shortness in the higher unbid suit; the third step (four diamonds) shows (A) 15-17 with shortness in the lower unbid suit; the fourth step (four hearts) shows (C) 15-17 with shortness in the higher unbid suit. If responder signs-off in three hearts, opener passes three hearts with (A) and (C) and raises to game with (B) and (D). Over one heart, opener bids three hearts holding (E) ♠A2♥A432♦32♣AK432; three spades holding (F) ♠A2♥AK32♦32♣AK432; four clubs holding (G) ♠2♥AK32♦32♣AKQ432; four diamonds holding (H) ♠432♥AK32♦AQ2♣AQ2; and four hearts holding (I) ♠2♥KQJ2♦2♣KQJ5432. (E) is the 15-17 HCP 2425 raise. (F) is game-forcing 2425 raise. (G) is 4-6 raise. (H) is the 3433 or 2434 game-forcing raise. (I) is the preemptive gambling raise -- with honors only in the two suits.

After one club - one spade, opener bids three hearts holding (A) ♠AK32♥A432♦2♣A432, (B) ♠AK32♥AK32♦2♣A432, (C) ♠A432♥2♦AK2♣A5432 or (D) ♠AK32♥2♦AK2♣A5432, the four hand types that contain shortness. (A), and (C) are limit raises, (B) and (D) are game-forcing raises. If responder is interested in slam over three hearts, he bids three notrump to learn opener's shape and strength. Opener bids four clubs with (B), four diamonds with (D), four hearts with (A), and four spades with (C). Over one spade, opener bids four diamonds holding (F) ♠AK32♥A2♦32♣AK432, four clubs holding (G) ♠AK32♥2♦32♣AKQ432, four hearts holding (H) ♠AK32♥432♦AQ2♣AQ2, and four spades holding (I) ♠KQJ2♥2♦2♣KQJ5432. Opener has an extra bid. Opener bids three diamonds holding (J) ♠AK32♥A32♦32♣AK32 and three spades holding (E) ♠AK32♥32♦32♣AK432. (F) is game-forcing 4225 raise. (G) is 4-6 raise with at most one loser in the six-card suit. (H) is the 4333 or 4234 game-forcing raise. (I) is the preemptive raise. (J) is the 18-point balanced raise and (E) is the 14-point semi-balanced raise.

After one diamond - one spade; opener bids three hearts holding (A) ♠AK32♥A432♦A432♣2, (B) ♠AK32♥AK32♦A432♣2, (C) ♠A432♥2♦AK432♣A32 or (D) ♠AK32♥2♦AK432♣A32, the four hand types that contain shortness. If responder is interested in slam, he bids three notrump to learn opener's shape and strength. Opener bids four clubs with (B), four diamonds with (D), four hearts with (A), and four spades with (C). Over one spade opener bids three spades holding (E) ♠A432♥K2♦A5432♣A2, four clubs holding (F) ♠AK32♥A2♦AK432♣32, four diamonds holding (G) ♠AK32♥2♦AKQ432♣32, four hearts holding (H) ♠AK32♥43♦AQ32♣AQ2, and four spades holding (I) ♠AKQJ2♥2♦KQJ5432♣2. (E) is the 15-17 HCP 2425 raise. (F) is game-forcing 4252 raise. (G) is the 4-6 raise. (H) is the 4342 game-forcing raise. (I) is the preemptive raise.

After one diamond - one heart; opener bids three hearts holding (A) ♠AK32♥A432♦A432♣2 or (C) ♠2♥A432♦AK432♣A32, the two limit-raise hand types that contain shortness and (E) ♠K2♥A432♦AK432♣32. Opener bids three spades holding (B) ♠AK32♥AK32♦A432♣2, or (D) ♠2♥AK32♦AK432♣A32, the two game-forcing hand types that contain shortness and (F) ♠A2♥AK32♦AK432♣32. If responder is interested in slam, he bids three notrump to learn opener's shape. Opener bids four clubs with (B), four diamonds with (D) and four hearts with (F). Over one heart, opener bids four diamonds holding (G) ♠2♥AK32♦AKQ432♣32, four clubs holding (H) ♠32♥AK43♦AQ32♣AQ2, and four hearts holding (I) ♠2♥KQJ2♦KQJ5432♣2. (E) is the 15-17 HCP 2452 raise. (F) is the game-forcing 2452 raise. (G) is the 4-6 raise. (H) is the 3442 game-forcing raise. (I) is the preemptive raise.

Opener	(1)	Responder		Opener	(2)	Responder	
♠AQ32	♦AKQJ2	♠K7654	♦43	♠AQ32	♦AKQJ2	♠K7654	♦43
♥KJ10	♣2	♥32 ♣Q543		♥KJ10	♣2	♥A43	♣543

Opener (1)	Responder	Opener (2)	Responder
1diamond	1spade	1diamond	1spade
3hearts	3spades	3hearts	4spades
4spades	Pass	4NT	5hearts
		6spades	

In examples (1) thru (6), opener jump reverses, showing shortness in one of the unbid suits and at least 15 points. In example (1), responder does not want to bid game opposite a 15-17 raise. Responder bids three spades, and opener with a game-forcing hand raises to game. In example (2), responder wants to be in game opposite a 15-17 raise, but is not interested in slam if opener has the stronger hand. Responder's jump to game shows some extras. Opener, who doesn't need much for slam, checks to make sure two keycards aren't missing.

Opener	(3)	Responder		Opener	(4)	Responder	
♠2 ♦A32		♠K543 ♦54		♠2 ♦A32		♠K543 ♦54	
♥A432 ♣KQJ32		♥K765 ♣654		♥A432 ♣KQJ32		♥KQ65 ♣654	
1club		1heart		1club		1heart	
3diamonds		3hearts		3diamonds		4hearts	

Opener	(5)	Responder		Opener	(6)	Responder	
♠AQ32 ♦AKJ2		♠K654 ♦Q3		♠AQ32 ♦AKJ2		♠K654 ♦Q3	
♥2 ♣A432		♥KQ3 ♣8765		♥A432 ♣2		♥KQ5 ♣8765	
1diamond		1spade		1diamond		1spade	
3hearts		3NT		3hearts		3NT	
4diamonds		4spades		4clubs		4hearts	
Pass				4NT		5diamonds	
				6spades		Pass	

Opener	(7)	Responder		Opener	(8)	Responder	
♠J2 ♦A2		♠A654 ♦54		♠2 ♦2		♠KQJ ♦KQJ	
♥A432 ♣AKQJ2		♥KQ65 ♣765		♥A432 ♣KQJ5432		♥KQ65 ♣876	
1club		1heart		1club		1heart	
3spades		4spades		4hearts		Pass	
4NT		6hearts					

In example (3), responder would pass a jump to three hearts. Therefore, he bids three hearts, which opener passes. In example (4), responder would raise a three-heart jump to game, but would not be interested in slam if opener has a stronger hand. In examples (5) and (6), responder is interested in slam if opener has a game-forcing raise with shortness, opposite his four-small suit. Responder bids three-spades, asking. In example (5), opener shows a game-forcing hand with heart shortness, and responder signs-off. In example (6), opener shows a game-forcing hand with club shortness, and responder bids four hearts, a slam try. Opener bids four notrump keycard, and bids six spades. In example (7), opener shows a 2425 game force. Responder bids keycard, and bids a slam. Slam has no play if opener has ♠J32♥AJ32♦A32♣AKQ. Playing Standard American, wouldn't you jump to four hearts with both hands? In example (8), opener jumps to four hearts, showing a preemptive raise. Responder, holding no aces, passes four hearts.

Opener bids one notrump, responder bids two clubs Stayman, and overcaller doubles. If opener has a four-card major, he bids it. If opener doesn't have a four-card major, he passes with a club stopper and bids two diamonds without a club stopper. Opener redoubles to show four very good clubs.

Opener bids one club, responder bids one heart and overcaller bids one spade. Pass by opener denies three-card support. To force, responder doubles or cuebids. A NEW SUIT BY RESPONDER IS NON-FORCING.

In Washington Standard, Inverted Minors is off by a passed hand. A passed hand can still show a limit raise. Over one diamond, a jump to three clubs is an artificial passed-hand limit raise. Over one club, a jump to two diamonds is an artificial passed-hand limit raise.

After opening two clubs, all doubles by opener and responder that are not conventional are penalty doubles. The only conventional double in Washington Standard is DOPI at the two-level, when playing control responses.

Opener bids one-of-a-minor and responder bids one notrump. Overcaller gets a lot more mileage if he defends against responder's notrump as if it were the opening bid. You could play my convention where double is a four-card major and a longer minor, a one-suited minor or a very strong hand; two clubs is takeout for the majors and could be 4-4 or even 4-3; two diamonds shows one major; two-of-a-major shows a five-card major and usually a four-card minor. You could play DONT, Cappelletti or any other notrump defensive system. Anything is better than standard methods.

If opener bids one heart and overcaller bids three spades, responder would like to be able to make a heart slam try below game. If you are willing to give up the natural four-club bid, you can use four clubs as a heart slam try. Holding clubs, make a negative double or jump to five clubs. If opener bids one-of-a-major and overcaller bids four clubs, four diamonds is the strong major-suit raise. Holding diamonds, make a negative double or jump to five diamonds.

Jumps to game are weak and deny four controls. After one spade - two clubs - two spades, responder jumps to four spades holding ♠Q32♥432♦AQJ♣K432. Holding ♠Q32♥432♦AQ2♣A432, responder bids three spades. Holding ♠AKJ432♥AKQ♦32♣32, opener passes responder's jump to four spades. Slam is poor unless responder has four controls.

Opener bids one-of-either-minor, overcaller bids one notrump. Double by opener in pass out seat shows both majors. Opener could have ♠A432♥A432♦32♣A32.

After anybid - double - redouble - pass - pass, the cheapest call is doubler's default and could be a three-card suit. Any other call shows a five-card or a very good four-card suit. Suppose you double one club holding ♠A432♥A432♦A32♣32. If it goes redouble - Pass - Pass, you bid one diamond. Bidding one heart shows five.

Playing standard Jacoby Two Notrump, opener jumps to game with a balanced minimum. Minimum is defined as a hand which you would NOT accept a limit raise. ♠KQJ32♥32♦32♣AK32 is not a minimum since you would bid game opposite a game invitation. With this hand show extras.

Suppose one spade - two clubs - two spades shows six spades. For slam purposes, it's very important for opener to know how many spades responder has. Responder's raise to three or four spades must still show three. If responder has two spades and wants to play in spades, he bids two notrump first, and then shows two-card support at the next opportunity. If opener then bids three spades or three notrump, responder bids four spades to show a minimum game-forcing hand such as ♠K2♥3♦KQJ2♣K65432, or cuebids to show a good hand such as ♠K2♥2♦AK32♣AQ5432.

Over one notrump, responder bids three diamonds to show a good hand with at least 5-5 in the minors. Responder has no way to show 5-4-2-2, 5-4-3-1 or 6-4 minor-suited slam hands. Responder can show 5-4-3-1 minor-suited slam hands, if he is playing methods in chapters 28.5 and 28.6. To fill these loopholes, transfer to one minor and then bid the other minor to show length, not shortness. Responder transfers to clubs, and follows with three diamonds, to show at least five clubs and exactly four diamonds. Responder transfers to diamonds and follows with four clubs to show at least five diamonds and exactly four clubs. Holding ♠2♥32♦KQ32♣KQ5432 or ♠A2♥32♦KQ32♣KQ432, responder bids two spades, transfer to clubs, and follows with three diamonds. Holding ♠2♥32♦KQ5432♣KQ32 or ♠A2♥32♦KQ432♣KQ32, responder bids two notrump, transfer to diamonds, and follows with four clubs. TRANSFERRING TO A MINOR AND BIDDING A MAJOR STILL SHOWS SHORTNESS.

Opener bids one notrump, responder bids two diamonds, transfer, and overcaller doubles showing diamonds. If opener passes the double showing two hearts, redouble by responder is a retransfer.

INDEX